D1601589

Michael Jay Polonsky, MA
Alma T. Mintu-Wimsatt, PhD
Editors

Environmental Marketing: Strategies, Practice, Theory, and Research

Pre-publication
REVIEWS,
COMMENTARIES,
EVALUATIONS . . .

"*E*nvironmental Marketing is a must-read book for anyone interested in environmental issues, whether from a theoretical basis, managerial perspective, public policy viewpoint, or for empirical evidence. It covers a wide array of topics from segmentation to product, advertising, and distribution strategies, and from a micro to a macro perspective. It represents an excellent source of material for understanding, researching, or teaching environmental marketing."

Michel Laroche, PhD
Professor of Marketing,
Concordia University

More pre-publication
REVIEWS, COMMENTARIES, EVALUATIONS . . .

"**M**ichael Polonsky and Alma Mintu-Wimsatt have pulled together first-rate writings on an absolutely critical subject at just the right time. These articles present a well-rounded picture of the latest in theory development and empirical research in environmental marketing.

The book and its editors are to be commended. They offer a global perspective that is essential for understanding environmental issues. The research and writings are all current, and the coverage is comprehensive, from consumer behavior to advertising claims to macromarketing issues.

Marketing scholars and managers alike simply must consider how the function of marketing has contributed to environmental problems and can also contribute to future solutions. This volume adds greatly to our understanding of the problems and issues."

D. Kirk Davidson, PhD
Professor of Marketing,
Mount Saint Mary's College,
Emmitsburg, Maryland

"***E****nvironmental Marketing* addresses a topic that is of great interest, yet is mainly discussed in popular media and is less researched in academia. Several contributors to this book call for a much stronger interest of and more effort by academics concerning the many issues within 'green marketing.' The book meets this plea by giving space to both theoretical and empirical articles covering areas such as consumer behavior, management, and the marketing mix.

It is a good source for putting certain ideas into perspective as well as inspiring further research."

Dr. Suzanne C. Grunert
Associate Professor,
Department of Marketing,
Odense University

More pre-publication
REVIEWS, COMMENTARIES, EVALUATIONS . . .

"**T**his book is a useful contribution to the marketing literature, not least because it succeeds quite well in placing the discipline in a strategic and more rigorously scientific context. Certainly no serious contemporary marketeer can afford to ignore the theme of this book. It appeals to those who want a better understanding of how the marketing profession can and ought to contribute to the dissemination of environmentally less harmful business practices."

J. P. Ulhøi, PhD
*Department of Organization
and Management,
The Aarhus School of Business,
Denmark*

"**A**fter many early publications that have addressed the issues of environmental marketing from a superficial level, this book reports substantial and in-depth analyses of the complex intricacies between marketing and environmental management. In this way it marks the coming of age of integrating environmental concern into business decision making.

The majority of contributions are from academia, and the quality shows that academic research need not be wholly theoretical. It will be of great benefit to practitioners and academics alike."

Dr. Walter Wehrmeyer
*Lecturer in Ecological Management,
The Durrell Institute,
University of Kent at Canterbury*

"**T**his book will prove quite useful to both practitioners and researchers in the rapid expansion of environmental management. The contributed selections include a variety of theoretical and practical pieces; all readers should find something of interest.

The many references cited by the numerous authors provide additional 'hooks' into the literature for those seeking further information. *Environmental Marketing* provides a welcome update to Henion and Kinnear's (1976) review of these issues."

Mark A. White, PhD
*Assistant Professor of Commerce,
McIntire School of Commerce,
University of Virginia*

The Haworth Press, Inc.

Environmental Marketing
Strategies, Practice, Theory, and Research

HAWORTH Marketing Resources
Innovations in Practice & Professional Services
William J. Winston, Senior Editor

New, Recent, and Forthcoming Titles:

Environmental Marketing
Strategies, Practice, Theory, and Research

Michael Jay Polonsky, MA
Alma T. Mintu-Wimsatt, PhD
Editors

The Haworth Press
New York • London

The Haworth Press, Inc., 10 Alice Street, Binghamton, NY 13904-1580

Library of Congress Cataloging-in-Publication Data

Environmental marketing : strategies, practice, theory, and research / Michael Jay Polonsky, Alma T. Mintu-Wimsatt, editors.
     p.   cm.
    Includes bibliographical references and index.
    ISBN 1-56024-927-7 (alk. paper)
    1. Green marketing. 2. Product management–Environmental aspects. 3. Social responsibility of business. I. Polonsky, Michael J. II. Mintu-Winsatt, Alma T.
HF 5413.E58 1995
658.8′02–dc20
                                                    94-28993
                                                     CIP

CONTENTS

SECTION XI. SOME CONCLUSIONS

ABOUT THE EDITORS

Michael Jay Polonsky, MA, is Lecturer in Marketing at the University of Newcastle in Australia where he coordinates the Marketing Group. He has taught in the United States, South Africa, New Zealand, and at several universities in Australia. His main interests are in areas relating to environmental marketing and the use of stakeholder theory in marketing strategy development. He has published articles in a number of international journals and has presented papers at various international conferences.

Alma T. Mintu-Wimsatt, PhD, is Assistant Professor of Marketing in the Marketing and Management Department at East Texas State University in Commerce. Her research interests include international negotiations, green marketing, and cross-cultural teaming. She has published in a variety of professional journals such as *Management Science, Marketing Education Review, Journal of Global Business,* and *Journal of International Consumer Marketing.*

CONTRIBUTORS

Jeff Allen, DBA, Department of Marketing, College of Business Administration, University of Central Florida, Orlando, FL.

Tom Suraphol Apaiwongse, PhD, Associate Professor in Marketing, Clark Atlanta University, Marketing Department, School of Business Administration, Atlanta, GA.

Greg M. Bohlen, BSc, Railfreight Research Fellow, European Business Management School, University of Wales, Swansea, U.K.

Don Michael Bradford, PhD, Department of Marketing, Georgetown University, Washington, DC.

Roger Calantone, PhD, Department of Marketing and Logistics, Michigan State University, East Lansing, MI.

Les Carlson, PhD, Associate Professor of Marketing, Department of Marketing, Clemson University, Clemson, SC.

Rajan Chandran, PhD, Professor and Chairman of Marketing Department, School of Business and Management, Temple University, Philadelphia, PA.

T. Bettina Cornwell, PhD, Department of Marketing, The Fogelman College of Business and Economics, Memphis State University, Memphis, TN.

Adamantios Diamantopoulos, PhD, Chair of International Marketing, European Business Management School, University of Wales, Swansea, U.K.

C. Anthony di Benedetto, PhD, Associate Professor of Marketing, School of Business and Management, Temple University, Philadelphia, PA.

Tabitha A. Doescher, PhD, Department of Marketing, College of Business Administration, Oklahoma State University, Stillwater, OK.

Cornelia DrÖge, PhD, Department of Marketing and Logistics, Michigan State University, East Lansing, MI.

Donald A. Fuller, PhD, Associate Professor of Marketing, College of Business, University of Central Florida, Orlando, FL.

Stephen J. Grove, PhD, Associate Professor of Marketing, Clemson University, Clemson, SC.

Curtis P. Haugtvedt, PhD, Department of Marketing, The Ohio State University, Columbus, OH.

Denise M. Johnson, PhD, Department of Marketing, School of Business, University of Louisville, Louisville, KY.

Scott D. Johnson, PhD, Assistant Professor of Marketing, School of Business, University of Louisville, Louisville, KY.

Norman Kangun, PhD, Professor and Director, Division of Management and Marketing, College of Business, The University of Texas at San Antonio.

Hector R. Lozada, PhD, School of Management, Binghamton University, Binghamton, NY.

Robert D. Mackoy, MBA, Department of Marketing and Logistics, Michigan State University, East Lansing, MI.

Morgan Miles, DBA, Department of Marketing, Georgia Southern University, Stateboro, GA.

Linda S. Munilla, EdD, Department of Marketing, Georgia Southern University, Stateboro, GA.

M. Bill Neace, PhD, School of Business and Economics, Mercer University, Macon, GA.

Atul Parvatiyar, PhD, Emory Business School, Emory University, Atlanta, GA.

Gregory M. Pickett, PhD, Associate Professor of Marketing, Department of Marketing, Clemson University, Clemson, SC.

Bodo B. Schegelmilch, PhD, Department of Marketing, American Graduate School of International Management (Thunderbird), Phoenix, AZ.

Charles H. Schwepker Jr., PhD, Department of Marketing and Legal Studies, Central Missouri State University, Warrensburg, MO.

Jagdish N. Sheth, PhD, Charles H. Kellsdat Professor of Marketing, Emory Business School, Emory University, Atlanta, GA.

Stephen M. Smith, PhD, Department of Psychology, North George College, Dahlonega, GA.

Joshua L. Wiener, PhD, Department of Marketing, College of Business Administration, Oklahoma State University, Stillwater, OK.

Foreword

In recent years, both producers and consumers have been turning towards more environmentally friendly goods and services. Environmental issues have become a major marketing focus.

Changes in patterns of consumption are just as important as changes to the production process, if we are to lighten demands on the Earth's resources and move towards ecologically sustainable development.

People are becoming increasingly aware of the links between major environmental problems, such as air pollution, land degradation and chemical contamination, and everyday consumption items, such as food, clothing, transport, and housing.

There are however considerable difficulties in the way of marketing "green" products. Producers seek to exploit new opportunities whilst consumers need more comprehensive and reliable information. One major problem is the dearth of knowledge about marketing and the environment, especially how consumers form their buying preferences. Research in this area would need to include consumer needs as well as behavior, trends in consumption generally, the assessment of environmental impacts, the advertising sector, and the credibility of claims.

I welcome this book as it addresses the most pressing research needs. I am delighted that the editors, Michael Polonsky and Alma Mintu-Wimsatt, have taken the initiative and have covered so effectively a wide range of topics.

I congratulate the editors and all the authors. I expect their collection of papers will make a vital contribution to the subject and to the directions which must surely be taken by continuing research and education on these vital issues.

Ros Kelly
Federal Minister for the Environment, 1989-1994
Australia

Preface

The preservation, conservation, and protection of our physical or "green" environment (i.e., environmentalism) pose a crucial challenge to business. Many executives believe that environmentalism will become one of the critical issues organizations will need to integrate into their activities for successful operations in the twenty-first century. Hence, concern over the environment has emerged as an important topic in the practice of marketing.

In the early 1970s, environmental issues were debated in both mainstream and academic marketing publications. Unfortunately, in the 1980s, this interest waned. While several of these environmental issues are still salient, many have changed since the 1970s. It appears that various publics–business community, society, government, and special interest groups, among others–have become more cognizant of environmental issues.

For example, the *Harvard Business Review*'s (1991) worldwide survey of 12,000 managers showed that environmental issues are among their second highest social priority. The findings from another study, sponsored by the American Marketing Association, report that concern over the physical environment has emerged as the most important issue affecting global marketing.

In addition, other studies have shown that consumers are now changing their behavior to integrate environmental considerations. This change includes consumers basing their purchasing decisions not only on how well products satisfy individual needs, but also how these products affect the natural environment. Consumers around the world have gone as far as paying a premium for environmentally friendly products.

Environmental activities initiated by various governments around the world have also expanded. Governments generally agree that environmental issues deserve their attention and action. They have now begun to address some of the basic environmental issues like greenhouse gases and global warming. Other issues are also being examined on a country by country basis.

In the practice of marketing, the phrase "green marketing" has become quite popular.* The conceptualization of green marketing re-evaluates the very tenants of our consumption society. For example, is the satisfaction of human needs and wants necessarily detrimental to our environment? Herein lies the dilemma posed by green marketing. Without continued support from the physical environment, the means to satisfy the needs and wants of consumers will be curiously absent.

While the above philosophical debate is important, it is not the sole component of green marketing. Other issues need to be addressed, such as:

- How can public policy makers modify consumer behavior?
- How do firms use green marketing claims?
- Can firms be environmentally friendly while still achieving "acceptable" profit levels?
- How do consumers view green products?

The main objective of this book is to introduce readers to a number of green marketing issues, such as the above questions. The materials included are presented to assist both practitioners and academics to better understand the implications of green marketing. However, from a practical standpoint, we will not be able to comprehensively cover all topics. Nonetheless, we hope that by presenting material relating to several green marketing issues, we will increase readers' awareness of how these issues can be integrated into marketing theory, practice, and research.

Upon reading this book, several unique qualities will become evident. First, we have included articles that are both conceptual and empirical in nature. This was done to represent the broad spectrum of work being undertaken in this topical area. Second, several internationally renowned scholars were invited to write green marketing articles. These eminent authors provided insightful analyses

---

*Green marketing is defined as the application of marketing concepts and tools to facilitate exchanges that satisfy organizational and individual goals in such a way that they preserve, protect, and conserve the physical environment.

and directions for green marketing. Finally, this book examines green marketing issues pertaining to a number of countries such as Australia, Germany, United Kingdom, and the United States. All the articles we have selected underwent a competitive review process, thus ensuring their relevance to the green marketing debate. In all cases, the articles included in this book seek to disseminate the most up-to-date information on green marketing theory, practice, and research.

This book is divided into 11 sections. Each section focuses on a different green marketing issue and includes no more than three chapters on any given topic. All chapters have practical implications to ensure that readers can better understand green marketing and use the information to improve their organizations' green marketing operations. Furthermore, we hope that the chapters presented will stimulate readers' interests and further the green marketing movement.

We would like to thank all our authors and colleagues for their support in this project. Without their quality submissions and efforts this project would never have reached its fruition. We would also like to thank our spouses, Clair and John, for their moral support and patience. Finally, we would like to thank the many manuscript reviewers for this book. Their efforts were invaluable, particularly in ensuring that the chapters included were of the highest caliber. The list of reviewers includes:

Mrs. Frances Edwards, Lecturer in Marketing, Griffith University

Dr. Susan Ellis, Senior Lecturer in Marketing, University of Sydney

Dr. Kwaku Atuhene-Gilma, Lecturer in Marketing, University of Wollongong

Mrs. Denise Jarratt, Lecturer in Marketing, Charles Sturt University–Mitchell

Dr. Bill Merrilees, Associate Professor in Marketing, University of Newcastle

Dr. Don Scott, Professor in Management, University of New England–Northern Rivers

Dr. Hazel T. Suchard, Associate Professor in Marketing, Australia Catholic University

Dr. Betty Weiler, Senior Lecturer in Tourism, University of Newcastle

Mr. Hume Winzar, Lecturer in Marketing, Murdoch University

Michael Jay Polonsky
Alma T. Mintu-Wimsatt

REFERENCES

AMA (1991), "Study Spots Global Marketing Trends," *Marketing News*, 25:21 (October 14), p. 9.

Kanter, Rosabeth Moss (1991), "Transcending Business Boundaries: 12,000 World Managers View Change," *Harvard Business Review* (May & June), pp. 151-164.

SECTION I.
INTRODUCTION

Chapter 1

Ecological Imperatives
and the Role of Marketing

Jagdish N. Sheth
Atul Parvatiyar

INTRODUCTION

The purpose of this chapter is to highlight the new role of marketing in improving our environmental condition. Our fundamental proposition is that sustainable development can be achieved only by proactive corporate marketing and active government intervention. While governments engage in mandatory intervention, corporate marketers can undertake proactive interventions at the marketplace and within their own corporations. In this chapter, we discuss four mechanisms of government intervention (regulation, reformation, promotion, and participation) and four R's of corporate marketing strategy (redirection of customer needs, reconsumption, reorientation of marketing mix, and reorganization) that are appropriate for promoting sustainable development. We suggest a two-dimensional shift in the approach to ecological problems: from consumption marketing to sustainable marketing and from invisible hand to a more visible hand of the government (Figure 1.1).

Public concern over environmental deterioration is rising and marketers have begun to recognize both the need and the value of environmental marketing. Some estimates suggest that manufacturers identified nearly 10% of all new products introduced in 1990 as "green" or otherwise "environmentally friendly." This was more than double the number of green products introduced just one year earlier and about 20 times more than the number of green products

3

FIGURE 1.1. New Orientation for Ecological Marketing

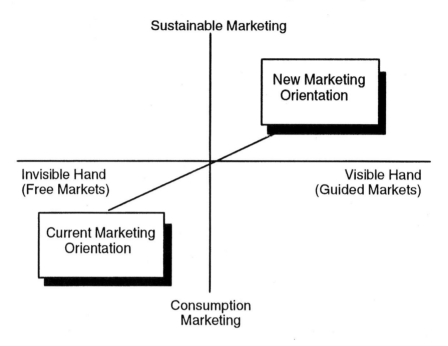

introduced in 1985 (Davis 1992). There was also a dramatic rise in green marketing references in news, business, and trade sources during 1990 and 1991 (Morgan 1992). However, academic literature relevant to this issue is less extensive. In fact, since the late 1970s very few scholarly references on this subject are available.

During the mid-1970s, many scholars made important contributions with respect to the ecological perspective of marketing (Cravens 1974; Fisk 1973, 1974, 1975; Henion 1976; Kangun 1974; Perry 1976; Shapiro 1978). Despite these early efforts, other marketing scholars did not channel their intellectual pursuits in this direction. Perhaps the fundamental belief that market process is sufficient to correct any environmental imbalances prevailed. Also, scientific uncertainty and the hesitant commitment by business leaders to this issue made it difficult for marketing scholars to wholeheartedly engage themselves in research in this area. Whatever may be the reasons for marketing managers and academicians to fend the issue then, it may no longer be possible to ignore it now. Environmental problems have since grown and so has the general awareness about it. While during the mid-1970s it remained mostly an issue of conservation of resources and local area pollution, ecological concerns of today are global and more compelling.

THE ECOLOGICAL IMPERATIVE

The following discussion is a description of some of the ecological imperatives to which marketing has to respond in this decade. Scientists bring to our attention complex but urgent problems that have a bearing on our very survival: a warming globe, acid precipitation, threats to Earth's ozone layer, accumulation of greenhouse gases, deserts consuming agricultural land, fast depletion of vital natural resources, the disappearance of rain forests, and loss of species (Chandler 1990). Although there may be scientific uncertainty about the extent of such ecological decline, there is evidence that the degradation of nature has begun to take its toll. Reports indicate that the Baltic Sea is dying from sewage and other pollution. Every year, we loose 25 billion tons of topsoil affecting 6 to 7 million hectares of agricultural land that convert into deserts. Another 1.5 million hectares of mostly irrigated agricultural land is affected by water logging, salinization, and alkanization (MacNeill, Winesmius and Yakushiji 1991). In places such as Mexico City and Eastern Europe, millions breathe toxic air; and China will soon have to cut all its harvestable forests (Smith 1992).

These and other dramatic changes are fundamentally impinging upon our global environment. An already crowded planet will have to support twice as many people within the next 40 years. To meet the needs of these people, world industrial output will have to quintuple (Smith 1992). About 90 percent of this population growth is expected in the already overpopulated poor countries who face tremendous shortage of resources for development. Already industrial production has grown more than 50 times over the past century, four-fifths of which has come since 1950 (WCED 1987). Such figures reflect and presage profound impacts upon the biosphere, as the world invests in houses, transport, farms, and industries. We all know that much of the economic growth pulls raw materials from forests, soils, seas, and waterways. The earth's vital resources are shrinking to alarming levels due to unsustainable development activities. The need for further economic activity is likely to impose colossal new burdens on the ecosphere.

The gains in human welfare over the past few decades have been outstanding. The potential for future gains is also promising. Marketing played a vital role in these gains by facilitating the use and development of products with new technologies in biology, materials, construction, chemicals, energy, and electronics. However, vast increases in the scale of human impact on the earth accompanied past gains, for which marketing is also responsible.

The interdependence between global ecology and global economy is clearly established. We are forced to be concerned with the impacts of ecological stress–degradation of soils, water regimes, atmosphere, and forests–upon our economic prospects. Economy and ecology are becoming more interwoven–locally, nationally, and globally. Marketing cannot insulate itself from these ecological problems. It needs to be concerned about the resources it uses to satisfy consumer needs and wants and also be concerned about the effects of this consumption on human life and its biosphere. Sustainable development requires "sustainable marketing"–marketing efforts that are not only competitively sustainable but are also ecologically sustainable.

MARKETING'S ROLE IN SUSTAINABLE DEVELOPMENT

Marketing's role in the development process is well recognized (Kinsey 1982; Riley et al. 1983; Dholakia 1984; Carter 1986; Kotler 1986). Much of the economic activity is triggered by the marketing process that offers and stimulates consumption opportunities to satisfy human needs and wants. However, marketing's critical role in development will be appreciated only when, through sustainable marketing, it meets the needs of the present without compromising the ability of future generations to meet their own needs. This means that it might have to shed its present profligacy that encourages an unsustainable development path. A marketing approach that aims at serving the material wants of consumers through an ever increasing volume of goods without any attempt to maximize life quality (Kotler 1988), draws too heavily, and too quickly, on already overdrawn environmental resources and is likely to mortgage the future. Life quality represents not only the quantity and quality of consumption goods and services but also the quality of the environment. Clearly, marketing has to assume a more responsible role for sustainable development.

A two-dimensional shift in the fundamental approach of marketing needs to take place so as to facilitate sustainable development: one with respect to shaping customer needs and expectations, and the other with respect to providing customers with appropriate choices to meet their needs. Marketing's claim that it serves societal needs by informing customers of the availability of goods and services to improve their quality of life can only be held tenable if its communication approach and techniques help in informing, educating, and channeling needs of its current and potential customers towards ecologically benign products, services, and/or activities. Implicit in this is the assumption that such marketing efforts are also directed to reforming inefficient and environmentally damaging consumption habits. Changing consumption patterns may call for positive incentives, new product and process developments, and price or non-price deterrents against certain customer practices.

Marketing's second and perhaps more critical role will be its ability to identify and develop such consumption choices for society that meet its current needs without sacrificing the ability to meet its future needs. This means that we not only look for green products that do not damage the environment, but also develop such products and services that will improve the poor condition of our environment. The concept of a "socio-ecological product" has to extend our understanding that environmental consequences (the product's aggregate impact on everyone affected by its use) are more important determinants of its acceptability than either user satisfaction or corporate profitability (Cracco and Rostenne 1971). The true socio-ecological product is one that becomes a consumer's first choice, since it meets his/her consumption needs along with his/her need for a healthy, sustainable physical environment. It is important to understand that customer needs are not, nor should they be, in conflict with the environmental needs. In fact, the two needs occur concurrently. People need and want to coexist with nature. The sooner this is understood, the better it will be for our discipline and our society. It is necessary to change the mindset that believes that what is good for one cannot be good for the other.

Those companies who make these shifts toward helping us achieve sustainable development will do more than clean up or prevent their own pollution. They will make and distribute products more efficiently, worry about their products' lifelong environmental impact, plan for their products' recycling, and get their suppliers to also follow suit. This may require a new mindset, new tools, and adjustments throughout the organization. Some companies like 3M, Dow Chemical, AT&T and BMW have already started work in this direction (Smith 1992). Such a marketing approach that promotes sustainable development and protection of our ecosystem can be called "sustainable marketing."

CORPORATE STRATEGIES FOR SUSTAINABLE MARKETING

Sustainable marketing requires proactive corporate strategies that would benefit both corporations and society. Such strategies must be aimed at redirecting customer needs and wants towards ecologically beneficial products and services, and providing the socio-ecological products to consumers.

It is an immense challenge for companies to advance simultaneously in economic development and environmental protection as sustainable development demands. However, this is something very attainable because companies have repeatedly demonstrated through their efforts in total quality management (TQM) that they can cope with the competing objectives–increasing quality while lowering costs (Schmidheiny 1992). Though the path towards sustainable development appears to be long and tortuous, corporations can effectively build a strategy for sustainable marketing through four distinct efforts: promoting reconsumption; redirecting customer needs and wants; reorienting the marketing mix; and reorganizing organizational efforts (see Figure 1.2).

Reconsumption

Companies need to think not just about the impact of their product in the hands of the consumer, but also the process by which the product is made and sold. They have to be concerned about every product's "eco-balance," the minimization of risks and impacts throughout its life cycle, and the resources required to make and dispose of it. A new marketing approach promoting "reconsumption"–the ability to use and reuse goods in whole or in part, over several use-cycles or generations–can become the industrial ideal of an economic system. Developing products that can be reconsumed over several generations and educating the consumers then become the tasks of marketers. There is already evidence that products made of high-density plastics, ceramics, and rare metals have a far lesser impact on our fast depleting natural resources than steel, aluminum, or other metals, because they possess higher strength appropriate for facilitating reconsumption. Those companies that succeed in developing such products and in convincing consumers regarding their benefits will have competitive advantage over others as consumers become more conscious about the ecosystem. This requires a new thinking about product life-cycle usage.

Life-cycle usage implies life-cycle responsibility. Marketing managers geared towards thinking that their role and responsibilities end with the transaction exchange will not be able to cope with this new situation. Conceptual and operational plans will be required to manage such responsibility. Conscious strategies that promote reconsumption could provide the competitive advantage to many products. This has already been demonstrated in the case of some environmentally sound products that have commanded almost 25% premium. For instance, people typically pay more for organically grown food. Similarly, Germany's AEG, a producer of white goods, recovered from near bankruptcy in the early 1980s by manufacturing a washing machine that used less detergent, energy, and water than its rivals (Cairncross 1992).

Sustainable marketing means more than pollution reduction and life-cycle responsibility. Businesses will be challenged to move toward "zero pollution," "zero waste," and redirection of product development efforts to meet ecological needs. The goal will be to

FIGURE 1.2. Strategies for Sustainable Marketing

Government Intervention

Corporate Strategy

Sustainable Marketing

Reorientation of the Marketing Mix

Reorganization

Participation

Promotion of Programs

Reform of Production and Consumption Processes

Regulatory Mandates and Policies

Reconsumption

Redirection of Customer Needs and Wants

make the manufacture, use, and disposal of products more compatible with sustainable development. These include efforts that help us produce more with less. These environmental marketing initiatives will be an integral part of corporate life in the 1990s.

Redirection

For the most ardent environmentalists, customers are the ultimate paradox. Their consumption uses up the earth's capacity to produce materials and absorb waste. Undoubtedly we agree that they should consume less, not differently. But until such human disposition comes about, it is necessary that they consume more environmentally friendly products. It is marketing's task to redirect their needs and wants towards consumption that is ecologically least harmful. Marketing's current tools can be geared towards such redirection. The role of advertising and promotion cannot be understated in this regard. However, the use of market research and in-depth customer analysis will provide the most sustainable results in this respect. First, market researchers and consumer analysts need to identify the current consumption options, the criteria being used by the customer for choice behavior, the relative importance being placed on these criteria, and the sources of information that are shaping these criteria. It is only then that marketers can intervene to appropriately change the criteria for consumer decision making in favor of ecologically benign consumption. Consumer attitude studies will help in designing proper communication messages for sustainable marketing.

Consumer sensitivity to environmental issues does not always translate into purchase behavior. It is the responsibility of marketers to use their communication and promotional tools to convert this latent desire for environmental quality of life into actions and activities that actually promote such environmental quality of life.

If marketing during the past few decades has been so successful in increasing societal consumption and in meeting human needs, we are confident that it will also be successful in redirecting consumption behavior in favor of environmentally sustainable consumption. Marketing's promotional ability cannot be underestimated. It only requires resolve and a cooperative effort. Large scale research on consumption behavior and net effect of interventions towards changing such consumption criteria could be effectively utilized by corporate marketers in their effort to redirect customer needs and wants.

Reorientation

Sustainable marketing requires the reorientation of the entire marketing mix, everything from product and packaging through positioning and promotion. Every marketer will have to assess the environmental impact of the manufacturing, content, package, label, advertising, distribution, use, and disposal of its products. Beyond assessment, strategic opportunities can be identified for a positive response that will earn the favor and support of environmentally conscious consumers, advocacy groups, media, and retailers. There may be strategic possibilities for new product development and acquisition opportunities. Retailers such as Wal-Mart, Kmart, and Safeway have already adopted aggressive environmental merchandising and promotional plans (Coddington 1990).

Reorienting the marketing mix means that marketers should consider options regarding repackaging, relabeling, reformulating, and/ or repositioning. We are already familiar with growing concerns regarding environmentally harmful product packaging. Several marketers have either started using biodegradable packages or are in the process of using recycled packaging. Product relabeling that includes more environment-related information has already begun to appear on retailer shelves. Many companies have initiated efforts to reformulate products to either remove the harmful ingredients, like phosphates in detergents, or make them more energy efficient. Repositioning products as environmentally friendly offers an opportunity to gain early market recognition and support of the conscious consumers and it also provides higher visibility in the already cluttered advertising media.

Reorientation is also required in selling approaches and sales incentive programs. Credible environmental themes based on appropriate environmental customer education can make the difference. Especially in business-to-business settings, those firms that provide vital environmental information to their clients on the use of supplies may make the difference. Chances are that as the pressure on companies to help the process of sustainable development increases, these companies will make similar demands on their suppliers. Retailers will favor those suppliers that carry products which help uplift their image as environmentally friendly organizations. The opportunities associated with proactive leadership far outweigh the risks.

Reorienting the marketing mix can lead to shifts in customer needs and also what we offer to the customers for consumption. Packaging, product-mix variables, and long lifetime warranties would be actions aimed at delivering ecologically beneficial offerings and advertising, labeling, and reorientation of selling efforts would help redirect customer needs for sustainable development.

Reorganization

Commitment to a vision of sustainable marketing must translate into strategies and action plans. This may often involve reorganization, restructure, and redesign of many processes and systems within a corporation. For example, some of these changes could include:

- Companies in the "sunset" industries develop environmentally sound substitutes.
- Alter the traditional roles of boards of directors and top management towards integrating the external and internal dimensions of a business, and to provide new vehicles for stakeholder participation.
- Develop a learning organization that involves middle management in the process of constantly rethinking and relearning the fundamentals of every aspect of business (Schmidheiny 1992).

Such reorganization must be complemented with proper incentive schemes within the organizational system that encourage its employees to adopt the philosophy of sustainable development. Providing meaning for employees beyond salaries is critical. Employee motivation can be further enhanced by providing technical and management training for environmentally sound operations. An organization that does not improve its own environment cannot market environmentally sound products or services. Focused education sets the orientations and attitudes of professionals and managers. Perhaps even a partnership with the government to provide education and training will help develop this capacity.

It should be realized that sustainable marketing efforts often require cross-functional teams. Promoting such cross-functional teams within the organization is essential . Those who think that marketing people will by themselves be able to develop green marketing orientation for the firm are sadly mistaken. Like total quality management, sustainable marketing requires the involvement of employees from all functional areas, including marketing, production, procurement, accounting, and information systems.

Corporate reorganization also signals new ways organizations are gearing themselves up to meet marketplace requirements. If corporations reorganize for environmental protection, customers will anticipate corporate marketplace offerings that are better for the ecosystem, and they will become interested in environmentally friendly offerings. Thus, customer needs will be redirected through corporate reorganization.

GOVERNMENT INTERVENTION FOR SUSTAINABLE DEVELOPMENT

Environmental policy is inevitably interventionist. Without intervention by the government, our environment cannot be fully protected (Cairncross 1992). Although the forces of unfettered competition can destroy the environment, this does not mean that we should replace markets with government. Such systems of absolute control by the government have not worked. This is made apparent by the scope of environmental catastrophe in the state-run countries of Eastern Europe. Bad governmental policies can further ruin the environment, even more so than unfettered competition. It is therefore important to identify mechanisms that the government can use to induce change. In this section we identify those mechanisms of governmental intervention that are necessary for environmental improvement. When free market process will not sufficiently promote sustainable development, government mandate is recommended. However, governmental intervention that too suddenly disrupts our industry and business practices could be catastrophic. Certainly, governmental measures must be strong enough to encourage everyone to follow the path of sustainable development and discourage those practices that cause environmental degradation. Yet these measures should be based on prudence (without delaying implementation) and should nudge businesses to internalize environmental costs or limit the damage to the environment. At the same time, government has to play the role of a champion in leading the world towards sustainable development. Its role has to extend beyond that of a watchdog to one of a promoter of better human life for current and future generations. Therefore, we suggest four interventionist roles for the government: regulatory, reformatory, promotional, and participatory.

Regulation

Through the process of regulations and policies, including performance standards for technologies and products, governments can command and control the industry to prevent it from damaging our environment beyond sustainable limits. For such command and control to be successful it has to be based on factors like what standards will lead to efficiency; the extent to which the regulations and policies permit flexibility of response regarding the manner in which the industry can comply to such regulations; stability of policy; and transparency of compliance whereby the same policy applies equally to all other parties. We suggest that government make long term explicit policies in this regard.

It is also important that national governments and international organizations such as the United Nations work towards policy coordination. If the greenhouse effect is to be abated, all nations must cut emissions of carbon dioxide and other gases. This requires international agreements and coordinated action. Quite often, the same government will take conflicting positions on the same issues in different forums, reflecting the disputes among various constituencies within that government. Specialized agency and UN department heads carry on the dispute at the international level, and there is no higher super agency capable of resolving the differences. Furthermore, in this situation there is only a limited possibility of a coordinated and integrated effort at solving a problem on which expertise from several sectors is required (The Stanley Foundation 1989).The actions of each national government must be coordinated and consistent with others because the problems of the environment, resources, and development transcend national boundaries.

Reforms

For sustainable development, major restructuring and reform of cultural, social, and political mores is in order. The systemic nature of these issues means that we recognize the linkages between production and consumption practices in most nations. Consumption reforms as well as production reforms must occur simultaneously. The commitment of the government towards such reforms is critical. A clear path in this direction would be that of raising the level of knowledge about environmentally sustainable consumption and production processes. Governments may have to invest in educational programs that educate consumers on how to effectively reduce their use of energy and other resources, reconsume products, and reduce wastage.

There is also a need to reform institutional practices that are widely accepted but dysfunctional for environmental purposes. For example, most pricing and accounting practices do not place the cost of using irreplaceable natural resources or emission of wastes and pollutants need to be changed. Firms inability to internalize all costs in decision-making yields a distorted view of costs and it is an institutional failure. Reforming production processes, marketing practices, and rewards for employee performance may all require government mandates at least in the short run so that we shed our dysfunctional practices and adopt the path of sustainable development.

Reform of political institutions and orientations may also be necessary for a reordered world. The international security system which features more concern for economic and environmental questions and relatively less for military concerns will soon have to be adopted. This may require reorganization or expansion of some of the formal institutions of government or international bodies that are vested with responsibilities relating to security, environment, or economy. It includes redefining the roles and authority of these formal institutions so that they can function effectively for the new task at hand.

Promotion

Through such market interventions as pollution taxes and charges, tradable pollution permits, deposit refund systems, performance bonds, resource-saving credits, differential prices, special depreciation provisions, and the removal of distorting subsidies or barriers to market entry, governments can potentially encourage the industry to change to cleaner technologies. To the extent that they may encourage industry to develop new technologies to overcome these costs, such economic measures are useful. If, however, these economic costs are being recovered through high market prices, then we are neither improving our environment nor is the system leading to improved efficiency. Therefore, governments also have to undertake positive measures that lead to continuous and speedy development of alternative technology for sustainable development.

Government's promotional role should therefore extend beyond the use of these economic instruments. The true promotional role of the government comes with support facilities and institutions that it helps establish. As in the case of export promotion whereby governmental organizations help business firms with information, training and other support services, they need to develop similar services and programs to help business firms make the transition towards sustainable business practices. Several suggestions can be made in this regard: sharing information through a more effective database on environmental products, consumers, and support service availability; providing training; raising additional funds for environmental work (including low cost loans); providing assistance in assessing the impact of current practices on environment and suggesting alternative processes; facilitating technology transfer; and identifying market opportunities for alternative products or technologies. The most effective and economical solutions will be those that work creatively with powerful market forces rather than trying to substitute them. Therefore, cooperation between industry and government is essential.

Participation

Through participative and cooperative action governments can help industry and the public move towards sustainable development. The participative role of the government spans over at least three areas: procurement, research and scientific development, and international agreements. In most countries of the world, government is the largest single customer. Through its purchase and procurement policies that are favorable to ecologically benign products, governments can make a substantial impact on what goods are produced in the nation and by what processes. A resolve not to buy ecologically harmful products or from companies that have environmentally defaulted would be appropriate.

Through cooperative measures such as participating in multilateral trade negotiations, promoting technology cooperation across companies and industry, and providing financial assistance for cooperative research, governments can foster sustainable development. Multilateral trade agreements are crucial for developing countries to afford investments in environmental improvement. As Gro Harlem Brundtland's commission on world environment and development observed, global ecology and economy are so interrelated that if we do not meet the needs of developing countries, we will be endangering our own ecology (WCED 1987). Similarly, technology cooperation is vital for enhancing our ability to solve the environmental problems. Very few industries are capable of developing the necessary technology on their own. Sharing their resources across industry helps share investment risks. Included in technology cooperation is the issue of technology transfer, especially to the developing countries. Government's role is important in facilitating such technology transfer is important.

Governments' participation in the past has brought handsome results through space programs. It is perhaps time that governments individually or collaboratively set up NASA-like institutions for research and development in the area of environmental improvement. Funds allocated for such purposes will have a snowballing effect on the quantity and quality of research at academic institutions in this area. This will signal the commitment of governments towards achieving sustainable development and sustainable marketing.

SUMMARY AND CONCLUSIONS

In this chapter, we have argued that the modern marketing concept (understanding customer needs and fulfilling them) is insufficient for sustainable economic development. At the same time, environmental conditions are deteriorating at an alarming speed mostly due to consumption-oriented marketing. We suggest that it will require a proactive corporate marketing strategy and active government intervention to encourage ecological marketing.

We suggest that marketing practice must redirect customer needs toward ecologically safe products and practices through technological innovations. In addition, it must encourage reconsumption of products through recycling of waste and excess capacity. Finally, it must reorient its marketing mix to develop and promote ecologically safe products and reorganize itself to achieve this aim.

Concurrently, the government must also proactively promote the balancing of ecological and economic activities through regulation policy; participation through procurement, research and development, and international cooperation; reforming the production and consumption practices through mandates and incentives; and finally actively promoting the environmental causes by partnering with the industry.

In short, we believe that the visible hand of the government must guide the markets toward environmentally sound production and consumption practices. And, at the same time, marketing practice must both shape customer expectations and deliver them in a manner which creates a win-win situation between cost efficiency and ecological protection. In other words, it must innovate to overcome the apparent trade-offs between economic value and environmental value of marketing practices.

REFERENCES

Cairncross, Frances (1992), *Costing the Earth: The Challenge for Governments, the Opportunities for Business*, Boston, Mass.: Harvard Business School Press.

Carter, Steve (1986), "Marketing in Less Developed Countries–Time for Dedicated Marketing Systems not Adaptive Transfer?" *Public Enterprise*, 6 (February), pp. 107-120.

Chandler, William U. (1990), "Development and Environmental Change," *Economic Impact*, 71 (Summer), pp. 18-25.

Coddington, Walter (1990), "How to Green Up Your Marketing Mix," *Advertising Age*, 3 (September), p. 30.

Cracco, Etienne and Jacques Rostenne (1971), "The Socio-Ecological Product," *MSU Business Topics*, 19 (Summer), pp. 28-29.

Cravens, David W. (1974), "Marketing Management in an Era of Shortages," *Business Horizons*, 17, (February), pp. 79-85.

Davis, Joel (1992), "Ethics and Environmental Marketing," *Journal of Business Ethics*, 11, pp. 81-87.

Dholakia, Nikhilesh (1984), "Marketing in the Less Developed Countries: Its Nature and Prospects," in G. S. Kindra (ed.), *Marketing in Developing Countries*, London and Sydney: Croom Helm, pp. 10-28.

Fisk, George (1973), "Criteria for a Theory of Responsible Consumption," *Journal of Marketing*, (April), pp. 24-31.

Fisk, George (1974), *Marketing and the Ecological Crisis*, New York: Harper & Row.

Fisk, George (1975), "Impact of Social Sanctions on Product Strategy," *Journal of Contemporary Business*, (Winter), pp. 1-20.

Henion, Karl E. II (1976), *Ecological Marketing*, Columbus, Ohio: Grid.

Kangun, Norman (1974), "Environmental Problems and Marketing: Saint or Sinner," in J. N. Sheth and P. L. Wright (eds.), *Marketing Analysis for Societal Problems*, Urbana: University of Illinois.

Kinsey, J. (1982), "The Role of Marketing in Economic Development," *European Journal of Marketing*, 16, 6, pp. 65-77.

Kotler, Philip (1986), "The Role of Marketing in Development," *Proceedings of the International Conference on Marketing and Development*, Istanbul, Turkey, September 1-4, 1986.

Kotler, Philip (1988), *Marketing Management: Analysis, Planning and Control*, Englewood Cliffs, NJ: Prentice-Hall, pp. 151-152.

MacNeill, Jim, Peter Winesmius and Taizo Yakushiji (1991), *Beyond Interdependence*, New York: Oxford University Press.

Morgan, Fred (1992), "On the Making of Environmental Managers: Is Marketing As "Green" as It Should Be?" in *Transcript of the Special Session at the 1992 AMA Winter Educators' Conference, San Antonio, Texas*, Binghamton: SUNY.

Perry, Donald L. (1976), *Social Marketing Strategies: Conservation Issues and Analysis*, Pacific Palisades, California: Goodyear.

Riley, H. Slater, et al. (1983), "Food Marketing in the Economic Development of Puerto Rico," Research Report No. 4, Latin American Studies Center, Michigan State University, Michigan.

Schmidheiny, Stephan (1992), *A Global Business Perspective on Development and the Environment*, Cambridge, Mass.: The MIT Press.

Shapiro, Stanley J. (1978), "Marketing in a Conserver Society," *Business Horizons*, 21 (April), pp. 3-13.

Smith, Emily T. (1992), "Growth vs. Environment," *Business Week*, (May 11), pp. 66-75.

Stanley Foundation, The (1989), *Environmental Problems: A Global Security Threat*, Report of the Twenty-Fourth United Nations of the Next Decade Conference, Hamilton Parish, Bermuda, June 18-23, 1989.

World Commission on Environment and Development (WCED) (1987), *Our Common Future*, New York: Oxford University Press.

SECTION II.
RE-EVALUATING THE TENETS
OF MARKETING

Chapter 2

The Eco-Marketing Orientation: An Emerging Business Philosophy

Morgan Miles
Linda S. Munilla

SUMMARY. The selection and implementation of appropriate strategic organizational responses to turbulent environments is one of the most important issues facing global corporations during the 1990s. Salient to this decision is the adaptation of a corporation's business orientation to the dynamics of domestic and international social concerns. The present study proposes that organizations may adopt an "eco-marketing orientation" as a response to increasing pressures by the international community to more fully meet their long-term social responsibilities in all aspects of society, including the global eco-system.

INTRODUCTION

How will organizations respond to the turbulent macro-environment of the 1990s? The decade of the nineties, like the sixties, appears to be an era in which social and cultural concerns are becoming increasingly paramount. As the "me" attitude of the 1980s becomes less prevalent, it is becoming apparent that consumers are looking at far more than a company's product offerings. These more sophisticated consumers are also concerned with a holistic view of corporate image, particularly with regard to social concern and responsibility, and are " . . . changing

This manuscript has been adapted from a previous work by the authors published in the *Journal of Marketing Theory and Practice* 1(2), 1993.

their purchasing patterns in accordance to their more socially responsible beliefs" (Hentze, 1991).

One of the most prominent of these social concerns is the determination of the level of a firm's ecological sensitivity. Ecological issues such as global warming, toxic waste disposal, resource depletion, and landfill management are items of public as well as legislative concern which have prompted organizations to interject pro-ecological values into their system of corporate heuristics. These issues are of increasing importance to the global community, with some of the more advanced nations even incorporating ecological regulations as an integral component of antitrust legislation (Polonsky, 1991). These changes typify the findings of strategy researchers (Khandwalla, 1977; Foxall, 1984; Smith, Arnold, and Bizzell, 1988; Covin and Slevin, 1989) who suggest that successful firms tend to adapt to the dynamics of their unique environments, typically resulting in changes in both organizational philosophy and behavior.

This ecologically sensitive corporate orientation, sometimes referred to as the "green" strategy, can originate with a firm's evaluation of current production and marketing practices and adjusting behavior to reflect an increased level of environmental awareness. This awareness is necessary since many consumers perceive that business is responsible for an "ample portion of the waste products generated in our country" (Munilla, 1990) and, therefore, should be held responsible for the current ecological crisis. For example, in the United States, Schwartz and Miller (1991) report that a recent Roper Organization study found approximately 78 percent of adult Americans believe that society must make major strides in the improvement of the environment. These same adults also feel, however, that while individuals can do little if anything to better the environment, changes should certainly be made by business.

PURPOSE

One potential organizational response to the increased level of "greenness" of the general public lies in the adoption of an ecological orientation, hereafter referred to as "eco-marketing orientation," as a response to social and environmental dynamics. The purpose of this chapter is twofold: first to examine the influence of environmental sensitivity on organizational style, climate, and culture; and second, to propose that the set of traditional business philosophies be augmented to include an ecologically sensitive orientation, the eco-marketing orientation.

THE INFLUENCE OF ENVIRONMENTAL SENSITIVITY ON ORGANIZATIONAL STYLE, CLIMATE, AND CULTURE

To understand how such a change in business orientation would affect an organization, it is necessary to examine how organizational philosophy evolves. Peterson (1989) suggests that a business orientation is a firm's latent philosophy that defines the nature and scope of the firm's relevant business domain.

It is important to differentiate between three different, but related, constructs which pertain to both an organization's philosophy and its behavior: (1) business orientation or style, (2) culture, and (3) climate. Strategy researchers define each construct by its own unique hypothetical domain.

Khandwalla (1977) describes an organization's style or orientation as an internal set of operating "beliefs and norms" which comprises management's philosophy of business. A firm's business orientation is the underlying business philosophy and consciousness that directs all internal and external activities of the firm (Borch, 1957; Kotler, 1988). Foxall (1984) suggests that this orientation colors how the organization defines itself, its mission, and its objectives. Hence, the organization's style or orientation is an underlying philosophy held by management that influences and flavors both its strategic and tactical decisions. An organization's orientation can be assessed by observing the organization's internal structure, staffing, and behavior as well as its external behaviors.

Deshpande and Webster (1989) state that culture is the pattern of shared values and beliefs that sets the norms for behavior within the organization. Organizational culture, therefore, indirectly "tells" an organization's employees the specific roles they are "expected" to play and the norms to be followed within the context of the organization.

Glick (1985) describes organizational climate as an antecedent to organizational behavior defined "as an organizational phenomenon" consisting of the "social, organizational, and situational influences on behavior." Likewise, Deshpande and Webster (1989) define climate to pertain to the "members' perceptions about the extent to which the organization is currently fulfilling their expectations." Thus, climate is more of a social psychology construct that pertains to the internal beliefs and expectations that members of an organization hold about the organization.

Culture and organizational climate are variables that relate primarily to the interrelations which exist within a firm's micro-environment. Orientation (or style) pertains to how the firm as an entity relates to all of its environments, specifically addressing how the firm defines its business. A summary of the definitions of culture, climate, style, and orientation is provided in Table 2.1.

DETERMINATION OF BUSINESS ORIENTATION

Different business orientations result from varied perceptions of organizational priorities, how the customer is viewed, and how the firm implicitly defines its business. McCarthy and Perreault (1984) describe three traditional, typically unique, business orientations as the following: (1) a production orientation, (2) a sales orientation, and (3) a marketing orientation. Ginsberg (1985) indicates that there is, in fact, a fourth underlying business philosophy, the entrepreneurial orientation.

The production orientation's major focus is internal. A production-oriented firm implicitly defines itself by the products manufactured, not by the customers served. Cost reductions, increases in production, and logistical efficiencies are of foremost importance to a firm that is production-oriented (Cravens, Hills, and Woodruff, 1987). Peterson (1989) describes the production orientation as an organizational focus upon the production of standardized, high value products that require minimum promotional efforts.

Sales orientation implies an external focus directed toward increasing sales volume (Zikmund and D'Amico, 1986). A sales-oriented firm implicitly defines itself to be in the business of selling specified products, not serving customer needs. A sales-oriented firm exclusively utilizes Ansoff's (1965) market penetration strategy, suggesting an emphasis on the promotional component of the marketing mix.

A marketing-oriented firm implicitly defines itself to be in the business of satisfying its customer groups, while achieving its own

TABLE 2.1. Comparison of Organizational Culture, Climate, Style, and Orientation

CULTURE:	"The system of Publicly and Collectively accepted meaning operating for a given group at a given time," Pettigrew (1979).
CLIMATE:	"The social, organizational, and situational influences (environmental) on (organizational) behavior," Glick (1985).
STYLE:	"The operating set of beliefs and norms about management held by key decision makers," Khandwalla (1976/77).
ORIENTATION:	"A philosophy that guides business and a way of life" (Borch, 1957), "A philosophy that guides all business activity" (King, 1965), "An overall business consciousness that directs all activities in the firm" (Kotler, 1972), "A marketing management philosophy" (Kotler, 1988).

objectives. Although typical definitions of the production and sales orientations exclude the customers' needs and preferences, the major focus of a marketing-oriented firm is the customer. The result is that the firm adapts to its task, micro, and macro environments in an organizational effort to best serve its customers' needs. Marketing scholars have suggested that customer needs are both implicit and explicit and can be satisfied by products, services, ideas, or socially responsible business behavior (Kotler and Levy, 1969; Kotler and Zaltman, 1971; Kotler, 1972; Hunt, 1976; Crosby, Gill, and Taylor, 1981; Marketing News, 1985; Houston and Gassenheimer, 1987).

The major focus of an entrepreneurial-oriented firm is its ability to innovate and to exploit both macro and task environmental opportunities, contain environmental threats, and then create innovative, highly profitable solutions by a proclivity to accept risks that offer positive and significant return/risk trade-offs. In a 1989 empirical study of the furniture industry, Miles and Arnold (1991) found support for the proposition that an entrepreneurial orientation is indeed a unique fourth business orientation, and not an extension of the marketing orientation. Ginsberg (1985) defines the entrepreneurial orientation as a firm's tendency to be: (1) innovative in product and logistical development, (2) aggressive in dealing with its competitors, and (3) willing to accept risks for more than compensatory returns.

Marketing scholars suggest that the movement from production to selling and ultimately to the marketing orientation is typically progressive in nature, starting with the production orientation and ending with the marketing orientation (Keith, 1959; King, 1965; Cravens, Hills, and Woodruff, 1987). Kotler (1988) suggests that all business orientations compete for dominance within organizations, implying that typically firms adopt only one of the competing orientations, described in the preceding paragraphs, as their primary orientation. McCarthy and Perreault (1984) propose, however, that well-managed firms have tended to adopt the marketing orientation as their dominant underlying business philosophy. The adoption of a marketing orientation by well-managed firms suggests that the marketing orientation is considered the current "state-of-the-art" business philosophy (Keith, 1959; King, 1965; McCarthy and Perreault, 1984; Kotler, 1988; Peterson, 1989).

However, due to consumers' increased ecological awareness, many firms are attempting to meet latent and long-term consumer needs by adopting a more ecologically friendly and socially responsive approach to product development, manufacturing, packaging, distribution, and promotion. This attempt to meet latent or future consumer needs by marketing management (Kotler, 1973) can be conceptualized as an extension of the marketing orientation augmented by: (1) innovation, (2) adaptation, and (3) a strong social and ecological conscious. Hence, the following recommendation to add such an augmented orientation to the set of traditional business philosophies is proposed.

PROPOSITION

The proposed fifth business orientation that may describe an organization's latent business philosophy is defined as the "eco-marketing orientation":

> P1. The "eco-marketing orientation" is a construct that may describe the ecologically oriented, latent business philosophies of environmentally sensitive organizations.

The adoption of an eco-marketing orientation by a firm is principally a response to the increased pressures by society for business to meet its comprehensive ethical and moral responsibilities, while adhering to the marketing concept's basic tenants as suggested by McCarthy and Perreault (1984) of meeting customer needs at a profit. In addition, an eco-marketing orientation may provide the organization with a strategic competitive advantage in both domestic and international markets. Crosby, Gill, and Taylor (1981) segmented U.S. consumers by their level of ecological concern, while the Roper Organization is currently utilizing consumers' self-designated "greenness" to segment consumer markets (Schwartz and Miller, 1991).

The eco-marketing orientation could be conceptually decomposed into Kotler's (1988) four components of the marketing orientation, augmented by both an explicit concern for ecologically and socially responsible business and consumer behavior and the innovative and environmental adaptive characteristics of the entrepreneurial orientation. Dimensions of the proposed eco-marketing orientation would include: (1) a market focus, (2) an obsession with both known and latent customer needs, (3) integrated and coordinated marketing throughout the entire organization, (4) focus on long-term profitability, (5) an explicit concern for the ecological and social aspects of all business activities and decisions, and (6) a proclivity to innovate and adapt to exploit environmental opportunities.

An eco-marketing orientation, adapting McNamara's (1972) framework for measuring an organization's degree of marketing orientation, may be measured by some combination of structural and behavioral indicators. Structural indicators may include: (1) employee, supplier, community, and customer eco-education programs; (2) toll free social concern and eco-hotlines; (3) a designated ecological and social concern marketing staff; (4) cradle to grave planned product eco-life-cycles; (5) explicitly considering ecological and social concerns in all strategic and tactical planning; and (6) a systematic environmental scanning procedure explicit in all business decision making.

Behavioral indicators of an eco-marketing orientation may include: (1) packaging in recyclable containers; (2) packaging in containers made of recyclable material; (3) having an active recycling program; (4) having a commitment to buy products which have been produced utilizing some proportion of recycled materials; (5) actively seeking input from ecological and social concern organizations on strategic decisions; (6) the abandonment of the archaic "planned obsolescence" product management framework; and (7) a tendency to adapt to environmental changes with innovations.

Behavioral indicators of a green orientation are currently measured by environmental and product testing organizations such as the Green Cross and the Green Seal organizations which assess product and packaging characteristics to determine if these characteristics meet minimum environmental criteria (Silver, 1990). A summary of four of the traditional business orientations compared to the proposed eco-marketing orientation is provided in Table 2.2.

SUPPORT FOR AN ECO-MARKETING ORIENTATION AS A STRATEGIC RESPONSE TO ENVIRONMENTAL DYNAMICS

Firms attempting to be perceived by consumers as legitimate global citizens must explicitly consider the impact of their business decisions and activities on both the ecology and society (Varadarajan, 1992). Business must transcend a concern for profits from individual product offerings to a vision of a managerial approach that consciously develops products that are congruent with global social and ecological needs.

Coddington (1990) surmises that ecological marketing must become an essential element of the marketing mix. Not only does there have to be a perception that ecological marketing is a principal component of a company's corporate ethics, but Coddington indicates that marketers should include the following initiatives in their environmental marketing plan (1990):

1. internal environmental marketing seminars
2. consumer research
3. product development
4. advertising and promotion
5. "green" retail manager
6. sales education and incentive programs
7. local marketing and promotion

TABLE 2.2. Underlying Business Philosophies Compared

ORIENTATION SYMPTOM[a]	PRODUCTION ORIENTATION[a]	SALES ORIENTATION[a]	MARKETING ORIENTATION[a]	ENTERPRENEURIAL ORIENTATION[b]
TYPICAL STRATEGY	Lower costs	Increase sales volume	Build market share and profitability	Seek high risk/high return opportunities
KEY SYSTEMS	Cost accounting	Sales projections	Strategic marketing plan	Growth, profits
TRADITIONAL STRENGTHS	Engineering, logistics	Sales	Marketing	Pragmatic, aggressive marketing, innovative
NORMAL FOCUS	Internal efficiencies	Short-term sales, distribution	Customer satisfaction, satisfy organization goals	Growth innovation, dominance
TYPICAL RESPONSE TO COMPETITIVE PRESSURE	Cut costs	Cut price, increase selling efforts	Consumer research, modification of marketing mix	Innovative solutions, aggressive response toward competition
OVERALL MENTAL SET	"What we need to do in this company is get our costs down and our quality up"	"Where can I sell what we make"	"What will customers buy that we can profitably make"	"What project offers the best opportunity"

a Adapted from Cravens, Hills, and Woodruff (1987)
b Adapted from Miles and Arnold (1991)

TABLE 2.2. (continued)

ORIENTATION SYMPTOM[a]	GREEN ORIENTATION
TYPICAL STRATEGY	Eco-friendly products and innovative business practices that engender an enhanced environment.
KEY SYSTEMS	Monitoring perceived corporate environmental sensitivity held by major market segments, environmental scanning, innovative product development, management of technology.
TRADITIONAL STRENGTHS	Marketing, product innovation, logistics innovation.
NORMAL FOCUS	Customer and societal satisfaction with the total product, including service, and organizational business practices.
TYPICAL RESPONSE TO COMPETITIVE PRESSURE	Educate consumers about the organization's eco-programs including (1) waste recycling and eco-friendly disposal; (2) packaging in recyclable containers; (3) packaging in containers made of recycled materials; (4) organizational commitment to buy products produced from recycled materials; (5) employee, supplier, community, and customer eco-education programs, and (6) innovation.
OVERALL MENTAL SET	"What we need to do in this company is to create high value, eco-friendly products; sold in high volumes, through traditional distributors, to a wide array of consumers. Our objectives include: (1) to educate non-green consumers to have product form insistence for green and eco-friendly products; (2) to produce high value eco-friendly products that will create brand preference for our brands by green consumers; and (3) to achieve sufficient distribution to minimize stockouts and brand switching."

a Adapted from Cravens, Hills, and Woodruff (1987)

The "green" consumer point of view cannot be ignored. In a survey conducted in the United States of 400 Midwestern consumers, 36 percent of the respondents were found to be "very likely" to change from one food brand to another competitive label which used a recycled carton; only 2.8 percent stated that they would be "somewhat unlikely" to make brand changes because of recycled packaging (Eisenhart, 1990). In many cases, mandatory environmental legislation is also forcing behavioral changes in consumers. Business may adopt an eco-marketing orientation as a strategic response to the dynamic environments of the nineties.

THE ADOPTION OF AN ECO-MARKETING ORIENTATION

What then, must corporations do to adapt an eco-marketing orientation? Prior to adoption of the eco-marketing orientation, the corporation must have internalized into its information processing and decision-making frameworks the basic tenants of the marketing orientation and the environmental adaptive and innovative characteristics of the entrepreneurial orientation. The optimal candidate for the adoption of the eco-marketing orientation will be an environmentally adaptive, comprehensively customer need-obsessed, market-focused, financially sound, future-oriented, innovative organization. The organization should then augment its information processing and heuristic frameworks with the explicit consideration of the ecological and social dimensions of all business actions and decisions. Suggestions for the adoption of an eco-marketing orientation are provided in Table 2.3.

CONCLUSION

The eco-marketing orientation appears to be an emerging strategic response by some organizations to the turbulent social and natural environments of the nineties. As a global society evolves, there appears to be an evolutionary process at work, resulting in the progression of organizational philosophies from the industrial-focused production orientation to the social ecology-focused eco-marketing orientation. As the natural environment becomes a paramount

TABLE 2.3. Suggested Strategies to Change from One of the Traditional Business Orientations to a Green Philosophy

ORIENTATION SYMPTOM	PRODUCTION ORIENTATION	SALES ORIENTATION	MARKETING ORIENTATION	ENTREPRENEURIAL ORIENTATION
TYPICAL STRATEGY	Seek cost saving by utilizing recycled materials, customer needs focus	Target sales communication by discussing eco-attributes, long-term exchanges focusing on customer needs	Determine the consumer's and society's long-term needs, consider social and ecological impacts	Exploit the high interest in green-oriented products via product development
KEY SYSTEMS TO ENGENDER ECO-MARKETING	Reverse logistics, Real time flexible manufacturing to reduce waste, Superior engineering	Market segmentation by green orientation, abandon planned obsolescence, consider ecological and societal impact of decisions	Focus on anticipating customer and society needs and alter demand for eco-products by education, de-market products that are harmful to society	Innovation in green or socially responsible venues
NEW STRENGTHS	Soft engineering, logistical responsibility from production to reuse, creation of durable products	Promoting superior green attributes	Demand modification, social responsive marketing, adopt a product durability standard	Innovation, product development, environmental assessments

constraint, more firms may need to consider the suggestions offered and adopt an eco-marketing orientation in the development of unique competitive advantages.

REFERENCES

Ansoff, Igor (1965), *Corporate Strategy*, New York: McGraw-Hill.

Borch, Fred J. (1957), *The Marketing Philosophy As a Way of Business Life*, New York: General Electric.

Coddington, Walter (1990), "How to Green Up Your Marketing Mix," *Advertising Age*, 61 (September 3), 30.

Covin, Jeffrey G. and Dennis P. Slevin (1989), "Strategic Management of Small Firms in Hostile and Benign Environments," *Strategic Management Journal*, 10 (January), 75-87.

Cravens, David W., Gerald E. Hills, and Robert B. Woodruff (1987), *Marketing Management*, Homewood, Illinois: Irwin.

Crosby, Lawrence A., James D. Gill, and James R. Taylor (1981), "Consumer/Voter Behavior in the Passage of the Michigan Container Law," *Journal of Marketing*, 45 (Spring), 19-32.

Deshpande, Rohit and Frederick E. Webster, Jr. (1989), "Organizational Culture and Marketing: Defining the Research Agenda," *Journal of Marketing*, 53 (January), 3-15.

Eisenhart, Tom (1990), "There's Gold in That Garbage," *Business Marketing*, (November), 24.

Foxall, Gordon (1984), *Corporate Innovation: Marketing and Strategy*, New York: St. Martin's Press.

Ginsberg, Ari (1985), "Measuring Changes in Entrepreneurial Orientation Following Industry Deregulation: The Development of a Diagnostic Instrument," *Proceedings of the First Biennial Conference of the U.S. Affiliate of the International Council for Small Business.*

Glick, William H. (1985), "Conceptualizing and Measuring Organizational and Psychological Climate: Pitfalls in Multilevel Research," *Academy of Management Review*, 10 (3), 601-616.

Hentze, Elizabeth A. (1991), "What Is the Corporate Message?" *Academy of Marketing Science News*, 12 (July), 12.

Houston, Franklin S. and Julie B. Gassenheimer (1987), "Marketing and Exchange," *Journal of Marketing*, 51 (October), 3-18.

Hunt, Shelby D. (1976), "The Nature and Scope of Marketing," *Journal of Marketing*, 40 (July), 17-28.

Keith, Robert J. (1959), "An Interpretation of the Marketing Concept," in *Advancing Marketing Efficiency*, Proceedings of the Forty-First National Conference, Chicago, Illinois: American Marketing Association.

Khandwalla, P. N. (1976/77), "Some Top Management Styles, Their Context and Performance," *Organization and Administrative Sciences*, 7 (Winter), 21-51.

Khandwalla, P. N. (1977), *The Design of Organizations*, New York: Harcourt Brace Jovanovich.

King, Robert L. (1965), "The Marketing Concept," in *Science in Marketing*, Schwartz, George (ed.), New York: John Wiley and Sons, Inc.

Kotler, Philip (1972), "A Generic Concept of Marketing," *Journal of Marketing*, 36 (April), 46-54.

Kotler, Philip (1973), "The Major Tasks of Marketing Management," *Journal of Marketing*, 37 (October), 42-49.

Kotler, Philip (1988), *Marketing Management, Analysis Planning, Implementation and Control*, Englewood Cliffs, NJ: Prentice Hall.

Kotler, Philip and Sidney J. Levy (1969), "Broadening the Concept of Marketing," *Journal of Marketing*, 33 (January), 10-15.

Kotler, Philip and Gerald Zaltman (1971), "Social Marketing: An Approach to Planned Social Change," *Journal of Marketing*, 35 (July), 3-12.

Marketing News (1985), "AMA Board Approves New Marketing Definition," (March 1), 1.

McCarthy, E. Jerome and William D. Perreault (1984), *Basic Marketing*, Homewood, Illinois: Richard D. Irwin, Inc.

McNamara, Carlton P. (1972), "The Present Status of the Marketing Concept," *Journal of Marketing*, 36 (January), 50-57.

Miles, Morgan P. and Danny R. Arnold (1991), "The Relationship Between Marketing Orientation and Entrepreneurial Orientation," *Entrepreneurship Theory and Practice*, 15 (4) 49-65.

Munilla, Linda S. (1990), "Organizational Communication and the Environment," *The Bulletin of Organizational Communication*, 2 (1) (August 6), 8-9.

Peterson, Robin T. (1989), "Small Business Adoption of the Marketing Concept vs. Other Business Strategies," *Journal of Small Business Management*, (January), 38-46.

Pettigrew, A. M. (1979), "On Studying Organizational Cultures," *Administrative Science Quarterly*, 24, 570-581.

Polonsky, Michael J. (1991), "Australia Sets Guidelines for 'Green Marketing,' " *Marketing News*, 25 (21), 6,18.

Schwartz, Joe and Thomas Miller (1991), "The Earth's Best Friends," *American Demographics*, (February), 26-35.

Silver, Marc (1990), "Seals for the Times," *U.S. News and World Report*, (November), 81-85.

Smith, Garry D., Danny R. Arnold, and Bobby G. Bizzell (1988), *Business Strategy and Policy*, Boston, MA: Houghton Mifflin Company.

Varadarajan, P. Rajan (1992), "Marketing Contribution to Strategy: The View from a Different Looking Glass," *Journal of the Academy of Marketing Science*, 20 (4), 335-343.

Zikmund, William and Michael D'Amico (1986), *Marketing*, New York: John Wiley and Sons.

Chapter 3

Environmental Marketing: Bridging the Divide Between the Consumption Culture and Environmentalism

Robert D. Mackoy
Roger Calantone
Cornelia DrÖge

SUMMARY. Development of successful environmental marketing strategies is rooted in an understanding of the relationship between environmentalism and the consumption culture. Critiques of the consumption culture, based in part on Schudson (1991), provide a framework for identifying distinct dimensions of environmentalism. Three types of environmental marketing–green marketing, demarketing, and societal issues marketing–are discussed within the framework. It is concluded that environmental marketing is probably most effective when it incorporates dimensions of environmentalism that do not dogmatically attack core consumption culture values.

INTRODUCTION

Environmentalism has had a significant impact on modern society, and indeed, continues to grab a significant share of media coverage and public attention. The 1992 Earth Summit in Rio, the continuing debate on global warming and the hole in the ozone, the "toxic trains" and "garbage barges," and the extent of pollution in Eastern Europe are visible recent examples. A recent Gallup poll reported that 75% of Americans consider themselves to be environmentalists.

Environmental marketing is rooted in the essential tension between environmentalism and modern mass consumption. To understand the strategic function and forms of environmental marketing, one must understand this relationship. On the one hand, one purpose of environmental marketing is to increase the consumption of a particular set of goods and services; on the other hand, it appeals to consumers' environmentalist sympathies, which may in part be a reaction against modern patterns of consumption. To be effective, environmental marketing must tap into, or at least be congruent with, environmentalism *and* the values of the modern "culture of consumption." We develop a framework for analyzing environmental marketing by examining environmentalism as a set of "critiques" of this consumption culture. It is our intention that the framework help managers and policy makers in business, not-for-profit, and governmental organizations to better understand the underlying forces affecting environmental marketing.

The analysis is organized as follows: First, essential terms are defined. Then, environmental orientations are classified as "critiques" of the consumption culture. The nature of the six critiques delineates the essential tension between environmentalism and consumption. The steps for effective environmental marketing are outlined. Using the framework for the analysis of the consumption culture-environmentalism tension developed previously, the alternatives at each step are delineated and evaluated.

DEFINITION OF TERMS

Environmentalism

Environmentalism may legitimately be defined in a variety of ways. For the purpose of this analysis, environmentalism will be a loosely defined umbrella term covering issues related to air and water pollution, land use, hazardous materials and related health problems, solid waste disposal, resource depletion, energy use, and biosphere integrity. This definition encompasses the topics covered in the Valdez Principles (Barnard 1990) and is consistent with the related concept of "ecological concern" as operationalized by Van

Liere and Dunlap (1982) and Gill, Crosby, and Taylor (1986). One notable omission from this definition is the issue of overpopulation; while this is a critical global issue with environmental implications, it is less central to this discussion of the western consumption culture and environmental marketing.

The "Consumption Culture"

The "consumption culture" is also an umbrella term. It refers to the complex set of phenomena which characterizes modern society's focus on producing and consuming goods above some minimum level. Numerous works have described and analyzed the consumption culture (e.g., Fox and Lears 1983; Galbraith 1958; Horowitz 1985; Mason 1984; McKenrick, Brewer, and Plumb 1982; Rassuli and Hollander 1986), so a detailed description will not be presented here. Most historical analyses posit the following three characteristics as necessary but not sufficient to define the consumption culture: (1) Division between production and consumption, and the crucial role of exchange; (2) Mass products and mass markets involving large numbers of consumers living above subsistence levels; and (3) New product proliferation and the high value placed on newness and fashion over durability and utility. Overall, goods and services are assigned value and symbolic meaning other than merely those related to the satisfaction of core needs.

CLASSIFICATION OF ENVIRONMENTAL ARGUMENTS: THE FRAMEWORK FOR ANALYSIS

Schudson (1991) systematically examined arguments against the consumption culture and classified them into five distinct "critiques" of the consumption culture. Note that Schudson classified critiques, not critics, and thus although each type of critique will be examined separately, a single individual may voice two or more critiques. The analysis that follows demonstrates that all five types of critique identified by Schudson are relevant to environmentalism, but a complete framework demands inclusion of a sixth critique (i.e., the systems perspective). It is important to understand these critiques because they are voiced in one form or another by consumers who comprise segments of interest to environmental marketers. Once the critiques are understood, strategies can be developed for addressing specific consumer segments on a managerial level and general issues on a public policy level.

Puritan

The Puritan critique expresses the belief that nature or "the earth" is itself a spiritual or mystical power, and that the consumption culture is dangerous for at least two reasons. First, it distracts individuals from the spiritual importance of the environment by focusing on the false meaning and significance of goods. This argument is most congruent with Schudson's (1991) original characterization of the Puritan critique. Second, the consumption culture defiles that which is holy by destroying land, polluting air and water, and needlessly killing flora and fauna.

Unlike the Quaker and Marxist critiques, the Puritan critique is rooted in a long tradition of "primitive" cultures. Nature formed the basis of religious beliefs of cultures widely dispersed geographically and temporally (Eliade 1963), typified by belief in the Great Spirit which is found in nearly every native American Indian tradition. A similar perspective was adopted by a more modern tradition of environmental Puritans which developed in parallel with the consumption culture. This perspective is clearly evident in the writings of Thoreau (1984) and Muir (1954) in the 1800s, and Leopold (1966) and Brower (1964) in the 1900s. In Table 3.1, examples are offered to illustrate the Puritan as well as the other critiques.

Environmental Puritan arguments appear not to be especially effective in motivating widespread environmental activities. However, such arguments are commonly expressed by leaders of environmental groups, and are often credited with being a leader's motivational source. Whether these beliefs are the cause or the effect of environmental fervor, however, is unclear.

Quaker

The Quaker critique centers on the notion that consumption culture is wasteful. Within the broad domain of environmentalism,

TABLE 3.1. Examples of Environmental Arguments Against Consumption Culture–Schudson's Five Critiques Perspective

Puritan
Summary: Consumption culture is aspiritual, anti-spiritual.

Example: "Man has not yet completed the full circle toward a realization that his own laws of life must conform in the long view with those greater laws to which he still and forever owes allegiance . . . . Man at last has conquered the land. But to what ultimate end no one can say. There is only a vague, inquiet feeling that in all his scheme of domination there is something he might have forgotten" (Waters 1946).

Quaker
Summary: Consumption culture is wasteful and ignores its true costs.

Example: "As the tide of chemicals born of the Industrial Age has arisen to engulf our environment, a drastic change has come about in the nature of the most serious public health problems . . . biological effects of chemicals are cumulative over long periods of time, and the hazard . . . may depend on the sum of exposures received throughout [one's] lifetime. For these very reasons the dangers are easily ignored" (Carson 1962, pp. 188-189).

Republican
Summary: Consumption culture encourages civic irresponsibility.

Example: "The conflict with hydroelectric development is . . . direct, for man wants to get energy from the water gravity brings down. . . . We need to remember that our choice to preserve is a temporary determination at best. Our choice to sacrifice, however, requires all future men to live by our choice" (Brower 1964, p. 57).

Marxist
Summary: Consumption culture is based on social injustices.

Example: "While the Kettlemen suit tests the theory of 'environmental racism,' the issue isn't just local. The EPA is studying whether minorities bear the brunt of nations' toxic pollution. And [other] studies . . . show that waste sites are mostly in black or Hispanic communities" (Siler 1991, p. 116).

Aristocrat
Summary: Consumption culture destroys natural beauty.

Example: "The marshlands that once sprawled over the prairie from the Illinois to the Athabasca are shrinking northward. Man cannot live by marsh alone, therefore he must needs live marshless. Progress cannot abide that farmland and marshland, wild and tame, exist in mutual toleration and harmony. So with dredge and dyke, tile and torch, we sucked the cornbelt dry, and now the wheatbelt. Blue lake becomes green bog, green bog becomes caked mud, caked mud becomes a wheatfield" (Leopold 1966, p. 172).

"waste" covers a wide range of specifics. Schudson (1991) characterized the Quaker critique as an attack on the lack of utility and durability of goods, with new product proliferation valued simply for its own sake. Environmentalism criticizes the wasted material and energy resources utilized to produce frivolous or poorly made goods. It is not consumption per se, but the waste associated with excesses which is criticized. Environmentalism has fashioned this type of critique into its most powerful attack on consumption culture: i.e., economic irrationality associated with waste (e.g., Siebert 1981). According to this argument, the true costs associated with waste are generally not factored into rational decision processes. If the true costs were considered, it is assumed that different decisions would follow.

The two major sources of ignored costs are true waste disposal costs and the replacement costs of resources consumed. The first type includes costs associated with intentional disposal of waste, such as incineration, as well as unintentional disposal, such as air pollution. There are costs associated with disposal, which if known and used in the planning stages, would have altered any cost benefit, return on investment, return on asset, or net present value calculations. For example, had the cost of nuclear fuel disposal been factored into the original investment calculations, it is doubtful as many nuclear power plants would have been constructed. If costs associated with air pollution such as the detrimental effects of acid rain, ozone depletion, and global warming (which many environmentalists assume exist and are caused by air pollution) were known and charged back to a firm, the firm might have chosen to produce differently or not at all. Waste production of any kind can be viewed as the result of production inefficiencies, and the fact that firms produce waste may be an indication of unnecessary direct costs (Kleiner 1991).

The second type of ignored costs are the true replacement costs of resources used. Consumers would choose to consume differently, the environmental argument states, if costs associated with resource replacement or substitution were factored into the price of goods. For example, fossil fuels have finite (though possibly large) supplies, and this ultimate limit should be carefully factored into current fossil fuel and alternative fuel prices.

The Quaker critique is perhaps the most sophisticated, and certainly the most effective, most visible argument used in political and policy discussions about environmentalism. For example, Lovins (1976) used this argument in his influential call for development of appropriate energy sources; Schumacher (1973) used this line of reasoning in his famous *Small Is Beautiful*. The Quaker critique is often seen in combination with the Puritan or with the Marxist, but Quaker arguments seem to be widely accepted as the most rational environmental argument against excesses in the buy-use-dispose consumption cycle.

Republican

The Republican critique focuses on the concept of social or civic responsibility. In environmentalism, the Republican critique translates into the idea that each citizen has a duty to the community and future generations to behave in an environmentally responsible manner, and to urge others to maintain intergenerational equity. In this way, social norms hopefully emerge to guide appropriate behavior. Social norms serve along with environmental activism to coalesce community action on specific issues such as river cleanups and voluntary recycling programs. Of course, the original rationale for an action may have been based on different reasoning. A good example of an environmental issue which was first marketed based on another critique is littering. Littering used to be tolerated much more so than it is today. In the United States, for example, early campaigns called for citizens to "beautify America" by not littering, which is basically an Aristocrat appeal. However, over time, anti-littering has become a social norm.

Like the Quaker critique, the Republican critique is not anti-consumption per se. Rather, it is opposed to some excesses specifically associated with the consumption culture. Republicans urge consumers, producers, and others to factor in the civic consequences of consumption.

Marxist

The Marxist critique is the most dogmatic in its criticism of the consumption culture. The environmental dimension of the Marxist critique focuses on the inequitable socioenvironmental implications of the consumption culture. According to this argument, the bourgeoisie support their extravagant and undeserved lifestyles by exploiting the working classes. Similarly, they exploit the natural resources of poorer countries and dispose waste in the neighborhoods (and countries) of the oppressed. The bourgeoisie are able to mask these social injustices by political oppression in poorer countries, and by numbing and distracting the masses with consumer goods.

In general, people do not like to live near environmentally negative vestiges of the consumption culture, such as dumps and incinerators. This phenomenon is commonly referred to as the NIMBY (not in my backyard) sentiment. Wealthy neighborhoods generally seem to be successful in stopping undesirable developments. Success is based partly on their knowledge of the system, their economic clout, and their political clout. Poor and minority neighborhoods mobilize less effectively behind NIMBY efforts, so that is where these sites are located (e.g., Siler 1991). Globally, the Marxist critique is illustrated by the well-publicized perceptions of a North-South division of nations at the Rio Earth Summit (Bidwai 1992), and in recent North American Free Trade Agreement discussions regarding extensive industrial pollution by relocated U.S. manufacturing facilities (Old, Baker, and Walker 1992). The Marxist critique stresses that such environmental quality inequities will persist as long as the consumption culture with its capitalist market system exists.

Aristocrat

The Aristocrat critique centers on the destruction of natural aesthetics by the consumption culture. Much of nature is beautiful, and that beauty has value in and of itself. Thus, the Aristocrat criticizes development in or near scenic areas. Park and wilderness expansion is supported, but making those areas too accessible is not. This position has been criticized as being elitist because it advocates using public funds and public land, but in such a way that the public is largely excluded from experiencing that natural beauty. The Aristocrat might respond that the exclusion is necessary to preserve the beauty, that it is logically necessary to make the commons less common, and that even those who do not physically visit the areas can benefit just by knowing they exist. Besides, only in this way can the beauty be preserved for "future generations."

The Aristocrat critique has been used successfully by a broad range of advocates. It forms the central argument President Teddy Roosevelt used to initiate the United States National Park system. It was also central to Greenpeace's campaign to protect baby harp seals.

The Systems Perspective

Systems theory rests on the observation that the world is dynamic. Systems theory seeks to impose order on complex dynamics by conceptualizing patterns of related objects and processes as systems. Two early systems theorists, Wroe Alderson and C. West Churchman, conceive of the environment as the largest general system, the system within which all other systems operate. As such, it and the sun are the ultimate *resources* for energy and material, and the ultimate *receptacles* of waste. Thus, to the extent that the consumption culture inputs from and outputs to the environment jeopardize the health of the environment, the survival of all other systems is jeopardized. This line of reasoning represents a sixth critique of consumption culture, referred to hereafter as the "Systems critique." The imperative behind this critique is the recognition that the stake is not simply economic, social, or personal efficiencies, or abstractions such as beauty, justice, or religious beliefs. The stake is survival itself.

Both Churchman and Alderson do, however, incorporate some of the rationales of other critiques in developing and explaining the decision maker's motivation to comply with the normative guidelines. Alderson (1964) adopts a Quaker perspective by stating that decision makers should take or avoid actions based on ". . . pursuit of rational self-interest" (p. 107). Churchman, on the other hand, adopts a Republican perspective and states that decision makers have the responsibility to behave in a way that future generations would want them to behave (1961). However, both ground their logic in the Systems critique, that real environmental limits threaten survival itself.

One of the best-known examples of the Systems critique is found in *Limits to Growth* (Meadows et al. 1972). The book details the perceived physical limits of the environment to support growth of both the consumption culture and world population. That many of the projections based on "facts" were so grossly inaccurate highlights the distinction between the Systems critique as a theoretical construct and the operationalization and use of its concepts.

Summary

The consumption culture's characteristics have been defined and the six main classes of critiques have been discussed. Each critique has its environmentally focused manifestation. All six would agree that the environmental credo of "reduce-reuse-recycle" is legitimate, but for different reasons. All agree that the present manifestation of "buy-use-dispose" is inappropriate, but for different reasons. This tension between "reduce-reuse-recycle" and "buy-use-dispose" has implications for marketing, as we examine in the next section.

ENVIRONMENTAL MARKETING: A HOLISTIC VIEW

Now that the basic rationales underlying the environmental critiques have been placed in context, the role of environmental marketing in effectively addressing the essential consumption-environmentalism tension can be addressed. The basic steps are outlined in this section.

The Identification of Stakeholders

Churchman recommends that to truly understand and evaluate a system, all stakeholders should first be identified. To analyze environmental issues, present and future stakeholders at both the micro and macro levels can be identified as follows: (1) on the micro/personal level are individuals and households; and (2) on the macro/external level are firms, other organizations, and governments. To facilitate the analysis, we follow Alderson's (1957) lead and focus on the household as the relevant unit of analysis at the micro level. Of course, any stakeholder category may be expanded to fit the situation being analyzed. For example, instead of having one stakeholder labeled "firms," a company may wish to list all major competitors. Instead of a single stakeholder labeled "household," all major market segments could be included.

The Impact of Actions

Next, Churchman (1968) recommends that implications of potential actions of any stakeholder on all others should be described. Secondary and tertiary effects should also be considered. One way to conceptualize the process is to construct a matrix. The stakeholders listed down the left side of the matrix represent initiating agents; stakeholders listed across the top represent affected agents. Any action contemplated by any particular stakeholder can be examined by considering its effect on each other stakeholder by moving across a row. The process becomes iterative when the response of an impacted party is considered.

The analysis should also include *future* stakeholders, even though their inclusion as initiating agents that may affect present stakeholders appears counterintuitive. However, it is clear that anticipated actions of a competitor or governmental agency may affect the present activities of a particular stakeholder. The primary use of this type of analysis is to ensure that decisions are made without the unintentional omission of relevant stakeholders.

The Resolution of Conflict

The explicit recognition of competition and disagreement among various stakeholders raises questions about how disputes might be resolved, especially on significant issues requiring policy decisions. Recall that *Limits to Growth* (Meadows et al. 1972) initiated a major debate over "the numbers" as well as over implied priorities. Indeed, the appropriate forum for resolving environmental issues on a policy level is unclear. Many conflicts can be traced to conflicting *values*, as the discussion about the five critiques of the consumption culture made clear. To the extent that the issues raised involve values, ethical and political sphere debates appear to be appropriate (Hardin 1968); to the extent that resolution revolves around questions of *fact*, science appears to be the most relevant sphere.

Most if not all significant environmental issues involve questions of both values and facts. Resolution is further hampered by the often conflicting discovery and presentation of "facts" by stakeholders with differing values. Questions of investigator integrity, methods validity and reliability, and logic cloud even supposedly straightforward "discovery of facts." Davis (1992) presents an example of this involving a dispute over the effects of exposure to cadmium. One potentially fruitful method of "working around" conflicting values and inconsistent facts en route to broadly supported policy development is through consensus formation; such an approach is being used in the regulated utility industry (A&C Enercom et al. 1990).

Even when consensus can be reached on the facts, disputes can arise over their use and presentation. For example, are Mobil's trash bags really biodegradable as claimed? The answer appears to be: "yes, but not in conditions commonly found in landfills." Mobil used the term biodegradable in advertising and packaging the bags. Later, the U.S. Federal Trade Commission ordered them to stop using the term because it was misleading. To lend credence to their factual claims, marketers have turned to independent environmental organizations for validation. Two such organizations, Green Cross and Green Seal, are testing and certifying the earth-friendly nature of consumer products, though it is unclear what the effects of such certification are.

IDENTIFICATION OF ENVIRONMENTAL MARKETING APPROACHES

Different organizational stakeholders tend to use different marketing approaches to deal with other stakeholders. Firms usually employ *demarketing* or *green marketing* concepts. Other organizations and governmental stakeholders also employ *social issues marketing* concepts. These three common marketing approaches, their goals and basic strategies, and the framework critiques with which they are compatible are shown in Table 3.2.

Demarketing is based on the notion that demand sometimes exceeds supply, and that to maintain optimal long-term profitability, demand must be managed (Kotler and Levy 1971). Traditionally, marketers have viewed their task as maximizing demand by satisfying consumer wants and needs. However, under conditions in which supply is limited or fluctuating, managing demand to match supply avoids shortages and minimizes customer frustration. An example of demarketing is time-of-use rates offered by electric utilities which operate near capacity. Customers are charged low usage rates

TABLE 3.2. Approaches to Environmental Marketing

Compatible Approach	Basic Goals	Strategy	Critiques*
Demarketing	Long term profits	Match demand with variable supply	S,Q,R
Green marketing	Maximum profits	Appeal to environmentally sensitive segment	Q,R,S
Societal Issue Marketing	Socio-political	Change attitudes and behavior in "socially desirable" directions	S,Q,R,A,P,M

*Q-Quaker, R-Republican, S-Systems, A-Aristocrat, P-Puritan, M-Marxist

when supply exceeds demand and high rates when demand approaches or exceeds supply.

As Table 3.2 indicates, demarketing is most compatible with the Systems, Quaker, and Republican critiques. The Systems critique is based on the premise that some resources are limited; as we have just seen, this scarcity provides the basic rationale behind demarketing. The Quaker critique stresses waste avoidance and "true" economic rationality, notions that are consistent with the scarce resource premise of demarketing. The Republican critique emphasizes civic responsibility; demarketing appeals often focus on the responsibility of preserving scarce resources for future generations. The demarketing-compatible outcomes desired by all three critiques are to ensure longer-term consumption by sacrificing unchecked short-term consumption.

Green marketing is a term that became popularized in the 1980s to describe efforts to address the needs and wants of a segment of consumers who express environmental concerns. Green marketers employ traditional marketing strategies by creating and adapting products, distribution channels, promotional efforts, and/or pricing strategies to target the new segment. Sometimes new promotional appeals were used to market products that had been in existence a long time (e.g., insulation). Sometimes new products and new industries arose (e.g., solar water heating). In all cases, however, green marketers have had the goal of maximizing demand and profits, and have attempted to do so by adopting traditional marketing practices.

Green marketing is most compatible with the Quaker, Republican, and Systems critiques (see Table 3.2). The market segments that express environmental concerns wish to consume, but they want to do so in a manner that is less wasteful (Quaker critique), more responsible (Republican critique), and more cognizant of limits of the environment to provide resources and/or absorb wastes (Systems critique) than the existing consumption culture. Green marketers increase the appeal of their products and services by explicitly addressing these three critiques in their design and promotion. Thus, Green marketing is not only compatible with these critiques, the critiques can be actively used to increase consumption of their products and services.

Government and other organizational stakeholders utilize concepts identified from *societal issues marketing*. Societal issues marketing, sometimes called social marketing, adapts marketing tactics and strategies to the development and promotion of social goals (Kotler and Zaltman 1971). For example, municipalities use such tools to encourage car pooling, promote recycling programs, and fight litter. Societal issues marketing strategies have been utilized by firms through both public relations and paid advertising channels because for-profit firms are often stakeholders in public policy issues.

Societal issues marketing is theoretically compatible with any of the six critiques (Table 3.2). Any goal of social change can be addressed using societal issues marketing tactics. A stakeholder may wish to implement a change within the context of the consumption culture, or may wish to change the consumption culture itself. The specific combination of stakeholder and issue will determine which critiques are most compatible with a specific issue, and societal issues marketers can utilize the most appropriate critique(s) in designing appeals.

Perceived Legitimacy of Marketing Messages

Table 3.2 lists environmental marketing approaches and matches them with *theoretically* compatible types of critiques. In choosing an appeal based on a critique, the marketer must consider the issue of *effectiveness* as well as compatibility. One key concept of social issues marketing is useful in determining effectiveness: ". . . . attempt to gain people's voluntary cooperation by sensing and satisfying their needs expressed by their attitudes and behaviors" (Sterngold and Kotler 1979, 196-197). Recall that some of the six critiques appeared to be more anti-consumption culture than others, but clearly virulent anti-consumption messages are incongruent with the dominant consumption values of society. We refer to this as anti-consumption culture dogmatism. Also, recall that some of the critiques appear to be more widely accepted as legitimate among environmentalists. Combining these two dimensions, *anti-consumption culture dogmatism* and *perceived legitimacy of critique*, yields a two by two matrix (see Table 3.3).

Environmental marketers who market traditional goods and services will probably want to present their appeals in a manner congruent with the Quaker or Republican critiques in the first cell. These are widely perceived as legitimate and they are not inherently inconsistent with consumption. Green marketers and demarketers seem to have embraced this strategy by using traditional marketing concepts and tools to promote everything from fuel-efficient automobiles to non-polluting detergents to greeting cards printed on recycled paper.

Appeals associated with the Aristocrat critique should be used cautiously to promote goods and services that are unique and beautiful, as well as being environmentally benign. By their nature, such goods and services will appeal to a segment that perceives itself as

TABLE 3.3. Categorization of Six Critiques

		Anti-Consumption Dogmatism	
		Low	High
Perception of Legitimacy by Environmentalists	*Widely Accepted*	Quaker Republican	Systems
	Narrowly Accepted	Aristocrat Marxist	Puritan

"select" or "special," but without the potentially damning label of "elitist." High performance canoeing and backpacking equipment and unique adventure vacations are examples.

Green marketers and demarketers are unlikely to sell many products using Puritan or Marxist appeals because the underlying ideas are inherently anti-consumption and not widely held. Books and magazines appear to be the only major products sold in a manner consistent with these two critiques. In addition, for-profit firms are unlikely to find a position of compromise when engaging in public discussion with those who focus on one of these dogmatic critiques. It seems advisable to avoid such discussions or to conclude them as quickly as possible.

Finally, although the systems perspective critique is generally accepted as a legitimate critique of the consumption culture, its high anti-consumption culture dogmatism precludes its wide use as a *primary* appeal by green marketers. However, it does form the basis for effective demarketing and societal issue demarketing, in part because it appears to be based on real physical limits rather than sociopolitical values.

CONCLUSION

The consumption culture, characterized by a "buy-use-dispose cycle" for goods and services, has evolved into one of the most powerful forces affecting both individual and social behavior. Widespread desire for greater consumption is credited with being a factor in the breakup of the Soviet Union and the radical changes to other centrally planned economies. It is also considered to be a motivating factor in the desire to develop poorer nations. The desire to participate in the buy-use-dispose cycle appears to be universal.

One unanswered question concerns the ultimate compatibility of environmentalism with the consumption culture. The environmental concerns as voiced by the six critiques presented here span a broad range of anti-consumption culture dogmatism. The two most radical, the Puritan and modern Marxist critiques, stand outside the consumption culture in a fervent but futile attempt to stop it. As such, their positions appear to be ultimately incompatible with the consumption culture's core values. In contrast, the Quaker, Republican, and Aristocrat critiques attempt to modify consumption. Environmental marketing offers one possible set of tools for incorporating the essence of these three moderate critiques within the reality of a powerful consumption culture. Thus, these critiques appear to offer the best platform for marketers in the foreseeable future.

REFERENCES

A&C Enercom et al. (1990), *Report of the Statewide Collaborative Process: An Energy Efficiency Blueprint for California.*

Alderson, Wroe (1957), *Marketing Behavior and Executive Action*, Homewood, IL: Richard D. Irwin.

Alderson, Wroe (1964), "A Normative Theory of Marketing Systems," in *Theory in Marketing*, Reavis Cox, Wroe Alderson, and Stanley J. Shapiro (eds.), Homewood, IL: Richard D. Irwin, 92-108.

Barnard, Jayne W. (1990), "Exxon Collides with the 'Valdez Principles,' " *Business and Society Review*, No. 74, 32-35.

Bidwai, Praful (1992), "North vs. South on Pollution," *The Nation*, 254:24, 853-854.

Brower, David R. (1964), "Wilderness–Conflict and Conscience," in *Wildlands in Our Civilization*, David R. Brower (ed.), San Francisco: Sierra Club.

Carson, Rachel (1962), *Silent Spring*, Cambridge, MA: The Riverside Press.

Churchman, C. West (1961), *Prediction and Optimal Decisions*, Englewood Cliffs, NJ: Prentice-Hall, Inc.

Churchman, C. West (1968), *The Systems Approach*, New York: Delacorte Press.

Davis, Bob (1992), "What Price Safety?" *The Wall Street Journal*, August 6, A1, A4.

Eliade, Mircea (1963), *Patterns in Comparative Religion*, New York: The World Publishing Company.

Fox, Richard W., and T. J. Jackson Lears (1983), *The Culture of Consumption*, New York: Pantheon Books.

Galbraith, John K. (1958), *The Affluent Society*, Boston: Houghton Mifflin Company.

Gill, James D., Lawrence A Crosby, and James R. Taylor (1986), "Ecological Concern, Attitudes, and Social Norms in Voting Behavior," *Public Opinion Quarterly*, 50:4, 537-554.

Hardin, Garret (1968), "The Tragedy of the Commons," *Science*, 162:3859, 1243-1248.

Horowitz, Daniel (1985), *The Morality of Spending: Attitudes Towards the Consumer Society in America: 1875-1940*, Baltimore: The Johns Hopkins University Press.

Kleiner, Art (1991), "What Does It Mean to Be Green?" *Harvard Business Review*, 69:4, 38-47.

Kotler, Philip, and Sidney J. Levy (1971), "Demarketing, Yes, Demarketing," *Harvard Business Review*, 49:6, 74-80.

Kotler, Philip, and Gerald Zaltman (1971), "Social Marketing: An Approach to Planned Social Change," *Journal of Marketing*, 35:3, 3-12.

Leopold, Aldo (1966), *A Sand County Almanac*, New York: Ballantine Books.

Lovins, Amory B. (1976), "Energy Strategy: The Road Not Taken?" *Foreign Affairs*, 55:1, 65-96.

Mason, Roger S. (1984), *Conspicuous Consumption*, New York: St. Martin's Press.

McKenrick, Neil, John Brewer, and J. H. Plumb (1982), *The Birth of a Consumer Society: The Commercialization of Eighteenth Century England*, London: Europa Publication, Ltd.

Meadows, Donella H., Dennis L Meadows, Jorgen Randers, and William Behrens III (1972), *Limits to Growth*, New York: Universe Books.

Muir (1954), "The Philosophy of John Muir," in *The Wilderness World of John Muir*, Edwin Way Teale (ed.), Boston: Houghton Mifflin Company.

Old, Joe, Stephen Baker, and Lynn Walker (1992), "How Do You Clean Up a 2,000-Mile Garbage Dump?" *Business Week*, July 6, 31.

Rassuli, Kathleen, and Stanley Hollander (1986), "Desire–Induced, Innate, Insatiable?" *Journal of Macromarketing*, 6 (Fall), 4-24.

Schumacher, E. F. (1973), *Small Is Beautiful: Economics as if People Mattered*, New York: Harper & Row.

Schudson, Michael (1991), "Delectable Materialism: Were the Critics of the Consumer Culture Wrong All Along?" *The American Prospect*, 5 (Spring), 26-35.

Siebert, Horst (1981), *Economics of the Environment*, Lexington, MA: Lexington Books.

Siler, Julia Flynn (1991), " 'Environmental Racism': It Could be a Messy Fight," *Business Week*, May 20, 116.

Sterngold, Arthur, and Philip Kotler (1979), "A Marketing Approach to Energy Conservation," in *The Conserver Society*, Karl E. Henion II and Thomas C. Kinnear (eds.), Chicago, IL: American Marketing Association, 193-207.

Thoreau, Henry David (1984), *The Natural History Essays*, Salt Lake City: Peregrine Smith, Inc.

Van Liere, K. D., and R. E. Dunlap (1982), "Environmental Concern: Does It Make a Difference How It's Measured?" *Environment and Behavior*, 13:6, 651-676.

Waters, Frank (1946), *The Colorado*, New York: Rinehart & Company.

Chapter 4

Marketing's Linear-Hierarchical Underpinning and a Proposal for a Paradigm Shift in Values to Include the Environment

M. Bill Neace

SUMMARY. This chapter reviews the philosophy of the linear economic model that underpins much of marketing thought and compares this model to an ecological model of the world. This leads to the proposal of a circular economic model incorporating both positions. Marketing is viewed as an integrating element at the business-environment interface.

INTRODUCTION

Every waste that is prevented or turned to profit, every problem solved, and every more effective process that is developed makes for better living in the material sense and for cleaner and more wholesome living in the higher sense.

–Dr. Arthur Dehon Little, 1905

We live in a remarkable world. This beautiful, blue, living orb is traveling through space at breakneck speed with its millions of fellow orbs, each following its own evolutionary path through time in a gigantic dynamic mosaic. This is also a remarkable time for the biosphere, that thin, irregular coverture of Earth where all species of life occurs. And like its celestial carriage, the biosphere is on an evolutionary journey that today is threatened because of human's economic behavior. This chapter discusses this threat, its historical roots, and how marketing can contribute to balancing our economic pursuits with the workings of the biosphere so that we can continue our evolutionary journey in concert with the biosphere, with Earth, with the cosmos.

Much of the developed world employs a linear economic model that has its philosophical roots in the civilizations that grew up around the Mediterranean Sea–Hellenism, Judaism, and Christianity. Today, after centuries of evolution, the resulting linear economic process is one that extracts resources from the earth, converts them into products and services, and returns the residue (waste) back to the biosphere. Until recently, little thought has been given by marketers to the impact this linear economic process has on the larger organism, Planet Earth. There is now substantial evidence to suggest that this supportive base–Planet Earth–is not capable of sustaining the continued rate of economic activity it has experienced over the past five decades. Marketing has been an important element in the development of this linear economic model whose purpose is to enhance the well-being of all participants in the economic exchange process. There is a growing group of environmentalists who have a different model of Planet Earth and its continued well-being.

The purpose of this chapter is to review the philosophical footings of the linear economic model that underpins much of modern marketing thought, and compare the linear model to an ecological perspective. This will lead to the proposal of a circular economic model that incorporates positions from both schools of thought–a shift from an anthropocentric value system to one biocentric in character–and its application to marketing.

WESTERN SOCIETY'S VIEW OF THE WORLD AND THE LINEAR ECONOMIC MODEL

The linear economic model employed by much of the Western world today can trace its origins to the civilizations that flourished around the Mediterranean basin from 500 B.C. up to the fall of the

Roman Empire–Hellenism, Judaism, and Christianity (Jones 1970; Royston 1979).

Hellenism–the life and culture of classical Greece–was the spawning ground of Western philosophy as we know it today. Through ideas developed by Socrates, Plato, Aristotle, Euclid, and Epicurus, Hellenism evolved a system of values that emphasized intellectual analysis. Humans were seen as searching minds rather than whole beings. Drawing heavily from Grecian thought, Judaism and later Christianity espoused a hierarchic view of the world with God at the top and a linear analytical approach, providing humans, maybe for the first time, the raison d'etre to exploit the natural world for their own advantage (Royston 1979).

Support and development of the hierarchical linear model, including humans' commerce, continued anew after Europe emerged from the Middle Ages. The Renaissance (fourteenth through seventeeth centuries) followed by the Enlightenment (eighteenth century) were periods of rich human development. The writings of Bacon, Locke, Descartes, and Adam Smith flowered during this period and provided much of the underpinning for the industrialization of Europe. Descartes' system of logic concentrated on the linear relation between parts, but ignored the affective and holistic dimensions. Smith showed clearly, through the use of Cartesian logic, that production could be increased through specialization. Coupled with his "invisible hand," Smith contended that the economic behavior of individuals seeking to maximize their own well-being in a free-market setting would have an internal self-regulating control system and the two would serve as the engine for economic development (Royston 1979).

Three of the founding fathers of modern sociology, Marx, Durkheim, and Weber, continued development of the hierarchical linear framework in the nineteenth and twentieth centuries. Marx, concerned with the concentration of economic power and wealth in fewer and fewer hands, developed a Cartesian linear model that replaced the mechanics of "free" markets as the allocator of Earth's bounty with economic planners. Linear economic processes, whether organized by free markets or economic planners, break the link between man and the natural environment. Weber and Durkheim continued the philosophical development of a higher integration of social processes, "man above Earth," refuting those of a simplistic evolutionary natural world (Redcliff 1987). As linear economic systems continued to develop through the nineteenth and twentieth centuries, becoming evermore specialized in their mechanizations, they also became evermore anthropocentric, void of any biological stigmatism. Theoretically and economically humans were distancing themselves from any impact their economic decisions were having on their natural resource base.

The natural environment is viewed by humans as a free resource to be exploited and used for our well-being, separating us from the environmental results of our economic decisions (Boulding 1966). (See Figure 4.1.) Our control over the natural environment has risen to the point that the natural order of the evolutionary process is moving ever closer to being an anthropogenic system rather than a biocentric system. By far the most important reason for the changes that have occurred in the land, in the air, and in the waters is the accretive scale of man's economic activity (Richards 1986). The next section critiques the linear-hierarchical model of man's eco-

FIGURE 4.1. Western Society's View of Its Hierarchical World

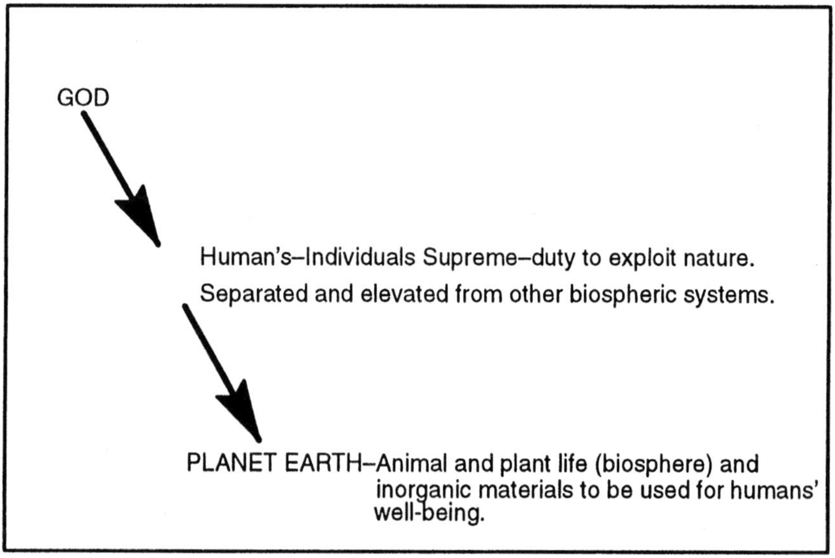

GOD

Human's–Individuals Supreme–duty to exploit nature.
Separated and elevated from other biospheric systems.

PLANET EARTH–Animal and plant life (biosphere) and
inorganic materials to be used for humans'
well-being.

nomic behavior as it impacts the natural environment from which all sustaining resources emanate.

CRITIQUE OF THE LINEAR-HIERARCHICAL MODEL

Development of the linear-hierarchical economic model has not gone unchallenged. Counter to mainstream thought of the eighteenth and nineteenth centuries, two outstanding treatises sounded warnings of man's intrusion into the biosphere: Malthus' *An Essay on the Principle of Population* (1798) and Darwin's *Origin of Species* (1859) claimed that humans and the environment were integral parts of a larger, long, evolving process, and that humans were not separate or immune from the boundaries and capacities of the larger biosphere.

More recently, a number of publications have raised serious questions about the linear model (see, e.g., Berry 1988; Boulding 1966; Hardin 1968; Odum 1971), but probably none more significant or impressive than Rachel Carson's *Silent Spring* (1962), a tour de force on the impact of chemical products specifically and the industrial technological society generally on the natural environment and the health and safety of the general population. Her book introduced ecology to the public and spurred a spate of legislative activity to protect the environment.

Today's industrial economies were founded on the access and use of boundless quantities of materials and energy. Extraction and processing of virgin raw materials along with maximal agricultural production are among the most environmentally destructive of economic activities. The system excretes as waste most of the raw materials used throughout the linear economic process; depletes the biosphere of its natural ability to replete itself requiring massive amounts of energy, machinery, and artificial stimulants; and presents enormous disposal problems. The capacity of natural systems to withstand disruptions through the intrusion of wastes, extensive use of unnatural fertilizers, or by harvesting some of the stock is limited. Continuing the linear expansion of the world economy on par with the pace of the past four decades is unsustainable (Repetto 1985; Boulding 1966; Young 1991).

Facing up to the erosion of the biosphere that underpins linear-hierarchical economic models, marketers and others are confounded by a host of issues, both ecological and human:

1. Ecological cycles, such as hydrological, carbon, and nitrogen, are much longer than human cycles, sometimes hundreds of years longer (Bolin and Cook 1983). Human cycles are generational in length and economic cycles are much shorter (Redcliff 1987). This disrelation has worked to our economic advantage until recently because of our ability to use knowledge and technology to manipulate, manage, and control the natural environment that supports our well-being. But this has worked to the disadvantage of the natural environment as it takes many years and sometimes centuries to adjust to intrusions of its natural evolutionary processes and cycles (Brown 1991; Odum 1971).
2. Individuals (and companies) pursuing their self-interests in free-market environments and de-linked philosophically from the biosphere are not disposed to put collective interests with regard to the underpinning role of the natural environment before private interests; therefore, natural environments are under constant abusive intrusions, which at a disaggregated level appears logical, but from a long-term "commons" perspective is disastrous (Hardin 1968).
3. Social and political institutions change too slowly to redress and adjust to environmental pressures before the onset of irreparable damage (Meyers 1979; Redcliff 1987).
4. Business and economic education and national accounting systems miss entirely the environmental debts the world is incurring. Rare is the economic or marketing text that discusses the underpinning role of the biosphere to production and marketing (Brown 1991).

Failure of the linear-hierarchical economic model to address environmental issues is a direct result of its intellectual inheritance. The environment has been systematically devalued as a result of the competitive production process in a market-driven global economy (Redcliff 1987). Figure 4.2 depicts the environmental economic interface, illustrating how the linear-hierarchical system of extrac-

FIGURE 4.2. The Linear-Hierarchical Economic Model and the Biosphere

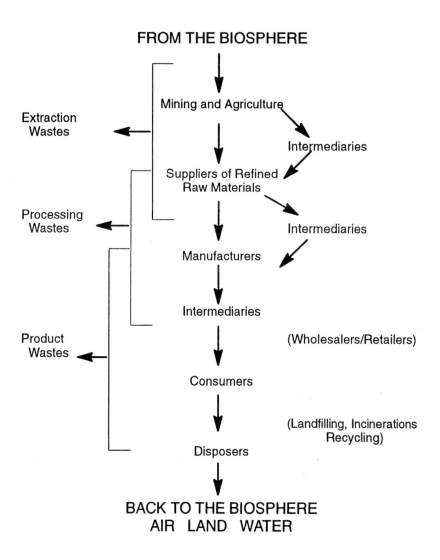

tion, processing, production, distribution, and disposal impinge upon the biosphere. Depending on the source consulted, only 10 to 20 percent of the resource throughput is recycled after its initial journey through the economic system. Approximately 80 percent is disposed as waste, hence the designation linear.

Despite the fact that most developed countries have specific agencies entrusted with the mission to protect the natural environment and the passing of hundreds of laws, significant progress to reverse the rate of biospheric degradation locally or globally has been elusive. There are several reasons for this seeming anomaly: (1) to date few national governments have been willing to make the necessary changes in their economic/social policies and structures to redress the problem; (2) the disconnectedness of production and consumption from their underlying biospheric base; and (3) lack of awareness and knowledge of the dynamic relationship between the natural environment and humans (Brown 1991; Clark 1986). What is lacking is a paradigm, both theoretical and operational, that re-unites humans and the biosphere. The discussion now turns to a view of the biosphere as perceived by ecologists/environmentalists.

ENVIRONMENTAL VIEW OF PLANET EARTH

Figures 4.3 and 4.4 are representative of environmentalist's view of Planet Earth. Figure 4.3 shows that the earth has five major dynamic interactive components: geosphere, hydrosphere, atmosphere, biosphere and noosphere. The first three are familiar and do not need a descriptive discussion.

The biosphere is that part of the earth where life occurs–a thin, discontinuous envelope that covers the surface of the earth. It varies in thickness and is quite incomplete in it coverture (Southwick 1985; Woodel 1985). The biosphere extends to altitudes that can reach 10,000 meters, below ground to the deepest plant roots, and ocean depths of thermal vents that can reach 10,000 meters. With few exceptions the zone of biospheric primary production is significantly thinner, from just a few meters on land to a few hundred meters in clear pristine waters. As noted by many ecologists, the biosphere is very limited, the source of all life support systems, and

FIGURE 4.3. Five Major Components of Planet Earth

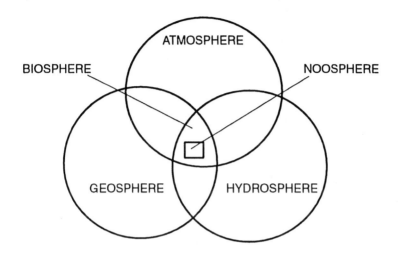

Source: Adapted from Berry 1988.

as viewed by one, the "grand oasis in space" (Berry 1988; Christensen 1984; Repetto 1985; Southwick 1985).

Noosphere is our storehouse of knowledge (and technology) and is a recent addition to the major components that shape the overall evolutionary processes of the earth (Teilard de Chardin 1959). The species known as Homo sapiens has evolved to where it has the knowledge and capacity to impact the course of earth development. After some 15 billion years of universe history and some 4.5 billion years of earth history, human beings, in just a few thousand years, find ourselves in a caretaker position of a living, dynamic, evolving orb called earth (Berry 1988; Lovelock 1979). No other single species has ever attained a position in the biosphere where such a high fraction of the earth's biota and other resources was diverted for its support. The impoverishing character of our linear-hierarchical modus operandi impedes the natural biotic processes that have evolved over millennia of time. Ecological evolution has inevitably

FIGURE 4.4. Model of the Biosphere

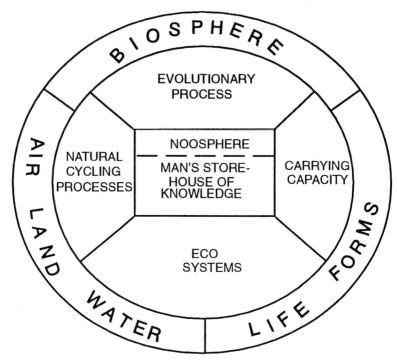

Sources: Adapted from Berry (1988), Brown (1991), Neace (1991)

led to greater specialization, more branching of the evolutionary tree, increasing dependence, and more species living in a more diverse and complex environment (Woodel 1985).

The impact of the noosphere will continue to increase with the outcome yet unknown. Most recent history does not bode well for the earth and its biosphere. In spite of our superior knowledge and capacities we are still quite ignorant of the workings of the earth and its biosphere. Regardless, the big question is, what kind of "garden" do we want? Will our basic instincts for survival and development (evolution?) bring us in harmony with the natural sustaining character of the biosphere? More to the point, how can business generally and marketing specifically, as children of the linear-hierarchical model, evolve a value system that incorporates an environmentalist's perspective so that the economic subsystem, in concert with biospheric systems, continue to provide goods and services and enhance our well-being.

MERGING THE TWO MODELS

The contrasting views developed above have their roots in the intellectual underpinnings of economics/business and ecology. In spite of these paradigms' differences, there is a growing body of literature that supports the interaction of the two disciplines (see, e.g., Clark and Munn 1986; Repetto 1985; and Royston 1979). It is interesting to note that the call for merging and linking the two models has essentially come from ecologists and environmental economists. Two of the most compelling reasons marketers should take heed of the business-environment interface are (1) rising costs associated with the impact of their products, packages, and processes on the environment, and (2) opportunities to exploit new markets for "green" products (Kleiner 1991; Porter 1991). More fundamentally, there is a growing awareness in the marketing and business community of the link between economic well-being and environmental health. In the long run the two are inseparable.

The linear-hierarchical economic model does not work in a world with growing populations and limited biospheric resources. To think that scarcity is the problem and technology is the answer is no longer tenable (Boulding 1966). The linear economic model should be modified; first by a value system that recognizes earth and its biosphere as the underfooting of all human activity; and second, that materials and energy flows are circular not linear. A biocentric economic model is proposed that recognizes the essential character of circular utilization of Earth's resources. The model is a move in the direction of mimicking nature. In nature, what goes around comes around; it wastes nothing (see Figure 4.5). For the circular model to be operative, marketers and other stakeholders will have to recognize the pluralistic nature of the biosphere–its diversity, including the diversity of stakeholders.

Wastes and pollution are now seen as economic inefficiencies that are not only costly but detrimental to the sustaining health of the biosphere and all of its inhabitants (Berry 1988). Figure 4.5 illustrates how a hierarchy of circular strategies can be used to make the paradigm shift from a linear-hierarchical economic paradigm to a circular-coevolutionary paradigm that incorporates principles from both the environmentalist discipline and the economic/business discipline, beginning with no-waste technology, life-costing analysis, and environmental audits. The paradigm shift is from an anthropocentric bias to a biocentric bias. Neither discipline is being asked to abandon its past, but to view the human (cultural, economic, technological, social organization)-environmental interface as coevolutionary. Both sides change, one to another through mutual feedback, as they continue their evolutionary journey (Berkes and Folke 1992; Neace 1991; Norgaard 1987). Norgaard (1985) describes the relationship as a linkage, not a synthesis of unlike paradigms, but a symbiosis whereby each enriches the other because of their differences.

The biosphere has a very long history of evolving into more diverse, more complex, and more interdependent life systems. From a biocentric perspective it follows that human diversity has paralleled biospheric diversity. And it is this diversity within human subsystems–diverse cultures, diverse philosophies, diverse ethics, diverse social organizations–that underpins the interplay between the two, fostering adaptation and thereby continued sustainability and yet higher forms of development. (Berkes and Folke 1992). Much the same can be said about marketing. Its evolution follows a similar path; from simple exchanges of goods to highly complex, diverse, and interdependent markets.

The next and final section of the chapter examines the role of marketing in a biocentric-oriented economic system.

MARKETING IN A BIOCENTRIC ECONOMIC PARADIGM

Figure 4.5 suggests several environment-friendly strategies businesses can use in their decision making. Although marketing, as a function, a profession, and a social institution, is the focus of this chapter, it is evident that environmental issues permeate all functional areas and levels of the enterprise (Gladwin 1992). Which strategies or combination of strategies are appropriate and applicable depends on the value creation activities in which the enterprise

FIGURE 4.5. Biocentric Economic Paradigm

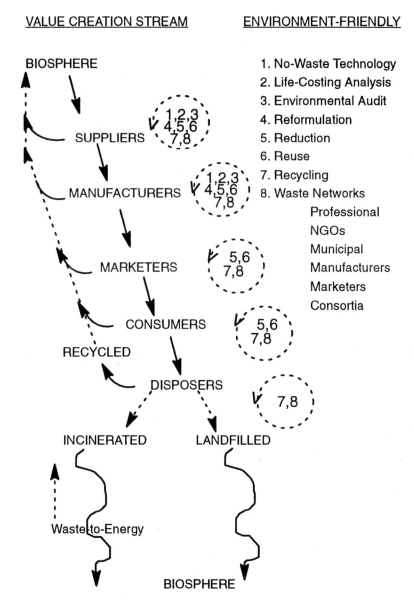

VALUE CREATION STREAM

BIOSPHERE

SUPPLIERS

MANUFACTURERS

MARKETERS

CONSUMERS

RECYCLED

DISPOSERS

INCINERATED   LANDFILLED

Waste-to-Energy

BIOSPHERE

ENVIRONMENT-FRIENDLY

1. No-Waste Technology
2. Life-Costing Analysis
3. Environmental Audit
4. Reformulation
5. Reduction
6. Reuse
7. Recycling
8. Waste Networks
   Professional
   NGOs
   Municipal
   Manufacturers
   Marketers
   Consortia

is engaged, as shown in Figure 4.5. Suppliers of raw materials (including processors and fabricators) and manufacturers, by the nature of their value-creating activities, have potential to use all of the environment friendly strategies.

For example, the Environmental Protection Agency of the United States (EPA), through powers mandated by the Clean Air Act of 1990, required petroleum distributors in 26 urban areas with stubbornly high levels of carbon monoxide (CO) to dispense *reformulated* oxygenated gasoline. As a result, just two days of unhealthy CO levels were recorded this past winter, down from 43 the year before, significantly *reducing* air toxicity and health risks (EPA 1993). In this case, reduced levels of CO and cleaner air resulted in benefits as well as costs. Petroleum manufacturers incurred higher costs in manufacturing, transportation, and storage that were passed on to consumers in higher prices at the pump (2 to 3 cents per gallon) and there were some reports of unpleasant odors (EPA 1993). The benefits are reduced sickness and disease, especially among children, the elderly, and persons susceptible to toxic pollutants. Additionally, the biosphere is more capable of continuing its sustaining, evolutionary, underpinning processes.

"Pollution Prevention Pays," a program initiated by 3M in the mid-1970s using a combination of strategies (reformulation, reduction, reuse, recycling, and waste networks), continues to have significant positive impacts on the natural environment because of what is not put back into the biosphere. Simultaneously, profits are increasing (over $37 million and counting) as a direct result. What is notable about the 3M program is that the application of biocentrically oriented strategies was not undertaken at the forfeiture of profit; quite to the contrary. From the outset, the two goals, biocentric economic behavior and profits, were viewed as harmonious. (Royston, 1979; Schmidheiny 1992).

Marketing and its primary activities of research, product and package design and development, distribution, promotion, and pricing offer excellent opportunities to use biocentric strategies. A growing number of major global enterprises are adjusting their marketing practices to include these biocentric strategies (Gladwin, 1992).

Within the area of marketing research, no-waste technology, life-costing analysis, and environmental audits are used to gather information and evaluate environmental impacts of product and packaging concepts and to search for less hazardous materials and processes.

Marketers can learn many things from Nature that contribute to a more harmonious business-environment interface. Probably more than any other biocentric economic concept, no-waste comes closest to mimicking nature. One company's "waste" becomes material input for another. For example, "waste" from nylon production has become material input in pharmaceuticals and coatings industries. In Denmark, farmers use converted nitrogen wastes from a biotechnology firm as fertilizer, the biotechnology firm purchases "waste" steam from a power station, and the power station buys "waste" water from a refinery for cooling. Interconnected waste streams–form of industrial symbiosis or industrial ecology–evolve over time, meeting both the needs of economic viability and environmental quality (Schmidheiny 1992; Smith 1992).

Life-costing analysis (LCA) is used to evaluate and identify environmental issues and opportunities associated with a product, process, or activity. (Blumenfeld, Earle, and Shopley 1991). For example, Arthur D. Little has reported on several LCAs (Polystyrene clamshell versus coated paper; disposable versus reusable diapers; beverage containers, comparing steel, aluminum, and glass) which identified environmental issues, opportunities, and cost (Blumenfeld, Earl, and Shopley 1991). These cradle-to-grave assessments enhance a company's understanding of a product's environmental strengths and weaknesses at every step throughout its entire life; from the time raw material is drawn from the earth, through manufacturing, sales and distribution, product use and maintenance, and final disposition. Green Seal, Inc., one of several environmental testing organizations, uses LCA to determine eligibility of products for being awarded and permitted to "wear" their green seal emblem (Weber 1990).

Environmental audits may be one of the most important tools marketers use to stay in biospheric touch with their markets. Like marketing and financial audits, they provide marketing managers and others with overviews of the environmental health of companies' products, packaging, distribution, and other marketing activities. Marketing strategies and policies are audited from an environmental perspective to inform marketers of the match, or lack thereof, between effort and potential to create competitive advantage. Additionally, environmental audits keep marketers informed with reference to being in compliance with internal corporate policy and with the escalating number of laws, regulations, and administrative procedures (record keeping and reporting) (Greeno, McLean, and Anneghofer 1990).

Utilization of no-waste research, life-costing analysis, and environmental audits points the way to using a variety of biocentric strategies such as reformulation, reduction, reuse, recycling (including composting), and waste networks. Application of these strategies cuts across all marketing tasks: identifying target markets; redesigning and reformulating products, packaging, and service delivery systems; and distribution networks, particularly waste and recycling networks, to minimize their environmental impact.

Not only does application of biocentric strategies in product development keep firms in compliance with laws, it is also a response to growing pressures from governments, consumers, and non-governmental organizations for "cleaner" products. For example, HENKEL, a German-based consumer products specialty chemicals company developed a phosphate substitute for its detergent because of mounting scientific evidence that linked phosphates to eutrophication–an excessive growth of algae in slow-moving rivers and lakes. The product development program took more than a decade of research and testing of environmental compatibility and performance efficacy before a satisfactory additive was found. Today, this biospheric additive is the world's leading phosphate substitute, has been very profitable for HENKEL, and has resulted in rivers and lakes that run much cleaner (Schmidheiny 1992).

Additionally, marketers should support pricing policies and regulatory mechanisms that fully reflect the costs associated with pollution and disposal. Marketers should take the lead in educating customers and other stakeholders about appropriate use, maintenance, storage, and disposal of their products and packaging with regard to environmental stewardship, health, and safety. (Gladwin 1992). Promotion using environmental claims should be done with great care. Messages should be conservative, clear, and backed by appropriate research. Even then, as some very well-intentioned companies have experienced, promotional claims can backfire, resulting in cancellations of programs, litigious stakeholders, and a damaged corporate image (Neace 1991).

A growing number of companies are making the paradigm shift in values–from anthropocentric to biocentric–not only because it is the right thing to do environmentally, but it synergistically benefits the bottom line. (Kleiner 1991; Porter 1991). Ciba-Geigy, Coca-Cola, ConAgra, Dow, Du Pont, Dwight-Church, Electrolux, S.C. Johnson, Kroeger, McDonald's, Mitsubishi, Norsk Hydro, Nippon Steel, Pacific Gas and Electric, Procter & Gamble, 3M, and Westinghouse are just a few of the companies that have experienced the benefits of a biocentric economic philosophy.

But the battle has just begun. There is much work to do and time is not on our side. These companies and many of their colleagues have begun the journey. There are many miles yet to go and the path is strewn with many stumbling blocks–ecological, economic, technological, political, and cultural. Marketers, because of their catalytic position, can and should take a leadership position. Not only will their companies profit, so will the earth and its biosphere.

The old ways are no longer adequate. It's time to think anew. We need to reorder our values to a paradigm that recognizes the partnership of humankind and Earth. If humans are to have dominion over the earth, its resources, and its biosphere, then we should have the foresight to appreciate its underpinning character. We need each other, not only for survival but also for continued growth–economically, socially, mentally, biocentrically, and spiritually.

REFERENCES

Berkes, Fikret and Carl Folke (1992), "A Systems Perspective on the Interrelations Between Natural, Human-Made and Cultural Capital," *Ecological Economics*, Vol. 5 (March), 1-8.

Berry, Thomas (1988), *The Dream of the Earth*. San Francisco: Sierra Club Books.

Blumenfeld, Karen, Ralph Earle III and Jonathan B. Shopley (1991), *Seizing Strategic Environmental Advantage: A Life Cycle Approach*. Cambridge: Arthur D. Little, Inc.

Bolin, Bert and Robert B. Cook (eds.) (1983), *The Major Biochemical Cycles and Their Interactions*, SCOPE 21. Chichester, U.K.: John Wiley.

Boulding, Kenneth E. (1966), "The Economics of the Coming Spaceship Earth," in *Environmental Quality in a Growing Economy*, Henry Jarrett (ed.). Baltimore: Johns Hopkins Press, 3-14.

Brown, Lester R. (1991), "A New World Order," in *State of the World 1991*, Linda Starke (ed.) New York: W. W. Norton and Co., 3-20.

Carson, Rachel (1962), *Silent Spring*. Boston: Houghton-Mifflin.

Christensen, John W. (1984), *Global Science: Energy, Resources, Environment*. Dubuque, Iowa: Kendall-Hunt Publishing Co.

Clark, William C. (1986), "Sustainable Development of the Biosphere: Themes for a Research Program," in *Sustainable Development of the Biosphere*, William C. Clark and R. E. Munn (eds.). London: Cambridge University Press, 5-48.

Clark, William C. and R. E. Munn (eds.) (1986), *Sustainable Development of the Biosphere*. London: Cambridge University Press.

Darwin, Charles, 1964 (1859, date of original publication), *Origin of Species*. Cambridge: Harvard University Press.

Environmental Protection Agency (EPA) (1993), *Carbon Monoxide Exceedances: All New Oxy Fuel Areas*. Washington, D.C.: Office of Mobile Resources (Preliminary).

Gladwin, Thomas N. (1992), *Building the Sustainable Corporation: Creating Environmental Sustainability and Corporate Advantage*. Washington, D.C.: National Wildlife Federation Corporate Conservation Council.

Greeno, J. Ladd, Ronald A. N. McLean and Frank Anneghofer (1990), "The New Environmental Stewardship," *Prism*, (Second Quarter), 47-61.

Hardin, Garrett (1968), "The Tragedy of the Commons," *Science* (13 December), 1234-1248.

Jones, W. T. (1970), *The Classical Mind: A History of Western Philosophy* (2nd ed.). New York: Harcourt Brace Jovanovich, Inc.

Kleiner, Art (1991), "What Does It Mean to Be Green?" *Harvard Business Review*, (July-August), 38-47.

Lovelock, James E. (1979), *Gaia: A New Look at Life on Earth*. New York: Oxford University Press.

Malthus, Thomas Robert (1960) (1798, date of original publication), *An Essay on the Principle of Population*. New York: Modern Library.

Meyers, Norman (1979), *The Sinking Ark*. Oxford, U.K.: Pergamon Press.

Neace, M. B. (1991), "Products and Packaging Disposal: Some Suggestions for Marketing Thought," in *Marketing Theory and Applications*, Terry L. Childers et al. (eds.). Chicago: American Marketing Association, 464-472.

Norgaard, Richard B. (1985), "Environmental Economics: An Evolutionary Critique and a Plea for Pluralism," *Journal of Environmental Economics and Management*, (December), 382-394.

Norgaard, Richard B. (1987), "Economics as Mechanics and the Demise of Biological Diversity," *Ecological Modelling*, Vol. 38, 107-121.

Odum, Howard T. (1971), *Environment, Power and Society*. New York: John Wiley and Sons.

Porter, Michael E. (1991), "America's Green Strategy," *Scientific American*, (April), 168.

Redcliff, Michael (1987), *Sustainable Development: Exploring the Contradictions*. London: Methuen.

Repetto, Robert (ed.) (1985), *The Global Possible*. Washington, D.C.: World Resources Institute.

Richards, J. F. (1986), "World Environmental History and Economic Development," in *Sustainable Development of the Biosphere*, William C. Clark and R. E. Munn (eds.). Cambridge, U.K.: Cambridge University Press, 53-71.

Royston, Michael G. (1979), *Pollution Prevention Pays*. New York: Pergamon Press.

Schmidheiny, Stephan (1992), *Changing Course: A Global Business Perspective on Development and the Environment*. Cambridge, MA: MIT Press.

Smith, Emily (1992), "Growth vs. Environment," *Business Week*, (May 11), 66-75.

Southwick, Charles H. (1985), "The Biosphere," in *Global Ecology*, C. H. Southwick (ed.). Sunderland, MA: Sinauer Associates, Inc., 1-4.

Teilard de Chardin, Pierre (1959), *The Phenomenon of Man*. New York: Harper & Row.

Weber, Peter (1990), "Green Seals of Approval Heading to Market," *World Watch*, (July/August), 7-8.

Woodel, George M. (1985), "On the Limits of Nature," in *The Global Possible*, Robert Repetto (ed.). Washington, D.C.: World Resources Institute.

Young, John E. (1991), "Reducing Waste, Saving Materials," in *State of the World 1991*, Linda Starke (ed.). New York: W. W. Norton and Co., 39-55.

SECTION III.
PROFILING
THE ENVIRONMENTALLY
CONSCIOUS CONSUMER

Chapter 5

An Examination
of the Conserving Consumer:
Implications for Public Policy Formation
in Promoting Conservation Behavior

Gregory M. Pickett
Norman Kangun
Stephen J. Grove

SUMMARY. A survey was conducted to identify conservation activity among the general populace to increase our understanding of those who do and do not engage in environmentally friendly behavior. Both demographic and psycho/social variables were explored as predictors of conserving behavior. Results and the implications for segmentation potential and public policy formation are provided.

INTRODUCTION

Marketers have become increasingly aware in recent years of the impact that company and consumer activities have on natural resources and the environment in general (Jay 1990). The concern is so great that environmentalism has been designated as potentially "the biggest business issue of the 1990s" (Kirkpatrick 1990). Affecting this surge of interest is a realization that the world's supply of natural resources is finite and the ecological balance of the environment can be easily disrupted (Hayes 1990). The product disposition behavior of American consumers alone accounts for over half of the world's trash, a figure that becomes more significant when one realizes that the U.S.A. accounts for only 5 percent of the world's population (Langone 1989). Much of the attention accorded to the predicament of environmental degradation is focused upon business practices (Ehrlich and Ehrlich 1970; Kleiner 1991), yet a measure of responsibility lies with the consumer as well.

Public policy makers have begun to comprehend the significant impact of consumer decisions upon environmental preservation. Unfortunately, public sector efforts directed toward preservation and conservation of natural resources have been undermined by severe budgetary shortfalls at local, state, and federal government levels. Officials have consistently been asked to "do more with less." Increasing pressure to develop consumer programs that encourage and/or force compliance with environmental directives coupled with a diminishing financial base available to achieve such initiatives has produced a complex situation necessitating that public policy makers fully understand the consuming markets they are trying to influence. The purpose of this chapter is to identify the conserving consumer, particularly as it pertains to consumers' disposition and conservation activities. The hope is that such understanding will allow public officials and managers to take appropriate actions to encourage conserving behavior.

THE ECOLOGICALLY CONSCIOUS CONSUMER

Efforts to identify the ecologically oriented consumer can be found in the marketing literature as far back as the early 1970s. That period is characterized by a flurry of research activity designed to profile those among the populace who exhibit a degree of environmental concern (Anderson and Cunningham 1972; Anderson, Henion and Cox 1974; Kassarjian 1971; Kinnear, Taylor, and Ahmed 1974). However, like so many topics of interest in marketing, the fervor for environmental issues eventually waned. Hence, the 1970s and 1980s passed with only a handful of similar studies marking the period (Webster 1975, Antil 1984, Balderjahn 1988). Meanwhile, contributions to the general literature concerning the ecologically conscious public continued to evolve in academic areas such as sociology (Buttel 1987; Van Liere and Dunlap 1981), education (Hines, Hungerford, and Tomera 1987) and psychology (Maloney,

Ward, and Braucht 1975; Arbuthnot 1977). Whether in marketing or elsewhere, most of these studies have commonly centered upon descriptive information such as demographic background, personality variables, and a host of psycho/social constructs such as alienation (Anderson and Cunningham 1972; Anderson, Henion, and Cox 1974, Arbuthnot 1977, Balderjahn 1988), attitudes toward pollution (Balderjahn 1988; Maloney, Ward, and Braucht 1975) and commitment to or knowledge of environmental issues (Antil 1984; Arbuthnot 1977; Hines, Hungerford, and Tomera 1987).

Overall, the results of these many investigations have been somewhat equivocal. For example, demographic variables such as income, education, and age have been found to be related to ecological concern in some studies and not related in others. Further, in some instances, contradictory findings emerge with respect to the direction of the relationships uncovered (Antil 1984). All of this leads to the conclusion that "the relationship between socio-demographic characteristics and environmental concern is still poorly understood" (Samdahl and Robertson 1989, p. 59). Other constructs such as personality measures and psycho/social indicants like tolerance, alienation, dogmatism, and attitudes toward pollution show some promise as predictors of ecological concern, yet vary in their strength across studies (Kinnear, Taylor, and Ahmed 1974; Webster 1975; Antil 1984).

Despite the inconclusive information concerning the ecologically conscious consumer, a couple of points bear noting. First, while quite appealing to public policy makers who might like to segment the populace with a good deal of ease, demographic variables demonstrate little predictive power and are, therefore, of limited use (Balderjahn 1988). Indeed, personality variables seem to be better predictors of environmental concern than demographics (Kinnear, Taylor, and Ahmed 1974; Webster 1975). Unfortunately, personality variables (e.g., dogmatism or tolerance) are seldom actionable from a public policy perspective. More direct measures of environmental concern and environmental knowledge seem to be more salient means of segmentation and may result in improved marketing strategies. In addition, much of the existing research has operationalized ecological concern in terms of attitudinal responses about environmentally sound activity, e.g., use of recycling centers (Anderson, Henion, and Cox 1974; Arbuthnot 1977) or concern about pollution (Kassarjian 1971; Kinnear, Taylor, and Ahmed 1974). However, since progress toward solving environmental problems is likely to be dependent upon pro-environmental behaviors more so than ecological consciousness (Van Liere and Dunlap 1981), it behooves researchers to focus upon consumers' actions with respect to the environment rather than simply their attitudes. In recognition of this, recent investigations have utilized multiple measures of ecological concern (e.g., Antil 1984; Balderjahn 1988; Samdahl and Robertson 1989) that include some behavioral component. Unfortunately, these behavioral measures often tap consumers' purchase activity to the exclusion of other forms of ecologically sound behavior (e.g., conservation activity and avoidance of environmentally unsafe products).

The research discussed here confronts many of these issues. First, our measure of ecological concern examines consumers' self-reported actions instead of simply their attitudes toward or intent to demonstrate environmentally safe behavior. Second, rather than focusing upon the direct purchasing behavior of consumers, our measure stresses non-purchasing conservation activity. This slant should be of interest to public policy makers in their attempt to move beyond remedies for ecological degradation that involve only the promotion of green products or green marketplace activity in general. Therefore, our orientation encompasses conservation behavior across a broad spectrum of concerns, including dispositional activity associated with consumer durables, recycling of non-durable goods and their packaging, avoidance of extensively packaged products, and preservation of public resources.

RESEARCH OBJECTIVES

Specifically, this investigation explores the incidence and type of conserving behavior among a broad population. Further, it examines the viability of segmenting a population in terms of that behavior. As noted earlier, efforts by market scholars to identify environmentally concerned consumers have seldom used actual behavior as their dependent measure. Knowledge of the psychological, social, and demographic composition of population groups that are likely to engage in environmentally sound practices, as well as groups that are not, should provide valuable information to aid the development of more effective public policy in this area.

METHODOLOGY

Data Collection

Data were collected for this research through a self-report questionnaire constructed to measure respondents' perception of pollution, knowledge of current environmental issues, and conservation practices. Information regarding psychological, social, and demographic characteristics was also collected. The original questionnaire was pretested on a small sample of the population and was changed to reflect needed simplification, instruction clarity, and questionnaire length. The final instrument contained approximately 100 items.

The research sample was drawn in early 1991 from a small college community (population = 45,000) located in the southwestern United States. Census data were used to divide the community into 24 enumeration districts which were then sub-divided into block groupings. Ultimately, a total of 520 households were selected from this sampling frame. Each of the sampling units was then personally contacted and household heads were asked to complete the research instrument. Questionnaires were collected the following day. This personalized request for participation resulted in an 88% response rate (n = 460).

Approximately 35% of the sample were students, a figure that roughly corresponds to the students' proportion of the city's population. However, due to the nature of this inquiry, the researchers believed that the student group would likely hold considerably different views of environmental issues compared to permanent residents of a city; hence, students were excluded from further analysis. Subsequently, 292 non-student residents comprised the transformed sample. Overall, it represented a fair cross section of the city's population and reflected significant diversity across all demographic variables included for investigation.

Dependent Variable

Past research suggests that conserving behavior may be achieved through both the purchase and/or non-purchase activity of consumers. The dependent variable in this study consisted of a seven-item scale (called ENVIROCON) which was designed to assess important resource conservation behaviors that are unrelated to the direct purchase activities of consumers. Specifically, ENVIROCON measures the extent to which consumers (1) abstain from the purchase of products that are excessively packaged, (2) engage in dispositional activities that are likely to encourage reuse of materials and/ or products, and (3) minimize usage of public resources (water and electricity).

Table 5.1 presents the ENVIROCON scale and selected properties associated with its development. Each item among the ENVIROCON scale identifies the frequency of respondent's conservation behavior by means of a five-category, Likert-type measure (1 = "never" and 5 = "always"). Scale items one, two, and six are dispositional activities (recycling of household garbage, the use of reusable containers to store food, and the recycling of durable products). Items three, four and five are precycling activities associated with using less water and electricity. Item seven assesses the frequency with which consumers elect to avoid the purchase of a product because of its extensive packaging.

Two items that were originally included among the inventory were removed from ENVIROCON due to low correlational fit with the overall item set. The resultant seven-item scale exhibited item-to-total correlations between .38 and .67 and an acceptable coefficient alpha of .75 (Nunnally 1967). The final scale was then factor analyzed to check for its unidimensionality. This principal component analysis produced a one-factor solution with an eigenvalue of 3.02 and an explained variation of 43%. All items loaded on the factor at or above the .5 level.

Independent Variables

Seven scales were included in this study as independent variables. The scales can be grouped into three broad categories of variables representing psychological, social, and cognitive (knowl-

TABLE 5.1. Dependent Variable (Conserv) Scale Properties

Item	Item-to-Total Correlation[a]	Factor Loadings[b]
1. How often do you separate your household garbage (i.e., aluminum, glass, newspapers, etc.) for either curbside pickup or to take to the nearest recycling center?	.46	.60
2. How often do you use reusable containers to store food in your refrigerator rather than wrapping food in aluminum foil or plastic wrap?	.46	.62
3. How often do you conserve water while washing dishes?	.50	.68
4. How often do you conserve energy by turning off light switches when leaving a room, turning down temperature controls when leaving home, etc.?	.55	.73
5. How often do you conserve water while brushing your teeth, shaving, washing your hands, bathing, etc.?	.67	.82
6. When disposing of durables like appliances, furniture, clothing, linens, etc., how often do you either give that item to someone else, sell it to someone else, or donate the item to a charitable organization (i.e., Goodwill, Salvation Army)?	.38	.54
7. How often do you refuse to buy products that you feel have extensive packaging?	.43	.55

[a] Two items were removed from this scale due to low item-to-total correlations. Coefficient alpha for this scale is .75.
[b] Principle component analysis produced a one-factor solution with an eigenvalue of 3.02 explaining 43% of the variation.

edge) constructs. The psychological scales that are employed include two subscales from Maloney, Ward, and Braucht's (1975) Ecology Scale; these subscales measure respondents' verbal commitment to environmental issues and general affect toward pollution. Past research has consistently demonstrated that one's attitude towards ecology and/or the environment and one's attitude toward taking environmental action are likely to affect one's behavior patterns (Hines, Hungerford, and Tomera 1987). However, an important mediating variable between these general attitudes and responsible environmental action appears to be the knowledge level that a person holds regarding ecology and pollution. Maloney and Ward (1973) suggest that "most people say they are willing to do a great deal to help curb pollution problems and are fairly emotional about it, but, in fact, they actually do fairly little and *know even less*" (p. 585). Therefore, a cognitive construct (i.e., a knowledge component) also was included in this investigation.

No currently relevant scale to assess ecological knowledge adequately could be found by the authors for use in this study. Consequently, a nine-item inventory involving true/false response categories was developed. The items were generated through examination of popular literature (i.e. *Newsweek, Time, The Wall Street Journal*) and they reflected issues/subjects that were repeatedly addressed across multiple sources. Statements were included about phenomena like the "Greenhouse Effect," "renewable resources," "methanol fuel," "degradable packaging," and "aerosol sprays," and respondents were asked to evaluate their truthfulness. Four of the original nine items were removed from the final knowledge scale because of low item-to-total correlations and insufficient scale reliability. The resultant five-item Environmental Knowledge Scale used in this research is shown in Table 5.2.

Two of the psycho/social scales employed in this study examine the impact of respondents' sense of attachment to community, society, and/or culture upon their conserving behavior. Several researchers have explored this basic relationship through the investigation of Middleton's (1963) Alienation scale (e.g., Anderson and Cunningham 1972; Balderjahn 1988, Webster 1975). While their results are somewhat conflicting, a logically derived proposition suggests that individuals who are less alienated from their social

TABLE 5.2. Environmental Knowledge Scale[a]

---

1. So called "acid rain" is really a natural type of rain in which dust particles mix with the moisture to form drops of dark-colored rain.

2. The Greenhouse Effect is the long-term cooling of our environment.

3. Methanol is a synthetic fuel used in anti-freeze and coolants.

4. All aerosol sprays contain chemicals that are harmful to the ozone layer.

5. "Organic" produce is grown with only the safest man-made fertilizers and pesticides applied to them.

---

[a] Four items were removed from this scale due to low item-to-total correlations and scale coefficient alphas. Final scale alpha is equal to .50.

world should exhibit a stronger sense of responsibility for their actions that may consume scarce resources. Consequently, one might expect those who are less alienated to behave in a more conserving manner.

Unfortunately, knowledge of one's sense of alienation is not a readily actionable variable for segmenting markets or developing public policy mandates. Therefore, in addition to alienation, this study includes a related fourteen-item scale proposed by Miller (1977) that measures a person's involvement in community affairs within the past year. This construct taps such activities as providing financial support to community groups, serving on civic boards, or keeping informed on community issues.

Finally, consumer behavior literature recognizes the importance that interpersonal influence may have on the development of attitudes, norms, values, aspirations, and purchase behavior of others (Bearden, Netemeyer, and Teel 1989; Stafford and Cocanougher 1977). Despite the fact that the present study does not examine the direct purchasing behavior of individuals, interpersonal influence is examined as a factor that may affect the behavioral decisions of consumers concerning dispositional/conservation choices. This premise seems particularly germane as communities promote the "rightness" of recycling, product reuse, and conservation, and as societal norms begin to change to reflect expected environmental responsibility (Kleiner 1991). Hence, a two-dimensional scale designed by Bearden, Netemeyer, and Teel (1989) to measure consumer's susceptibility to interpersonal influence was selected for inclusion in this research. The first dimension is comprised of eight normative statements representing the extent to which a consumer's purchasing action is influenced by expectations of others. The second dimension contains four statements that focus on information acquisition and the informational role others play in one's behavior.

All totaled, seven scales are employed in the present research as independent variables to investigate the dependent variable ENVIROCON. These seven psychological, social, and cognitive scales are combined with ten demographic variables to complete the set of independent measures utilized in this research (see Table 5.3).

PROCEDURE

Fisher's Linear Discriminant Analysis (Fisher 1936) was used to assess the effects of the independent variables on respondents' conserving behavior (ENVIROCON). This was accomplished through dichotomizing the sample into two groups: those who practiced conserving behavior less frequently (low ENVIROCON) and those who engaged in such activity more frequently (high ENVIROCON). Group membership was determined by each respondent's summated score on the ENVIROCON scale items. Respondents' scores that fell below or equal to the median score on ENVIROCON were classified in the low ENVIROCON group (52% of the sample), while all others were classified in the high ENVIROCON group (48% of the remaining elements). Scores on the summated variable ranged from seven to 35 with a score of 26 representing the median point. Twenty cases were not classified due to incomplete responses on one or more of the ENVIROCON items.

Utilizing a stepwise procedure, three separate discriminant analyses were performed on the data to examine the discriminating potential of the independent variables. The discriminant functions that were generated represent the ability of the demographic variables, psycho/social variables (which includes the cognitive scale),

TABLE 5.3. Summary of Research Variables

Variable Type	Number of Items	Type of Measurement	Number of Categories
DEPENDENT			
conserving behavior	7	Likert	5
INDEPENDENT (DEMOGRAPHICAL)			
sex	1	categorical	2
marital status	1	categorical	2
age	1	categorical	6
income	1	categorical	6
occupation	1	categorical	9
education	1	categorical	5
number of children	1	open-ended	N/A
length of residence	1	open-ended	N/A
expectation of permanence	1	open-ended	N/A
home ownership	1	open-ended	N/A
INDEPENDENT (PSYCHO/SOCIAL)			
verbal commitment	10	true/false	2
affect toward pollution	10	true/false	2
ecological knowledge	15	true/false	2
alienation	6	Likert	5
sense of community	14	check list	N/A
normatively influence	8	Likert	5
informational influence	4	Likert	5

and the combined set of all independent measures to differentiate between the high and low ENVIROCON groups. All scales included in this research were summed to form a single measure for each of the constructs that they were designed to represent.

RESULTS

Several preliminary investigations were conducted prior to the discriminant analyses to check for the viability of including the independent measures in a multivariate procedure. Tables 5.4 and 5.5 present these results. Table 5.4 depicts the findings from a Chi-square analysis of the demographic variables and high/low EN-VIROCON. Note that three of the ten demographic variables (sex, age, and number of children) were significant ($p \leq .05$). These results suggest that some demographic variables may discriminate between low and high ENVIROCON groups, but their combined discriminating ability is likely to be disappointing.

In contrast to the preliminary analysis of the demographic variables, most of the singular, psycho/social scales exhibited significant differences between the high/low ENVIROCON groups. Results of T-test analyses examining this group of variables is presented in Table 5.5. Each of the resulting significant relationships occurred in the anticipated direction. For instance, individuals classified as low ENVIROCON were (1) less verbally committed to action to correct ecological problems (PVC total), (2) less disturbed by pollution in general (PAFF total), (3) more alienated toward society (ALIEN total), (4) less active in community affairs (COMUN total), and (5) more susceptible to normative interpersonal

TABLE 5.4. Preliminary X^2 Analysis of the Demographic Variables

Variable	d.f.	P-Value
Sex	1	<.001
Marital Status	1	.14
Age	4	.04
Income	5	.99
Occupation	5	.06
Education	3	.09
Children	4	.05
Years Lived in Community	4	.13
Community Home	1	.72
Home Ownership	1	.60

TABLE 5.5. Preliminary T-Test Analysis of the Psycho/Social Variables

Variable	d.f.	T-value	Probability
PVC Total	242	−3.80	<.001
PAFF Total	242	−6.25	<.001
K Total	233	−1.10	.273
ALIEN Total	247	−3.29	.001
NPI Total	254	−4.25	<.001
IPI Total	255	−1.46	.153
COMUN Total	242	−2.88	.004

influence (NPI total). Given the number (five or seven) and strength of the relationships between the seven scales and the different EN-VIROCON groups, there is evidence to support the likelihood of their discriminating potential.

Additionally, a series of multivariate stepwise discriminant analyses were conducted to provide a more rigorous test of the relationships suggested above. These results are presented in Tables 5.6-5.8. As seen in Table 5.6, each of the three discriminant analyses utilizing the demographic, psycho/social, and combined set of independent measures produced statistically significant canonical functions. These results indicate that the independent variables in this study were capable of some discrimination between the high and low conserving groups among our sample. However, the ability of the demographic variables to discriminate high/low ENVIRO-CON respondents was much weaker than the psycho/social variables effect.

Table 5.7 presents the standardized canonical discriminant function coefficients across the independent variables generated by each stepwise discriminant analysis. Larger coefficients indicate a greater discriminating contribution attributable to that individual variable. For instance, education level contributed the most (coefficient .90) to

TABLE 5.6. Stepwise Discriminant Analysis: Canonical Discriminant Functions

Function[a]	Canonical Eigenvalue	Wilks Correlation	Lambda	X^2	X^2-Prob
Demographic	.139	.35	.87	19.86	<.001
Psycho/Social	.251	.45	.79	21.88	<.001
Combined	.615	.62	.62	239.32	<.001

[a] Four variables were retained in the final functions for both the individual demographic and psycho/social analysis, while ten variables entered in the combined group. In each of the investigations, Box's M indicates the equality of the covariance matrices.

the composite set of demographic variables' separation ability. The variable among the psycho/social set of predictors that produced the greatest discriminating power is respondents' general attitude toward pollution (PAFF) (coefficient .81).

An examination of the combined effect of demographic and psycho/social variables revealed only marginal changes in the set of independent discriminating variables. Two additional psycho/social scales enter in this function (PVC and K), but they are relatively unimportant in their discriminating contributions (coefficients between .2 and .3). Also, in the combined function, the demographic variable sex drops out and is replaced by the number of years an individual has lived in the community. Moreover, like the additional psycho/social variables, it provides a relatively weak discriminating influence.

In total, these results indicate the importance of including psychological and social descriptors in the identification of differences among individuals conserving behavior. However, the ultimate value of a discriminant function is determined by its ability to predict group membership correctly. Hit rates utilizing the discriminant functions are presented in Table 5.8. A holdout technique was employed to assess the classification rates for each group of independent variables. As expected, the classification rates for the validation sample using the demographic discriminant function were

TABLE 5.7. Standardized Canonical Discriminant Function Coefficients

Function	Coefficients
Demographic:	
Sex	.46
Income	−.28
Education	.90
Children	.33
Psycho/Social:	
PAFF	.81
ALIEN Total	.38
NPI Total	.38
COMUN Total	.28
Combined:	
PVC Total	−.27
PAFF Total	.74
K Total	−.26
ALIEN Total	.33
NPI Total	.45
COMUN Total	.41
Income	−.64
Education	.39
Children	.35
Years Lived in Community	.21

poor. Only 49% of this total holdout sample were correctly classified as high or low ENVIROCON members by virtue of the demographic variables. This classification rate is below the expected hit rates using either the Cmax or Cpro comparison criterion often employed to determine classification excellence. Hit rates improve dramatically as the psycho/social and combined functions are examined. The psycho/social function correctly predicts membership of the low ENVIROCON group 71% of the time and 57% of the time for the high ENVIROCON group for a total of 64% correctly

TABLE 5.8. Hit Rates for the Discriminant Functions

Function[a]	Low CONSERV	High CONSERV	Total[b]
Demographic:			
Construction	70.0%	63.4%	67.1%
Validation	43.3%	54.3%	49.2%
Psycho/Social			
Construction	68.1%	74.1%	70.8%
Validation	71.1%	57.6%	64.1%
Combined:			
Construction	77.2%	79.1%	78.0%
Validation	65.2%	63.0%	64.0%

[a] The function developed to establish the decision rule utilized 67% of the sample, while 33% of the sample was randomly held out and used in its validation.

[b] The maximum chance criterion (Cmax) = 52%. The proportional chance criterion (Cpro) = 49%.

classified. The combined function shows similar improvement over the demographic analysis (65% of the low ENVIROCON group, 63% of the high ENVIROCON group, and 64% of the correctly classified).

Overall, these results suggest that discrimination between those who less frequently engage in conserving activities and those who are more conservationally active may be possible particularly in this type of discrete analysis. The identification of individuals belonging to the latter group is particularly clear, as evidenced by the higher hit rates. Among the various sets of predictor variables, it appears that demographics offer little to the accurate profile of these groups, while psychological and social variables are considerably more powerful.

IMPLICATIONS FOR PUBLIC POLICY
IN FOSTERING CONSERVING BEHAVIOR

According to our results, many individuals engaged in conserving activities at least some of the time. Yet it bears noting that a significant number of respondents either did not engage or only infrequently engaged in the simple and easy-to-perform conservation tasks our ENVIROCON measure represented. Increased adherence to publicly sponsored conservation programs may be enhanced if this group of less frequent conservers can be convinced to engage more frequently in environmentally sound practice. This goal might be achieved through policy makers' development and implementation of targeted communication. Obviously, this would require public officials to more fully understand the low ENVIROCON market and any differences it may exhibit from those more actively engaging in conservation behavior.

As this study indicates, low ENVIROCON individuals were distinguishable from those more actively involved in conservational activities. In particular, segmentation of high vs. low ENVIROCON markets appears most feasible with respect to psychological and social constructs. Low ENVIROCON individuals appear to be less affected by problems that pollution may cause, are less involved in their community, feel less integrated into their social world, and are more susceptible to normative pressure from others. This information might be quite valuable in addressing the low ENVIROCON group and designing persuasive communication. For instance, due to their susceptibility to normative influences, service announcements targeting the group might be improved by employing local opinion leaders and/or celebrities to deliver the conservation appeal. The ad copy would logically need to emphasize how each individual is affected by problems that pollution may cause. Finally, given the low involvement of these individuals in community affairs, conservation activities that municipalities hope to encourage must be designed with implementation simplicity in mind. Low ENVIROCON individuals appear unlikely to be among those who give most freely to the community.

While these general suggestions may certainly be embraced by public policy makers in their attempt to communicate with their markets, public officials need to recognize that many in the low ENVIROCON group may *never* respond to persuasive appeals in isolation. In consumer behavior terminology, they represent the last category of adopters, i.e., the laggards. Laggards generally cling to established patterns of behaviors long after the majority of consumers have embraced new behaviors.

This fact points to the need for governmental institutions to consider other public policy measures (i.e., market incentives, mandates, prohibitions, etc.) as a means to encourage source reduction, reuse, and recycling among citizens. At the municipal level, public officials might consider instituting curbside pickup of separated recyclables and provide and/or sell special containers for these materials to be placed in. Similarly, market incentives (or disincentives) can be utilized, i.e., a charge for garbage by the can or, even better, some type of variable price system (a higher price charged for the second container and a still higher price for the third container and so on). Where recycling facilities don't exist for certain materials, outright bans may be appropriate policy initiatives.

While recycling earns high marks as a way to encourage environmentally sound behavior, public policy must be organized to reflect environmental priorities. Environmentally, reuse is preferable to recycling, while reduction and/or conservation is the most desirable. Government (and industry) have embarked on ambitious programs to encourage recycling, yet an even better option is overlooked–greater emphasis upon reusable products/packages. For instance, in the beverage industry in the U. S., the market share for refillables has declined to 11 percent (Young 1991b). Why the decline in popularity? Industry leaders contend that returnable bottles are too inconvenient to consumers. This argument is specious since return rates approach 90 percent in states that have mandatory deposits on beverage containers (Young 1991a). The advantages of refillables vis-à-vis recyclables are substantial. Refillables save both material resources and energy. A shift back to refillables by consumers (and industry) is possible, but this requires strong action from government. Deposit legislation, preferably at the national level, is an important first step. Standardization of bottle shapes and colors would avoid the need for complex sorting procedures and complicated distribution systems.

Finally, disposition of garbage is likely to be perceived by most consumers as a serious environmental and economic problem. Increasing pollution of our soil and air with its impact on health and safety, and escalating costs of garbage disposal are well understood by most citizens. Landfills are reaching capacity in most places. Furthermore, citizens, particularly those with strong attachments to their community, do not want landfills or incinerators in their neighborhoods. Consequently, much of the public is likely to recognize that recycling of solid waste has an immediate benefit, hence, they may be more likely to recycle on their own or support government initiatives in this area.

In summary, consumer markets can be segmented based on frequency of conservational activity performed. Evidence exists which supports the contention that public policy actions can affect people's conserving behaviors. For those conserving behaviors where the problems are readily apparent and the pay-offs quick, high ENVIROCON people may not require external prodding. However, for those low ENVIROCON members, government initiatives (i.e., market incentives, price adjustments, bans, etc.) may be needed to encourage appropriate disposition and conservation behaviors.

MANAGERIAL IMPLICATIONS

As in other industrialized countries, environmental concern in the United States is not a recent phenomenon. What seems to be different today is that significant numbers of consumers recognize that their consumption activities contribute to the environmental degradation that surrounds them. Consequently, environmentally conscious citizens appear to be willing to change their buying behavior to improve the environment (Chase 1991). Our data confirms this. Further, organizations that attend to the concerns of these consumers may find the effort to be a profitable endeavor. A few firms have taken the lead in catering to this "green" market segment. For example, Procter & Gamble and Colgate-Palmolive now market refillable packs which help to reduce the volume of waste attributed to plastic containers. Kimberly Clark and Fort Howard, manufacturers of a broad line of paper products, are utilizing more recycled paper in many of their products (Freeman 1989). Other companies have embraced environmental concern in the design stage of the new product development process. For instance, Whirlpool Corporation has been a pioneer in the appliance industry through its design of many products for future disposability. Further examples include BMW and Minnesota Mining and Manufacturing, who have designed some of their products so that they may be easier dissembled into parts that are readily recyclable (Holusha 1991). Such product attributes may go a long way toward attracting those who are already environmentally conscious, but significant efforts to demonstrate the utility of these offerings may be necessary to convince others.

Simply developing environmentally sound products is not a sufficient means to serve the "green" market segment, much less those who are not yet among it. Effective positioning and communication strategies also need to be employed. As more companies target the environmentally conscious market, it becomes increasingly important to differentiate one's products from those of its competitors and to communicate those differences effectively. Many organizations use advertising to project a positive environmental image. However, an emphasis upon the unique environmental benefits of one's products is more likely to influence the behavior of those who consider themselves to be environmentally concerned. The differential advantage found in the environmentally sound product may also be a critical focus when communicating to others, particularly if it can be linked to their currently held psycho/social orientation. The content of such promotional efforts should attend to the special psycho/social characteristics evident among both groups of consumers. For instance, our results suggest that an emphasis upon normative influence of peer pressure might be an appropriate appeal in ads targeted to those currently outside the green segment, while information regarding the effect of one's offering upon pollution reduction may be effective in targeting the environmentally conscious.

As a caveat, it is important to note that when our data are disaggregated, environmentally concerned consumers are not homogeneous. Efforts to target them specifically should consider this point. Those among this group may regard some environmental issues as being more serious and important than other issues. For some, energy conservation may be more important than dealing with solid waste; for others, the reverse may be true. As one might expect, individual behaviors and activities are likely to vary based upon such judgements. Consequently, understanding the particular concerns of consumers within the "green" segment is vital if firms are to develop appropriate marketing strategies.

CONCLUSIONS

Although this study provides meaningful insights regarding the conservation behaviors of consumers, it is not without limitations. First, the community chosen is not a typical American town. With a university in its midst, the population is above average in education, occupational status, and income. However, the representativeness of the sample should not be a significant issue since the research was directed at predicting differences within the sample population. Second, the study focused exclusively on disposition and conservation behaviors. Clearly, environmental actions include other consumer activities, such as that involved in the acquisition or purchase of ecologically sound products. Finally, the conservation tasks composing our dependent measure were easy to perform and required little or no investment of time and money on the part of respondents. Consequently, the extent of conserving behaviors exhibited by consumers may be somewhat inflated. Undoubtedly, a study with a larger, randomly selected national sample which delves into a wider range of behaviors would provide greater understanding and more generalizable information than found in the present investigation.

Nonetheless, an important fact emerges from this study and other studies investigating environmentally conscious behavior. All of our environmental problems–the garbage glut, pollution, waste of energy and materials, etc.–are the result of conscious human choices. All can be solved, or significantly mitigated, by making other, more environmentally sound choices. Consequently, citizens need to make their consumptive behaviors more compatible with environmental imperatives. The private and public sector must work together in this endeavor. Further, government at all levels must play a major role because of its ability to shape the context within which private choices are made. Through tax policy, bans, market incentives (or disincentives,) and the provision of information to enhance the knowledge base of people, government can move citizens in the direction of appropriate conserving behaviors. The public is not averse to either government or business involvement in environmental matters (see Samdahl and Robertson 1989). Clearly, we have made some progress in this area, but we still have a long way to go.

REFERENCES

Anderson, W. Thomas, Jr. and William H. Cunningham (1972), "The Socially Conscious Consumer," *Journal of Marketing*, 36 (July) 23-31.

Anderson, W. Thomas, Jr., Karl E. Henion, and Eli P. Cox (1974), "Socially vs. Ecologically Responsible Consumers," in *The Combined Conference Proceedings*, No. 36, Ronald C. Curhan (ed.), Chicago: American Marketing Association, 304-311.

Antil, John H. (1984), "Socially Responsible Consumers: Profile and Implications for Public Policy," *Journal of Macromarketing*, 4 (Fall), 18-32.

Arbuthnot, Jack (1977), "The Roles of Attitudinal and Personality Variables in the Prediction of Environmental Behavior and Knowledge," *Environment and Behavior*, 9, 217-232.

Balderjahn, Ingo (1988), "Personality Variables and Environmental Attitudes as Predictors of Ecologically Responsible Consumption Patterns," *Journal of Business Research*, 17 (August) 51-56.

Bearden, William O., Richard G. Netemeyer, and Jesse E. Teel (1989),"Measurement of Consumer Susceptibility to Interpersonal Influence," *Journal of Consumer Research*, 15 (March) 473-481.

Buttel, Frederick H. (1987), "New Directions in Environmental Sociology," *Annual Review of Sociology*, 13, 465-488.

Chase, Dennis (1991), "The Green Revolution: P&G Gets Top Marks in AA Survey," *Advertising Age*, 62:5 (January 29), 8-10.

Ehrlich, Paul R. and Ann H. Ehrlich (1970), *Population, Resources, Environment: Issues in Human Ecology*, San Francisco: W.H. Freeman.

Fisher, R.A. (1936), "The Use of Multiple Measurements in Taxonomic Problems," *Annals of Eugenics*, 7, 179-188.

Freeman, Lauria (1989), "Government Questions Downy Refill," *Advertising Age*, 60: 50, 42.

Hayes, Denis (1990), "The Green Decade," *The Amicus Journal*, 12 (Spring), 24-29.

Hines, Jody M., Harold R. Hungerford, and Audrey N. Tomera (1987), "Analysis and Synthesis of Responsible Environmental Behavior: A Meta-Analysis," *Journal of Environmental Education*, 13 (Winter), 1-8.

Holusha, John (1991a), "Recyclable Claims Are Debated," *The New York Times* (January 8), D1, D5.

Jay, Leslie (1990), "Green About the Tills: Markets Discover the Eco-Consumer," *Management Review*, 79, (June), 24-29.

Kassarjian, Harold H. (1971), "Incorporating Ecology into Marketing Strategy: The Case of Air Pollution," *Journal of Marketing*, 35 (July), 61-65.

Kinnear, Thomas C., James R. Taylor, and Sadrudin A. Ahmed (1974), "Ecologically Concerned Consumers: Who Are They?" *Journal of Marketing*, 38 (April), 20-24.

Kirkpatrick, David (1990), "Environmentalism: The New Crusade," *Fortune*, 121 (February 12), 44-51.

Kleiner, Art (1991), "What Does It Mean to Be Green?" *Harvard Business Review*, 69 (July-August), 38-47.

Langone, John (1989), "A Stinking Mess," *Time*, (January 2), 45.

Maloney, Michael P. and Michael P. Ward (1973), "Ecology: Let's Hear it from the People: An Objective Scale for the Measurement of Ecological Attitudes and Knowledge," *American Psychologist*, 28 (July), 583-586.

Maloney, Michael P., Michael P. Ward, and G. Nicholas Braucht (1975), "A Revised Scale for the Measurement of Ecological Attitudes and Knowledge," *American Psychologist*, 30 (July) 787-790.

Middleton, Russell (1963), "Alienation, Race, and Education," *American Sociological Review*, 28 (December), 973-977.

Miller, Delbert C. (1977), *Handbook of Research Design and Social Measurement*, 3rd ed., New York: David McKay Co.

Nunnally, Jum C. (1967), *Psychometric Theory*, New York: McGraw-Hill Book Company.

Samdahl, Diane M. and Robert Robertson (1989), "Social Determinants of Environmental Concern: Specification and Test of the Model," *Environment and Behavior*, 21 (1), 57-81.

Stafford, James E. and Benton A. Cocanougher (1977), "Reference Group Theory," in *Selected Aspects of Consumer Behavior*, Washington, D.C.: Superintendent of Documents, U.S. Government Printing Office, 361-380.

Van Liere, Kent D. and Riley E. Dunlap (1981), "Environmental Concern: Does It Make a Difference How It Is Measured?" *Environment and Behavior*, 12 (6), 651-676.

Webster, Frederick E. (1975), "Determining the Characteristics of the Socially Conscious Consumer," *Journal of Consumer Research*, 2 (December), 188-196.

Young, John E. (1991b), "Refillable Bottles: Return of a Good Thing," *Worldwatch*, 4 (March-April), 35-36.

Chapter 6

Eco-Attitudes and Eco-Behaviors in the New German States: A 1992 Perspective

Scott D. Johnson
Denise M. Johnson

SUMMARY. The empirical research describes eco-attitudes and eco-behaviors of consumers in the new German states, which formerly comprised East Germany. Factor analysis suggests underlying dimensions exist in consumer attitudes and behaviors toward environmental issues. Cluster analysis suggests relatively homogenous groupings or segments of consumers in the context of their environmental attitudes. The results point to the need for approaches to environmental marketing which recognize distinct consumer groups which transcend a "green" or "non-green" dichotomy. The chapter also discusses potential environmental issues specific to developing economies.

INTRODUCTION

The environment has recently become a critical issue that is influencing how products are developed, promoted, and disposed of. Consumers in Western countries have been deluged with product claims of "eco-friendliness," "biodegradable," and "recyclable" (Olney and Bryce 1991). A new breed of eco-entrepreneurs is

The authors would like to thank the College of Business and Public Administration and the University of Louisville for a grant that facilitated the completion of this research.

attempting to meet the needs of a new class of eco-consumers (Wang 1991; Adams 1990; Hardy 1990; Jay 1990) by using eco-speak (Vandervoort 1991). Regulatory issues are coming to a head in terms of defining what constitutes a "green" product (Landler, Schiller, and Smart 1991). Finally, to point further to the legitimacy of the environment as a major concern of marketers today, the First Annual Green Marketing Summit was held in New York in January of 1991 (Smyth 1991).

A unique facet of environmental concern is its global reach as witnessed by the 1992 United Nations International Conference on the Environment in Rio de Janeiro, Brazil. When the nuclear accident occurred at Chernobyl, the spreading radiation was an international problem. When the topic of ozone depletion is discussed and debated, it is inevitably framed in a global context of how the entire climatic structure of the earth will be affected. When energy alternatives are the focus of attention, broad multinational eco-system changes are of concern.

The focus of this research is to delineate empirically eco-attitudes and eco-behaviors of consumers in the newly formed states that formerly comprised East Germany. As such, the research sheds light on a general topic of growing concern from the unique perspective of a former East Bloc country. The chapter begins with a review of some of the environmental issues facing Eastern Europe and the new German states in particular. Next, the discussion turns to the methodology and then to the findings. Finally, a general discussion is presented which is then followed by limitations of the research and the conclusion.

EAST GERMAN ENVIRONMENTAL ISSUES

The socialist mandate for economic growth in countries controlled by the Soviet Union following World War II contributed greatly to the creation of what some later termed an environmental disaster (Bryson 1984). Recent figures compiled by a German government task force in early 1991 estimated there were between 15,000 and 90,000 potentially toxic dump sites in the five new German states (Cezeaux 1991; Henzler 1992). The specific contents of these dump sites are unknown, but are believed to range from photochemical to nuclear waste.

Much of the environmental problem in the new German states is attributed to fuel sources. Ancient furnaces burning brown coal resulted in this area having the dubious distinction of generating the most sulfur dioxide in the world on a per capita basis (Henzler 1992; French 1990). In a similar vein, Burant (1988) notes that: by the mid-1980s, East Germany's heavy reliance on lignite, the only fuel source it possessed in great quantity, was exacting a heavy price from the country's natural environment, resulting in a high level of atmospheric pollution, particularly from sulfur dioxide. In the 1980s, increasing use of nitrate fertilizers and pesticides was also creating problems. The country has become one of the most polluted regions of Europe.

In an effort to reclaim polluted air and water, the East German government did set up a Ministry of the Environment and Water Management (Bush 1974). However, the efforts to recycle and meaningfully protect the environment did not gather momentum until the late 1980s. Prior to this time, it was generally accepted that the socialist state would not admit to negative social situations that existed. East Germans were expected to recycle some materials, but this was primarily motivated by economic necessity rather than a concern for the environment. The Communist state subsidized drop-off centers in order to save valuable hard currency for purchasing needed raw materials (Menke-Gluckert 1992). Bryson (1984) notes that according to official party ideology, ecological consciousness and the avoidance of a super-abundance of industrial effluents were characteristics of socialism rather than capitalism. It is sadly ironic that such an ostensibly ecologically conscious state could in fact become a world leader in air and water pollutants.

METHODOLOGY

Survey Instrument

The survey instrument was developed to tap consumer attitudes and behaviors toward the environment. A review of the academic literature showed no scales in existence for measuring the specific eco-attitudes and eco-behaviors of interest to the authors, with the exception of one that was very recently developed. The scale to measure eco-attitudes was adapted from the survey instrument entitled "Solid Waste Management Survey" (West, Feiock, and Lee 1992). Additional items were generated by the authors to try to tap a variety of environmental attitudes that had been noted as important issues in prior articles.

The scale measuring eco-behaviors was also adapted from West, Feiock, and Lee (1992). Some changes to their scale were made to account for the differences in products that are more typical in Europe as opposed to the United States. For example, the Solid Waste Management Survey (West, Feiock, and Lee 1992) did not distinguish between white glass and green glass, something that is commonly done in Germany, as these two items are recycled separately.

Data Collection

Pre-addressed stamped return envelopes were provided to the respondent within a larger envelope with the respondent's name on the outside. Each questionnaire was placed into the respondents home mailbox after his or her name was viewed on the mailbox and then written onto the outer envelope. This sampling process was used for a variety of reasons. First, there was no reliable mailing list available at the time. Second, current phone directories were unavailable for either mailing or telephoning possibilities. Third, only a small percentage of households had telephones even if telephone numbers could be obtained either through a listing or through random digit dialing.

Sample

A total of 1200 questionnaires were distributed in the new German states. Out of the 1200 distributed, 184 questionnaires were returned for a response rate of 15.3% (184/1200). The returned questionnaires were further screened to ensure that they were properly completed. Of the 184 returned, 39 were not included in the sample primarily because they were incomplete. Consequently, the usable sample was 145.

Three cities (Wismar, Meissen, and Potsdam) were selected in the effort to obtain a representative sample from different geographic locations and population magnitudes. For each city selected, 400 questionnaires were distributed to home addresses. For each of the three cities selected, the population of city streets were randomly numbered and then a simple random sample was taken from the population of streets. Once a street was selected, a census of the entire block was sampled in a clockwise manner. If the street was more than one block long, the block selected was in the northern or eastern end of the street such that only one block per street was selected.

Table 6.1 describes the gender, education, and age of the respondents. In terms of gender, the population was quite evenly split with 53% of the respondents being male while 47% were female. There is a 99% literacy rate in the new German states, and the education variable reflected this finding. No one in the sample had less than seven years of education. However, 22% of the sample did indicate having between 7 and 9 years of formal education. The modal response was 10 and 12 years for 49% of the sample. Finally, 14% of the sample had between 13 and 15 years, while 15% of the respondents indicated that they had 16 or more years of education. The age of respondents was quite evenly distributed. Slightly less than half (45%) of the respondents were 44 years old or less, while 55% indicated that they were 45 years of age or older.

Statistical Analysis

The first statistical procedure was an examination of the means and standard deviations of the items in each of the scales in order to become more familiar with the general nature of the responses. Next, correlation coefficients for the scales were examined to determine whether or not factor analysis would be appropriate. Since the data indicated that some underlying dimensions might exist, factor analytic procedures were completed. Following these tests, individual respondents were separated into groups using cluster analysis, and consumer profiles based on eco-attitudes were examined. Finally, mean values of demographic variables were computed for each

TABLE 6.1. Sample Profile: Gender, Education, and Age

Gender	Relative Frequency
Male	53%
Female	47%
	100%

Education	Relative Frequency
< 7 years	0%
7-9 years	22%
10-12 years	49%
13-15 years	14%
16 or more years	15%
	100%

Age	Relative Frequency
< 25	13%
25-34	13%
35-44	19%
45-54	13%
55-64	30%
> 64	12%
	100%

of the clusters and discriminant analysis was performed to determine significant differences in the demographic composition of each cluster.

FINDINGS

Attitudes toward the environment, which we have termed eco-attitudes, are listed in Table 6.2. A five-point Likert response format was provided ranging from strongly agree (1) to strongly disagree (5). The mean scores range from a low of 1.147 (showing agreement) for the statement "I prefer to recycle products that can be recycled," to a high of 4.007 (showing disagreement) for "Economic development is more important than protecting the environment."

Eco-behavior results are presented in Table 6.3. The statement "How often do you recycle the following materials" was followed by a listing of materials. For each item, the respondent could choose from "almost always" (1) to "almost never" (5). Glass and newspapers appeared to be the most frequently recycled materials while plastic and aluminum cans were comparatively less frequently recycled by former East Germans.

Examination of the correlation matrix indicated that a number of significant correlations were present, thus, principal components factor analysis was performed to further investigate the dimensionality of the eco-attitude scale items. The results of the factor analysis are shown in Table 6.4. This analysis indicated that the data were composed of four dimensions or factors that accounted for 70.3% of the variance. The first factor, which accounted for 26.4% of the variance, included variables that were related to recycling attitudes and opinions and was called "recyclers." The second factor contained items regarding water pollution, accounted for 16.7% of the variance, and was named "safe water." The third dimension, accounting for 14.5% of the variance, contained variables which indicated that the environment should take precedence over economic

TABLE 6.2. Eco-Attitude Scale Responses

	Statement	mean	std. dev.	n
1.	Economic development is more important than protecting the environment.	4.007	1.162	141
2.	I prefer to recycle products that can be recycled.	1.147	.744	140
3.	Pollution is the responsibility of the government.	2.790	1.502	138
4.	I prefer to purchase environmentally friendly products.	1.524	.777	143
5.	It is more important to reduce environmental pollution than to build up the economy.	2.560	1.161	141
6.	The water that I drink is, in general, unpolluted.	2.727	1.290	139
7.	Water pollution is a big problem in the region where I live.	3.204	1.378	137
8.	If I had the opportunity, I would buy recycled products.	1.550	.916	140

1 = strongly agree, and 5 = strongly disagree

development, and hence, this factor was called "environment over economy." The last factor, accounting for 12.7% of the variance in the data, related to the government's involvement in controlling pollution, and hence, it was labeled "government problem."

Undertaking this same procedure for the eco-behavior scale, examination of that correlation matrix indicated that the data may have several underlying dimensions. Principal components factor analysis yielded a three-factor solution accounting for 75.9% of the variance (see Table 6.5). The first factor included batteries, tires,

TABLE 6.3. Eco-Behaviors: Recycling

"How often do you recycle the following materials?"

Materials	mean	std. dev.	n
9. Newspapers	1.513	0.546	144
10. Aluminum Cans	2.861	1.787	137
11. Glass (white)	1.210	0.615	143
12. Glass (green and brown)	1.259	0.719	143
13. Plastic	2.688	1.674	144
14. Oil	2.098	1.577	132
15. Batteries	2.104	1.561	135
16. Automobile tires	2.024	1.511	124

1 = almost always, and 5 = almost never

and oil, accounted for 33.8% of the variance, and was labeled "auto." The second factor accounted for 25.6% of the variance, included white glass, green glass, and newspapers, and was labeled "commonly recycled." The final factor consisted of plastic and aluminum cans. It accounted for 16.5% of the variance and was labeled "not used often," since these materials were not commonly used in the eastern part of Germany in the past.

The next part of the investigation entailed the use of cluster analysis to develop consumer profiles based on the eco-attitudes of the respondents. Cluster analysis is a widely accepted statistical procedure to segment consumers based on lifestyle data. Thus, it is presumed that people can be separated into different groups according to their attitudes toward environmental variables (eco-attitudes). Factor scores on the eco-attitude variables were saved to cluster individuals into groups using the Quick Cluster hierarchical algorithm in SPSS-X. Use of factor scores to do this procedure rather than surrogate variables representing the factors has the advantage of representing a composite of all variables loading on that dimension (Hair et al. 1992). A dendrogram

TABLE 6.4. Factor Matrix of Eco-Attitudes

Statement	Factor 1 "recyclers"	Factor 2 "safe water"	Factor 3 "environment over economy"	Factor 4 "government problem"
4.	.88063			
2.	.81519			
8.	.63328			
6.		.81184		
7.		−.79842		
5.			.81282	
1.			−.72967	
3.				.88733
Eigenvalues	2.11	1.33	1.16	1.02
% variance	26.4	16.7	14.5	12.7

analysis indicated that a four-cluster solution was appropriate as did a noticeable jump in the fusion coefficients (Aldenderfer and Blashfield 1984). In addition, the distance between the cluster centroids indicated that a four-cluster solution was better than other solutions. The results of the cluster analysis are shown in Table 6.6.

The first cluster, comprising 19% of the sample, was composed of individuals who answered that they themselves do not recycle but they think that the environmental protection is important. In other words, the profile of this cluster is such that they believe there is a problem but it is not their particular problem. Consequently, this cluster was named "not *my* problem." Twenty percent of the sample, comprising the second cluster, consisted of individuals who do not think an environmental problem exists. They do not recycle, think the water is safe, think development is more important than pollution, and see the problem as being a government concern. Thus, we characterized this cluster of individuals as "there *is* no problem." The third cluster, consisting of 13% of the sample, was

TABLE 6.5. Factor Matrix of Eco-Behaviors:
Recycling

Statements	Factor 1 "auto"	Factor 2 "commonly recycled"	Factor 3 "not used often"
15. Batteries	.85705		
16. Auto. Tires	.85417		
14. Oil	.85343		
11. Glass (white)		.90863	
12. Glass (green & brown)		.89240	
9. Newspapers		.61768	
13. Plastic			.94023
10. Aluminum Cans			.91705
Eigenvalues	2.70	2.05	1.32
% variance	33.8	25.6	16.5

comprised of people who recycle and think the water is not safe but believe that development must take priority over environmental concerns. They also think that the government should not be involved. Thus, these individuals may believe that, although there is a problem, development should be of primary concern. Therefore, this third cluster was named "*delay* the problem." Finally, the last cluster contained 48% of the sample and consisted of individuals who do not recycle but do not believe the water to be safe. Since the profile of this group is such that they realize there is a problem but they choose not to recycle, and they believe that development is more important and that government should not be involved, we believe that this group chooses not to acknowledge the problem and so were named "*forget* the problem."

In order to determine how these profiles differed in terms of demographic variables, discriminant analysis was performed to examine the means of these variables. The results showed that the clusters did not differ significantly in terms of education and gender; however, there was a significant difference with regard to age,

TABLE 6.6. Cluster Analysis Results

	Cluster 1 **"Not *my* problem"** 19%	Cluster 2 **"There *is* no problem"** 20%	Cluster 3 **"*Delay* the problem"** 13%	Cluster 4 **"*Forget* the problem"** 48%
Factor 1	do not recycle	do not recycle	recycle	do not recycle
Factor 2	water not safe	water safe	water not safe	water not safe
Factor 3	environment before economy	economy before environment	economy before environment	economy before environment
Factor 4	govt. problem	govt. problem	govt. problem	not govt. problem

with Cluster 3 having the youngest average age, followed by Clusters 2, 4 and 1, respectively.

DISCUSSION

Results of the factor analysis showed four dimensions of eco-attitudes. These dimensions encompassed recycling, water pollution, economic development, and government involvement. As this scale is expanded and further refined, it would be interesting to see if these same eco-attitude dimensions hold across cultures. Further, factor analysis findings showed three dimensions of eco-behaviors. These dimensions included auto products, common recyclables (newspapers and glass), and products not often used (plastic and aluminum). It is notable that the common recyclables are those that have been recycled for years, in part due to scarce resources in the former East Germany. The dimension containing auto products may have occurred not just because the products are automotive in nature, but because these products are difficult or require a special effort to recycle. Finally, plastic and aluminum cans are products that were not widely available in the former East Germany. As a result, recycling efforts for these products is relatively new.

The finding that plastic and aluminum cans are not yet widely recycled suggests that other newly emerging democracies with a scarcity of Western products may exhibit similar recycling patterns. Consequently, the material that was once scarce will become more abundant yet the recycling mechanisms will not be in place initially to handle the influx of these new materials. Former East Germans are now amazed at the plastic and disposable diapers building up in garbage facilities (Henzler 1992). Consequently, both public and private enterprises would benefit by anticipating these predictable changes.

In addition, one can examine the cluster analysis results and postulate that there is not a "typical" eco-consumer. Only 13% of the sample comes close to being eco-consumers in the sense that they recycle. However, these consumers also believe that development should take precedence over the environment and may be referring to a type of sustainable development. A substantial group indicated that they want to forget about the environmental problem.

The other groups believe that either there really is no problem, or if there is a problem, it is not their problem.

LIMITATIONS

A potential limitation with the study is the generalizability of the attitudinal and behavioral dimensions to other countries around the globe. While the new German states do have commonalities with other East bloc countries, they are also unique in terms of their problems and historical circumstances. Another area that could be further developed is the research instrument itself. This study represents one of the first efforts to systematically measure eco-attitudes and eco-behaviors. As such, further development of the scales used in this study would contribute to a more accurate representation of the consumer eco-attitude and eco-behavior delineations.

The sampling procedure may appear to be different from what we may typically expect compared to populations where extremely reliable mailing lists or telephone numbers are available to facilitate communication with the respondent. Nevertheless, Peterson (1988) notes that response rates of 15 to 25% are not unusual for single-wave questionnaire mailings. While a higher response rate is preferable, years of political oppression have likely reduced the willingness of consumers in newly emerging democracies in Eastern Europe to voluntarily give out seemingly private information. The East German secret police (*Stasi*) is reported to have accumulated files that amassed to 125 miles of shelf space (Kinzer 1992). Consequently, a certain cloud of suspicion will probably continue to plague market researchers in the new German states into the near future.

CONCLUSION

The research presented suggests the existence of numerous identifiable consumer groupings that represent particular eco-attitude and eco-behavioral dimensions. Consequently, it is important to recognize the richness of the constructs surrounding environmental/ ecological consumption behavior. For example, to suggest that someone may or may not be "green" does not capture properly the true complexity of the issue. One must also remember that terms such as "environmentally friendly" or "ecologically aware" may vary from culture to culture. A "green" individual in Mexico may differ tremendously from a "green" individual in Sweden, since their frames of reference are so dissimilar. Thus, private and public organizations must be aware that not all eco-consumers have the same perspective when these organizations attempt to influence attitudes and behaviors in relation to environmental issues.

In terms of consumer products, former East Germans and East bloc consumers in general were used to letting the State make consumption decisions for them. Consequently, the State essentially determined needs and wants of consumers by ostensibly using scientific criteria of efficiency and equitability to determine what should be produced and distributed. This perspective has been labeled the "socialist marketing concept" (Naor 1986). An obvious result of this approach to providing for consumer needs was a marked lack of variety and the lack of brand and price competition typically found in the more advanced economies.

In the context of this lack of consumer goods in lesser developed countries, it is interesting to note that advanced economies that have enjoyed mass consumption for generations are now beginning to embrace conservation (Ritchie and McDougall 1985). An obvious question arises with respect to this ecological awareness. Should one expect deprived consumers of newly emerging democracies to essentially skip the culture of consumption that many have ostensibly craved? As Western Europe moves from this culture of consumption to a culture of conservation, will (or should) the East follow by moving from a culture of deprivation directly to a culture of conservation? Now that the West is moving from consumption to conservation, are they not asking newly emerging democracies as well as other developing countries essentially to skip the consumption stage, something that these countries may apparently prefer to experience? Western countries may take on the paternalistic attitude of not wanting these nations to make the same "mistakes" they made.

Recent environmental legislation in Germany has focused on putting pressure on manufacturers and retailers. Consumers are encouraged to recycle materials used in the home such as glass, newspapers, and increasingly, aluminum and plastic. However, more importantly, consumers can now leave superfluous packaging with the retailer. The retailers in turn are pressuring vendors and packaging firms to cut back on unnecessary packaging materials (Menke-Gluckert 1992). Despite these measures, the new German states still lag behind the former West Germany. Henzler (1992) notes that if Western German environmental laws were uniformly applied today, 70% of industry in the new German states would have to be shut down. In addition, the water pollution problem in the new German states is so bad that it is unlikely to meet minimal European Community standards even after receiving an extended 1995 deadline (Reicherzer 1993).

One interesting perspective suggests that the East is now in a position to not just catch up with the West but to surpass the West and lead the world into the twenty-first century with a model program for sustained growth (Henzler 1992). In such a case, economic development would take place, but within certain ecological parameters that would serve to protect the environment (Ruckelshaus 1989). Or, to phrase sustained growth somewhat differently, profitability would be maintained, but the environment would not be exploited (Davis 1991). Natural gas and solar energy, for example, are energy sources that provide numerous environmental advantages if used effectively (Eisenhart 1991). Hence, it may be beneficial for policymakers to shift attitudes to a more sustainable approach to consumption and economic development before environmentally dangerous behavior patterns have been formed.

REFERENCES

Adams, Richard (1990), "The Greening of Consumerism," *Accountancy*, June, 81-82.
Aldenderfer, Mark S. and Roger K. Blashfield (1984), *Cluster Analysis*, Beverly Hills, CA: Sage Publications.
Bryson, Phillip J. (1984), *The Consumer Under Socialist Planning*, New York: Praeger.
Burant, Stephen R. (1988), *East Germany: A Country Study*, Washington D.C.: U.S. Government Printing Office.
Bush, Keith (1974), "The Soviet Response to Environmental Disruption," in *Environmental Deterioration in the Soviet Union and Eastern Europe*, New York: Praeger Publishers, 8-36.

Cezeaux, Andrea (1991), "East Meets West to Look for Toxic Waste Sites," *Science*, Vol. 251, 620-621.

Davis, Joel J. (1991), "A Blueprint for Green Marketing," *The Journal of Business Strategy*, July/August, 14-17.

Eisenhart, Tom (1991), "Energy Report: Out of Crisis Comes Opportunity," *Business Marketing*, May, T1-T8.

French, Hilary F. (1990), "Clearing the Air: A Global Agenda," *Columbia Journal of World Business*, Spring/Summer, 64-81.

Hair, Joseph F. Jr., Rolph E. Anderson, Ronald L. Tatham, and William C. Black (1992), *Multivariate Data Analysis*, Third Edition, New York: Macmillan Publishing Company.

Hardy, Ed (1990), "Eco-Entrepreneurs," *American Demographics*, July, 49-50.

Henzler, Herbert (1992), "Managing the Merger: A Strategy for the New Germany," *Harvard Business Review*, January-February, 24-29.

Jay, Leslie (1990), "Markets Discover the Eco-Consumer," *Management Review*, June, 24-28.

Kinzer, Stephen (1992), "East Germans Face Their Accusers," *The New York Times Magazine*, April 12, 24-52.

Landler, Mark, Zachary Schiller, and Tim Smart (1991), "Suddenly, Green Marketers Are Seeing Red Flags," *Business Week*, February 25, 74-76.

Menke-Gluckert, Wanda (1992), "A Solution to Waste Disposal," *Europe*, March, 36-37.

Naor, Jacob (1986), "Toward a Socialist Marketing Concept," *Journal of Marketing*, 50, January, 28-39.

Olney, T.J. and Wendy Bryce (1991), "Consumer Responses to Environmentally Based Product Claims," in *Advances in Consumer Research*, Vol. 18, Rebecca H. Holman and Michael R. Solomon (eds.), 693-696.

Peterson, Robert A. (1988), *Marketing Research*, Plano, Texas: Business Publications, Inc.

Reicherzer, Judith (1993), "Trüber Cocktail," *Die Zeit*, February 26, 29.

Ritchie, J.R. Brent, and Gordon H.G. McDougall (1985), "Designing and Marketing Consumer Energy Conservation Policies and Programs: Implications from a Decade of Research," *Journal of Public Policy and Marketing*, (4), 14-32.

Ruckelshaus, William D. (1989), "Toward a Sustainable World," *Scientific American*, September, 166-174.

Smyth, Sandy (1991), "The Competitive Advantage of Green Leadership," *Telemarketing*, June, 68-71.

Vandervoort, Susan Schaefer (1991), "Big 'Green' Brother Is Watching," *Public Relations Journal*, April, 14-26.

Wang, Penelope (1991), "Going for the Green," *Money*, September, 98-102.

West, Jonathan P., Richard C. Feiock, and Stephanie J. Lee (1992), "Municipal Solid Waste Management and Recycling: Strategies and Issues," *Municipal Yearbook 1992*, Washington D.C. International City Management Association, 27-35.

Chapter 7

Ecologically Concerned Consumers and Their Product Purchases

T. Bettina Cornwell
Charles H. Schwepker, Jr.

SUMMARY. Packaging is a major contributor to the escalating solid waste stream. This chapter presents results of a study attempting to determine variables that can be used to discriminate between groups who are and are not willing to purchase ecologically packaged products. Attitude toward ecologically conscious living, attitude toward litter, locus of control, and the perception of pollution as a problem were found to be significant discriminating variables. Implications for marketers and public policymakers are provided, as well as directions for future research.

INTRODUCTION

A recent national survey found that Americans ranked solid waste disposal second, after improved education, as one of the most serious problems facing local officials (Environmental Protection Agency 1989). As landfills become exhausted, business comes under pressure to design and use more "environmentally friendly" product packaging (Stuller 1990). Meanwhile, business and government continue to debate the extent of legislative action needed to mitigate the growing solid waste problem.

Valuing the right to choose in a free market, both businesses and consumers typically desire less regulation, and voluntary measures taken by both may help avoid future legislation concerning solid waste disposal. However, the question remains, are marketers and consumers willing to take voluntary actions that will avoid extensive legislation? Furthermore, will businesses find meaningful consumer markets in the environmentally concerned? Previous research that identified ecologically concerned consumer segments (Anderson and Cunningham 1972) was discounted due to "the existence of a substantial segment that exhibits little or no concern about the pollution aspect of products" (Kinnear, Taylor, and Ahmed 1974, p. 23). Clearly, the mindset of consumers has changed since the early 1970s and the viability of the ecologically concerned consumer is undeniable.

Recently, Balderjahn (1988), working in Germany, developed a model of ecologically conscious consumer behavior in which personality variables and environmental attitudes were used to predict five ecologically responsible consumption patterns. One consumption pattern of particular interest to marketers is the ecological purchase and use of products. Balderjahn measured this consumption pattern by assessing the extent to which consumers intended or actually used returnables, used fewer detergents, and bought fewer packaged products. The consumption pattern dealing with packaging appears to be a particularly important issue as evidenced by a recent call for research on consumer response to packaging practices (Corey and Fitzgerald Bone 1990).

Given the increasing concern over packaging's contribution to the solid waste stream, the present research seeks to develop a fuller understanding of consumer consumption patterns of ecologically packaged products that make efficient use of materials and lead to less solid waste. Specifically this research (1) attempts to isolate useful variables for identifying the ecologically concerned consumer, (2) measures intentions to purchase ecologically packaged products, and (3) replicates aspects of Balderjahn's work with a U.S. sample. As a result, marketers may be better equipped to target the ecologically concerned consumer and policymakers may be better able to encourage consumers who are willing to voluntarily reduce packaging consumption.

We begin by examining how packaging affects the solid waste stream. This is followed by an investigation of the present roles played by policymakers, marketers, and consumers in consumer goods packaging control, production, and disposal. After presenting previous research on the ecologically concerned consumer, we describe our method, analysis, and results. We conclude with a discussion of research implications, and future topics to be investigated.

PACKAGING IN THE SOLID WASTE STREAM

At the rate of two to four pounds of household trash per day, per person, Americans dispose of roughly 160 million tons of solid waste each year (Beck et al. 1989, Larkin 1986. See Figure 7.1). Two major components of solid waste are packaging material and scrapped durable goods (Fishelson 1985). According to Rathje (1984), the average household in Tucson each year discards 1,800 plastic items (both wraps and containers) and more than 13,000 individual items of paper and cardboard (largely packaging). Tucson is a typical example; nationwide consumers dispose of approximately nine-tenths of all packaging materials consumed each year (Kovacs 1988).

A 1980 study for the U.S. Department of Agriculture found that more than 600 pounds of packaging per year were required to wrap the food and beverages bought by each American, resulting in packaging costs of $34 billion or nine cents on every dollar consumers spend on food and beverages (Johnson, Sommer, and Mayes 1985). Packaging, the largest category of consumer household refuse, now accounts for one-third of all household trash (Stuller 1990) and is expected by the year 2000 to account for 50.7 million tons of municipal waste per year (Lewis 1989). Clearly, packaging is costly to the American consumer in both economic and environmental terms.

PACKAGING REDUCTION

Government's Role

In an attempt to lessen packaging's contribution to the solid waste stream, government agencies have begun to take action at various levels. On a national level, packaging legislation is being

FIGURE 7.1. Total Quantity of Municipal Solid Waste Per Year

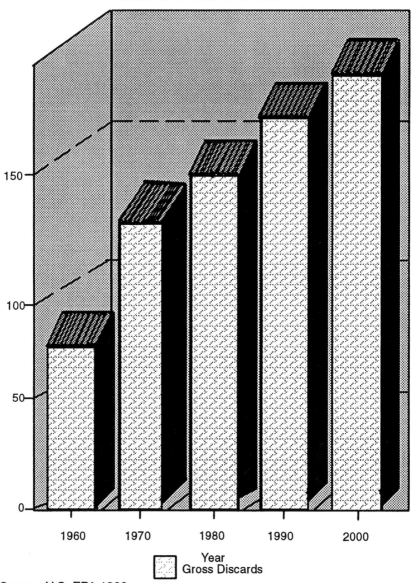

Millions of Tons Per Year

Source: U.S. EPA 1988

initiated and programs developed to deal with source reduction. Despite resistance, state and municipal legislatures are also tenaciously addressing the waste problem.

Presently there exists little national legislation addressing the issue of packaging. However, there is proposed legislation such as the "Recyclable Materials and Technology Development Act," which would require food and beverage containers for use in the sale of goods for immediate consumption to be photodegradable or biodegradable. Also, the Commerce Department's National Bureau of Standards is working with industry associations and groups to set package quantity standards in product areas where there is excess (*Packaging's Encyclopedia* 1988). Hearings were recently conducted on a bill which would set minimum standards for waste reduction and disposal, and would require states to develop plans for dealing with their solid waste (*Nation's Business* 1990).

National policy efforts by the Environmental Protection Agency (EPA) are providing leadership on source reduction (Popkin 1989). For example, the EPA has set goals of increasing source reduction and recycling efforts from 10 to 25% by 1992 (Weddle and Klein 1989). To do so the EPA plans to work closely with industry to find opportunities for packaging reduction (*EPA Journal* 1989). Additionally, the federal government plans on performing market studies to identify incentives and other means for reducing volume and toxicity (Weddle and Klein 1989). The Environmental Defense Fund, an environmental research and lobbying group, has proposed a sales and user tax based on the quantity of packaging in a product, and a national sales tax on disposable items such as diapers, razors, and plates (Begley and King 1989).

There is also concern at the state level. For example, all states have laws encouraging glass container recycling (even though some are not enforced). At least 35 state legislatures are now considering more than 250 bills on plastic disposability and recycling, as are hundreds of counties and municipalities (Stuller 1990). For the most part, state legislatures have focused on bans of certain types of plastic packaging and the imposition of packaging taxes (Kovacs 1988).

Response to national and state initiatives has been mixed. Seattle residents responded positively to government initiatives by purchasing more recyclables, fewer packaged goods, and more large-size boxes (Beck et al. 1989). Studies indicate that positive reinforcers may be used to reduce the amount of litter (Cone and Hayes 1980). For instance, bottle bills, such as the one in New York State have been found to be effective in reducing the amount of returnable litter (Levitt and Leventhal 1986). Conversely, negative reinforcers, such as pay-per-bag trash collection programs, have even enjoyed some success (Riggle 1989). Likewise, taxes on packaging have been found to induce reductions in solid waste generation (Bingham et al. 1974). However, it is often difficult to derive the appropriate tax or subsidy for such measures (Conn 1988). Despite these successes, many government interventions are impotent in dealing with environmental issues.

Regulatory controls often receive limited public support. In November, 1990, California voters rejected a far-reaching environmental initiative by nearly a two-to-one margin. According to McCoy (1990, p. A16), "Big Green seems to have fallen prey to voters' economic jitters and general disgust with government." In New York, voters turned down a $2 billion bond issue that would have funded recycling programs, land acquisitions, and the closing of dumps. Initiatives in Oregon met with voter resistance as measures to close down a nuclear plant and to require that packagers use more recycled and recyclable materials were both soundly defeated (McCoy 1990). In light of strong consumer concern for the environment, failure to pass the initiatives appears to be a rejection of further government regulation.

Rejection of environmental initiatives stems in part from the enormous economic cost of environmental regulation and liability. According to Environmental Protection Agency estimates, private industry spent $64 billion in 1988 to prevent or clean up pollution, and federal, state, and local governments spent an additional $31 billion (Cross 1990). These costs are passed along to the consumer in terms of higher product costs or increased taxes. Although environmental contamination has economic costs, it takes its toll on public health and quality of life in ways that are not always immediately apparent.

The Firm's Role

In recent years, there has been a call for industry to undertake a major redesign effort to cut excess packaging (Larkin 1986; Rice 1988; Thompson and Bluestone 1987). Several methods exist for doing so. For instance, by using marginal analysis, Fishelson (1985) showed that by increasing the size of packages and decreasing the range of package sizes, solid waste could be decreased. Conversely, for some types of containers, slightly reducing the size of a package can save thousands of dollars in materials costs and reduce excess packaging (Erickson 1988). Additionally, the shape of the package affects the quantity of packaging needed (Stoops and Pearson 1989). Such package changes result in less solid waste and are profitable in terms of materials reduction costs and higher profit contributions per unit (Bishop 1986; Russell 1976; Stoops and Pearson 1989).

Increased awareness and concern for the environment presents marketers with an excellent opportunity. Michman (1985) finds a firm's image has a definite relationship on the ability of the firm to sell its products. Therefore, if society finds ecology-mindedness a positive attribute, a firm can enhance its image by producing and marketing more ecologically packaged products.

The Consumer's Role

If there is to be solid waste reduction without mandate, the manufacturer must be willing to initiate, and the consumer willing to accept, ecological packaging changes for the betterment of society. Recent research indicated that 84% of consumers expressed concern on environmental issues, and a similar number of consumers are changing some buying patterns because of their concern (Schlossberg 1990). Likewise, a Gallup poll showed that 76% of Americans consider themselves "environmentalists" (Fisher 1990). There is evidence that consumers are willing to purchase ecologically sound products and/or services and make ecologically conscious investments. Examples of marketers successfully targeting the environmentally conscious consumer include mail order catalog companies selling environmentally friendly products, magazines focusing on environmental issues, and investment opportunities in companies that deliver environmentally safe products and services (Antilla 1985).

In addition, consumers appear to be interested in purchasing ecologically packaged products. A 1989 survey found that 77% of Americans say a company's environmental reputation affects what they buy (Kirkpatrick 1990). Moreover, 53% said they did not buy a product in the past year because of concern that it or its packaging might harm the environment. Similarly, a *Good Housekeeping* poll indicated that 83.7% of the consumers surveyed were interested in buying foods in environmentally safe packaging, and that 77.6% indicated willingness to pay a little more for environmentally safe packaging (Jay 1990). Other research indicates that consumers are willing to pay up to 5% or more for a product in an environmentally sound package (Miller 1990).

While consumers seem willing to purchase environmentally sound products, they may do so only within certain constraints. For instance, there may exist a price difference limit beyond which consumers are no longer willing to purchase the environmentally sound product. Similarly, inconveniences associated with an environmentally sound product may result in resistance. Nevertheless, it appears as though consumers are concerned about the environment and stand ready to exhibit purchase behaviors reflecting this concern. Hence, the marketer can and should play a pivotal role in facilitating such behaviors.

Government, manufacturers, and consumers all appear poised to deal with the impending solid waste disposal crisis. If consumers are willing to purchase ecologically packaged products, and manufacturers are willing to produce them, then perhaps valuable government resources needed for planning and implementing policies to curb excessive packaging can be utilized in the pursuit of other worthy causes. The remaining question is, "Can these consumers be identified?" Previous research on the ecologically concerned consumer indicates it may be possible.

PROFILING THE ECOLOGICALLY CONCERNED CONSUMER

Researchers have used demographic, socioeconomic, cultural, and personality variables, as well as attitudes, to identify the ecologically concerned consumer. Research in this area has been plagued with mixed results and inconsistent measures (Van Liere and Dunlap 1981) and is therefore at times inconclusive. It is for this reason that the current study is in part a replication attempting to supplement the existing literature. Table 7.1 provides a synopsis of the various measures used to examine the ecologically concerned consumer. Interestingly, there was little concern with the package as a form of pollution until the mid-1970s. Package-related measures have focused primarily on consumers' concern with beverage container's contribution to pollution or their interest in the use of recyclable or returnable containers. Following is a discussion of previous research in the area.

Demographic and Socioeconomic Variables

Previous research has utilized demographic and socioeconomic information to predict ecological concern (Table 7.1). While the findings are inconsistent, the ecologically concerned consumer tends to be white, better educated, higher in income, higher in occupation status, and higher in socioeconomic status. Also, younger, well-educated, and politically liberal persons are more concerned about the environment than their counterparts (Van Liere and Dunlap 1980). Nevertheless, these variables are limited in explaining variation in environmental concern (Balderjahn 1988; Samdahl and Robertson 1989; Van Liere and Dunlap 1980). Perhaps this explains why they received less emphasis during the late 1970s and the 1980s.

Cultural Variables

As indicated in Table 7.1, cultural variables have not received much attention. Webster (1975) found that those who were highly involved in community activities scored high on a social responsibility scale. Social responsibility has been conceptualized as the willingness of an individual to help other persons even when there is nothing to be gained (Anderson and Cunningham 1972). Furthermore, those who are considered socially responsible are influenced by accepted social values (Webster 1975). Thus, it is possible that

TABLE 7.1. Synopsis of Measures Used to Examine the Ecologically Concerned Consumer

Author	Ecological Concern & Related Measures	Package-Related Measures	Personality Measures	Demographic & Socioeconomic Measures	Cultural & Geographic Measures
Kassarjain (1971)	included questions about concern for air pollution	none	none	age, sex, education, social class, home value, occupation, marital status, political party	none
Anderson & Cunningham (1972)	used 8-item social responsibility scale (SRS) as a surrogate measure for environmental concern	none	alienation, dogmatism, personal competence, status consciousness, cosmopolitanism conservatism	occupation, income, education, age, stage in family life cycle, socioeconomic status	none
Kinnear & Taylor (1973)	8-item index of ecological concern	none	none	none	none
Anderson, Henion & Cox (1974)	compared recyclers with non-recyclers across different dimensions	whether or not subject participated in recycling	alienation, dogmatism, personal competence, status consciousness, cosmopolitanism, conservatism	age, occupation, education, income, socioeconomic status	8-item SRS

Kinnear, Taylor & Ahmed (1974)	8-item index of ecological concern; 1-item perceived consumer effectiveness	none	aggression, anxiety, self-esteem, play, desirability, dominance, sentience, understanding, harm-avoidance, tolerance	age, education, income, occupation	none
Webster (1975)	8-item measure of socially conscious consumer, 2-item perceived consumer effectiveness	concern for use of returnables; use of recycling service	dominance, tolerance, socialization, responsibility	age, education, gender, income marital status, occupation	8-item SRS
Henion & Wilson (1976)	8-item index of ecological concern; 1-item perceived consumer effectiveness; 128-item ecology scale	use of recyclables	24-item locus of control	none	none
Murphy, Kangun & Locander (1978)	environmental importance score through use of simulated product choice	concern for solid waste; interest in recyclable or returnable package	none	race, social class	none
Murphy (1978)	simulated brand choice of environmentally correct product	whether or not returnable soft drink container was chosen	none	age, education, income, occupation, marital status, family size	none

TABLE 7.1 (continued)

Author	Ecological Concern & Related Measures	Package-Related Measures	Personality Measures	Demographic & Socioeconomic Measures	Cultural & Geographic Measures
Tremblay & Dunlap (1978)	8-item pollution concern measure	none	none	none	population density
Belch (1979)	20-item measure of concern with social & ecological dimensions	concern over littering	AIO inventory	none	none
Crosby, Gill & Taylor (1981)	voter preference with regard to container law; 7-item revised index of ecological concern	2-item litter index	alienation	age, education gender, income	population density
Crosby & Taylor (1982)	satisfaction with container deposit law; likes and dislikes about recycling system	perception of reduction in beverage container litter	none	none	none
Crosby & Taylor (1983)	7-item revised ecological concern index	2-item litter index; returnable usage	none	none	none

Study	Measure				
Gill, Crosby & Taylor (1986)	21-item measure combining items from previous research on the ecologically concerned	concern with beverage containers	none	none	none
Balderjahn (1988)	2-item attitude toward ecologically conscious living; 3-item ecologically responsible buying and using of products; 1-item environmental concern; attitude toward pollution	use of returnables; purchase of less packaged products	alienation, ideology control	age, education, income	size of dwelling
Samdahl & Robertson (1989)	5-item perception of environmental problems; 4-item ecological behavior; 5-item support for environmental regulations	none	none	age, education, income	population of residential community

those who are highly involved in community activities and/or are socially responsible might respond to ecologically packaged goods should such behavior become the accepted norm. Given the increased concern and sensitivity toward environmental issues, it appears that environmental concern is becoming the socially accepted norm.

Personality Variables

Kinnear, Taylor, and Ahmed (1974) found personality variables to be better predictors of ecologically concerned consumers than socioeconomic variables. As Table 7.1 illustrates, the use of personality variables as predictors subsided in the late 1970s. Although several personality variables have been examined, two in particular appear to be worthy of further consideration: locus of control and alienation. Locus of control has only been examined in one study with regard to ecological concern. Alienation, however, has periodically appeared in research on the ecologically concerned consumer.

Locus of control refers to the extent to which an individual perceives that a reward or reinforcement is contingent upon his/her behavior (Rotter 1966). An individual may be classified as either externally or internally controlled. Externally oriented individuals are believers in luck or fate, whereas internals perceive themselves to have greater control (Quick and Quick 1984).

When investigating the relationship between locus of control and ecological concern, Henion and Wilson (1976) found a positive correlation between internal locus of control and perceived consumer effectiveness with regard to pollution, an index of ecological concern, and an ecology scale. The ecology scale measures what an individual knows, thinks, feels, and actually does regarding ecology and pollution (Maloney, Ward, and Braucht 1975). It is important to note that some of the items in the scale are concerned with ecological packaging and purchase. The results suggested that product merchandising and advertising which recognized that the ecologically concerned consumer can by his/her own effort improve environmental quality may appeal to this group.

Locus of control may also indicate one's degree of learned helplessness. According to Barber, Winfield, and Mortimer (1986, p. 312),

The obvious parallel between external locus of control and learned helplessness has led authors both from within the learned helplessness tradition (e.g., Hiroto 1974) and from within the social learning theory tradition (e.g., Lefcourt 1980) to conclude that locus of control is an adequate personality equivalent of the state of helplessness.

Therefore, those with an internal locus of control may exhibit a positive attitude toward ecologically conscious living, and subsequently a higher probability of purchasing ecologically packaged products. Conversely, those with an external locus of control may experience learned helplessness. Hence, their feelings of helplessness concerning the pollution problem may inhibit them from seeing how purchasing ecologically packaged goods could help solve the solid waste disposal problem.

Alienation, or the feeling of being isolated from one's community, society, and/or culture, has produced conflicting results in identifying the ecologically concerned consumer. Anderson and Cunningham (1972) found the socially responsible consumer to be less alienated and more involved in community activities, while Webster (1975) found a stronger positive correlation between alienation and social consciousness. However, the socially conscious consumer participates in consumption behaviors consistent with his/her *own* standards of responsibility, whereas the socially responsible individual adheres to generally accepted values of the society at large. Anderson, Henion, and Cox (1974) found the ecologically concerned consumer to be more alienated, while Nelson (1974) found the converse to be true. Crosby, Gill, and Taylor (1981) found alienation to be negatively related to the ecological behavior of voting for a deposit law, while Balderjahn (1988) recently found a positive correlation between alienation and attitude toward ecologically conscious living. Mixed results may be due to researchers employing different measures of alienation and behavior.

While the results are inconsistent, it appears that the less alienated individual may be more concerned about community or society. Hence, she/he may express dissatisfaction with environmental pollution, and be inclined to purchase ecologically packaged products. The alienated individual, however, may be less concerned about community or society, and may make no special effort to purchase such products.

Attitudes

By definition, the ecologically concerned consumer's attitude must express concern for ecology (Kinnear, Taylor, and Ahmed 1974). The impact of ecological concern on consumption and voting behavior has frequently been assessed (Balderjahn 1988; Crosby, Gill, and Taylor 1981; Crosby and Taylor 1982, 1983; Henion 1976; Kassarjain 1971; Kinnear and Taylor 1973). Research indicates that ecological concern is related to, but is not highly correlated with consumption behavior. Additionally, attitude toward pollution has been found to affect one's attitude toward ecologically conscious living (Balderjahn 1988). This suggests that those who are genuinely concerned about pollution are inclined to take measures to circumvent further pollution. Also, Balderjahn found that those having a positive attitude toward ecologically conscious living participated in the ecological buying and consuming of products. Attitudes have likewise served as predictors of energy conservation behavior, and environmental concern and recycling (cf. Balderjahn 1988).

It is also likely that one's perception of the pollution problem could have a bearing on one's attitude toward pollution. Crosby, Gill and Taylor (1981) found that an individual's concern with beverage container's contribution to pollution and litter had a strong positive relationship with his/her ecological concern. However, they found little association between litter concern and the purchase of returnable containers. Thus, those who believe there is a solid waste disposal problem are apt to be more concerned about pollution than those who do not, and vice versa.

Finally, the extent to which the consumer believes she/he can be effective in pollution abatement is considered to be a predictor of the ecologically concerned consumer (Kinnear, Taylor, and Ahmed 1974; Webster 1975). The ecologically concerned consumer believes his/her actions will make a difference. Similarly, the more consumers believe in the power of the individual, the more they buy and use non-polluting products (Balderjahn 1988).

While prediction at the individual level proves difficult, ecological concern is often a good explanatory variable of group behavior (Gill,

Crosby, and Taylor 1986). Traditionally, the link found between attitudes and behavior in the ecology and social marketing literature has been weak (Gill, Crosby, and Taylor 1986; Rothschild 1979). This may be partially explained by the finding that the effects of ecological concern on ecological behavior are mediated by attitudinal, normative, and behavioral intention variables (Gill, Crosby, and Taylor 1986).

Place of Residence

Place of residence, a potentially useful segmenting variable, has often been overlooked by marketing scholars investigating the ecologically concerned consumer (Table 7.1). According to Tremblay and Dunlap (1978), urban residents should be more concerned with environmental problems since they are generally exposed to higher levels of pollution and other types of environmental deterioration. Although there is some evidence that environmental concern is related positively to urban residence, the results are again mixed (Samdahl and Robertson 1989; Van Liere and Dunlap 1980). A recent review by Samdahl and Robertson (1989) suggests that residence is largely inadequate in explaining the variance in perceptions of environmental problems or ecological behavior. Based on its potential use for segmentation, and the conflicting results concerning it, residence should not be omitted in a study of environmental consciousness. Clearly, it is plausible that one's place of residence may influence one's perception of the solid waste disposal problem, which in turn may influence one's attitude toward pollution or litter.

As discussed, previous research has found several variables useful for identifying the ecologically concerned consumer. Hence, these variables are incorporated in a study that attempts to identify characteristics of those who are willing to purchase ecologically packaged products.

METHOD

Data Collection

A questionnaire was developed and initially pretested on a sample of 30 students from a large university located in the central southern United States. Information gained from the pretest was used to revise the test instrument before distributing it to a convenience sample of 150 individuals in a major metropolitan area in the same locale. A modified mall intercept technique was used to administer a self-report questionnaire. To obtain information from individuals living in diverse areas with different population densities, approximately half of the questionnaires were administered at a shopping mall and the remainder at an airport. Four questionnaires were deemed unusable, resulting in a final sample of 146. The characteristics of the sample are presented in Table 7.2.

Measurement

The instrument was based largely on variables deemed important in previous theoretical research on the ecologically concerned consumer. Seven scales were included, three of which were utilized by previous researchers investigating environmental concern: (1) Rotter's (1966) 29-item locus of control scale (LOCUS); (2) Middleton's (1963) six-item alienation scale (ALIEN); and (3) Berkowitz and Lutterman's (1968) eight-item social responsibility scale (SRS).

Three scales were developed that attempted to capture the following constructs: one's *attitude toward litter* (AL), *perception of pollution* (PP), and *attitude toward ecologically conscious living* (AECL) (scale items are listed in Appendix A). The purpose of assessing these dimensions was to determine whether those with favorable inclinations towards the environment and those aware of pollution would also be more likely to purchase ecologically packaged goods. Previous research suggests that these dimensions are useful indicators for identifying the ecologically concerned consumer. Finally, a five-item scale was developed to measure one's *purchase intentions* (PI) with respect to ecological packaging (Appendix B).

For each item of the locus of control scale, respondents were asked to indicate which of two statements they more strongly believed to be the case for them. The remaining measures contained statements scored on a five-point scale ranging from (1) "strongly disagree" to (5) "strongly agree." Several items were reverse scored to avoid response bias.

In addition to measuring attitudinal and personality variables,

TABLE 7.2. Characteristics of the Sample

Characteristic	Percent	Frequency
Gender		
Male	63.0	92
Female	37.0	54
Marital Status		
Single	54.5	79
Married	37.2	54
Other	8.3	12
Age		
Under 25	38.2	55
25-34	31.9	46
35-44	17.4	25
45-54	4.9	7
55-64	6.9	10
65 +	0.7	1
Education		
Some high school	12.5	18
High school graduate	18.8	27
Some college	32.6	47
College graduate	19.4	28
Some graduate work	8.3	12
Graduate degree	8.3	12
Income		
Under $10,000	22.5	32
$10,000 - $19,999	26.1	37
$20,000 - $29,999	19.0	27
$30,000 - $39,999	12.7	18
$40,000 - $49,999	7.7	11
$50,000 +	12.0	17
Race		
Black	19.2	28
White	76.7	112
Hispanic	1.4	2
Other	2.7	4
City size		
Population < 100,000	30.8	45
Population > = 100,000	69.2	101

place of residence and demographic information was obtained. Included in the study were questions regarding: (1) one's place of
residence, from which the city size in terms of population was extracted (CITYSZ); (2) whether there was a public or private recre-
ation area within 50 miles of one's place of residence (REC); and (3)
the number of hours a week spent involved in outdoor leisure activities (LEISURE). LEISURE and REC were included on an exploratory basis to see if these variables could be used as discriminators. It
was expected that those who live near a recreational area may be
more sensitive to pollution given that such areas are more pristine.
Additionally, it was expected that those more involved in outdoor
leisure activities would have a greater awareness and concern about
the environment and pollution. In light of previous research, the
following demographic variables were also included: (1) number of
community organizations to which one belongs (ORG); (2) sex
(GENDER); (3) race (RACE); (4) marital status (MS); (5) age
(AGE); (6) education (EDUC); and (7) income (INC).

Data Analysis

Linear Discriminant Analysis (Fisher 1936) was used to assess the
effects of the socio-psychological (LOCUS, SRS, ALIEN, AL, PP,
AECL) and demographic variables (CITYSZ, REC, LEISURE,
ORG, GENDER, RACE, MS, AGE, EDUC, INC) on the intensity of
each respondent's purchase intentions (PI). Respondents were classified into two groups: those with low purchase intentions with regard
to ecologically packaged products (low PI), and those with high
purchase intentions with regard to ecologically packaged products
(high PI). Respondents whose scores fell above or equal to the median score (17.0) on the PI measure were classified as having high
purchase intentions. All other respondents were classified in the low
PI group.

The analysis was conducted in two parts. First, only the socio-psychological variables were used to discriminate between the two
groups. Then, both the socio-psychological and demographic variables were combined. This was done to determine if the socio-psychological variables alone could discriminate between the two
groups, or if better results would be obtained by adding the demographic variables. Since interval measurement was not used for

collection of the demographic variables, these variables were not deemed appropriate for separate analysis.

RESULTS

The analysis was conducted by setting the prior probabilities based on the sample size, which included 72 respondents in the low PI group and 74 in the high PI group. The discriminant function coefficients for the variables for each group are presented in Table 7.3. The canonical correlation is .619 for the socio-psychological variables alone and .644 for the combined variables. This indicates that in each case, there is a fairly strong relationship between the two groups and the discriminant function, with the combined variables being slightly higher. Additionally, a Wilks' Lambda of .617 (chi-square = 68, signf. = 0.00) indicates that the socio-psychological variables are significant in discriminating between the two groups, as is the combined group (Wilks' Lambda = .585, chi-square = 72.28, signf. = 0.00).

Table 7.3 also includes the standardized canonical discriminant function coefficients. At .606 and .615 (combined variables), AL appears to be the most important variable in discriminating between low PI and high PI. The structure matrix indicates that the function is carrying the most information from AL, while AECL and LEISURE are contributing the least.

In an attempt to eliminate any weak or redundant variables, stepwise variable selection was performed on the same set of data. Results indicate that most variables are still significant in discriminating between the groups. However, ALIEN was no longer significant for either set of variables, and all the demographic variables, barring RACE and INC, failed to enter the equation for the combined set of variables. Table 7.4 provides the coefficients for the two sets of variables. For the socio-psychological variables, AL was again the most important variable for discriminating between the two groups. However, for the combined variables, PP has the highest standardized canonical discriminant function coefficient at .587, indicating it is the most important, discriminating variable.

TABLE 7.3. Discriminators of Intention to Purchase Ecologically Packaged Products[a]

Canonical Discriminant Functions

Variables	Eigen-Value	Canonical Correlation	Wilks' Lambda	Chi-Squared	df	Signif.
Socio-Psychological	.620	.619	.617	68.00	6	0.000
Socio-Psychological & Demographic	.708	.644	.585	72.28	16	0.000

Classification Function Coefficients
(Fisher's Linear Discriminant Functions)

Variables	High Purchase Intentions	Low Purchase Intentions
Socio-Psychological		
Locus of Control	0.857	0.752
Alienation	1.553	1.504
Social Responsibility	1.178	1.151
Attitude toward Litter	0.042	0.441
Perception of Pollution	1.544	1.986
Attitude toward ECL	1.905	2.116
Constant	49.909	−58.479
Socio-Psychological & Demographic		
Locus of Control	1.258	1.139
Alienation	1.635	1.589
Social Responsibility	1.363	1.134
Attitude toward Litter	−0.246	0.187
Perception of Pollution	1.155	1.680
Attitude toward ECL	1.659	1.891
City Size	11.404	11.722
Organizations	5.801	5.600
Recreation	12.811	12.033
Leisure Activities	2.124	2.064
Gender	11.413	11.429
Race	3.373	2.609
Marital Status	2.542	2.501
Age	3.703	3.912
Education	7.171	7.228
Income	0.165	−0.460
Constant	−94.266	−101.036

Standardized Canonical Discriminant Function Coefficients

Socio-Psychological Variables		Socio-Psychological & Demographic Variables	
Locus of Control	−0.221	Locus of Control	−0.236
Alienation	−0.120	Alienation	−0.147
Social Responsibility	−0.095	Social Responsibility	−0.097
Attitude toward Litter	0.606	Attitude Toward Litter	0.615
Perception of Pollution	0.548	Perception of Pollution	0.610
Attitude toward ECL	0.262	Attitude toward ECL	0.267
		City Size	0.087
		Organizations	−0.049
		Recreation	−0.159
		Leisure Activities	−0.018
		Gender	0.005
		Race	−0.252
		Marital Status	−0.016
		Age	0.056
		Education	0.017
		Income	−0.208

Structure Matrix
Pooled Within-Groups Correlations Between
Discriminating Variables and Canonical Discriminant Functions

Socio-Psychological Variables		Socio-Psychological & Demographic Variables	
Attitude toward Litter	0.761	Attitude toward Litter	0.707
Perception of Litter	0.690	Perception of Pollution	0.644
Attitude toward ECL	0.462	Attitude toward ECL	0.424
Social Responsibility	0.369	Social Responsibility	0.341
Locus of Control	−0.270	Locus of Control	−0.261
Alienation	−0.131	City Size	−0.160
		Marital Status	0.118
		Alienation	−0.118
		Gender	0.104
		Education	0.066
		Race	−0.054
		Income	−0.051
		Age	0.020
		Recreation	−0.007
		Organizations	0.004
		Leisure Activities	−0.001

TABLE 7.3 (continued)

Test of Equality of Group Covariance Matrices Using Box's M

Variables	Box's M	F	df	Signf.
Socio-Psychological	46.005	2.093	21, 76144.3	.002
Option 11[b]	0.022	0.020	1, 62176.0	.887
Socio-Psychological & Demographic Option 11[b]	159.370	1.099	136, 62925.7	.202

[a]SPSSX Direct Entry Method
[b]SPSSX Option 11 approximates the quadratic classification technique by using individual-group covariance matrices of the discriminant functions for classification.

Hit Rate Estimation

The "hit rate" in discriminant analysis refers to the probability of correctly classifying an observation into a particular group. In an additional analysis, hit rates for each group, as well as an overall hit rate, were calculated for both the socio-psychological variables, and the combination of socio-psychological and demographic variables. The findings show that a fairly large improvement in classification is attributed to the power of the discriminating variables.

Additional Analysis

Since CITYSZ did not appear to be a significant discriminating variable, but AL and PP did, t-tests were conducted to examine the relationship between CITYSZ and each of these constructs. CITYSZ was divided into two groups. One constituted individuals from cities with a population of 100,000 or more, and the other from cities with less than 100,000. Over 40 different cities were represented. The t was statistically significant in each case. Apparently those living in larger cities are more concerned about pollution than those living in smaller cities. Furthermore, those living in larger cities are more inclined to believe there is a pollution problem. Given these findings,

TABLE 7.4. Discriminators of Intention to Purchase Ecologically Packaged Products[a]

(Alternative Approach)

Canonical Discriminant Functions

Variables	Eigen-Value	Canonical Correlation	Wilks' Lambda	Chi-Squared	df	Signif.
Socio-Psychological	.612	.616	.620	67.78	4	0.000
Socio-Psychological & Demographic	.677	.635	.596	72.36	6	0.000

Classification Function Coefficients
(Fisher's Linear Discriminant Functions)

	Low Purchase Intentions	High Purchase Intentions
Variables Socio-Psychological		
Locus of Control	1.014	0.929
Attitude toward Litter	1.165	1.539
Perception of Pollution	1.839	2.329
Attitude toward ECL	1.928	2.136
Constant	−29.541	−42.006
Socio-Psychological & Demographic		
Locus of Control	1.126	0.998
Attitude toward Litter	1.035	1.429
Perception of Pollution	1.155	2.045
Attitude toward ECL	1.903	2.109
Race	4.275	3.532
Income	2.937	2.377
Constant	−33.925	−42.006

Standardized Canonical Discriminant Function Coefficients

Socio-Psychological Variables		Socio-Psychological & Demographic Variables	
Locus of Control	−.239	Locus of Control	−.259
Attitude toward Litter	.571	Attitude toward Litter	.573
Perception of Pollution	.544	Perception of Pollution	.587
Attitude toward ECL	.258	Attitude toward ECL	.243
		Race	−.251
		Income	−.190

TABLE 7.4 (continued)

Structure Matrix
Pooled Within-Groups Correlations Between
Discriminating Variables and Canonical Discriminant Functions

Socio-Psychological Variables		Socio-Psychological & Demographic Variables	
Attitude toward Litter	.766	Attitude toward Litter	.724
Perception of Pollution	.694	Perception of Pollution	.659
Attitude toward ECL	.465	Attitude toward ECL	.434
Social Responsibility	.406	Social Responsibility	.383
Locus of Control	−.271	Locus of Control	−.267
Alienation	−.049	City Size	−.248
		Gender	.126
		Recreation	.118
		Marital Status	.102
		Education	.061
		Race	−.055
		Income	−.052
		Alienation	−.038
		Age	−.032
		Leisure Activities	.001
		Organizations	.000

Test of Equality of Group Covariance Matrices Using Box's M

Variables	Box's M	F	df	Signf.
Socio-Psychological	26.412	2.562	10, 98963.6	.004
Option 11[b]	0.096	0.095	1, 62176.0	.758
Socio-Psychological & Demographic	48.103	2.188	21, 74935.7	.001
Option 11[b]	0.175	0.174	1, 61275.0	0.677

---

[a]SPSSX Stepwise Entry Method
[b]SPSSX Option 11 approximates the quadratic classification technique by using individual-group covariance matrices of the discriminant functions for classification.

perhaps CITYSZ could be used as a surrogate for AL and PP, when attempting to target consumers of ecologically packaged products.

SUMMARY AND IMPLICATIONS

The results of this study indicate that there are consumers who are willing to purchase ecologically packaged products and that certain socio-psychological variables are significant for discriminating between consumers having low and high purchase intentions concerning these products. The analysis showed that individuals with an internal locus of control, who are concerned about litter, who believe there is a pollution problem, and who have a favorable attitude toward ecologically conscious living, are more inclined to purchase ecologically packaged products. Thus, as people become aware of the solid waste problem, their attitudes and purchase intentions may in turn change. Hence, even those not currently favoring environmentally conscious purchasing are candidates for ecologically packaged products if they can be convinced that there is a problem.

Consistent with previous findings (Balderjahn 1988; Kinnear, Taylor, and Ahmed 1974; Webster 1975), the results here indicate that demographic variables are not as important as socio-psychological variables in understanding the ecologically concerned consumer. Also, it appears that locus of control, attitude toward pollution, and attitude toward ecologically conscious living used by Balderjahn in Germany (1988) are also useful indicators of the ecologically concerned consumer in the U.S.

It was expected that city size may be useful in discriminating between low and high PI. Contrary to what was expected, those living in large cities evidently do not develop learned helplessness and are actually more likely to purchase ecologically packaged products. They are more inclined to believe there is a pollution problem and are more concerned about it than those living in smaller communities. This suggests that marketers may need to educate those consumers living in less densely populated areas in order to influence them to purchase ecologically packaged products.

The results further suggest that increased awareness about the solid waste disposal problem may result in attitude and purchase behavior change. Both marketers and policymakers may wish to use advertising to educate the consumer with regard to the solid waste problem. Increased awareness of the problem may enhance attitude changes, which in turn may result in behavioral changes such as the purchase of ecologically packaged products. If consumers are convinced that they can make a difference, they are likely to attempt to do so.

Also, the results suggest that consumers would be willing to make changes in their consumption behaviors related to package changes. For instance, they are willing to purchase products in larger packages with less frequency, products in less attractive packages that eliminate unnecessary packaging, and products in redesigned packages that contribute less solid waste. Consumers are also willing to purchase products in recyclable and biodegradable packages over similar products whose packages are not.

Implications for policymakers are interesting. Rather than placing more stipulations in the form of laws for consumers and/or marketers, policymakers might benefit more from informing the public of the solid waste disposal problem, and attempting to influence attitudes toward pollution. More importantly, if marketers take an active role in educating the public, the government's role may be attenuated. The more willing consumers and manufacturers are to help solve this problem, the less the need for government intervention. While it is recognized that packaging is only one component of the solid waste stream, it is a significant one, and one that may be amenable to voluntary action.

Although this study provides several insightful findings, it is not without limitations. A larger randomly selected national sample would provide more generalizable information than the present regional sample. Though the sample included different size cities, many are adjoining and from the same region. Furthermore, the reliabilities of the scales are somewhat low, perhaps due to the limited number of items per scale. However, significant relationships were found despite the fact that measures low in reliability tend to attenuate the correlation between measures (Peter 1979). Finally, future researchers should be cognizant of the wording they use to measure purchase intentions. Instructions provided in this study asked respondents to indicate their purchase intentions. However, it could be argued that some of the words used in the purchase intentions scale suggest an attitudinal component. Our research indicates that close attention to word choice and instructions that clearly delineate attitude from behavior should be used in order to avoid confounding effects.

Future studies might investigate consumers' price elasticity with regard to ecological packages. In other words, how much more would the consumer be willing to pay? The present investigation assumed all things remained equal, except for the package change. Furthermore, what types of packaging will consumers tolerate? In other words, how much can the manufacturer deviate from current norms in packaging practices before encountering consumer resistance? It is possible that some package changes may result in significant inconveniences to the consumer. Therefore, the trade-offs involved in purchasing ecologically packaged products need to be investigated.

Additionally, several potential areas for research concerning the advertising and promotion of the ecological package emerge. What is the best way to present a new package change? How much information should be provided to consumers concerning the package's contribution to waste reduction? For example, it would be interesting to test whether *information* concerning packaging's contribution to solid waste has an effect on one's purchase intentions. Such additional research might be enlightening for advertising and labeling purposes. Can the ecological package be used as a differentiating technique?

In summary, the findings suggest that there is a viable and identifiable market segment with high purchase intentions concerning ecologically packaged products. As consumers become more concerned with the environment, marketers must take a closer look at present business practices. As pointed out earlier, ecological package changes are feasible from both a technological and marketing perspective. Perhaps the expansion of the ecologically concerned consumer segment will create a win-win situation for both marketers and society.

The following statements concern your opinions about solid waste, pollution, and packaging. Please circle the number that corresponds with your feelings about each statement. There are no right or wrong answers.

Attitude Toward Litter (AL)

AL1: I am concerned with the amount of pollution in my city.
AL2: Seeing litter in streets and parks bothers me.
AL3: Seeing someone litter upsets me.

Attitude Toward Ecologically Conscious Living (AECL)

AECL1: When I buy products, I try to consider how my use of them will affect the environment and other consumers.
AECL2: Whenever possible, I buy products that I consider environmentally safe.
AECL3: I recycle whenever possible.

Perception of Pollution (PP)

PP1: The United States is facing a solid waste disposal problem.
PP2: The city in which I live is running out of places to dispose of its solid waste.
PP3: I believe that industry could reduce the amount of packaging it presently uses for some consumer packaged goods.

APPENDIX B:
Purchase Intentions Scale (PI)

The statements in this section are concerned with your purchase intentions. Given that you are made aware through advertising or some other means that the following packaging practices would help to eliminate packaging's contribution to solid waste, please circle the number that corresponds with your feelings about each statement. If the characteristics of alternative products were the same, how would you respond to the following statements:

1. I would purchase a product in a biodegradable package before purchasing a similar product in a non-biodegradable package.

2. I would purchase a product in a recyclable package before purchasing a similar product in a package that is not recyclable.

3. I would be willing to purchase some products (now bought in smaller sizes) in larger packages with less frequency.

4. I would purchase a product with a nontraditional package design (for example, round where most are square) if it meant creating less solid waste.

5. I would purchase a less attractively packaged product if I knew that all unnecessary plastic and or paper covering had been eliminated.

REFERENCES

Anderson, W. Thomas Jr. and William H. Cunningham (1972), "The Socially Conscious Consumer," *Journal of Marketing*, 36 (July), 23-31.

Anderson, W. Thomas Jr., Karl E. Henion II, and Eli P. Cox III (1974), "Socially vs. Ecologically Concerned Consumers," in *1974 Combined Proceedings*. Chicago, IL: American Marketing Association.

Antilla, Susan (1985), "Socially Responsible Investments," *Working Woman*, 10 (April), 38-41.

Balderjahn, Ingo (1988), "Personality Variables and Environmental Attitudes as Predictors of Ecologically Responsible Consumption Patterns," *Journal of Business Research*, 17 (August), 51-56.

Barber, James G., Anthony H. Winfield, and Karl Mortimer (1986), "The Personal Interests Questionnaire: A Task Specific Measure of Locus of Control and Motivation for Use in Learned Helplessness Research," *Personality and Individual Differences*, 7 (3), 311-318.

Beck, Melinda, Mary Hager, Patricia King, Sue Hutchison, Kate Robins, and Jeanne Gordon (1989), "Buried Alive," *Newsweek*, 114 (November 27), 66-76.

Begley, Sharon and Patricia King (1989), "The Supply-Side Theory of Garbage," *Newsweek*, 114 (November 27), 16.

Belch, Michael A. (1979), "Identifying the Socially and Ecologically Concerned Segment Through Life-Style Research: Initial Findings," in *The Conserver Society*, Karl E. Henion II and Thomas C. Kinnear (eds.), Chicago, IL: American Marketing Association.

Berkowitz, Leonard and Kenneth G. Lutterman (1968), "The Traditional Socially Responsible Personality," *Public Opinion Quarterly*, 32 (Summer), 169-185.

Bingham, T.H., M.S. Marquis, P.C. Cooley, A.M. Cruze, E.W. Hauser, S.A. Johnston and P.F. Mulligan (1974), *An Evaluation of the Effectiveness and Costs of Regulatory and Fiscal Policy Instruments on Product Packaging*. EPA: U.S.

Bishop, Willard (1986), "DPP–Direct Profit Product Squeeze," *Marketing Communications*, 11 (October), 67-76.

Cone, J.D. and S.C. Hayes (1980), *Environmental Problems: Behavioral Solutions*. Monterey, CA: Brooks/Cole.

Conn, W. David (1988), "Reducing Municipal Solid Waste Generation: Lessons from the Seventies," *Journal of Resource Management and Technology*, 16 (April), 24-27.

Corey, Robert J. and Paula Fitzgerald Bone (1990), "Ethical Packaging: Directions for the 1990's," in *AMA Educators Proceedings 1990: Enhancing Knowledge Development in Marketing*," William Bearden et al. (eds.), Chicago, IL: American Marketing Association, 387.

Crosby, Lawrence A. and James R. Taylor (1982), "Consumer Satisfaction with Michigan's Container Deposit Law–An Ecological Perspective," *Journal of Marketing*, 46 (Winter), 47-60.

Crosby, Lawrence A. and James R. Taylor (1983), "Psychological Commitment and Its Effects on Post-Decision Evaluation and Preference Stability Among Voters," *Journal of Consumer Research*, 9 (March), 413-431.

Crosby, Lawrence A., James D. Gill, and James R. Taylor (1981), "Consumer/ Voter Behavior in the Passage of the Michigan Container Law," *Journal of Marketing*, 45 (Spring), 19-32.

Cross, Frank B. (1990), "The Weaning of the Green: Environmentalism Comes of Age in the 1990's," *Business Horizons*, 33 (September-October), 40-46.

Environmental Protection Agency (1989), *Promoting Source Reduction and Recyclability in the Marketplace: A Study of Consumer and Industry Response to Promotion of Source Reduced, Recycled, and Recyclable Products and Packaging*. Washington, D.C.: Environmental Protection Agency.

EPA Journal (1989), "An Interview with Sylvia Lowrance," 15 (March/April), 10-13.

Erickson, Greg (1988), "High-Profit Packages," *Packaging*, 33 (June), 8-10.

Fishelson, Gideon (1985), "Package Size and Solid Waste," *Resources and Energy*, 7 (June), 203-215.

Fisher, Anne B. (1990), "What Consumers Want in the 1990's," *Fortune*, 121 (January), 108-112.

Fisher, R.A. (1936), "The Use of Multiple Measurements in Taxonomic Problems," *Annals of Eugenics*, 7, 179-188.

Gill, James D., Lawrence A. Crosby, and James R. Taylor (1986), "Ecological Concern, Attitudes, and Social Norms in Voting Behavior," *Public Opinion Quarterly*, 50 (Winter), 537-554.

Henion, Karl E., II (1976), *Ecological Marketing*. Columbus, OH: Grid, Inc.

Henion, Karl E., II and William H. Wilson (1976), "The Ecologically Concerned Consumer and Locus of Control," in *Ecological Marketing*, Karl E. Henion and Thomas C. Kinnear (eds.), Chicago, IL: American Marketing Association.

Jay, Leslie (1990), "Green About the Tills: Markets Discover the Eco-Consumer," *Management Review*, 79 (June), 24-29.

Johnson, Scott Lee, Robert Sommer, and Lora Mayes (1985), "Prices of Unpackaged and Packaged Foods," *The Journal of Consumer Affairs*, 19 (Winter), 305-315.

Kassarjain, Harold H. (1971), "Incorporating Ecology into Marketing Strategy: The Case of Air Pollution," *Journal of Marketing*, 35 (July), 61-65.

Kinnear, Thomas C. and James R. Taylor (1973), "The Effect of Ecological Concern on Brand Perceptions," *Journal of Marketing Research*, 10 (May), 191-198.

Kinnear, Thomas C., James R. Taylor and Sadrudin A. Ahmed (1974), "Ecologically Concerned Consumers: Who Are They?" *Journal of Marketing*, 38 (April), 20-24.

Kirkpatrick, David (1990), "Environmentalism: The New Crusade," *Fortune*, 121 (February 12), 45-55.

Kovacs, William L. (1988), "The Coming Era of Conservation and Industrial Utilization of Recyclable Materials," *Ecology Law Quarterly*, 15 (4), 537-602.

Larkin, Andrew (1986), "Environmental Impact and Institutional Adjustment: Application of Foster's Principles to Solid Waste Disposal," *Journal of Economic Issues*, 20 (March), 43-61.

Levitt, Lynn and Gloria Leventhal (1986), "Litter Reduction: How Effective is the New York State Bottle Bill?" *Environment and Behavior*, 18 (July), 467-479.

Lewis, Jack (1989), "What's in the Solid Waste Stream?" *EPA Journal*, 15 (March/April), 15-17.

Maloney, Michael P., Michael P. Ward, and G. Nicholas Braucht (1975), "A Revised Scale for the Measurement of Ecological Attitudes and Knowledge," *American Psychologist*, 30 (July), 787-790.

McCoy, Charles (1990), "Environmental Initiative Rejected in California," *The Wall Street Journal*, 216 (November 8), A16.

Michman, Ronald D. (1985), "Linking Ecology and Public Policy with Marketing Planning," *Akron Business and Economic Review*, (Fall), 24-29.

Middleton, Russell (1963), "Alienation, Race, and Education," *American Sociological Review*, 28 (December), 973-977.

Miller, Cyndee (1990), "Use of Environmentally Friendly Packaging May Take Awhile," *Marketing News*, 24 (March 19), 18.

Murphy, Patrick E. (1978), "Environmentally Concerned Consumers: Demographic Dimensions," in *Proceedings of the 1978 Educators' Conference*, Subhash C. Jain (ed.), Chicago, IL: American Marketing Association.

Murphy, Patrick E., Norman Kangun, and William B. Locander (1978), "Environmentally Concerned Consumers–Racial Variations," *Journal of Marketing*, 42 (October), 61-66.

Nation's Business (1990), "Congressional Alert: Solid-Waste Management," 78 (April), 70.

Nelson, James E. (1974), "An Empirical Investigation of the Nature and Incidence of Ecologically Responsible Consumption of Housewives," unpublished PhD dissertation, University of Minnesota.

Packaging's Encyclopedia (1988), "Legal Aspects of Packaging," 33 (5), 221-227.

Peter, J. Paul (1979), "Reliability: A Review of Psychometric Basics and Recent Marketing Practices," *Journal of Marketing Research*, 16 (February), 6-17.

Popkin, Roy (1989), "Source Reduction: Its Meaning and Its Potential," *EPA Journal*, 15 (March/April), 27-29.

Quick, James C. and Jonathan D. Quick (1984), *Organizational Stress and Preventive Management*. New York: McGraw-Hill Book Company.

Rathje, William L. (1984), "The Garbage Decade," *American Behavioral Scientist*, 28 (September/October), 9-29.

Rice, Faye (1988), "Where Will We Put All That Garbage?" *Fortune*, 118 (April 11), 96-100.

Riggle, D. (1989), "Only Pay for What You Throw Away," *Biocycle*, 30 (February), 39-41.

Rothschild, Michael L. (1979), "Marketing Communications in Nonbusiness Situations or Why It's So Hard to Sell Brotherhood Like Soap," *Journal of Marketing*, 43 (Spring), 11-20.

Rotter, Julian B. (1966), "Generalized Expectancies for Internal Versus External Control of Reinforcement," *Psychological Monographs*, 80 (1), 609.

Russell, Charles B. (1976), "Economical, Ecological Packaging," in *Ecological Marketing*, Karl E. Henion II and Thomas C. Kinnear (eds.), Chicago, IL: American Marketing Association.

Samdahl, Diane M. and Robert Robertson (1989), "Social Determinants of Environmental Concern: Specification and Test of the Model," *Environment and Behavior*, 21 (January), 57-81.

Schlossberg, Howard (1990), "Environmental Concerns Lead Some Consumers to Change Buying Habits," *Marketing News*, 24 (December 24), 7.

Stoops, Glenn T. and Michael M. Pearson (1989), "Direct Product Profit: A Sensitivity Analysis," in *Developments in Marketing Science*, Vol. 12, Jon M. Hawes and Hohn Thanopoulos (eds.), Greenvale, NY: Academy of Marketing Science.

Stuller, Jay (1990), "The Politics of Packaging," *Across the Board*, 27 (January/February), 40-48.

Thompson, Terri and Mimi Bluestone (1987), "Garbage: It Isn't the Other Guy's Problem Anymore," *Business Week*, (May 25), 150-154.

Tremblay, Kenneth R., Jr. and Riley E. Dunlap (1978), "Rural-Urban Residence and Concern with Environmental Quality: A Replication and Extension," *Rural Sociology*, 43 (Fall), 474-491.

Van Liere, Kent D. and Riley E. Dunlap (1980), "The Social Bases of Environmental Concern: A Review of Hypotheses, Explanations and Empirical Evidence," *Public Opinion Quarterly*, 44 (Summer), 181-197.

Van Liere, Kent D. and Riley E. Dunlap (1981), "Environmental Concern: Does It Make a Difference How It Is Measured?" *Environment and Behavior*, 13 (November), 651-676.

Webster, Frederick E., Jr. (1975), "Determining the Characteristics of the Socially Conscious Consumer," *Journal of Consumer Research*, 2 (December), 188-196.

Weddle, Bruce and Edward Klein (1989), "A Strategy to Control the Garbage Glut," *EPA Journal*, 15 (March/April), 30-32.

Chapter 8

Implications of Understanding Basic Attitude Change Processes and Attitude Structure for Enhancing Pro-Environmental Behaviors

Stephen M. Smith
Curtis P. Haugtvedt

SUMMARY. Even though most people now report attitudes that are highly favorable to the environment, changes in pro-environmental behavior have been seemingly minimal. We suggest five factors that might account for part of the attitude-behavior discrepancy that has been observed in the realm of pro-environmentalism, focusing our discussion on characteristics of the attitudes themselves that may be influential in determining when attitude changes will be accompanied by significant behavioral changes.

INTRODUCTION

Significant changes occurred over the last decade in the way people view the natural environment. In the United States, citizen contributions to environmental lobbying organizations grew to unprecedented levels, pro-environmental legislation was passed even in the presence of conservative Presidential leadership (1981-1992), and many large corporations rushed forward to posi-

Preparation of this manuscript was facilitated by NIMH grant MH10118-02 to Stephen Smith and Ohio State University Research Professorship and College of Business Research grants awarded to Curtis Haugtvedt.

tion themselves as "green," or at least as less harmful to the environment than had been the case in the not-so-distant past. In addition, the results of many polls suggested that concern over environmental problems had risen substantially, and that public support for environmental protection had "become a truly consensual issue" (Dunlap 1991, p. 15).

In the midst of the growth of the green movement, marketers of "green" products, pro-environmental activist groups, and environmental educators have been faced with the seemingly paradoxical coincidence of rapid, broad adoption of pro-environmental attitudes, and yet changes in pro-environmental behaviors that have been frequently marginal or nonexistent. A recent meta-analysis of 51 studies showed the correlation between pro-environmental attitudes and pro-environmental behaviors to be only about .35 (Hines, Hungerford, and Tomera 1987). In other words, not many people appear to be actually engaging in the kinds of behavior their pro-environmental attitudes would seem to dictate.

In this chapter, we discuss five factors that may help account for the low degree of attitude-behavior consistency observed with respect to pro-environmental behaviors. Drawing on recent theoretical and empirical advances, we outline the obstacles we feel are most important to consider when attempting to increase pro-environmental behavior via persuasion. We also suggest the types of research that we feel are most needed in each area.

We do not discuss the now well-known measurement issues that also need to be taken into consideration in attitude-behavior correspondence research (see e.g., Davidson and Jaccard 1979; Pieters 1989; Weigel and Newman 1976).[1] Instead, we discuss how greater understanding of theoretical ideas regarding the nature of pro-environmental attitude formation and change may be used to guide the development of promotional campaigns designed to engender behaviors more in line with expressed attitudes. Understanding of these issues should be of interest to pro-environmental advocacy groups as well as marketers interested in encouraging consumers to purchase particular brands or kinds of products on the basis of environmental attributes.

UNDERSTANDING THE BASES
OF PRO-ENVIRONMENTAL ATTITUDES

Much advertising and promotion focuses on increasing levels of awareness and creating positive attitudes toward a product or issue. At this point, promotion in the area of pro-environmental issues should perhaps focus on strategies to alter attitudes in such a way as to enhance their influence on behavior. That is, as discussed above, significant percentages of Americans now claim to hold pro-environmental attitudes. Basic research in social psychology and consumer behavior suggests, however, that even though two individuals may express evaluatively similar and equally extreme attitudes toward a brand, product, or issue, their attitudes may still differ, leading to different patterns of behavior. For example, the manner in which the attitudes were formed and other, often unmeasured, characteristics of the attitudes, may be critical factors in guiding behavior (cf. Haugtvedt, Leavitt, and Schneier, forthcoming).

1. Central Route vs. Peripheral Route Attitude Changes

Research guided by the Elaboration Likelihood Model (ELM; Petty and Cacioppo 1986) has shown that evaluatively similar and equally extreme attitudes can be developed via very different kinds of processes. In brief, the ELM suggests that, in some cases, individuals may develop and express pro-environmental attitudes largely because of the kinds of positive cues associated with persuasive appeals. Attitude changes based on simple inferences or cue associations are characterized as attitude changes via the peripheral route. On the other hand, some individuals may develop pro-environmental attitudes as a result of careful consideration of very cogent arguments contained in persuasive appeals. Attitude changes due largely to greater levels of issue-relevant elaboration are characterized as attitude changes via the central route.

Based on the ELM framework, greater attitude-behavior consistency would be expected for individuals whose attitudes are based on greater message-relevant elaboration. Relative to attitudes formed on the basis of a few simple inferences or associations (peripheral route), central route attitudes are hypothesized to be based on a greater diversity of associative structures. Because of the differences in structures underlying the attitudes, attitudes formed via the central route have been shown to decay slower than attitudes formed via the peripheral route (Haugtvedt and Petty 1992, Experiment 1), to be more resistant to change in the face of attack (Haugtvedt and Petty 1992, Experiment 2), and to be better predictors of behavior (Cacioppo, Petty, Kao, and Rodriguez 1986). Attitudes formed via the central route therefore may be characterized as "stronger" than attitudes formed via the peripheral route and more likely to guide behavioral choices. Thus, two individuals (Joe and Mary) may have similarly positive environmental attitudes, but if Mary's attitude is formed via the central route while Joe's attitude is formed via the peripheral route, we expect Mary to demonstrate higher attitude-behavior consistency.

2. *Other Factors Related to Attitude Strength*

One of the methods used to induce higher or lower levels of processing motivation (and thus influence the route to persuasion) in ELM research is a manipulation of the situational relevance or importance of a topic. While manipulation of the relevance or importance of an issue is useful and possible in experimental research, self-rated judgments of attitude importance have also been used in other kinds of research. Findings from this research are also seen as supportive of the ELM view. Thus, for example, research by Krosnick (1988) suggests that consistency between attitudes and actions is more likely for more important attitudes than for those that are less important to the individual. A related notion is that individuals with strong *convictions* with respect to a particular attitudinal position (cf. Abelson 1988) will demonstrate greater attitude-behavior consistency (see, e.g., Balboa and Bodenhausen 1992).

Part of the process by which important or centrally formed attitudes guide behavior appears to be related to the speed with which an individual retrieves his or her attitude in response to stimuli. This is generally referred to as the attitude's *accessibility.* Just as the ELM analysis suggested that two individuals could hold evaluatively similar and equally extreme positive attitudes, other theory and research has shown that two persons can hold what appear to be equivalent attitudes but that the attitudes can differ in accessibility. The process of how more accessible attitudes may guide behavioral choice has been outlined in a program of research by Fazio and colleagues (e.g., Fazio, Powell, and Herr 1983; Fazio and Williams 1986; Fazio, Powell, and Williams 1989; see Fazio, forthcoming, for a review). The speed with which a person responds to an attitudinal probe (e.g., a question, the presentation of an attitude object) is thought to reflect the accessibility of the attitude-object association. Many experiments have demonstrated the construct validity of these response time measures of attitude accessibility as measures of the strength of association between an attitude object and the individual's evaluation of the object (e.g., Powell and Fazio 1984; Fazio et al. 1986).

Two types of manipulations have been used to increase the accessibility of an individual's attitudes. One type of manipulation has involved having individuals gain experience with the attitude object (e.g., Fazio and Zanna 1981) and another has simply varied the number of times individuals rehearse the attitude–through repeated reporting of the attitude, for example (e.g., Powell and Fazio 1984). In general, Fazio and his colleagues find that increasing attitude accessibility strengthens the attitude-behavior relationship. However, in our view, manipulations like increased experience are more likely than repeated-expression manipulations to lead to the development of more elaborative supportive structures (cf. Haugtvedt, Leavitt, and Schneier, forthcoming) and are thus more likely to lead to increases in the durability of the attitude (cf. Haugtvedt 1989) and persistence of the changes in accessibility.

The above discussion has highlighted the idea that the evaluative direction and extremity of two individuals' attitudes may be equal, yet one individual's attitude is more likely to guide actual behaviors than the other by virtue of being a more important, strongly held, or persistently more accessible attitude. Part of the discrepancy between pro-environmental attitudes and pro-environmental behaviors, therefore, may be attributable to deficits in the strength or conviction with which the pro-environmental attitudes are held, their lack of importance relative to other attitudes, and/or their reduced accessibility when the individual is presented with behavioral opportunities.

3. Attitude Functions

Attitudes have long been thought to play an important role not only in guiding behavior, but also in serving psychological needs for people (e.g., Katz 1960; Smith, Bruner, and White 1956). The psychological functions that attitudes are thought to serve include, for example, utilitarian and social identity functions. Utilitarian attitudes are those which an individual holds to the extent that they lead to explicit rewards or punishments. Other attitudes might be held primarily in order to obtain rewards from peers, hence the term "social identity."

The reason an individual holds an attitude is potentially quite important in devising a strategy for changing his or her attitude. For example, research has shown that the attitudes of high "self-monitors" (who are more interested in obtaining social acceptance; see Snyder 1974) are less susceptible to "quality-based" persuasion strategies than are the attitudes of low "self-monitors" (e.g., DeBono and Packer 1991; also see Shavitt, Lowrey and Han 1992). It may also be the case that attitude functions play a role in attitude-behavior consistency. Consistent with this hypothesis, low self-monitors have been shown to demonstrate greater attitude-behavior consistency than high self-monitors (Snyder and Swann 1976).

Regarding pro-environmental behavior, some individuals are thought to be highly sensitive to what others are doing, and will not, for example, participate in a recycling program unless they are confident that others are participating as well (see Wiener and Doescher 1991). This may be partly attributable to the fact that some individuals' attitudes about recycling serve a social identity function. Hence, getting them to recycle may entail persuading them that others are also participating, and that social rewards will accompany their own participation. Others may care little or not at all about the social benefits of recycling, perhaps being more concerned about whether a pro-recycling position is consistent with their values (i.e., the attitude serves a value-expressive function). Thus, pro-environmental attitudes may differ from one person to the next in terms of the psychological functions they serve, with important implications for persuasion strategies and for attitude-behavior relations. Future research in this area could focus on identifying the personality variables that are most strongly associated with particular attitude functions, the extent to which different functions are associated with attitude-behavior consistency, and on clarifying the processes through which persuasion strategies can work to either alter the functional bases of attitudes or appeal to the functional basis that exists.

4. *"Ideal" versus "Ought" Psychological Systems*

Two individuals' pro-environmental attitudes may also differ importantly in terms of the psychological consequences of acting contrary to them. If the consequences of attitude-discrepant behavior for Joe are more negative than the consequences for Mary, we might expect Joe to exhibit higher attitude-behavior consistency.

Strategies aimed at promoting pro-environmental behavior often use appeals designed to get individuals to consider discrepancies between their current behaviors and some other desired behavior. For example, an appeal might describe the ideal attitudes and behaviors for an individual as well as others (as in, "Wouldn't it be nice if . . ."). On the other hand, an appeal might focus on the discrepancy between a current or actual level of behavior and a level of behavior that is demanded by a situation or by other individuals (as in, "As a society we must . . ."). The importance of the difference between socially suggested "ideals" and socially demanded "oughts" has recently been systematically explored in the work by E.T. Higgins and colleagues on what is broadly characterized as "self-discrepancy theory" (Higgins 1987). Empirical findings in this realm may have important implications regarding the kinds of strategies most likely to stimulate pro-environmental behavior by individuals. It has been demonstrated, for example, that discrepancies between "actuals" (e.g., true performances) and oughts are more emotionally distressing than discrepancies between "actuals" and ideals, and recent evidence suggests that the distress induced by the actual/ought discrepancy is likely to motivate behavior to reduce the discrepancy, whereas discrepancies between the actual and ideal are likely to lead to depression and inactivity (Higgins, Tykocinski, and Vookles, 1990).

On the other hand, meeting an ideal should lead to feelings of satisfaction or happiness. It could be argued that this incentive outweighs the advantage of emphasizing actual/ought discrepancies outlined above. However, the reward value of avoiding an unpleasant state (as reflected in the psychological literature on negative reinforcement) has consistently been demonstrated to be as powerful as that of obtaining a pleasant state (i.e., positive reinforcement). For example, animal studies of avoidance learning (e.g., Solomon, Kamin, and Wynne 1953) have documented the impressive degree to which negatively reinforced behavior persists over time. Indeed, Skinner (1953) decried the underutilization of negative reinforcement techniques by parents, and therapists generally consider it to be highly effective (although practical and ethical considerations severely limit its application; cf. Spiegler 1983).

The logical fallout from the above reasoning is directly applicable to the reasoning on attitude-behavior (A-B) consistency. If an attitude is tied into an "ought" system, then A-B consistency should be high, because failure to act consistently with the attitude (or, at least, awareness of having acted inconsistently) should induce in the individual feelings of guilt. Attitudes that are connected to "ideal" systems may be less influential in guiding behavior (because of resultant depression and inactivity in the face of discrepancies). It is interesting to note in this regard that, in the Hines, Hungerford, and Tomera (1987) meta-analysis, an individual's sense of duty or obligation to the environment was a significant predictor ($r = .33$) of environmental behavior. These "psychological system" differences may also have important implications for persuasion. For example, recent research has found that manipulations of actual and ought self-discrepancies with respect to individuals' pro-environmental behavior affected the extent to which they systematically processed a pro-environmental message (Smith and Petty 1992). People in whom actual/ought discrepancies had been induced were more likely to differentiate between strong and weak argument versions of the persuasive appeal than were those experiencing actual/ideal discrepancies (resulting in a significant Discrepancy Type X Argument Quality interaction, $F = 4.49$, $p < .05$). However, more research is needed to clarify the processes through which these "psychological system" differences affect behavior and judgment.

It is also noteworthy that the Hines, Hungerford, and Tomera

(1987) study revealed substantially higher A-B consistency for individuals with ties to environmental organizations (r = .59) than for
the rest of the population (r = .33). Several possible explanations for
this between-group discrepancy are evident from the above discussion. First, people involved in environmental organizations are likely to have stronger environmental attitudes, and these attitudes are
probably more important to them than to those in the general population. Further, the environmental organization members may have
more direct experience with the environment than do others (see
e.g., Kellert 1985). Such direct experience has been demonstrated to
enhance A-B consistency (e.g., Regan and Fazio 1977). Further,
direct experience with the environment has been found to strength-
en the affective aspects of pro-environmental attitudes (e.g., Ryan
1991). Thus, a related possibility is that the attitudes of these people
have stronger affective components. Along these lines, Newhouse
(1990) has observed that environmentalists typically have experienced a sense of loss with respect to the environment, and have
stored vivid images of environmental degradation. Such vividly
represented information has been shown to be more likely to influence behavior than less vivid attitudinal components (e.g., Borgida
and Nisbett 1977). Others have hypothesized that strong pro-environmental attitudes are typically formed early in life (i.e., age 15),
when affective information tends to be more important than cognitive information (Hendee, Catton, Marlow, and Brockman 1968).
These and other factors suggest another way in which two individuals' pro-environmental attitudes may be equally positive yet differ-
entially influence behavior. Specifically, one individual's attitude
may have greater affective strength or a more substantial affective
component.

5.1 Affective Influences on Attitudes

Consistent with the above notions, Zajonc (1980) argues that
affective responses to stimuli are primary, and affective dimensions
are an important determinant of attitude accessibility. Along these
lines, a recent set of experiments by Edwards (1990) suggests that
affectively based attitudes may also be held more confidently than
cognitively based attitudes. Preliminary hypotheses to account for
this effect include the notion that affectively based attitudes are less

complex and hence more uniform. Although this notion has yet to be tested, it has clear implications for A-B consistency if true. An attitude that is uniform and simple may be a more reliable guide (assuming that the attitude is accessed) than an attitude whose basis includes a mixture of supportive and nonsupportive components. These simple, uniform, affectively based attitudes may also be less subject to contextual influences (see, e.g., Shavitt and Fazio 1991).

For example, certain contexts might make salient aspects of a more complex and mixed attitude that lead to behavior that is inconsistent with the overall valence of the attitude.

Consider an individual who holds a positive attitude toward environmentally friendly products, but also believes that they are generally more expensive. When price is made temporarily salient to such an individual, this belief may disproportionately influence their behavior, leading them to purchase a less environmentally sound product–perhaps without even carefully checking the price of the pro-environmental alternative. On the other hand, an individual whose attitude toward environmentally friendly products is based solely on positive feelings associated with these products is perhaps less likely to be influenced by price considerations, since no negatively evaluated attributes are integrated into the attitude.

It is also possible that attitudes that are affectively based are less influenced by cognitive appeals, as Edwards (1990) has shown, and also less likely to influence behavior after exposure to such appeals (while perhaps being more likely to influence behavior following additional affective appeals). An alternative is suggested by Millar and Millar (1990), who found that cognitive appeals produced more attitude change than affective appeals when the initial attitude was affectively based (i.e., a "mismatching" strategy worked better than a "matching" strategy). Given the discrepancies in findings, it is unclear whether affectively based attitudes respond more to affective than to cognitive appeals. More research is necessary to identify the conditions under which either "matching" or "mismatching" persuasion strategies are more appropriate.

In sum, although advertisers have long believed the use of emotions to be an effective persuasion tool (e.g., Ogilvy 1983, p. 109) there is little research examining the possible role of affect in creating or sustaining attitudes that are more predictive of behavior.

There is reason to suspect that affect plays an important role, particularly in the realm of pro-environmental attitudes and their subsequent influence (or lack thereof) on pro-environmental behaviors. Before much progress can be made in this area, however, some agreement needs to be reached as to how to assess the relative attitudinal contributions of affective and cognitive components.

5.2 Affective Influences on Behavior

Not only are pro-environmental attitudes subject to affective influences, but the pro-environmental behaviors themselves may be directly determined by affect. First, people generally will engage more frequently in activities that they enjoy than those which cause displeasure. Thus, we would expect that individuals who experience pleasant affective states subsequent to engaging in pro-environmental activities will be more likely to repeat such behaviors than individuals who experience negative affect, or even a lack of positive affect (i.e., reinforcement) upon engaging in pro-environmental actions.

More interestingly, affect can influence whether the activities will be performed in the first place. For example, some research has shown that people experiencing pleasant emotional states are more likely to engage in pro-social behaviors, such as helping (e.g., Isen and Levin 1972; note, however, that other studies have found similar patterns for negative emotional states, e.g., Cialdini, Kenrick, and Baumann 1981, see Schaller and Cialdini 1990 for a review).

Although scholars have generally assumed that emotional influences on behavior are mediated by attitudes, recent evidence suggests that this may not be entirely true. For example, Allen, Machleit, and Schultz Kleine (1992) found that attitudes toward blood donation did not completely mediate the influence of emotional experiences associated with blood donation, when predicting future donation behavior. A conceptual replication focusing on recycling has yielded similar results (Smith, Haugtvedt, and Petty 1994). Results from the above inquiries also suggest that affective influences are greater for individuals whose attitudes are relatively low in importance or accessibility, or who have relatively little experience with the attitude object. This would seem to imply that their behaviors might best be influenced through strategies geared toward changing their affective associations.

A related perspective on the influence of affect on behavior can be found in the literature on decision-making. Specifically, while decisions are influenced by both normative and idiosyncratic beliefs, research has shown that decisions are also influenced by *anticipated* emotions, above and beyond the effect of the actual emotions experienced upon performing the behavior. Related to this idea, Ritov and Baron (1992) recently provided evidence that people have a bias toward inaction that results in part from the fact that they anticipate more negative emotional outcomes from action that results in negative consequences than inaction that results in equally negative consequences. In addition, Baron (1992) also demonstrated that anticipated emotions can remain intact even after the beliefs that underlie these anticipated emotions are changed. This implies that people may report quite honestly that their attitudes have become more pro-environmental, yet their behaviors do not change because they anticipate negative post-behavior emotions, an anticipation that might be considered a residual of the former attitude and that must also be changed before pro-environmental behaviors will mirror the pro-environmental attitude.

For example, some people may feel that pro-environmental behavior is a good thing, but also think they would feel like a "sucker" if they expended the effort to engage in the behavior and others did not (Wiener and Doescher 1991). The anticipated emotional response thus impedes pro-environmental behavior, even though the individual might well express a pro-environmental attitude. Perhaps such people would act more consistently pro-environmentally were they persuaded that they would not experience these negative post-behavior emotions.

DISCUSSION

Our review has focused on the ways in which attitudes that are evaluatively similar can be quite different in terms of their implications for behavior. We have suggested five factors that we consider critical in understanding these differences, as well as why attitudes might not be strongly associated with behavior. Our findings are

TABLE 8.1. Factors Affecting Attitude-Behavior Relations and Supporting Evidence

Factor	Method of Influence	References
1. Central vs. Peripheral Route Formation	centrally formed attitudes are more predictive of behavior due to increased elaborations	Cacioppo et al. (1986) Haugtvedt and Petty (1992) Petty and Cacioppo (1986)
2. Other Factors Related to Strength (e.g., Importance, Accessibility)	stronger attitudes are more predictive of behavior due to increased likelihood that they will be remembered, outweigh other attitudes, etc.	Balboa and Bodenhausen (1992) Fazio et al. (1989) Kallgren and Wood (1987) Krosnick (1988, 1990) Powell and Fazio (1984)
3. Attitude Function	attitudes held for social reasons are less predictive of behavior than those held for utilitarian reasons	Shavitt et al. (1992) Snyder and Swann (1976)
4. "Ought" vs. "Ideal" Psychological Systems	attitudes toward "oughts" are more likely to predict behavior than those toward "ideals'"	Higgins et al. (1990) Smith and Petty (1992) Solomon et al. (1953)
5. Affective Basis of Attitudes	attitudes may be positive even though associated affect is not, affect may be more important than attitude for some people; also, affectively based attitudes may respond to different persuasion strategies than cognitively based attitudes	Allen et al. (1992) Baron (1992) Edwards (1990) Millar and Millar (1990) Smith et al. (1993) Zajonc (1980)

summarized in Table 8.1. Below we consider some of their implications for marketers and for the directions future research might take.

SUMMARY OF IMPLICATIONS FOR MARKETING

Approaches to environmental marketing follow logically from the reasoning outlined in this chapter. First, it should be clear that merely providing information is not enough. Attitudes toward "green" products are becoming increasingly positive, but they are not leading to a tremendous change in consumer behavior. The first suggestion we outlined is derived from the ELM (Petty and Cacioppo 1986). Advertisements should be designed so as to induce individuals to think about their reasons for holding pro-environmental attitudes. An example would be an ad that suggests that perhaps most people are only pretending to be in favor of pro-environmental changes. Similarly, ads that mildly attack an individual's pro-environmental attitude (for example, wryly noting that we have plenty of space left in the U.S. for more landfills) should work to strengthen the attitude and enhance its influence on behavior. Other techniques that have been shown to increase people's cognitive elaboration of a message include the use of rhetorical questions (Burnkrant and Howard 1984), personal pronouns such as "you" (Burnkrant and Unnava 1989), and framing messages in terms of potential costs of *not* engaging in a behavior rather than the benefits of performing the behavior (Smith and Petty 1993).

Consistent with the notion that more important attitudes will be more predictive of behavior, strategies should obviously attempt to highlight the importance of pro-environmental action. Further, successful marketing must elicit a reconsideration of an individual's attitudinal priorities. If one's attitude toward some other behavior is more important than, say, one's attitude toward recycling, then whenever a conflict between these two behaviors exists, recycling will lose out. Consistent with Fazio's work on accessibility, it may be useful to simply repeat messages about pro-environmental behavior, so as to encourage consumers to "rehearse" their attitudes, although we question whether such a strategy will have much long-term influence.

The reemergence of interest in attitude functions has highlighted the importance of understanding *why* an individual holds a particular attitude. Although not enough research has accumulated in this area to provide strong suggestions for improving attitude-behavior consistency in any given area of behavior, it seems clear that strategies for changing behavior can be greatly improved if differences in attitude functions can be anticipated and targeted. One possibility is a demographic segmentation approach that attempts to assess functions across a broad sample and determine covariations between particular functions and other sample characteristics. This information could then be used to devise relatively individualized persuasion strategies.

Another potentially useful approach follows from the discussion on "ought" versus "ideal" systems. It was noted that inconsistency (i.e., behavior that does not match the person's attitude) is more aversive when it violates an ought goal than when it violates an ideal goal. This suggests that changes in consumer behavior may be more likely if pro-environmental attitudes and behavior are portrayed as oughts rather than ideals. That is, advertisements or promotions that induce consumers to feel that it is their duty to make environmentally responsible purchases may be more effective than those that portray this behavior as idealistic.

Finally, the use of affective appeals to bolster pro-environmental attitudes may prove particularly fruitful. In addition, the use of vivid, affective appeals should make the information contained in an ad more likely to be retrieved. Most U.S. readers will doubtless remember an advertisement that aired during the early 1970s, in which a Native American was shown weeping after seeing garbage dumped by a roadside. The ease with which this ad is remembered provides anecdotal evidence of the strength of affective appeals.

The use of affectively oriented strategies seems particularly useful in getting people started–that is, it may work best for those who have little or no direct experience engaging in a given behavior (see Allen, Machleit, and Schultz Kleine 1992; Smith, Haugtvedt, and Petty 1994). Needless to say, this would be an important group to reach with respect to pro-environmental behavior, since success in this area is contingent upon mass participation. It may be that information-based appeals work better in sustaining pro-environmental behavior after it has been initiated.

SUMMARY OF IMPLICATIONS FOR RESEARCH

Investigations into the effectiveness of cognitive versus affective persuasive appeals suggest that significant differences may exist in the effectiveness of these different types of appeals, and that these differences may be contingent upon the nature of the original attitude; that is, whether the attitude is primarily affectively or cognitively based. It is important to point out, however, some important differences between existing research and the kind of situation faced in pro-environmental marketing and advertising. Most studies conducted so far, for example, have employed counterattitudinal communications. Since changing attitudes from anti- to pro-environmental does not appear to be the problem in our case, interesting questions from an applied standpoint may not receive sufficient answers from such research paradigms. That is, instead of changing attitudes from anti- to pro-environmental, our earlier discussion suggested that changing the structure underlying the attitude may be useful–for example, changing factors related to the importance, strength, or accessibility of the attitude.

With respect to the above proposition, we know relatively little about the implications of pre-existing positive attitudes toward the target of the ad or persuasive appeal for marketing and persuasion. However, a number of plausible effects deserve consideration here. Foremost is that the presence of a positive attitude toward the advocated position (i.e., toward engaging in environmental behaviors such as recycling or buying "green" products) may mean that individuals will actually put less effort into thinking about what is being said in the appeal. After all, one of the main reasons we are theorized to hold attitudes is because it saves us the cognitive effort of carefully processing all the information we are presented with. However, such a state of affairs suggests that typical pro-attitudinal appeals may have little impact on individuals whose attitudes are already positive. Even if an individual was at one time persuaded via effortful thinking and/or elaboration based upon experience, most pro-attitudinal appeals may not encourage persons to "reactivate" or "reinvigorate" the cognitive or affective structures underlying the attitude. The challenge for theorists and practitioners, therefore, is to consider ways in which initially positive attitudes can be strengthened, or otherwise altered to enhance their influence on behavior (cf. Haugtvedt, Leavitt, and Schneier, forthcoming).

Ideas derived from the Elaboration Likelihood Model (Petty and Cacioppo 1986) and Cognitive Response approaches (Greenwald, Brock, and Ostrom 1968) provide some insight into the kinds of strategies that may be useful. In brief, techniques that cause individuals to question reasons for holding positive attitudes may actually strengthen such attitudes by inducing individuals to think about and consider the basis for the positive attitudes. The process of reactivating and potentially reinvigorating the structures underlying the attitudes may enhance attitude behavior consistency (Haugtvedt, Leavitt, and

Schneier forthcoming). The process of engaging in pro-environmental behaviors may also provide additional elaboration and strength, leading to a self-reinforcing pattern of behavior and thoughts.

In line with the above arguments, research should also focus on the longer-term effects of attitude change on actual behavior change (i.e., longer-term than immediately post-message or even "day-after" effects). Further, the majority of research in the areas of persuasion and marketing has been limited to the cognitive domain; that is, the focus has been on whether facts are being represented accurately in the minds of the consumer or educational targets, and how these cognitive representations can be manipulated. Such a focus is likely to fall short of identifying optimal strategies for producing attitudes that maximize behavior change. Affective change is equally if not more important than cognitive change in yielding meaningful attitude change–i.e., attitude change which translates into behavior change–and this affective change may be induced best by affective appeals.

Affectively based appeals may usefully supplement cognitive information and assist in the formation of more complex and strong attitude structures. That is, many people may have recently developed positive attitudes toward pro-environmental behavior only as a result of factual knowledge that environmental problems exist, but these attitudes may not yet contain strong affective components. People's awareness that there are problems is not often the result of direct contact with the problems themselves. Major environmental catastrophes, for example, have often been very distant geographically (e.g., Exxon Valdez oil spill, Chernobyl nuclear disaster), and more common environmental problems in the U.S. remain either largely out of the public eye (e.g., landfills, groundwater contamination), or invisible to the naked eye (e.g., surface water pollution, ozone depletion). Because of this fact, strong affective reactions are less likely, and existing attitudes, in many cases, have probably not been extensively influenced by affective considerations.

NOTE

1. We have also excluded a number of other factors that could account for part of this gap, and summarize them briefly here. First, some of this gap is readily explained by the inability of infrastructural change to accommodate sweeping changes in human practices. For example, there aren't enough recycling facilities

in many areas to accommodate demand. Some of the discrepancy probably derives from citizen apathy, low self-efficacy, and even self-presentational influences–people may fail to act in accord with their stated attitudes because they are simply too lazy to do so, or don't believe there is a problem. Perhaps they do detect a problem, but they doubt their behavior makes any difference. Or perhaps their stated attitudes do not reflect their true attitudes; they may be merely reporting what they perceive to be a "politically correct" attitude. Many other factors can work to constrain the attitude-behavior (A-B) relationship as well. Knowledge of the appropriate behaviors is certainly important if one is to act in line with one's attitudes, and there seems to be room for improvement in the complex realm of pro-environmental action. People may desire to act to help the environment, yet be unaware of the behaviors that would accomplish this objective. Similarly, incomplete knowledge may occasionally serve to disrupt the A-B link. For example, a consumer may be interested in purchasing "green" products, but may lack important information about certain attributes of a given pro-environmental alternative; the consumer, being risk-averse, may subsequently assign negative values for these unknown characteristics, making the pro-environmental alternative less likely to be selected (e.g., Yates, Jagacinski, and Faber 1978; Yates and Zukowski 1976).

Some other factors working to deflate the A-B relationship might include the extent to which the behavior is under volitional control (e.g., Ajzen and Fishbein 1977) or normative control (e.g., Sheppard, Hartwick, and Warshaw 1988), or the extent to which the individual sees the particular behavior as useful in achieving a goal relevant to the attitude (e.g., Berger and Corbin 1992). These factors have nothing to do, however, with the attitudes themselves, nor do knowledge, self-efficacy, or any of the other factors described above.

REFERENCES

Abelson, Robert P. (1988), "Conviction," *American Psychologist*, 43, 267-275.

Ajzen, Icek, and Martin Fishbein (1977), "Attitude-Behavior Relations: A Theoretical Analysis and Review of Empirical Research," *Psychological Bulletin*, 84, 888-918.

Allen, Chris T., Karen A. Machleit, and Susan Schultz Kleine (1992), "A Comparison of Attitudes and Emotions as Predictors of Behavior at Diverse Levels of Behavioral Experience," *Journal of Consumer Research*, 18(4), 493-504.

Balboa, Roberto T., and Galen V. Bodenhausen (1992), "Conviction and the Attitude-Behavior Relation," paper presented at the annual meeting of the Midwestern Psychological Association, Chicago, IL.

Baron, Jonathan (1992), "The Effect of Normative Beliefs on Anticipated Emotions," *Journal of Personality and Social Psychology*, 63, 320-330.

Berger, Ida E., and Ruth M. Corbin (1992), "Perceived Consumer Effectivenesss and Faith in Others as Moderators of Environmentally Responsible Behaviors," *Journal of Public Policy and Marketing*, 11(2), 79-89.

Borgida, Eugene, and Richard E. Nisbett (1977), "The Differential Impact of

Abstract vs. Concrete Information on Decisions," *Journal of Applied Social Psychology*, 7, 258-271.

Burnkrant, Robert, and Daniel J. Howard (1984), "Effects of the Use of Introductory Rhetorical Questions Versus Statements on Information Processing," *Journal of Personality and Social Psychology*, 47, 1218-1230.

Burnkrant, Robert, and H. Rao Unnava (1989), "Self-Referencing: A Strategy for Increasing Processing of Message Content," *Personality and Social Psychology Bulletin*, 15, 628-638.

Cacioppo, John T., Richard E. Petty, Chuan F. Kao, and Regina Rodriguez (1986), "Central and Peripheral Routes to Persuasion: An Individual Difference Perspective," *Journal of Personality and Social Psychology*, 51, 1032-1043.

Cialdini, Robert B., Douglas T. Kenrick, and Donald J. Baumann (1981), "Effects of Mood on Prosocial Behavior in Children and Adults," *The Development of Social Behavior*, ed. Nancy Eisenberg-Berg, New York: Academic Press.

Davidson, Andrew R., and James J. Jaccard (1979), "Variables that Moderate the Attitude-Behavior Relation: Results of a Longitudinal Survey," *Journal of Personality and Social Psychology*, 37, 1364-1376.

Debono, Kenneth G., and Michelle Packer (1991), "The Effects of Advertising Appeal on Perceptions of Product Quality," *Personality and Social Psychology Bulletin*, 17, 194-300.

Dunlap, Riley E. (1991), "Public Opinion in the 1980s: Clear Consensus, Ambiguous Commitment," *Environment*, 33, 10-15, 32-37.

Edwards, Kari (1990), "The Interplay of Affect and Cognition in Attitude Formation and Change," *Journal of Personality and Social Psychology*, 59, 202-216.

Fazio, Russell H. (forthcoming), "Attitudes as Object-Evaluation Associations: Determinants, Consequences, and Correlates of Attitude Accessibility," *Attitude Strength: Antecedents and Consequences*, eds. Jon A. Krosnick and Richard E. Petty, Hillsdale, NJ: Erlbaum.

Fazio, Russell H., and Carol J. Williams (1986), "Attitude Accessibility as a Moderator of the Attitude-Perception and Attitude-Behavior Relations: An Investigation of the 1984 Presidential Election," *Journal of Personality and Social Psychology*, 51, 505-514.

Fazio, Russell H. and Mark P. Zanna (1981), "Direct Experience and Attitude-Behavior Consistency," *Advances in Experimental Social Psychology*, vol. 14, ed. Leonard Berkowitz, New York: Academic Press.

Fazio, Russell H., Martha C. Powell, and Paul M. Herr (1983), "Toward a Process Model of the Attitude-Behavior Relation: Accessing One's Attitude Upon Mere Observation of the Attitude Object," *Journal of Personality and Social Psychology*, 44, 723-735.

Fazio, Russell H., Martha C. Powel, and Carol J. Williams (1989), "The Role of Attitude Accessibility in the Attitude-to-Behavior Process," *Journal of Consumer Research*, 16, 280-288.

Fazio, Russell H., David M. Sanbonmatsu, Martha C. Powell, and Frank R. Kardes (1986), "On the Automatic Activation of Attitudes," *Journal of Personality and Social Psychology*, 50, 229-238.

Greenwald, Anthony G., Timothy C. Brock, and Thomas M. Ostrom (1968), *Psychological Foundations of Attitudes*. New York: Academic Press.

Haugtvedt, Curtis P. (1989), "Persistence and Resistance of Communication-Induced Attitude Changes," *Proceedings of the Division of Consumer Psychology*, ed. David W. Schumannm, Knoxville, TN: University of Tennessee.

Haugtvedt, Curtis P., and Richard E. Petty (1992), "Personality and Persuasion: Need for Cognition Moderates the Persistence and Resistance of Attitude Changes," *Journal of Personality and Social Psychology*, 62, 308-319.

Haugtvedt, Curtis P., Clark Leavitt, and Wendy L. Schneier (forthcoming), "Cognitive Strength of Established Brands: Memory, Attitudinal, and Structural Approaches," *Brand Equity and Advertising: Advertising's Role in Building Strong Brands*, eds. David A. Aaker and Alexander L. Biel, Hillsdale, NJ: Erlbaum.

Hendee, John C., William R. Catton, Larry D. Marlow, and C. Frank Brockman (1968), "Wilderness Users in the Pacific Northwest: Their Characteristics, Values, and Management Preferences," *USDA Forest Research Paper (PNW-61)*. Portland, OR: U.S. Department of Agriculture.

Higgins, E. Tory (1987), "Self Discrepancy: A Theory Relating Self and Affect," *Psychological Review*, 94, 319-340.

Higgins, E. Tory, Orit Tykocinski, and Jennifer Vookles (1990), "Patterns of Self-Beliefs: The Psychological Significance of Relations Among the Actual, Ideal, Ought, Can, and Future Selves," *Self-Inference Processes: The Ontario Symposium on Personality and Social Psychology*, vol. 6., eds. James M. Olson and Mark P. Zanna, Hillsdale, NJ: Erlbaum, pp. 153-190.

Hines, Jody M., Harold R. Hungerford, and Audrey N. Tomera (1987), "Analysis and Synthesis of Research on Responsible Environmental Behavior: A Meta-Analysis," *Journal of Environmental Education*, 18, 1-8.

Isen, Alice M., and P.F. Levin (1972), "Effects of Feeling Good on Helping: Cookies and Kindness," *Journal of Personality and Social Psychology*, 21, 384-388.

Kallgren, Carl A., and Wendey Wood (1986), "Access to Attitude-Relevant Information in Memory as a Determinant of Attitude Behaviour Consistency," *Journal of Experimental Social Psychology*, 22, 328-338.

Katz, Daniel (1960), "The Functional Approach to the Study of Attitude," *Public Opinion Quarterly*, 24, 163-204.

Kellert, Stephen R. (1985), "Attitudes Toward Animals: Age-Related Development Among Children," *Journal of Environmental Education*, 16, 29-39.

Krosnick, Jon A. (1988), "The Role of Attitude Importance in Social Evaluation: A Study of Policy Preferences, Presidential Candidate Evaluations, and Voting Behavior," *Journal of Personality and Social Psychology*, 55, 196-210.

Krosnick, Jon A. (1990), "Government Policy and Citizen Passion: A Study of Issue Publics in Contemporary America," *Political Behavior*, 12, 59-92.

Millar, Murray G., and Karen U. Millar (1990), "Attitude Change as a Function of

Attitude Type and Argument Type," *Journal of Personality and Social Psychology*, 59, 217-228.

Newhouse, Nancy (1990), "Implications of Attitude and Behavior Research for Environmental Education," *Journal of Environmental Education*, 21, 26-32.

Ogilvy, David (1983), *Ogilvy on Advertising*. New York: Crown.

Petty, Richard E., and John T. Cacioppo (1986), *Communication and Persuasion: Central and Peripheral Routes to Attitude Change*. New York: Springer-Verlag.

Pieters, Rik G.M. (1989), "Attitudes and Behavior in a Source Separation Program: A Garbology Approach," published doctoral dissertation, Netherlands: Tilburg University.

Powell, Martha, C., and Russell H. Fazio (1984), "Attitude Accessibility as a function of Repeated Attitude Expression," *Personality and Social Psychology Bulletin*, 10, 139-148.

Regan, Dennis T., and Russell H. Fazio (1977), "On the Consistency Between Attitudes and Behavior: Look to the Method of Attitude Formation," *Journal of Experimental and Social Psychology*, 13, 28-45.

Ritov, Ilana, and Jonathan Baron (1992), "Status-Quo and Omission Bias," *Journal of Risk and Uncertainty*, 5, 49-61.

Ryan, Chris (1991), "The Effect of a Conservation Program on Schoolchildren's Attitudes Toward the Environment," *Journal of Environmental Education*, 22(4), 30-35.

Schaller, Mark, and Robert B. Cialdini (1990), "Happiness, Sadness, and Helping: A Motivational Integration," *Handbook of Motivation and Cognition: Foundations of Social Behavior*, eds. Richard Sorrentino and E. Tory Higgins, New York: Guilford, pp. 265-296.

Shavitt, Sharon, and Russell H. Fazio (1991), "Effects of Attribute Salience on the Consistency Between Attitudes and Behavior Predictions," *Personality and Social Psychology Bulletin*, 17, 507-516.

Shavitt, Sharon, Tina M. Lowrey, and Sang-Pil Han (1992), "Attitude Functions in Advertising: The Interactive Role of Products and Self-Monitoring," *Journal of Consumer Psychology*, 1(4), 337-364.

Sheppard, Blair H., Jon Hartwick, and Paul R. Warshaw (1988), "The Theory of Reasoned Action: A Meta-Analysis of Past Research with Recommendations for Modifications and Future Research," *Journal of Consumer Research*, 15, 325-343.

Smith, M. Brewster, Jerome S. Bruner, and Robert W. White (1956), *Opinions and Personality*. New York: Wiley.

Smith, Stephen M., and Richard E. Petty (1992), "Acute Self-Discrepancies and Message Processing," unpublished manuscript, The Ohio State University, Columbus, OH.

Smith, Stephen M., and Richard E. Petty (1993), "Framing Effects in Persuasion," paper presented at the annual meeting of the Midwestern Psychological Association, Chicago, IL.

Smith, Stephen M., Curtis P. Haugtvedt, and Richard E. Petty (1994), "Attitudes and Recycling: Does the Measurement of Affect Enhance Behavioral Prediction?" *Psychology and Marketing* (forthcoming).

Snyder, Mark (1974), "Self Monitoring of Expressive Behavior," *Journal of Personality and Social Psychology*, 30, 526-537.

Snyder, Mark, and William B. Swann (1976), "When Actions Reflect Attitudes: The Politics of Impression Management," *Journal of Personality and Social Psychology*, 34, 1034-1042.

Solomon, Richard L., Leon J. Kamin, and L.C. Wynne (1953), "Traumatic Avoidance Learning: The Outcomes of Several Extinction Procedures with Dogs," *Journal of Abnormal and Social Psychology*, 48, 291-302.

Spiegler, Michael D. (1983), *Contemporary Behavioral Therapy*. Palo Alto, CA: Mayfield Publishing Co.

Weigel, Russell H., and Lee S. Newman (1976), "Increasing Attitude-Behavior Correspondence by Broadening the Scope of the Behavioral Measure," *Journal of Personality and Social Psychology*, 33, 793-802.

Wiener, Joshua L., and Tabitha A. Doescher (1991), "A Framework for Promoting Cooperation," *Journal of Marketing*, 55, 38-47.

Yates, J. Frank, and Lisa G. Zukowski (1976), "Characterization of Ambiguity in Decision Making," *Behavioral Science*, 21, 19-25.

Yates, J. Frank, Carolyn M. Jagacinski, and Mark D. Faber (1978), "Evaluation of Partially Described Multiattribute Options," *Organizational Behavior and Human Performance*, 21, 240-251.

Zajonc, Robert A. (1980), "Feeling and Thinking: Preferences Need No Inferences," *American Psychologist*, 35, 151-175.

SECTION IV.
GREEN-BASED
PRODUCT TRENDS

Chapter 9

Green-Based Innovation: Sustainable Development in Product Management

Hector R. Lozada
Alma T. Mintu-Wimsatt

SUMMARY. This chapter explores how the new environmental movement may present opportunities for business firms to engage in a constructive search for creative solutions to the ecological plights facing them. In particular, the authors examine the impact that such creative solutions may have on the process of innovation and product development. The authors also consider the possibility of achieving organizational goals such as growth and profitability through the capitalization of green-based creativity and innovation.

INTRODUCTION

As you move through the process of greening, new business opportunities will undoubtedly emerge in the form of markets for products you require for your own clean-up, for green versions of your existing goods or for services you can offer to help other companies go green. (Carson and Moulden, 1991: 41)

Every organization occupies a position that is in some respects unique. Its location, product offering, operating methods, customer relationships and/or customer base tend to set a firm off in some degree from every other firm. In turn, each organization competes by making the most of its individuality and its special character.

179

Competition is kept dynamic as a result of this unending search for differential advantage. However, differential advantage is subject to change over time, and firms could only strive to preserve it in dynamic markets through continuous innovation. Kuczmarski (1992) submits that the companies that will survive the turbulent transition into the twenty-first century are "those that are able to accommodate change, that strive to create an entrepreneurial culture for [their] employees–in short corporations that can and do innovate" (p. 10).

Several companies innovate through the creation of new products. Organizations engage in new product activities because they expect increased profitability and growth from the exploitation of market opportunities from the introduction of new products (see, for example, Cooper and Schendel 1976; Hymer 1972; Simmonds 1986). A failure to respond to changes in the market structure or bypassing opportunities (ignoring strategic windows; see Abell 1978) may result, in the long run, in a severe alteration of the organization's competitive position.

To summarize, the quest for differential advantage and the drive to innovate go hand-in-hand. Ultimately, the goal is to generate growth and profitability. However, this would require keeping an eye on the windows of opportunity that may open up as a result of changes in the external environment of organizations.

A major change currently stemming from the external environment is the renewed interest of the marketplace in the preservation, conservation, and protection of the physical (or green) environment. This in turn is having an impact on the corporate thinking of the 1990s. Consider, for example, the findings of a study reported in a recent issue of *Harvard Business Review* (Kanter 1991). The report indicates that environmental business issues, e.g., waste disposal and pollution, are among the top social priorities of the almost 12,000 world managers surveyed. In addition, environmental clean-up has been widely proclaimed as one of the major corporate investment responsibilities of the 1990s (cf. *Business Week* 1989). The recent Earth Summit resulted in, among other things, a non-binding 800-page document outlining suggestions for cleaning up the global environment and urging development in an economically sound manner (Lewis 1992). These events suggest that corporate interest in green marketing is on the rise.[1] Green marketing, thus, presents managers with the challenge to turn environmentalism into a source of differential advantage and growth. A window of opportunity has opened up for those firms willing to take the lead in establishing positions of advantage based on greenness.

As an example, note how McDonald's has been coping with growing protests about the environmental damage caused by the fast-food industry (cf. *The Economist*, August 29, 1992). The company saw such protests as a threat to its future. But instead of fighting the environmentalists, McDonald's turned to them for help. In August 1990 it signed a unique agreement with the Environmental Defense Fund (EDF), one of America's more inventive environmental research and lobbying groups, to collaborate on ways to reduce the company's solid waste. One reason that McDonald's was willing to embark on the EDF deal was that it had already tried to come up with an environmental policy of its own and had found the task immensely complicated. By turning a threat into an opportunity, McDonald's has put itself in the forefront of corporate environmentalism.

WHAT WE CALL GREEN MARKETING

In the 1970s, leading marketing thinkers like Philip Kotler and Gerald Zaltman mandated that "social marketing" become an important concept in the discipline (cf. Kotler and Zaltman 1971). Social marketing was defined as "the application of marketing concepts and techniques to the marketing of various socially beneficial ideas and causes instead of products and services in the commercial sense" (Fox and Kotler 1980: 25). This definition implicitly includes ideas on the preservation, conservation, and protection of the physical environment as a component of social marketing.

Building on the tenets of social marketing, Henion and Kinnear (1976) offer a definition of *ecological marketing*:

> . . . [E]cological marketing is concerned with all marketing activities: (1) that served to help cause environmental problems, and (2) that may serve to provide a remedy for environmental problems. Thus, ecological marketing is the study of

the positive and negative aspects of marketing activities on pollution, energy depletion and nonenergy resource depletion. (p. 1)

More recently, Mintu and Lozada (1993) have defined *green marketing* as "the application of marketing tools to facilitate exchanges that satisfy organizational and individual goals in such a way that the preservation, protection, and conservation of the physical environment is upheld" (p. 2). Through this definition, Mintu and Lozada note that green marketing goes beyond image-building activities. The ecological concerns espoused by Henion and Kinnear (1976) would be integrated into the strategies, policies, and processes critical to the organization. More importantly, this definition of green marketing parallels what practitioners such as Coddington (1993) are embracing as *environmental marketing:*

> Marketing activities that recognize environmental stewardship as a business development responsibility and business growth opportunity is what I mean by *environmental marketing.* (p. 1)

> The environmental marketer adds the environment to the standard mix of decision-making variables. (p. 2)

Thus, *green marketing*, as we use the term here, conveys a more proactive role for marketers. It fosters not only sensitivity to the impact that marketing activities may have on the natural environment, but also encourages practices that reduce or minimize any detrimental impact.

THE ENVIRONMENTAL REVOLUTION'S SECOND WAVE

The environmental advocates of the 1970s warned about economic stagnation as a result of depletion of energy resources. In this first wave of the environmental revolution, our knowledge of environmental science was limited but our perceptions of the threats to the standard of living and quality of life were quite real. Today, the second wave of the environmental revolution is under way.

When the environment resurfaced on the political agenda of the

1980s, the issues associated with it had become international: acid rain, depletion of the ozone layer, global warming. Scientists are warning that excessive burning of fossil fuels threatens the health of the planet. Recent studies have identified four major environmental risks: acid rain, ozone depletion, deforestation, and the greenhouse effect. Now, the threats to our standard of living and quality of life have so intensified that environmental protection became a key issue in the 1992 Presidential Campaign in the U.S. So, where do we go from here? How will the role of government, society, and industry change in the foreseeable future?

FROM LIMITS TO GROWTH TO SUSTAINABLE DEVELOPMENT

The first wave of the environmental revolution brought about the philosophy of *limits to growth,* which put businesses and society's interests on the warpath. The crux of this philosophy was that both population and economic growth should be limited in favor of an alternative low-technology lifestyle in symbiosis with nature (Pearce 1991). The end result was that the "lifestyle environmentalism" was labeled as another form of extremism, and dismissed by both government and business organizations as a threat to economic stability. Although lifestyle environmentalism has not gone away, it has helped establish a form of environmentalism that is more acceptable to business and government.

Moving away from the "limits to growth" advocation of the green movement of the 1970s, the new environmentalism is based on the philosophy of *sustainable development.* Sustainable development, a concept originally popularized by the 1987 report titled *Our Common Future,*[2] proposes that future prosperity depends on preserving "natural capital"–air, water, and other ecological treasures–and that doing so will require balancing human activity with nature's ability to renew itself. In simple words, this idea refers to development that meets the needs of the present without compromising the ability of future generations to meet their own needs (World Commission on Environment and Development 1987). As simple as the phrase may be, it can also be misleading. Sustainable development could be construed as economic growth that has been made more equitable and environmentally careful. Schmidheiny (1992) alerts us to the illusive suggestion that sustainable development is a chore for "developing" nations only:

> But development is more than growth or quantitative change. It is primarily a change in quality. . . . Sustainable development will command the greatest changes in the wealthiest nations, which consume the most resources, release the most pollution, and have the greatest capacity to make the necessary changes. (p. 6)

Thus, we must start by first recognizing that growth is necessary to eliminate poverty, which leads to the plunder of resources *(Business Week*, May 11, 1992: 68). With the cooperation of industrial nations and developing nations alike, worldwide development might proceed without risking constraint from overpopulation, resource depletion, and ecological breakdown.

However, sustainable development is a complicated process. Industrial nations would have to shift from resource-intensive production systems and lifestyles to ones that consume vastly fewer resources and dramatically cut pollution. Developing nations would have to practice less destructive agriculture, industrialize with unprecedented care, and cut birth rates, with all that implies for improving women's rights. *Business Week* (1992) submits that we may be confronting the new industrial and social revolution. Some of the tenets of the philosophy of sustainable development are presented in Table 9.1.

Note that the concept is primarily geared around helping people to consider the stock of natural resources that are available now, and those that will be available to future generations. Cairncross (1991) admonishes that sustainable development encourages countries to think about whether they are currently living beyond their means. More importantly, she warns that a country that believes it is too costly to live with the tenets of sustainable development will certainly find it too costly to live without them. We certainly adhere to her admonition.

TABLE 9.1. What Sustainable Development Would Entail

1. **Boost efficiency:** Adopt innovations that slash the resources used and pollution emitted per unit of output. These include clean technology such as electric cars, energy efficiency, recycling, "closed-loop" production, less destructive agriculture, and designing products with less packaging, fewer materials, and longer lives.

2. **Build a framework for change:** Account for environmental costs and benefits in economic transactions and revise GNP calculation. Forge international compacts to protect common resources and address global problems. Enact taxes and other incentives to curtail destructive actions. Boost international aid for poverty alleviation, family planning, sound agriculture, and resource protection in developing nations. Liberalize trade and promote industry investment in developing nations.

3. **Stabilize population:** Improve standards of living and the status of women and make family planning widely available to help lower the birth rates in developing nations.

4. **Restrain consumption:** Foster lifestyles that lower the burden on the environment, especially in industrial nations: Depend more on public transportation, less on gas-guzzling cars; consume more information-based goods and services, husband consumer goods more carefully; encourage *green consumerism.*

Adapted from *Business Week* (May 11, 1992)

OVER-HYPED "GREENING"
AND CONSUMER SKEPTICISM

Business Week (1989) predicts that one of the business trends of the 1990s will include investments into America's physical landscape to protect, and, if possible, to improve the environment. The American public has openly expressed its demands for action against smog that clogs urban air, acid rain that kills lakes and forests, and pollutants that taint drinking water and soil. Responses from the business community abound. According to Scott Jay Wollins, an environmental analyst for Tucker, Anthony Inc., "regulations and fear of liability, not conventional economic forces, drive spending on the environment." Robert Keefer, president of EnvironQuest, an environmental information company, estimates that for every dollar spent by the government, companies will spend $5 to $10 for environmental clean-up.

The surge of environmental consciousness that followed Earth Day in 1990 washed over the marketplace rapidly. In poll after poll, consumers claim they are willing to change their buying habits–and even pay more for products–to protect the environment (*Consumer Reports* 1991). Manufacturers got the message and fast. The Marketing Intelligence Service (Consumer Reports 1991), which tracks new product introductions, reports that the percentage of new packaged products making some kind of green claim more than doubled between 1989 and 1990, rising from 4.5% to 11.4% of the total. During the same year, the number of green advertisements appearing on television and in major print outlets more than quadrupled, according to an audit by the advertising agency J. Walter Thompson (Consumer Reports 1991).

Suddenly, consumer-product companies are being confronted with millions of newly aroused consumer consciences. Marketers discovered that catering to environmental worries might be the hottest sales strategy since advertising agencies discovered in the 1950s that sex sells. Between 1989 and 1990, industries were hastily setting up various "institutes" and "councils" to establish the green credentials of their products or materials. Unfortunately, *The Economist* (1990) affirms that exaggerated claims of greenery on product packaging and in advertisements may be making shoppers cynical.

We do not dispute the validity of the criticism from skeptics in some instances. However, we submit that business organizations who have declared a genuine commitment to the resolution (or betterment) of ecological conditions have discovered that there need not be a contradiction between environmentalism and capitalistic drives, just realignments. Some of these realignments will be spurred by creativity and innovation, and not necessarily from a limits to growth philosophy. We believe that the new environmentalism presents a gamut of opportunities for business organizations in terms of creativity, innovation, and, conceivably, growth.

INNOVATION AND GREEN MARKETING

The basic ideas behind environmentalism dictate that corporations have responsibilities that go beyond the production of goods and services. These responsibilities involve helping to solve important social problems, especially those they have helped create (Buchholz 1991). Corporations such as McDonald's, Wal-Mart, Procter & Gamble, and Du Pont acknowledge that the environment must be protected and enhanced for economic growth to take place, and have taken action towards that goal (Lodge and Rayport 1991). McDonald's has made a $100 million commitment to its consumers for recycling purposes. Wal-Mart encourages the purchase of environmentally friendly products and reports that the green labeling program that they initiated in 1989 contributed to an overall 25% increase in sales for the year. Procter & Gamble has pledged to spend $20 million per year to develop a composting infrastructure.

Yet, note that the Procter & Gamble example is quite telling. To a large extent, the company has been under fire by environmentalists mostly for its disposable diapers and its detergents. As a response, Procter & Gamble has implemented a strategy that takes the concepts of recycling and reusing to heart, particularly regarding packaging. Still, they have discovered that the synergistic relationship between issues and trends can yield criticism and consumer resistance. Even though their formula for Cheer laundry detergent (or Ariel outside of the U.S.) has been changed to minimize the amount of phosphates in the product, the company is still being strongly criticized for its overt reliance on animal testing.

In spite of some setbacks, green marketing efforts on the part of corporate America continue to grow. As a result of the re-greening of society, *environmentalism* has slowly become a buzz word for corporate policies of the 1990s. Within the context of corporate activities, environmentalism is interpreted as a higher level of corporate consciousness geared toward the protection, preservation, and conservation of the physical environment.

All in all, environmentalism could act as a trigger to innovation, one that is desperately needed and most welcomed. Relating it to our previous discussion, the activities associated with sustainable development may be construed by business either as a potential threat (increased regulatory action on the part of government, consumer resistance to or avoidance of environmentally unfriendly products), or as an opportunity to achieve their goals by doing what is right for the planet and for society at large. However, Coddington (1993) forewarns that green-product development may not be an easy sell to senior management due to an apparent widespread perception that the introduction of green-product lines may have a negative impact on sales.

We firmly believe, though, that at a time when corporate America is coming to terms with the inefficacy of some of their short-sighted alternatives implemented in the pursuit of growth, green-based innovation may represent an invigorating alternative. The ability to launch new products that are internally developed provides more control over the desired growth that the corporation seeks, especially when a strategic window opens up. Today, integrating environmental and growth concerns presents new challenges for the long-term, for which creativity is imperative. Green products represent a substantial product opportunity, the opening of a provocative strategic window.

Take, for instance, the following corporate examples. The Royal Dutch/Shell Group is one of a growing minority of companies that are forming task forces, mounting experiments, and revising their planning based on the idea of balancing growth and the environment. Braden R. Allenby, AT&T's senior environmental attorney, suggests that corporate leaders are tiptoeing to a new approach to management that drives a different set of design and cost considerations (*Business Week* 1992). 3M has as a goal for 1995 to reduce air and water emissions by 90% and solid waste 50% from the levels of 1990. This will cut the inflation-adjusted cost per unit of most products by 10%. Monsanto, Du Pont, and AT&T, like 3M, are planning to sharply cut air emissions and waste. Dow Chemical may replace, within two years, chlorinated solvents used for cleaning industrial equipment with less-polluting, water-based systems. BMW is using design for disassembly in a pilot project aimed at building cars so they can eventually be taken apart and recycled more easily. This concept is also being implemented by IBM-

Germany to dismantle and recycle computer parts. All of these corporate attempts are not only meant to capitalize on the potential profitability and cost reduction associated with green-product development. It is also an opportunity "to improve their bona fides with a populace that is demanding exemplary environmental behavior from the corporate community" (Coddington 1993: 149).

Equally vital is the integration of environmental issues into all aspects of the corporation's activities, from strategy formulation, planning, and construction through production and into dealings with consumers. There is no doubt that environmental considerations will open new business opportunities in the development of new technology. On the product side, environmental problems also require creative and, perhaps, innovative solutions. For example, manufacturers of products sold as canned sprays (e.g., Gillette's Right Guard Deodorant Spray, or more recently, the introduction of the Cool Wave line) have been replacing CFCs in their products before the deadline for their elimination. Additionally, we are currently seeing the revival of some old product forms, usually with minor (cosmetic) modifications (e.g., the pump spray bottle).

Similarly, several products have been reintroduced to the market (e.g., Procter & Gamble's Downy) in more environmentally friendly forms. Hampson (1991) contends that almost all business will in fact be affected by environmental considerations. Hence, firms' failure to be sensitive to these influences can make them lag behind in the competitive race.

Although some would prefer to look at these changing circumstances as threats, visionaries within business firms are realizing that there also are real opportunities in environmental developments for those companies ready to recognize and capitalize on them. To support our contention, we borrow from Cairncross (1991), who suggests that developing products that use nature more frugally will call forth whole generations of technology.

The change will be more pervasive than those that followed the invention of the steam engine or the computer. Fortunes await those who devise less expensive ways to dispose of plastics or to clean up contaminated soil. The great engineering projects of the next century will not be the civil engineering of dams or bridges, but the bio-engineering of sewage works and waste tips. Industry has before it that most precious of prospects: a spur to innovate (Cairncross 1991: 178).

THE GREENING OF A TRIAD

The decade of the 1990s has been heralded as the "Decade of the Environment." The rude awakening pertaining to the environment as a limited resource is forcing us to face the unique challenge of becoming citizens of the world. As such, our major concern stems from the accelerated way in which Mother Earth is being de-structed. We are three-quarters down that path. This problem is mainly the result of the actions of businesses, governments, and the public at large.

The triad presented in Figure 9.1 is crucial to the understanding of environmental problems and to the identification of creative solutions. Several strategists recommend that in order to effectively understand environmental problems and provide solutions, a symbiotic relation-ship or partnership has to exist between the triad members.

Governments

Governments and their agencies have to adopt a consistent na-tional regulatory scheme to provide businesses some environmental guidance and direction. Even when businesses and society engage in behavior that fosters recycling and reusing, a major concern facing governments is waste reduction. For example, ABC News (1993) reports that even though there is heightened interest in re-cycling in the U.S., our government is still concerned with the increasing amount of waste. This keeps increasing the cost of col-lecting and disposing of waste.

The German government has found a way of tackling this issue head on. They have enacted a law that requires manufacturers to take back the packaging from their products and recycle it. Klaus Topfer, Environmental Minister, has boldly stated that handling waste cannot continue to be the task of the state (ABC News 1993). In spite of initial reluctance and resistance from manufacturers, the

FIGURE 9.1. The Triad

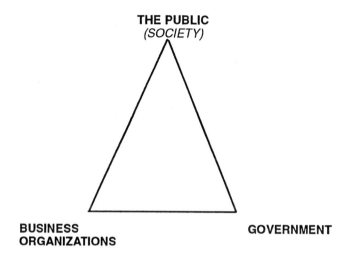

THE PUBLIC
(SOCIETY)

**BUSINESS
ORGANIZATIONS**   **GOVERNMENT**

program was implemented. To avoid turning stores into trash collection centers, the retailers and the manufacturers have banded together to create a dual collection system by which privately funded trucks go through neighborhoods collecting packaging left in special containers. Even though the costs are passed along to consumers in the form of slightly increased prices, the average German consumer pays less than $3 a month for the government's recycling policy.

The dual system has triggered various responses from manufacturers. Since less packaging literally means less in payments to the dual system, companies like Braun have significantly reduced the amount of packaging in their product offerings.

Manufacturers are now expecting the German government to enact new laws that will require them to take back their products and recycle them. All products, including cars, television sets, and computers, will be targeted. In anticipation, IBM-Germany now has a program that dismantles old computers, separates circuit boards, wiring and precious metals, recycles what they can, and sells the rest. Other European countries are looking into the German dual collection system as a model for their own programs.

Business Organizations

Businesses need to conscientiously include environmental management in their list of top strategic priorities. From an industry perspective, corporate managers have recognized that environmental management is a critical component for gaining competitive advantage. Private industry has been quick to respond to environmental quandaries. Their motives notwithstanding, private industry has acknowledged that the environment is a new imperative to business success in the 1990s, for it triggers creative thinking, gives impetus to innovation, and moves companies towards achieving growth potentials. Consequently, we are seeing a rapid proliferation of *environmental development programs* in most businesses' agendas.

Perhaps the second wave of the environmental revolution has as its most important contribution the provision of momentum to the management of creativity and innovation. Intriguingly enough, this in turn is reshaping the product management function in directions that were previously inconceivable. For example, Friedman (1992) advocates that Total Quality Management (TQM), an increasingly popular concept related to the management of both the product and the production processes, needs to integrate environmental management issues. Commitment to quality now refers not only to the traditional production concept, but to environmental quality as well. Currently, our concern is with the total yield of the production and product marketing processes, including waste and pollution.

Schmidheiny (1992) maintains that business has taken the challenge, not only at the sectoral and national levels, but at the international level as well. The *Business Charter for Sustainable Development*, launched in 1991 by the International Chamber of Commerce and endorsed by over 600 firms worldwide, encourages companies to pledge a commitment to the improvement of their environmental performance, to implement management practices to effect the improvements, to measure their progress, and to report progress accordingly. Still, the stipulation for clean, equitable, economic growth prevails as the biggest single difficulty within the larger challenge of sustainable development (Schmidheiny 1992).

Concepts such as *eco-efficiency, demanufacturing,* and *remanufacturing* have gained momentum as the recycling of materials and energy and resource conservation are more plausible due to technological change. More importantly, since all natural and industrial processes generate waste, and waste becomes pollution when it exceeds the carrying capacity of the environment (Schmidheiny 1992), finding ways to prevent pollution before it happens has become critical. To a large extent, companies are realizing that pollution is a sign of inefficiency and added cost, and that waste represents raw materials not sold in final products. Schmidheiny (1992) contends that the combination of the above with mounting public expectations, increasing regulatory pressures, and the tightening of competitive conditions may account for the adoption of the logic of pollution prevention by a significant number of companies worldwide.

Note that oftentimes an implication inherent in pollution reduction programs is restructuring in the form of materials substitution. The search for substitutes is acting as a trigger for innovative solutions. Volkswagen switched to water-based paints for their automobiles and IBM promised to phase out CFCs in electronic production by 1993. The *zero pollution* targets set by many U.S. companies (e.g., Monsanto, General Dynamics) approximate the zero defects pledge brought about by Total Quality Management.

In a related vein, Coddington (1993) asserts that *Design for the Environment* (DFE) has emerged as a philosophy of integrating environmental considerations into the design process, including both product and packaging. There are two basic tenets: (1) the firm engaged in DFE must internalize environmental considerations and constraints, and (2) the firm must evaluate environmental issues systemically, in conjunction with associated manufacturing, economic, regulatory, social, and political factors (Allenby 1991). Additional considerations inherent in DFE as applied to product and package design are designing for disposal, designing for nondisposal (recycling), designing for pollution prevention, and designing for resource conservation.

The Public (Society)

In turn, society must not remain apathetic to the solutions that both governments and businesses offer to resolve environmental dilemmas. The throwaway mentality will be perpetuated unless society stops subsidizing the generation and disposal of garbage. This means changes in current consumers' behavior. They need to be proactive towards green consumerism, by which consumers favor those products that are friendly to the environment not only as they are consumed, but through their production and later disposal.

The importance of the local or grass roots level also comes into focus. Sustainable development requires the internalization of necessary trade-offs to meet basic needs while protecting the environment and empowering the poor. Realizing that the society is the primary beneficiary of any attempts at sustainable development, individuals will have to readjust their consumption and realign the satisfaction of needs with the more environmentally friendly options that industries would offer. Governments in turn must keep up the pressure to comply with environmental standards that society at large can set as appropriate for a better quality of life.

CONCLUSION WITHOUT CLOSURE

We are convinced that the preservation, protection, and conservation of nature should not be considered an option, but an obligation. Coddington (1993) advises that businesses have two fundamental approaches to green marketing. On the one hand, there is the shallow approach, by which lip service and green coloring are added to marketing activities. Through this approach, the environment becomes just another marketing tool, and no basic changes in attitude on the part of marketing managers or top managers is involved. Coddington (1993) describes the shallow approach as "business-as-usual, colored green" (p. 222).

The second approach, which Coddington advances and to which we utterly subscribe, is "more complex, more comprehensive, and ultimately more effective" (p. 222). This approach would entail a fundamental change in attitude regarding the role of firms in relation to the environment:

> It asks companies to have a much stronger sense of fiduciary responsibility than is embodied in the extractive or exploitative relationships they have traditionally enjoyed with the

environment. It calls for companies to think beyond the short-term bottom line, i.e., to factor the environment into all of their strategic planning. (Coddington 1993)

We admit that this approach may be faced with resistance from managers who believe that the implementation of such an approach may seriously harm the firm. Yet, we do not suggest that companies go alone on this journey. Environmental initiatives require collaboration or alliances between governments, businesses, and society at large. That was the emphasis in citing at the beginning of this article what McDonald's has accomplished in the past few years through their association with the EDF. Note that environmental education becomes critical to the successful implementation of *the right approach* (Coddington 1993). Hopefully, in the end we–individuals, communities, businesses, industries, government–will all be on the most appropriate track to be better prepared for the jarring transition into the twenty-first century.

NOTES

1. A minority view, however, goes so far as to suggest that green products may actually be fading in appeal, being nothing more than a short-lived response to the twentieth anniversary (June 1990) of Earth Day (National Public Radio 1992).

2. *Our Common Future* is the title of the report generated in 1987 by the World Commission on Environment and Development, an international commission set up under Gro Harlem Brundtland, then prime minister of Norway.

REFERENCES

ABC News (1993), *World News Tonight with Peter Jennings*, Capital Cities-ABC, broadcast March 10.

Abell, Derek (1978), "Strategic Windows," Journal of Marketing, *42 (July), 21-26.*

Allenby, Braden R. (1991), *SSA Journal*, Semiconductor Safety Association, Washington, September, 5-9.

Buchholz, Rogene (1991), "Corporate Responsibility and the Good Society: From Economics to Ecology," *Business Horizons*, July-August, 19-31.

Business Week (1989), "Cleaning Up on the Coming Cleanup," (October 16), 96-102.

Business Week (1992), "Growth vs. Environment," (May 11), 66-75.

Cairncross, Frances (1991), *Costing the Earth*, Boston, MA: Harvard Business School Press.

Carson, Patrick and Julia Moulden (1991), *Green Is Gold*, Toronto, Canada: Harper Business.

Coddington, Walter (1993), *Environmental Marketing*, New York: McGraw-Hill.

Consumer Reports (1991), "Selling Green," (October), 687-692.

Cooper, Arnold and Dan Schendel (1976), "Strategic Responses to Technological Threats," *Business Horizons*, (January), 61-69.

The Economist (1992), "Food for Thought," (August 29), 64-66.

The Economist (1990), "Friendly to Whom?" (April 7), 83.

Fox, Karen F.A. and Philip Kotler (1980), "The Marketing of Social Causes: The First Ten Years," *Journal of Marketing*, 44 (Fall), 24-33.

Friedman, Frank B. (1992), "The Changing Role of the Environmental Manager," *Business Horizons*, (March-April), 25-28.

Hampson, Chris (1991), "ICI and the Environment," in *The Greening of Business*, Rhys A. David (ed.), Brookfield, VT: Gower Publishing Co., 80-90.

Henion II, Karl E. and Thomas C. Kinnear (1976), "A Guide to Ecological Marketing," in *Ecological Marketing*, Karl E. Henion II and Thomas C. Kinnear (eds.), Chicago: American Marketing Association.

Hymer, Stephen (1972), "The Multinational Corporation and the Law of Uneven Development," in *Economics and World Order from the 1970s to the 1990s*, Jadish N. Bhagwati (ed.), New York: Macmillan, 113-140.

Kanter, Rosabeth Moss (1991), "Transcending Business Boundaries: 12,000 Managers View Change," *Harvard Business Review*, (May-June), 151-164.

Kotler, Philip and Gerald Zaltman (1971), "Social Marketing: An Approach to Planned Social Change," *Journal of Marketing*, 35 (July), 3-12.

Kuczmarski, Thomas D. (1992), *Managing New Products*, Englewood Cliffs, NJ: Prentice Hall.

Lewis, Paul (1992), "The Earth Summit," *The New York Times*, (June 15), A1.

Lodge, George and Jeffrey Rayport (1991), "Knee-Deep and Rising: America's Recycling Crisis," *Harvard Business Review*, September-October, 128-139.

Mintu, Alma T. and Héctor R. Lozada (1993), "Green Marketing Education: A Call for Action," *Marketing Education Review*, forthcoming.

National Public Radio (NPR) (1992), "All Things Considered," broadcast May 22.

Pearce, David (1991), "Environmentalism and Business," in *The Greening of Business*, Rhys A. David (ed.), Brookfield, VT: Gower Publishing Co., 1-10.

Schmidheiny, Stephan (1992), *Changing Course: A Global Business Perspective on Development and the Environment*, Cambridge, MA: The MIT Press.

Simmonds, Kenneth (1986), "Marketing as Innovation: The Eighth Paradigm," *Journal of Management Studies*, 23 (September), 479-500.

World Commission on Environment and Development (1987), *Our Common Future*, Oxford: Oxford University Press.

SECTION V.
WHAT ABOUT
GREEN ADVERTISING?

Chapter 10

Cleaning Up Green Marketing Claims: A Practical Checklist

Michael Jay Polonsky

SUMMARY. Firms that attempt to capitalize on the increased demand for "green" products are faced with a variety of strategic options ranging from the development of new products to repositioning established products. The strategies adopted will be influenced by the way the business views the opportunities, and threats in the business environment, and how these relate to organizational strengths and weaknesses.

This chapter discusses some of the attempts in the U.S. and Australia to develop green marketing guidelines. It then discusses how green marketing claims relate to a business's strategic options, i.e., opportunities, threats, strengths, and weaknesses. A green marketing checklist is presented, based on the Australian work. Following this checklist will help organizations in any country to remove a large amount of the uncertainty regarding what is acceptable "green" marketing.

INTRODUCTION

While there is no one accepted definition of green marketing, in general, the term relates to how an organization's activities affect the natural environment. This definition includes the activity of promoting products as having characteristics that do not harm the natural environment, i.e., green marketing claims. Effective green marketing claims will help consumers overcome the "greatest environmental hazard," the lack of factual environmental information (Schlossberg 1993).

Concern as to how firms' activities influence the natural environment is one of the main reasons for the growth in green marketing. Business activities have both short- and long-term environmental effects. In the past, many organizations did not consider these implications, now they are being forced to do so.

The increased interest and concern from management, consumers, and policy makers has resulted in an increased environmental awareness. This concern has significant implications for all groups. Moreover, businesses are most heavily influenced as their success is dependent on the behavior of the other groups, consumers, and government.

As firms integrate green marketing into their overall strategy, they must consider how it affects the business environment. As shown in Figure 10.1, green marketing, or the lack of it, can impact on organizations at both the external (macro) and the internal (micro) level. In the external environment, green marketing affects the opportunities and threats. It can have the effect of either creating a new opportunity or reducing the potential of an existing opportunity. It also can create a new threat or reduce the potential negative impact of an existing threat. In the internal or micro context, green marketing affects firms' strengths and weaknesses. It can have the effect of either improving or reducing the benefits of an existing strength. It can also increase or reduce the effect of a firm's internal weakness.

The goal of any strategic analysis of green marketing is for organizations to minimize the weaknesses and threats that arise and/or to maximize the opportunities and strengths. How firms cope with environmental uncertainty determines how successful their strategic activities are. Firms want to ensure that they carefully consider the implications of green marketing activities. A green marketing SWOT analysis will allow the firm to effectively evaluate how green marketing relates to their activities. How green marketing can affect the various components of the SWOT analysis are discussed later in this chapter.

Making environmental claims clearly understood is one of the

FIGURE 10.1. Impact of Green Marketing on Organizations at the External (Macro) and Lateral (Micro) Levels.

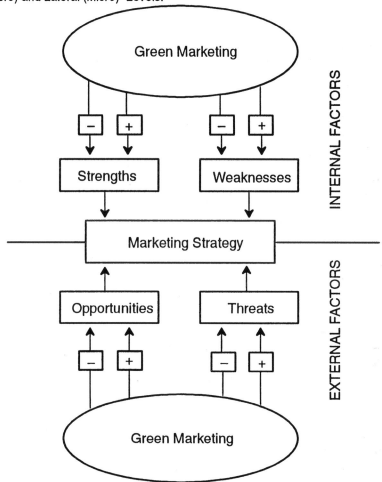

difficulties firms face. Much of the uncertainty of green marketing relates to the factual accuracy of advertising claims and how well consumers understand the claims being made. Consumer and governmental understanding of green claims is dependent on organizational behavior and how that behavior affects the natural environment. Claims need to be made so that consumers believe a firm's behavior is consistent with what is being claimed.

One way for firms to reduce "factual" uncertainty is for governmental bodies to set down guidelines or regulations detailing what green marketing activities are acceptable, i.e., what is fair and legal. Many governments are attempting to assist in the reduction of green marketing uncertainty. The U.S. and Australian attempts to do this will be discussed in the second section of this chapter.

The importance of a uniform set of guidelines should not be understated. One common set of guidelines will simplify the marketing process for all organizations. Fragmented regulation causes many problems for organizations that market goods in various regions. These firms must ensure that their activities comply with the most stringent set of regulations in their target area.

In the fourth section of this chapter a generalizable set of guidelines will be presented. Firms may be able to use this checklist to ensure that their green activities are as effective as possible, enabling them to maximize their green marketing potential.

SOME PAST U.S. AND AUSTRALIA EXPERIENCE

U.S. Background

In mid-1992, the U.S. Federal Trade Commission (FTC) introduced a set of green guidelines for organizations to follow in an attempt to ensure that a firm's green marketing activities are clear and not misleading (Trade Practices Commission 1992). As recently as 1991 it was reported that the FTC's Bureau of Consumer Protection favored using a case-by-case analysis for green claims to show other marketers the FTC's direction (Lawerece and Colford 1991). This ad hoc mentality put organizations in a very vulnerable position.

The U.S. guidelines put forward by the FTC are much more prescriptive than their Australian counterparts and therefore not as generalizable internationally. The areas addressed in the U.S. guidelines include:

1. All qualifications and disclosures "should be clear and prominent to prevent deception." (FTC 1992)

2. Distinctions made between product and packaging benefits.
3. Environmental claims do not overstate their environmental benefit or attribute.
4. Comparative claims give sufficient information for comparisons to be made.
5. It is deceptive to use "general" environmental claims without sufficient explanation.
6. The following terms can only be used if they meet specific criteria:
   - Degradable
   - Biodegradable
   - Photogradable
   - Compostable
   - Recyclable
   - Recycled Content
   - Source Reduction
   - Refillable
   - Ozone Safe
   - Ozone Friendly

In the U.S. prior to 1992 there were attempts to give green marketing direction to business. In 1990, the National Association of Attorneys-General (NAAG) formed a task force and held a forum on environmental marketing (NAAG 1991). 1991 also saw the introduction into congress of a bill entitled "Environmental Marketing Claims Act of 1991" (EMCA), though this bill failed to become law (Lautenberg 1992).

The NAAG investigation generated two reports: *The Green Report* and *The Green Report II* (NAAG 1990; NAAG 1991). The second report stated: "These final recommendations of the task force are intended to serve as interim guidance to the business community and to provide a framework upon which more concrete definitions and standards can be developed" (NAAG 1991). These suggestions relate to a broad spectrum of environmental marketing issues and should help in minimizing uncertainty. However, the report went on to state: "These recommendations are not law," therefore all uncertainty would not be completely removed. This is still the case with the 1992 guidelines, i.e., they are in themselves still not law.

NAAG's recommendations cover four major areas, each with several subsections discussing very specific issues. The recommendations suggested that:

1. Environmental claims should be as specific as possible, not general, vague, incomplete or overly broad.
2. Claims should reflect current solid waste management options.
3. Claims should be substantive.
4. Claims should be supported.

In NAAG's reports, each of the four areas are discussed in detail, including subsections that specifically relate to the various activities. The recommendations made "could" be used as a checklist of some description, but many subsections are somewhat prescriptive. One example under point two is: "(P)roducts that are currently disposed of primarily in landfills or through incineration . . . should not be promoted as 'degradable,' 'biodegradable,' or 'photodegradable'" (NAAG 1991). While this is a useful statement, it may be too specific for a generalized checklist that all marketers in all industries can easily utilize. The statement also falls under the general intent of point two and therefore a specific restatement in a checklist is unnecessary.

The Environmental Marketing Claims Act (EMCA) incorporated five objectives. These were:

1. Prevent the use of fraudulent, deceptive, and misleading environmental marketing claims;
2. Empower consumers with reliable and consistent guidance to facilitate value comparisons with respect to environmental marketing claims;
3. Establish uniform and accurate standards and definitions that reflect the best available manufacturing practices, products, and packaging;
4. Encourage the development of innovative technologies and practices to be adapted by manufacturers in considering the environmental effects when producing products and packages; and

5. Encourage both consumer and industry to adopt habits and practices that favor natural resource conservation and environmental protection. (Lautenberg 1992)

The EMCA wanted to ensure that environmental marketing was not misleading as well as "encourage" modifications in consumer and industrial behavior. Within the detail of the act there were concrete directions to marketers as to what would be acceptable. Specific sections of the act established criteria under which environmental marketing terms could be used. In this way the EMCA was exceedingly prescriptive and therefore could not be effectively used as a checklist. Many points made by NAAG, the EMCA, and the FTC were incorporated in a generalizable form, within the Australian checklist.

Prior to the FTC regulations, all of the green marketing regulation was established at the State level. By late 1991, at least six states had some green legislation and at least five or more states had legislation pending (Watman 1992, Colford 1991). These activities often were directed at specific activities such as defining what are the requirements for something to claim it is "recyclable" or "recycled." None of the states put forward a checklist that applies to all green claims.

For any set of guidelines to be effective, they must be well-distributed to and adopted by the business community. Neither the NAAG reports, the EMCA, nor the FTC guidelines have received the prominence in the marketing community necessary for them to be effective. There were some attempts to develop the NAAG guidelines into "A Blueprint for Green Marketing" (Davis 1991). These attempts were not in the generalizable form of a checklist that marketers could easily adopt. The FTC guidelines are less than a year old and it may be too soon to expect the business community to fully appreciate them. In any event, organizations need some concrete guidance that they can follow to evaluate the legality and factuality of their environmental marketing claims.

Australian Background

The same environmental marketing issues that have plagued U.S. firms have surfaced in Australia. The Australian Trade Practices

Commission (TPC), under the Trade Practices Act, has national responsibility for a broad range of issues relating to competition and consumer protection, including false and misleading advertising (Collinge and Clarke 1989). It is for that reason that the TPC became involved in the debate over environmental marketing claims. This includes ensuring that advertising claims are factual and not misleading.

The TPC has charged very few organizations with using misleading environmental marketing claims. This is reasonable given that no national guidelines existed before February 1992. Consumer backlash against organizations using green marketing in Australia has occurred in a few cases. It is only a matter of time before governmental backlash begins in earnest.

In early 1992, the Australian government, through the TPC, released a document entitled *Environmental Claims for Marketing–A Guideline* (TPC 1992). The guidelines incorporated an eight-point checklist that marketers could follow to minimize the possibility that their green claims would fall under TPC examination. The guidelines and checklist developed by the TPC are the result of a long, detailed discussion with many interest groups, similar to NAAG's public forum. These groups include consumer groups, government bodies and regulatory bodies, individual industries, industry groups, and other special interest groups. In Australia, draft guidelines were developed and distributed in December of 1990, where interested parties were asked to make submissions in writing to the TPC (TPC 1990). The final environmental marketing guidelines and checklist were developed by integrating the draft guidelines and submissions. The Australian guidelines have the same problem as their U.S. counterpart, i.e., they are not set out as enforceable regulations, but only as guidelines that may or may not be followed.

The Australian checklist serves as a good foundation from which to proceed further. The original Australian checklist had two main deficiencies. First, the points were not ranked in order of importance. Rearranging the points allows organizations to minimize any overlap in effort, i.e., address the most critical factors first, reducing the number of major modifications to claims. The modified Australian checklist also incorporates a ninth point, which ensures that uncertainty is minimized. The areas addressed in the Australian checklist include:

1. Use "truly" meaningful terms and pictures;
2. Clearly and simply state benefits;
3. Explain product characteristics that are beneficial;
4. Make provable claims;
5. Detail benefits that are achieved;
6. Claims should allow for negative product characteristics;
7. Real differences in product characteristics should be used;
8. Define composition of environmental endorsement schemes; and
9. Address all other potential environmental questions (listed in the documentation but not included as a specific point in the checklist).

Much of the information contained in the first five points of the U.S. guidelines are covered in the Australian guidelines, though in a more generalized format. Table 10.1 lists all key points presented in both sets of national guidelines. It is easy to see that there is extensive overlap, though it must be emphasized that the generalizable Australian guidelines are much more useful as a checklist.

The modified checklist discussed in the fourth section of this chapter contains all the components of the Australian government's policy; many of these points were also made by the National Association of Attorneys-General, EMCA, and the FTC (NAAG 1990, NAAG 1991, FTC 1992, Lautenberg 1992). The proposed checklist has the advantage of ordering the points in terms of importance. As an organization moves down the list, it can be assured that it's green claims are becoming clearer and more factual. The points further down the list examine some subtle issues of green marketing, whereas the first points deal with ensuring that consumers understand the meaning of the relevant green claims. The nine-point framework could be easily applied to any organization, in any country.

HOW GREEN MARKETING FITS IN THE SWOT ANALYSIS

In the rapidly changing business environment, green marketing issues are only one area of change that organizations must contend

TABLE 10.1 Comparison of Australian and U.S. Environmental Marketing Guidelines

Guideline Characteristic	Australian Trade Practices Commission	United States Federal Trade Commission
Clearly Stated Environmental Benefits	YES	YES
Explains Environmental Characteristics	YES	YES
Explains How Benefits Are Achieved	YES	YES
Comparative Differences Are Justified	YES	YES
Claims Can Be Proven	YES	NO*
Negative Factors Taken into Consideration	YES	YES
Uses Meaningful Terms and Pictures	YES	YES**
Clearly Defines Endorsement Schemes	YES	NO
Addresses Potential Other Questions on Claims	YES	NO

* Referred to in section dealing with meaningful terms, but in itself not specifically mentioned as a guideline criteria.

** Also includes specific criteria established for the use of the following ten environmental terms: degradable, bodegradable, photogradable, compostable, recyclable, recycled content, source reduction, refillable, ozone safe, ozone friendly.

with. Green marketing can affect each firm differently, as was shown in Figure 10.1. Changes that create an opportunity for one firm may create a threat for another. There has been little research into how green marketing fits into the SWOT analysis. This is an area that could benefit from additional industry case studies and academic research.

Opportunities

Green marketing has caused several apparent opportunities in the business environment to arise (Cross 1990). These include:

1. Marketing to segments who are becoming more environmentally aware and concerned. These consumers are demanding goods that conform to these new attitudes.
2. Organizations perceive green marketing to be a competitive advantage, relative to their competitors. Firms therefore strive to improve their societal awareness. This complements the increase in consumers' socially conscious behavior and will therefore give them an advantage over competitors who do not address these issues.

Examples of the attempts to capitalize on opportunities abound in the "real world." Some examples are:

- As consumers began to boycott tuna products that killed dolphins, some firms modified their behavior to ensure that their production did not harm dolphin populations (Anonymous 1991).
- As consumer's demand for unbleached paper products increased, one firm who produced coffee filters increased their market share through the sale of unbleached filters (Ottman 1993).
- When consumers demanded packaging waste material be reduced, some detergent firms introduced "refillable" packages (Shearer 1990).

The coffee filter and detergent examples demonstrate that meeting consumer demands may also result in firms becoming more cost effective by reducing production and packaging costs. Opportunities to meet consumers' needs also may be turned into a competitive advantage.

Threats

There are three threats that organizations experience in terms of green marketing. These are:

1. Uncertainty as to the environmental impact of present activities, including those that are perceived to be less environmentally harmful.
2. Uncertainty as to which green marketing activities are acceptable from a governmental perspective.
3. The possibility of a backlash from consumers or government based on existing green marketing claims. Threats one and two above may cause backlash to arise.

Uncertainty of Environmental Impacts

The first threat that all firms experience is that their products or production processes have unknown long-term effects on the environment. There are many examples of firms changing the production techniques or the materials incorporated into a product only to find out in the future that the "new" process is also environmentally harmful.

One example of new knowledge revealing that "environmental improvements" are also harmful is the aerosol industry. Manufacturers moved from "harmful" propellants that were CFC-based to "safe" HCFC-based propellants only to find that these HCFC propellants were harmful as well (Ottman 1992). To counter this problem, some firms switched to a propellent known as DME. While this propellant is "less" harmful, it is still a hydrocarbon (i.e., a greenhouse gas) and therefore contributes to the ozone problem (Anonymous 1992). In the future, companies who use DME may again be forced to change their behavior.

The environmental implications of any organization's changes are often only apparent in the future. What happens when a company that presents itself as highly concerned changes its product in an "environmentally friendly" manner and it is latter discovered that the change is also environmentally harmful? If at the time of the change the firm used the most up-to-date scientific information, could they reasonably be expected to predict the future? Scientific knowledge regarding the environmental influence of products and their inputs is a dynamic process. Product composition changes, but not as rapidly as environmental knowledge. Environmental solutions often become obsolete as knowledge and technology become more advanced.

Re-introduction of an older technology may be an alternative green solution. An interesting example of this would be McDonald's. At one point in time McDonald's replaced paper wrapping on products with polyfoam, in an attempt to reduce paper consumption (Ottman 1992). Now they have moved back to paper wrappings because the other packaging is too harmful (Anonymous 1991). There is no uniform opinion, which is actually more environmentally harmful, paper or the newer polyfoam package. In any case, McDonald's changed their behavior to address consumer concerns.

There is no way to remove the uncertainty of firms' future environmental influences completely. Organizations could utilize additional research and scan the technical and business environment to learn if their activities are as "safe" as possible. Just as they monitor trade and scientific journals to look for new opportunities, they can monitor the relevant scientific literature to learn about future threats. This allows firms to modify behavior as environmental knowledge changes. As the McDonald's example points out, there may be continual debate on the environmental impact of a product or its inputs. In times of "environmental crises," firms may simply choose to move in the direction of popular opinion rather than scientific data.

Uncertainty in Governmental Behavior

Lack of concrete governmental direction towards green marketing is another threat facing all organizations. In many countries there is no clear indication of which green marketing activities are legally acceptable and which are not. Even the recently established guidelines of Australia and the U.S. are non-enforceable and are suggestions to business at best. (TPC 1992, FTC 1992). Green regulatory uncertainty is a difficult problem for firms to overcome.

Governmental attempts to clarify green marketing activities through the introduction of guidelines can reduce this uncertainty, but it can never be completely removed until legislative direction is determined. Some environmentally aware organizations have attempted to "minimize" this threat by not using green marketing claims. Though even in instances where firms do not directly make green marketing claims, consumers may still perceive that implied environmental claims exist. These implied claims are equally vulnerable to the uncertainty of governmental behavior and backlash.

Consumer and Governmental Backlash

All organizations face the threat that the use of green marketing claims may result in consumer or governmental backlash. This may occur if either of the groups believe that organizations' green marketing activities imply they are more "responsible" than their behavior suggests. Confusion over claims may result in consumers and government believing that firms are not acting responsibly or that firms are attempting to "mislead" them. The result may be consumers and/or government reacting in a "negative" fashion, i.e., backlash (Miller and Sturdivant 1977).

Organizations must ensure that green marketing claims are reflected in their behavior. This requires that firms fully understand the implications of the claims they make, thus reducing the probability of unforeseen "problems" arising. An additional method of minimizing backlash is through clearer communication, i.e., using marketing tools that do not mislead in any way. If all groups have a clear understanding of what is actually being claimed, there should be a lower probability of consumer and governmental confusion. It is hoped that following a checklist like the one proposed will assist in clarifying claims.

Consumer backlash may take several forms, including change in purchasing behavior (i.e., stop buying specific products), protests about the organization's environmental inconsistencies, or the extreme situation of boycotting all the company's products.

Consumer backlash will cause a reduction in sales (i.e., profits) and a loss in consumer goodwill. This latter point may be much more detrimental to the firm than the loss in profits. New markets may be found, but regaining consumer confidence is often more difficult. The degree of consumer commitment to a specific issue will determine the amount of backlash experienced. Issues that have a high degree of consumer involvement may result in more adverse consumer behavior.

Backlash also can arise from government or regulatory bodies. In these cases the firms may be required to either change their behavior, compensate consumers, or pay fines for their activities or lack of activity (Schlossberg 1992). Often governmental backlash stems from consumer backlash. In either case, it is harmful financially and in terms of corporate image.

Mobil, one of the largest producers of plastic garbage bags, marketed some of their products as "biodegradable." One unexpected result of this activity was consumer and governmental backlash (NAAG 1990, Lawerece 1991, Watman 1992). The bags were only biodegradable under very specific conditions that did not in fact occur under the present method of disposal. When consumers became aware of this, they stopped buying the products, protested against the firm and even boycotted some of the firm's other products. Governmental backlash to this firm arose in some U.S. states where the organization was forced to modify its marketing claims. Other states used their consumer protection legislation to prosecute Mobil (Watman 1992, Associated Press 1991). While other firms used this example to learn what types of environmental marketing claims were acceptable, this is of little comfort to Mobile.

Changes in market threats and opportunities will encourage the firm to modify its behavior. Firms' behavior modification will relate to the organization's internal strengths and weaknesses. Any changes made should attempt to maximize strengths and minimize weaknesses.

Strengths

Companies' green strengths can take many forms. A well-defined corporate policy with procedures and guidelines that ensure it's effective implementation is one important strength (Friedman 1991). It could be argued that having a "socially aware" policy allows the firm to conform to the societal marketing concept, i.e., meeting the needs of consumers and society. Being a "good corporate citizen" also may be reflected in the organization's ability to respond to the green marketing opportunities. Organizations whose policies and actions are consistent also reduce the factors that could result in a green backlash.

Well-established environmental policies are an important component of a total environmental management program. To implement a strong environmental program requires an integrated management process (Buzzelli 1991). "Policies should be broad based, outlining the key aspects of an environmental program and establishing the company's commitment to that program" (Friedman 1991). According to the Vice President of Health, Environment, and Safety at Occidental Petroleum, Frank Friedman, for a firm's environmental policy to be a strength, it must have a strong degree of corporate commitment, be integrated within all corporate levels, be financially supported, and should adapt as knowledge changes. Friedman listed ten points that would make for a strong environmental policy. It should:

- be established by the Board and senior executives;
- incorporate an allocation of funds to ensure effective implementation;
- allocate responsibility for environmental performance at the line management level;
- ensure that the environmental objectives are incorporated to all operations and functional areas;
- implement the most modern procedures, processes, and control methods;
- have an internal compliance system in place to monitor performance;
- require that each division have an environmental monitor system;
- ensure that an information system is in place;
- have environmental training for all employees; and
- emphasize the need and importance of conducting R&D, developing new technology, and utilizing new developments (Friedman 1991).

Planning is another area where an organizational green strength can arise. A well-developed organizational planning process enables the firm to anticipate opportunities and threats. This is an important strength, for many environmental threats will not be "considered" unless there is a long-term planning process designed to examine changes in the business and scientific environment. A further strength may be that organizations have "environmentally aware" managers. These managers may be better able to consider the implications of green marketing claims than their unaware counterparts. This is not to imply that aware managers are a necessity, but these managers will ensure that decisions incorporate consideration of green activities. Aware managers also may be better able to ensure that environmental policies and programs are accurately carried out.

Weaknesses

Organizations that simply jump on the green bandwagon, although exploiting an opportunity, would not be exploiting their strengths. They may place themselves in a position of high exposure to the threat of consumer and governmental backlash. Firms that jump on the bandwagon may reduce the effectiveness of all green marketing activities due to consumers becoming increasingly skeptical of the proliferation of green claims. Inaccurate activities of one organization may taint all green marketing activities. Organizations that do not have both a well-defined environmental policy and the implementation procedures described in the strength section, would indeed be opening themselves up to backlash from consumers and government.

Poor planning is another weakness that affects all organizations no matter what the threat. It is too easy to exploit the apparent opportunities that green marketing presents without considering the consequences. In their excitement to utilize green marketing, firms often do not evaluate these activities with the same vigor used in other potentially risky decisions. Firms may not realize potential problems exist, or they may underestimate the potential for problems to arise.

Organizations that do not realize that green marketing claims could have a detrimental impact are deficient in their knowledge of the environmental issues, and that deficiency is a substantial weakness. Another weakness some organizations exhibit is that they do not appreciate the societal trends that occur and how these trends impact on organizational activities. Not realizing that green marketing issues are important to society may result in a firm not giving them the consideration they deserve, thus exposing the organizsation to a variety of risks.

HOW A CHECKLIST ASSISTS FIRMS

There are links between the factors influencing the business environment (opportunities and threats) and factors relating to internal organizational variables (strengths and weaknesses). Reduction of governmental uncertainty is an area that would generate internal and external benefits. The reduction of external threats would allow a firm to develop clearer policies, thus creating internal strengths.

It is important that government be consistent, otherwise organizations will not be able to understand and react to governmental policy. Given there is limited green marketing "policy" for organizations to follow, any activity that reduces uncertainty will allow more confident modification of corporate behavior. Attempts to ensure that green marketing claims are as valid, clear, and understandable as possible would be beneficial to all organizations.

Firms that progress through a green marketing SWOT analysis with the assistance of an effective checklist such as the one put forward here will reduce corporate uncertainty. Figure 10.2 shows how the introduction of a green marketing checklist reduces uncertainty and how this flows through the SWOT analysis. Following the checklist described here will ensure that firms increase their opportunities and strengths and reduce their threats and weaknesses.

THE CHECKLIST

The checklist below is an adaptation of the Australian Trade Practices Commission's checklist. The modified checklist covers the most important points first. Clarification of the nine points makes implementation easier and more effective. Firms that follow this checklist will ensure that their claims are not misleading and that consumers are made more aware of the relevance and significance of the claims being made.

1. *State or spell out exactly what makes your product environmentally beneficial.* Explain environmental characteristics in terms that the average consumers can understand. The more simplistic the language, the better. The average consumer may not be that well environmentally informed. This will reduce the chances that any activities are "misunderstood," resulting in a lower probability of consumer or governmental backlash.

2. *Discuss exactly what part or aspect of your product has the environmental benefit.* Environmental benefits often relate to usage, production, transportation, disposal, packaging, or some combination of these factors. Claims should only relate to the areas where benefits arise. This factor will reduce potential consumer and governmental backlash that could arise from groups perceiving that claims are generalizable to all product characteristics.

3. *Explain how the beneficial factors your product incorporates impact on the environment.* An example would be that a reduction in packaging saves X many trees or reduces energy consumption, etc. This relates directly to discussing the beneficial environmental factors. Explaining the benefits will ensure that consumers understand the implications of changes in their behavior. Also, they will become more environmentally informed. This will address the uncertainty of future environmental impacts as people will understand the implications of changes, given the existing technology and information.

4. *Make claims that are relevant to your product.* To claim that your product does not contain CFCs when none of products in that category contains CFCs would be inappropriate, as there has been no change in the product or the production process. Claims must be made in the appropriate context. This will ensure that claims are not misunderstood and therefore reduce the probability of backlash. One important factor here is that

competitors will be unable to "suggest" that claims are irrelevant or misleading.

5. *Make sure that any claims that you make can be substantiated.* To say that your product contains the lowest amount of a chemical for that product category must be provable. If the claim cannot be proved then it should not be used or it should be modified so it can be proved. This will have many benefits: it will ensure that claims are not misleading, reduce chances of backlash, and remove the uncertainty of the environmental impact of the activities, since the claims can be or are already proved.

6. *Do not use broad brush environmental statements for all facets of your products, if there are also negative environmental factors.* An example would be to say a product is produced from recycled plastic when plastic is a minor component of the product and the impact on the environment is therefore negligible. This is one area that will greatly reduce the chances of backlash, since there will be no justification to claim that there are "misleading green marketing claims." Clarification of statements also will reduce uncertainty caused by unclear governmental regulations.

7. *Do not use words or pictures that are meaningless.* This will ensure that organizations do not receive undue criticism from consumers or governmental groups. Meaningless words or pictures may be misinterpreted and therefore misleading, since they may have more than one meaning. This type of ambiguity allows people to interpret the message differently, which could lead to a backlash when people or governmental bodies "believe" you claimed something when actually you did not.

8. *Explain any environmental endorsement or emblem schemes that are used.* This information should include:

   a. the standards the product met;
   b. the benefits to the environment of meeting these standards;
   c. how schemes were formulated. Some of these factors may include:
      • program design (private, governmental, or industrial);

- program involvement (mandatory or voluntary);
- associated fees attached to using the program;
- body that set the standards to be used;
- where the relevant testing occurred.

Clarification of emblem and endorsement schemes will reduce the probability of backlash due to ambiguity. If the endorsement scheme used is an industry standard, it will be understood what that means. Consumers and governmental groups understand the scheme and will not "believe" that more stringent conditions apply.

9. *Be able to answer* __any__ *other question relating to the environmental marketing claims made.* This activity forces organizations to answer the tough questions before they're asked and modify any claims for which answers cannot be formulated. This point is important, for it ensures that areas that may not be obvious to management are considered. This is where the reduction in backlash and uncertainty may be most prevalent.

By following the preceding nine steps, most of the "tricky" questions should already have been addressed. Since all the hard questions are answered in advance, changes in governmental guidelines or regulations should have a small impact on the firm.

Following the checklist enables any organization to ensure that they maximize the "truthfulness" of their claims and therefore reduce the risk of consumer and governmental backlash. This self-monitoring will ensure that organizations can easily adapt to governmental regulations as they come about. Organizations will therefore be minimizing the impact of governmental uncertainty, although no concrete governmental policies may be in place.

The checklist may be an important strategic tool for business. Organizations that follow the nine steps put forward will consider how the green marketing activities "could" be viewed by the various stakeholders. This will be useful in ensuring not only that the claims are effective, but that the potential problems are also minimized. (Though these problems can never be completely removed.)

Firms following the checklist will only be minimizing their exposure to risk, since consumers who do not fully understand claims may still believe that firms are being misleading. Marketers may

FIGURE 10.2.

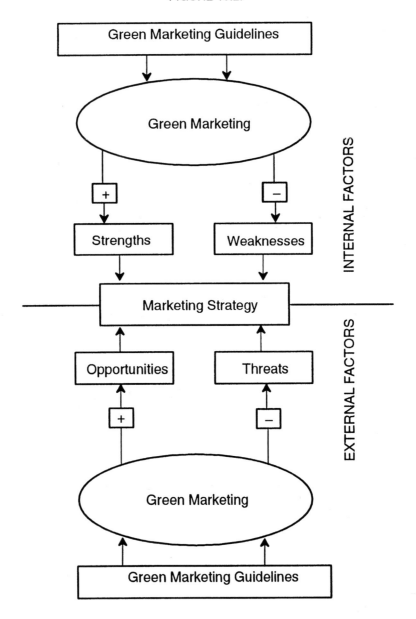

feel that the checklist is too restrictive and changes their role to that of an educator. When government finally becomes more involved, there may be significant regulating costs, both for firms and society. Once claims are disputed in a regulatory system, there are always problems with regulator's interpretations.

CONCLUSION

The nine steps of the checklist are not only simple to follow, but relatively inexpensive. There are no additional direct financial outlays to be incurred from following the checklist that would not have been incurred if the claims were challenged and then verified. In the long run, organizations may experience cost savings, because they will not need to cover the legal fees associated with future legal suits, since these suits will be avoided.

By following these nine steps, organizations will minimize both the threats and weaknesses they face through using green marketing claims. This will prevent uncertainty in the minds of both consumers and government officials, who may be weary of environmental marketing claims. The added benefit is that any green marketing activities will be more effective and therefore increase the benefits to using factual green marketing tools. Any checklist that has all of these benefits available at a small cost is a management tool worth further investigation.

Rigid self-monitoring systems like the suggested checklist will help organizations to meet future environmental marketing regulations when and if they should arise. Following this or some equally stringent checklist will enable organizations to ensure that environmental marketing messages are correctly understood and are therefore more effective.

Until some widely accepted set of generalizable guidelines or regulations is developed, the Australian-based checklist is one that will reduce the potential risks to organizations who use green marketing claims. The reduction of uncertainty is an important area where guidelines will help organizations cope with an uncertain business environment.

REFERENCES

Anonymous, (1991) "Spurts and Starts: Corporate Role in '90s Environmentalism Hardly Consistent" *Advertising Age* (Oct 28) Vol. 62 No. 46 pp. GR14-GR16.

Anonymous, (1992) "New Preen Not So Green" *Choice* (February) Vol. 22 No. 2 p. 9.

Associated Press, (1991) "New Jersey Probes Claims of Environmentally Safe Products" *Marketing News* (Dec 9) Vol. 25 No. 25 p. 7.

Buzzelli, David T., (1991) "Time to Structure Environmental Policy Strategy" *The Journal of Business Strategy* (March/April) Vol. 12 No. 2 pp. 17-20.

Colford, Steven W., (1991) "The State of Legislation" *Advertising Age* (October 12) p. GR12.

Collinge, John and Bruce R. Clarke, (1989) *The Law of Marketing in Australia and New Zealand*, 2nd edition. Butterworths.

Cross, Frank B., (1990) "The Weaning of Green: Environmentalism Comes of Age in the 1990s" *Business Horizons* (September-October) Vol. 33 No. 5 pp. 40-46.

Davis, Joel J., (1991) "A Blueprint for Green Marketing" *The Journal of Business Strategy* (July/August) Vol. 12 No. 4 pp. 14-17.

Friedman, Frank B., (1991) *Practical Guide to Environmental Management* (July) The Environmental Law Institute, Washington DC, USA.

FTC, (1992) *Guidelines for the Use of Environmental Marketing Claims Federal Trade Commission* (July) Washington DC.

Lautenberg, Frank R., (1992) "Environmental Marketing Claims Act: Pulling the 'Green' Over Our Eyes" *Seton Hall Legislative Journal* Vol. 16 No. 2 pp. 305-340.

Lawerece, Jennifer, (1991) "From Hero to Villain" *Advertising Age* (January 29) Vol. 62 No. 5 pp. 12-13.

Lawerece, Jennifer and Steven W. Colford, (1991) "Seeking Uniform Guidelines" *Advertising Age* (January 29) Vol. 62 No. 5 pp. 28-30.

Miller, Kenneth E. and Fredrick D. Sturdivant, (1977) "Consumer Responses to Socially Questionable Corporate Behavior: An Empirical Test" *Journal of Consumer Research* (June) Vol. 4 No. 2 pp. 1-7.

National Association of Attorneys-General (NAAG), (1990) *The Green Report: Findings and Preliminary Recommendations for Responsible Advertising*, (November) National Association of Attorneys-General.

National Association of Attorneys-General (NAAG), (1991) *The Green Report II: Recommendations for Responsible Environmental Advertising* (May) National Association of Attorneys-General.

Ottman, Jacqueln, (1992) "Brand 'Stewards' Will Guide Environmental Planning" *Marketing News* (April 13) Vol. 26 No. 8 p. 15.

Ottman, Jacqueln, (1993) "Consumer Attitude Shifts Provide Grist for New Products" *Marketing News* (January 4) Vol. 27 No. 1 p. 16.

Schlossberg, Howard, (1992) "Marketers Told to Heed Consumers Before Big Brother Steps In" *Marketing News* (April 27) Vol. 26 No. 9 p. 10.

Schlossberg, Howard, (1993) "Envirothon Attracts Students, Corporate Sponsors" *Marketing News* (January 4) Vol. 27 No. 1 p. 6.

Shearer, J.W., (1990) "Business and the New Environmental Imperative" *Business Quarterly* (Winter) Vol. 54 No. 3 pp. 48-52.

Trade Practices Commission, (1990) *Draft for Discussion of Environmental Claims in Marketing*. Trade Practices Commission, (December).

Trade Practices Commission, (1992) *Environmental Claims in Marketing–A Guideline*. Trade Practices Commission, (February).

Watman, Joanna L., (1992) "Whose Grass is Greener? Green Marketing: Toward a Uniform Approach for Responsible Environmental Advertising" *Fordham Environmental Law Report* Vol. 3 No. 2 pp. 163-181.

Chapter 11

A Classification Schema
for Environmental Advertising Claims:
Implications for Marketers
and Policy Makers

Les Carlson
Norman Kangun
Stephen J. Grove

SUMMARY. Consumers seem to experience some confusion about environmental advertising claims, yet it appears that no research has attempted to investigate the nature of claims that are being made in environmental advertising. This study posits a system for classifying environmental ad claims and then applies that system by content analyzing 100 environmental ads. Results indicate that organizations seem to be generating environmental claims that present themselves as "good environmental citizens" or they are stating environmental facts rather than those that extol the ecological virtues of their products or process attributes. This emphasis may contribute to consumer confusion regarding environmental advertising.

INTRODUCTION

During the past decade, an increasing number of companies have attempted to position themselves as environmentally conscious in order to secure a competitive advantage in the marketplace. The driving force behind this effort appears to be broad-based concern expressed by a significantly large number of consumers who feel that business is simply not doing enough to preserve the environment (*Advertising Age* 1991). Recent opinion polls indicate consumer preference for products that are perceived to be more environmentally benign; further, it appears that consumers are willing to pay somewhat higher prices for such products (Chase 1991). A recent survey revealed that 85% of those polled preferred brands labeled "biodegradable" over brands not so identified; unfortunately, nearly two-thirds of those queried were uncertain as to what "biodegradable" actually meant (*Consumer Reports* 1991). Similar confusion exists for other environmental terms like "recycled," "ozone-friendly" and "compostable" (*Consumer Reports* 1991). Hence, it is not surprising that consumers are skeptical about environmental claims.

Some of the ambiguity and consumer mistrust regarding environmental claims may be traced to manufacturers' use and/or misuse of environmental terminology in their advertising. For example, the Federal Trade Commission has charged that certain products contain an ozone-destructive propellant in their product canister even though they are promoted as ecologically and ozone safe (*Consumer Reports* 1991). Against such a backdrop, consumer confusion exists concerning certain "green" terms that are commonly employed by marketers. However, before an accurate appraisal and basic understanding of consumer response to environmental claims can be established, certain questions must be addressed. For example, how is "green" terminology actually used in environmental advertising and what specifically constitutes an environmental claim? Further, can a taxonomy for environmental claims be developed, and, if so, which types of claims appear to be the most prevalent? Answers to these questions and further clarification of the scope of environmental advertising claims may help to explain why consumers appear to be confused by, and perhaps distrustful of, the environmental positioning of many advertisers.

This study confronts these various questions via a content analysis of environmental advertising claims. To accomplish this, we assembled environmental ads that had appeared over a two-year period (1989-1990) in one medium–magazines. In selecting titles to represent the general categories for this medium, we utilized the categorization system periodically provided in *Advertising Age*. We then ascertained the number and nature of the environmental claims made in the advertisements. We determined from our analysis of the claims that three general categories could be used to describe the scope and nature of the claims in our sample. Our categories included environmental claims (1) relating directly to the specific product being sold; (2) relating to the production and/or disposal process for a firm's output; and (3) focusing on image and depicting (promoting) the firm as a "good environmental citizen." Independent judges then categorized the claims found among the ads according to these categories. Frequencies of claim assignment to the various categories were examined to discern underlying patterns. Based on our analysis, policy and managerial implications and suggestions for future research are set forth.

THE RISE OF ENVIRONMENTAL CONCERN AMONG MARKETERS

Many businesspeople believe that the 1990s will be the "environmental decade" (Fisher 1990; Gross 1990; Hayes 1990). The public has begun to realize that their consumption activities contribute to environmental problems. Many of these problems are national and/or global in scope and are manifested in such phenomena as the accumulation of solid waste, underground water contamination, global warming, and acid rain. As a consequence, there appears to be a growing desire to protect the environment as evidenced by a seeming willingness of consumers to avoid products that they believe contribute to environmental degradation. For example, in a recent survey conducted by the Gallup Organization for *Advertising Age,* a majority of respondents indicated an eagerness to change their buying behavior to improve the environment (Chase 1991, p. 9). Eighty percent of those polled favored a ban on chlorofluorocarbons, a chemical known to damage the ozone layer, regardless of the higher prices it would bring for air conditioners, refrigerators, and some other appliances. In short, consumer interest in purchasing products that are less harmful to the environment appears to be sincere.

Many business organizations have made an effort to accommodate the growing consumer interest in "environmentally safe" products. In the past two years, a number of companies have attempted to

position themselves in the minds of the consuming public as environmentally concerned organizations. Some have openly acknowledged
that every business has an inherent obligation to be environmentally
responsible and that this obligation encompasses a concerted effort to
minimize the adverse environmental impact of its products (National
Association of Attorneys-General 1990). Industry leaders such as
Procter & Gamble (Bremmer 1989) and McDonald's Corporation
(McDonald's 1990) have begun to explore and to implement ways to
embrace a more ecological orientation.

Associated with the developing consumer interest in the environment has been a concomitant increase in the incidence of environmental advertising. American companies and international firms
conducting business in the U.S. have advertised a plethora of products as "degradable," "recycled" or "recyclable," "ozone-friendly," or otherwise good for the environment. According to Marketing
Intelligence Service, Ltd., "Green" products constituted 4.5% of all
new products introduced in 1989 and 9.2 percent of those introduced
in the first six months of 1990 (National Association of Attorneys-
General 1990, p. 5) and, overall, marketers have been quick to emphasize their green commitment in their advertising.

Amid the rush of businesses to engage in environmental advertising, some environmental groups (i.e., the Environmental Defense
Fund, the Media Foundation, etc.) and several state attorneys-general note a growing confusion on the part of many consumers regarding the environmental claims that appear in advertising (National Association of Attorneys-General 1990). While a number of
reasons for this confusion may exist (unclear terminology, incomplete product comparisons, overreliance on difficult-to-comprehend
scientific information, etc.), no explicit examination of the nature of
environmental claims has been attempted. Critics of environmental
advertising have coined the term "green-washing" to describe advertisements in which the environmental claims are either trivial,
misleading, or deceptive. Yet, before this and other phenomena
relevant to environmental advertising can be explored, a systematic
assessment of the nature (or kind) of claims appearing in such
advertising is needed. Such an effort requires that a typology which
captures the frequency of various types of environmental advertis-

ing claims be developed and applied. This study represents an initial effort in these regards.

METHOD

As noted, a purpose of this research is to investigate the types of claims that are used in environmental advertisements. In keeping with this objective, a typology for classifying environmental ad claims was developed and then applied to a sample of environmental advertisements to ascertain the incidence and type of claims present in environmental advertising.

To generate an ad pool for our research, three referees were briefed on environmental advertising and shown examples of advertisements with environmental claims. Referees were assigned 18 magazines from the popular and environmental press. Overall, they examined 15 titles from the popular press (e.g., *Scientific American, Popular Mechanics, Time*) and three environmental publications (e.g., *Garbage*). A complete list of all magazines used in the study is included in the Appendix. The referees were instructed to search these periodicals for examples of environmental advertising for all issues of a magazine title during the calendar years 1989 and 1990. This span roughly coincides with the time period in which environmental advertising became more prevalent in the popular press, and, concomitantly, emerged as an issue in the marketing discipline. Overall, these searches resulted in a set of over 200 ads.

Next, the authors independently examined this set and eliminated advertisements that did not provide a specific environmental claim, e.g., automobile ads that only cited the EPA gas mileage estimate. Disagreements among authors on specific ads were assuaged through either exclusion of the ad from further consideration or discussion leading to consensus concerning its retention. In addition, duplicate and/or incomplete ads were discarded and only full page ads were used to enhance readability. The authors also included two advertisements from 1991 issues of *USA Today* in order to arrive at a final tally of 100 ads. This ad pool encompassed a wide variety of product categories, e.g., automobiles, energy, food, appliances, and services. The authors then examined each ad to determine the location and number of environmental claims that it possessed and resolved any differences concerning a claim's presence. Once agreement was achieved, the environmental claims were highlighted and the advertisements were numbered for identification purposes.

Three judges were used in the study to assess the incidence and type of environmental claims present among the 100 ads. An assistant professor of marketing and an economics instructor from the same university and a learning lab coordinator from a small college were recruited for this purpose.

To aid them in the task of classifying environmental claims, the judges were given a typology developed by the authors. Since no classification schema existed at the time of the study, the authors found it necessary to create such a system. This was accomplished by first examining a number of environmental ads to identify a preliminary set of mutually exclusive and exhaustive categories for classifying the claims found among them. The authors then applied these categories to a subsequent set of environmental claims in order to establish the validity of the typology. Several iterations were necessary before a "final" classification system was developed. Ultimately, the original typology was found to be remiss and an additional category was required. The resulting schema contained the following categories of environmental claims:

1. PRODUCT ORIENTATION–The claim focuses on the environmentally friendly attributes that manufactured goods or service possess.

   Example: This product is biodegradable.

2. PROCESS ORIENTATION–The claim deals with an organization's internal technology, production technique, and/or disposal method that yields environmental benefits.

   Example: Twenty percent of the raw materials used in producing this item are recycled.

3. IMAGE ORIENTATION–The claim associates an organization with an environmental cause or activity for which there is broad-based public support.

   Example (a): We are committed to preserving our forests.

Example (b): We urge that you support the movement to preserve our wetlands.

4. ENVIRONMENTAL FACT–The claim involves an independent statement about the environment at large or its condition that is ostensibly factual in nature.

Example: The world's rain forests are being destroyed at the rate of two acres per second.

The final version of the typology included one other category. Judges were offered the opportunity to note whether a claim seemed to encompass more than one of the classification categories noted above. This was devised to provide additional evidence as to whether typology categories were mutually exclusive. To aid their understanding, verbal and written descriptions and explanations of the typology were provided to judges.

All judges were briefed on environmental advertising and the purpose and methods of the study, and were provided a chance to ask questions concerning the task. They were instructed to examine each of the 100 ads and to classify the ad claims according to the typology described above. Judges were asked to complete the task in one time period and to perform the evaluations independently.

RESULTS

Table 11.1 presents a breakdown of the judges' assessment of the environmental claims by classification category and magazine type in which the ad containing the claim(s) appeared. Calculations based on Perreault and Leigh (1989) resulted in an interjudge reliability coefficient of .88. The coefficient's magnitude provides justification for further interpretation of the results. Overall, 22% of judgements made fell into the multiple category classification (100 multiple assignments divided by 465 claim judgments–3 judges × 155 claims; see Table 11.1). Analysis across the four unique classification categories indicated that more claims were environmental facts or image orientation claims than process orientation claims (X^2 = 18.49, p < .01; Table 11.1). Moreover, on an aggregate basis, there were significantly more image orientation and environmental facts

TABLE 11.1. Environmental Advertising Claims Classified by Type and Media Category

Media Category*	Ads	Claims				N
	Total Environmental Ads	Product Orientation Claims	Process Orientation Claims	Image Orientation Claims	Environmental Facts	
Weekly/ Bi-weekly*	28	10	4	23	22	59
Environmental*	24	9	7	17	8	41
Science/ Mechanical*	13	3	5	6	8	22
Business/ National*	29	8	3	7	1	19
General*	2	0	0	1	1	1
Men's*	1	0	0	1	0	1
Home*	1	1	0	0	1	2
Newspaper	2	1	0	0	1	2
Total	100	35(23)**	20(13)	57(37)	43(28)	155

* Categories of magazines as used by *Advertising Age*
** Indicates the percentage of claims in each category to total claims (N = 155)
There were more environmental facts or image-oriented than process-oriented claims (X^2 = 18.49, p < .01, df = 3).
There were more image-oriented and environmental facts than product- and proces- oriented claims (X^2 = 13.06, p < .001, df = 1).

232

than product and process orientation claims ($X^2 = 13.06$, p < .001; Table 11.1). In terms of raw numbers and percentage of total claims identified, image orientation claims were most prevalent, followed by environmental facts, product orientation and process orientation claims, respectively.

DISCUSSION

The ultimate utility of a classification system depends on the ability of judges to assign observations reliably to categories that are assumed to describe and differentiate among the phenomena of interest. When judges are unable to make consistent classifications, questions arise regarding the usefulness of the categories and adequacy of the classification system.

As noted, a primary objective of this research was to develop a classification typology for categorizing environmental advertising claims. The magnitude of the interjudge reliability coefficient derived here indicates that our classification system may indeed be adequate, particularly given the exploratory nature of this research (Perreault and Leigh 1989). Furthermore, the reliability coefficient may have been greater if the judges and their backgrounds had been more homogeneous. Their prior experience and current affiliations were quite varied and this diversity may have contributed to tendencies to evaluate claims differently.

As indicated, 22% of the claim assessments resulted in an assignment to the multiple claim response category. While higher than multiple claim responses found in similar research on deceptive/misleading advertising claims (see Kangun, Carlson, and Grove 1991) the frequency exhibited here still is within a range of acceptability for exploratory research of this nature. Nevertheless, the assignment of many claims to multiple categories would suggest that the classification system contains response categories that are not unique. However, it should be noted that offering the judges the opportunity to assign a claim to more than one category may have created a demand characteristic such that they may have felt compelled to find instances of multiple assignments. Debriefing comments offered by the judges seemed to support this conjecture. Moreover, even though judges may have recognized that a claim sometimes reflected more than one response classification, they demonstrated considerable homogeneity in the multiple responses that they chose. Future research may necessitate fine-tuning the typology to more effectively accommodate the requisite that classification systems be comprised of mutually exclusive categories.

Another criterion for evaluating a typology is how well its categories span the range of classification possibilities, i.e., are the categories "collectively exhaustive?" (Hunt 1991). A review of the judges' protocols indicated that only one judge had failed on two occasions to assign a claim to one of the existing categories. Thus, even though assignment to multiple categories was higher than in previous, similar, research, the judges seemingly regarded the categories in the typology as adequately spanning the range of environmental claims to which they were exposed. In sum, the typology developed here appears to meet at least one of Hunt's (1991) criteria for creating a new classification schema and could, perhaps, be improved by accommodating or deleting the multiple response category for future applications of the typology.

Judges also appear to have identified more claims that reflect an organization's effort to promote itself as an environmental "good citizen" or that simply report a so-called environmental fact than claims that stressed environmentally sound product features or production/disposal processes. The relatively high incidence of environmental good citizen and environmental fact statements (37% and 28% of the claim total, respectively) suggests that such claims form an integral component of environmental ads. We believe that this circumstance may, in fact, contribute to much of the consumer confusion about claims made in environmental advertising.

MANAGERIAL IMPLICATIONS

Given the nature of today's marketplace, it is evident that marketers may benefit by segmenting consumers based on their propensity to consume environmentally benign products. However, consideration must be given to how one might best reach these consumers. Examination of the ads in our sample suggests that organizations are already attending to this concern. Many companies promote the "green" features of their products in magazines that are targeted primarily at environmentally conscious consumers. For example, one can find in *Utne Reader*, a magazine that attracts a broad-based environmentally conscious readership, various ads such as those placed by Aveda, a company whose personal care products are touted as containing pure and natural compounds.

In conjunction with such a segmentation strategy, one key implication deriving from our research is that managers must carefully consider the unique environmental benefits of their products and production processes. It may be simpler and more expedient to attempt enhancement of an organization's overall "green" image by stating environmental facts and promoting one's institution as a good environmental citizen. However, one is cautioned to consider the fact that such promotions may not carry the same weight with the public as would examples of the organization's unique and environmentally benign product and process benefits. In short, the latter may provide consumers with a more concrete base for differentiating among the competitors. Consumers may be able to judge an organization's offering(s) more positively from an environmental perspective when their advertisements emphasize comparison points that readily and easily distinguish the institution from its competition. To make these comparison points more viable and convincing, managers should stress the environmental features that are unique to the organization/offering and that are salient in terms of consumers' decision making.

We believe the types of environmental claims that we have termed "product" and "process" hold the most potential for serving as these bases for comparison because they reflect explicit environmental features. Simply stating/restating environmental facts or attempting to showcase the organization as a good environmental citizen are less likely to aid consumers in determining how an organization and its products are environmentally exceptional. Unfortunately, our data suggest that there are more of these types of environmental claims being made than product and process claims. If these trends continue and our results are predictive of the types of environmental claims found in general, it may become increasingly difficult for organizations to differentiate themselves or their products on an environmental basis. As the number of firms making these claims increases, simply citing environmental facts and pro-

moting oneself as a good environmental citizen will not be sufficient to develop or maintain a positive environmental presence. We
believe the attempt to differentiate oneself with these types of
claims poses the likelihood of one's message becoming blurred due
to the potentially high degree of clutter found with such claims and
the failure to portray explicit features of the organization's offerings
and/or production processes.

CONCLUSIONS

The study described here and the resultant framework for classifying environmental claims that it proposes represent an important
foundation for further examination of environmental ads. By fine-
tuning and combining it with other classification schemes (e.g., a
system to categorize deceptive advertising), a greater wealth of
information concerning the description of environmental advertising claims is possible. Such an effort could help establish the types
of claims that are more likely to be perceived as misleading and
alert marketers and public policy concerns to this circumstance.
This, of course, first requires that a broad typology that captures the
nature of environmental claims be in place. The present research
offers a step in that direction. In addition, longitudinal assessment
of the type of claims being made seems to be justified.

In sum, this exploratory research is designed to help fill a gap in
our understanding of environmental advertising. Certainly, the
reader is cautioned to recognize those caveats normally associated
with a preliminary investigation of a phenomenon such as this
study. Replication with a different set of judges and/or another set
of environmental ads is desirable. Nevertheless, our research results
provide reasonably strong, initial evidence that it is possible to
delineate the nature of environmental advertising claims and that
relatively few of those claims are based upon product or process
attributes. Further research to substantiate and to extend beyond
these conclusions is advised to identify more fully the scope and
composition of environmental advertising.

APPENDIX

Frequency of Environmental Ads by Magazine Title

Title	Total Environmental Advertisements	Title	Total Environmental Advertisements
Atlantic	2	Omni	2
Better Homes and Gardens	1	Popular Mechanics	1
Business Week	14	Popular Science	1
Buzzworm	7	Rolling Stone	3
Discover	3	Scientific American	6
Esquire	1	Time	2
Fortune	15	U.S. News and World Report	9
Garbage	14	Utne Reader	3
New Yorker	2	Newspaper	
Newsweek	12	USA Today	2

Frequency of Environmental Ads by Product Category

Product	Total Environmental Advertisements	Product	Total Environmental Advertisements
Energy	21	Automobiles	5
Food	4	Appliances	2
Services	9	Gardening	3
Forest-Related	14	Clothing/Apparel	3
Financial	3	Infant Care	2
Wildlife-Related	5	Personal Care	5
Household/Office	15	Chemicals/Plastics	9

REFERENCES

Advertising Age (1991), Special Issue on "The Green Marketing Revolution," (January 29).

Bremmer, Brian (1989), "A New Sales Pitch: The Environment," *Business Week* (July 24), 50.

Chase, Dennis (1991), "P&G Gets Top Marks in AA Survey," *Advertising Age*, (January 29), 8-10.

Consumer Reports (1991), "Selling Green" (October), 687-692.

Cross, Frank B. (1990), "The Weaning of the Green: Environmentalism Comes of Age in the 1990s," *Business Horizons*, 33 (September-October), 40-46.

Fisher, Anne B. (1990), "What Consumers Want in the 1990s," *Fortune*, 121 (January 16), 108-112.

Hayes, Dennis (1990), "The Green Decade," *The Amicus Journal*, 12 (Spring), 10-21.

Hunt, Shelby D. (1991), *Modern Marketing Theory: Critical Issues in the Philosophy of Marketing Science*, Cincinnati, Ohio: South-Western Publishing Co.

Kangun, N., L. Carlson, and S. J. Grove (1991), "Environmental Advertising Claims: A Preliminary Investigation," *Journal of Public Policy and Marketing*, 10 (Fall), 47-58.

McDonald's Corporation (1990), "McDonald's and the Environment."

National Association of Attorneys-General (1990), *The Green Report: Findings and Preliminary Recommendations for Responsible Environmental Advertising,* (November).

Perreault, William D. and Laurence E. Leigh (1989), "Reliability of Nominal Data based on Qualitative Judgments," *Journal of Marketing Research*, 26 (May), 135-148.

SECTION VI.
REVERSE
CHANNEL SYSTEMS

Chapter 12

A Typology of Reverse Channel Systems for Post-Consumer Recyclables

Donald A. Fuller
Jeff Allen

SUMMARY. Today, marketers must be concerned with reducing the pollution that accompanies high levels of product consumption. One potential solution to the post-consumer solid waste problem involves the collection, processing, and returning waste materials back to productive use. From a marketing perspective, recyclable materials extracted from the waste stream need to be efficiently matched with end-markets. This article reviews some important concepts and issues associated with the recycling of post-consumer solid waste and suggests a typology of reverse distribution channels to describe the process.

INTRODUCTION

The average American is estimated to generate more than 4 pounds of solid waste a day of which approximately 76 percent is landfilled, 10 percent is incinerated, and only 14 percent is recycled for further use (Glenn 1992a). Recent articles by Weiner and Sukhdial (1990), Neace (1990), and Fuller (1991), however, indicate a renewed interest by marketers in the area of post-consumer recycling as a potential solution to the solid waste disposal-pollution problem. Given that municipal solid waste from all sources totaled an estimated 281 million tons in the United States in 1991 (Glenn 1992b), these articles represent a timely and relevant contribution to the growing body of marketing-recycling literature and also serve to raise ecological consciousness in general.

At the macromarketing level, the challenge for marketing is to reduce the pollution associated with high levels of consumption. Pollution is not necessarily a function of waste generation, but rather, inappropriate waste disposal. Obviously, one approach to pollution abatement is to reduce the amount of waste needing disposal–a strategy called pollution prevention by the U.S. Environmental Protection Agency (Freeman et al. 1992). However, as Fisk (1974) points out, the process of consumption inevitably produces waste, so the continuing disposal of solid waste remains a major challenge in any high level macromarketing system. Therefore, an approach that is complementary to pollution prevention is the development of large-scale resource recovery systems that systematically render the waste stream ecologically benign by diverting it from traditional landfill and other polluting forms of final disposal.

Materials recycling is one form of resource recovery that collects, processes, and returns former waste materials to productive use. While recognizing that achieving pollution abatement via source reduction and other forms of resource recovery are equally important issues, this chapter focuses on the channels aspects of the post-consumer recycling problem. Specifically, it reviews the key concepts and issues associated with the recycling of post-consumer materials from municipal solid waste, examines the nature and structure of the reverse distribution channels involved, and then suggests a typology of reverse channel systems that collectively describes the overall process. Implications are drawn for channel types that are apt to predominate given unique market conditions.

POST-CONSUMER RECYCLING: BACKGROUND

Post-consumer recycling is a term that applies to the recycling of waste materials generated by personal consumption activity as opposed to those generated directly by industrial processes. More generally, post-consumer recycling has become identified with one major source, the municipal solid waste stream that is created by households. From a macromarketing perspective, the overall objective is to efficiently match the material resources extracted from this waste stream with end-users (industrial users) on a continuing basis.

This process parallels the well-known sorting model described by Alderson (1965).

Insight into the nature of recycling is gained by examining the definition of the term *recycle,* which is ". . . to extract and reuse useful substances found in waste" (*American Heritage Dictionary* 1985). While the traditional approach to product disposition can be described as a linear flow (Neace 1990) in which waste materials are interred in landfills or indiscriminately dumped, the definition of *recycle* clearly demonstrates that the goal is to reverse this result by achieving a circular flow that effects a reintegration of materials with markets.

Figure 12.1 diagrams this reintegration process as it applies to wastes generated at different levels in a hypothetical production-consumption cycle over time. Since this work focuses on post-consumer waste, heavy lines are used to demarcate the through-put waste flows associated with this source and their eventual routing either through resource recovery or unsecured landfill/dumping alternatives. It should also be noted that other sources (i.e., extraction industries, production facilities, marketing intermediaries) also produce waste that follows this same routing, and that the overall effect of the diversion of materials through resource recovery is not only to conserve resources but to eliminate additional, on-going pollution from unsecured landfilling/dumping.

As shown in Figure 12.2, materials recycling is one of three basic subsystems within the broader waste management strategy of resource recovery. However, materials recycling is clearly differentiated from the other subsystems by the fact that it creates a marketable physical product that is essentially a substitute for virgin source raw materials in primary production/manufacturing processes. In contrast, the reuse and incineration subsystems have as their respective objectives the development of returnable (reuse) container systems and the reduction of waste volume/energy harvesting (Korzum, Duyar, and Villaneuva 1990). When used together, materials recycling, reuse, and incineration represent the major elements of an integrated waste management program.

As a unique form of materials recycling, post-consumer re-

FIGURE 12.1. Production-Consumption Cycle: Waste Sources, Flows, and Disposal Alternatives Over MacroTime

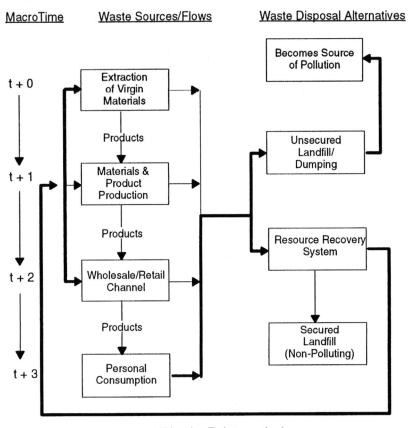

(Circular Reintegration)

cycling is distinguished by the nature of the waste generators involved and the types of materials sought. As noted by Fuller (1979):

> Post-consumer wastes are generated by thousands/millions of scattered households, each of which continuously generates small quantities of co-mingled materials produced through day-to-day consumption. In contrast, industrial generators, on

the other hand, are typically relatively few in number (i.e., industrial/commercial locations), and each typically produces much larger quantities of relatively homogeneous wastes which are by-products of their operations. For example, a local bar (commercial establishment) may generate and set aside thousands of aluminum cans per week as a normal part of the business routine, while a household may generate only 6-12 cans weekly which are totally co-mingled with other household refuse. (p. 567)

The important point is that under normal conditions, the initial collection, sorting, and accumulation of desired materials from post-consumer sources is a costly, labor-intensive endeavor. However, the types of materials sought are basic, that is, ferrous and non-ferrous metal, glass, newspaper, and plastic, most of which derives from various forms of product packaging.

THE CONCEPT OF REVERSE CHANNEL SYSTEM

Since a marketable product is involved, post-consumer recycling is properly viewed as a problem in the development of reverse channels (Fuller 1978). That is, the initial collection, sorting, and accumulation of materials is only the starting point of a broader, continuing process that must result in repeat market transactions with industrial users. Maintaining the desired circular flow is dependent on four basic conditions (Boone and Kurtz 1992):

1. A technology for efficiently processing the material being recycled must be available (i.e., upgrading to acceptable purchasing specifications);
2. A substantial and continuous quantity of secondary materials/products (i.e., recyclable aluminum, steel, paper, plastics, glass) must be available in the solid waste stream;
3. A marketing system (channel) that can profitably bridge the gap between suppliers of secondary products and end-users must be developed; and
4. A market must be available for the end product.

FIGURE 12.2. Resource Recovery Subsystems

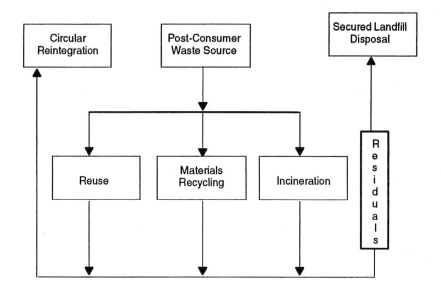

As with any channel design challenge, consideration must be given to the nature of the target markets, the types of materials involved and associated processing requirements, the sources of materials, the anticipated roles of the channel member participants, and the profitability of the overall enterprise. While reverse channels are conceptually similar to the traditional notion of forward channels in many ways, there are major differences.

First, as explained by Guiltinan and Nwokoye (1974), recyclable materials can flow backwards through reverse channels to any of three generalized industrial markets: (1) original manufacturers, (2) firms in the raw materials-producing industry, or (3) other industries that can use recyclables as virgin materials substitutes. In general, these markets require a steady flow of known quality materials in large quantity over time, and most buyers focus on one generic category (e.g., aluminum, steel, old newspapers, glass, plastic, etc.). Quality factors, which dictate processing requirements, are established through published and informal trade specifications and vary across end-use applications.

As in traditional forward channels, Alderson's (1958) four basic functions of sorting, accumulation, allocation, and assorting are generally considered to be essential. However, because of the nature of the waste sources, reverse channel systems for post-consumer materials must emphasize the collection functions of sorting and accumulation in order to generate the large volumes of single commodities that are required by industrial buyers as well as necessary to achieve economies of scale in processing/handling. In the past, this has made it relatively important for reverse intermediaries to accomplish accumulation by maintaining levels of customer service (Crosby, Gill, and Taylor 1981). This meant emphasizing time and place convenience, and offering stable prices to stimulate repeat business (Fuller 1977). As will be discussed later, sorting and accumulation objectives are now also being accomplished in the post-consumer sector through mandated curbside collection programs at the local level.

In addition, the roles of the various reverse channel participants are changed. As noted by Zikmund and Stanton (1971):

> The consumer has a product to sell, and, in essence he assumes the same position as a manufacturer selling a new product. The consumer's (seller's) role is to distribute his waste materials to the market that demands his product. (p. 35)

But the typical consumer does not emulate the proactive role of the typical commercial channel member (i.e., producers or intermediaries), so the conventional marketing roles of producers, intermediaries, and consumers are reversed along with the physical flow of materials (Ginter and Starling 1978). Specifically, some consumers are likely driven to participate by their genuine desire to improve ecological conditions, while others are simply obeying local waste collection statutes. Overall, buyers in these channels (i.e., intermediaries and manufacturers) are generally the instigators and controllers of marketing initiatives while the sellers (consumers) tend to play a more passive role.

A TYPOLOGY OF REVERSE CHANNEL SYSTEMS

Determining the most efficient channel for the reverse distribution of recyclable materials is an important undertaking. An examination of current practices in the post-consumer arena has produced the following suggested typology (see Figure 12.3): (1) manufacturer-integrated systems, (2) waste-hauler systems, (3) specialized reverse dealer/processor systems, (4) traditional "forward" wholesaler-retailer systems, and (5) temporary/facilitator systems. Figure 12.3 depicts the reverse flows of recyclable materials from generalized post-consumer sources to generalized industrial user markets through the various types of reverse channel systems. Some of the principal functions performed at each level of the recycling process are shown at the bottom of Figure 12.3. In addition, some of the general characteristics of each type of reverse channel system are summarized in Figure 12.4.

Manufacturer-Integrated Systems

Forward vertical integration in the form of manufacturer-owned recycling centers is desirable for producers wishing to strategically control the accumulation process as a means of supplying a specialized, high-volume internal company market. Corporate integration requires a high level of investment in the buyback facilities and processing and transportation equipment required to establish the intensive reverse collection network necessary to maximize volume. These costs, however, may be more than offset when recovering high unit value recyclables on a volume basis. For example, the creation of aluminum container sheet stock from recycled materials results in an energy savings of over 90 percent in comparison to processing virgin bauxite ore (Chandler 1984). For the manufacturer, this energy savings makes it profitable to maintain continuous reverse channels to tap this source, and also reduces dependence on virgin sources (*Business Week* 1977).

The program operated by the Reynolds Aluminum Recycling Company in Florida meets the four conditions previously cited as necessary for recycling success. Reynolds initiated a fully-integrated reverse channel system in Florida in the early 1970s because the area was one in which beverages were heavily marketed in aluminum containers (Fuller 1977). After over two decades of growth, the system has expanded to a nationwide total of over 900 redemption locations in the United States, which include fixed facilities, mobile units, and freestanding reverse vending locations

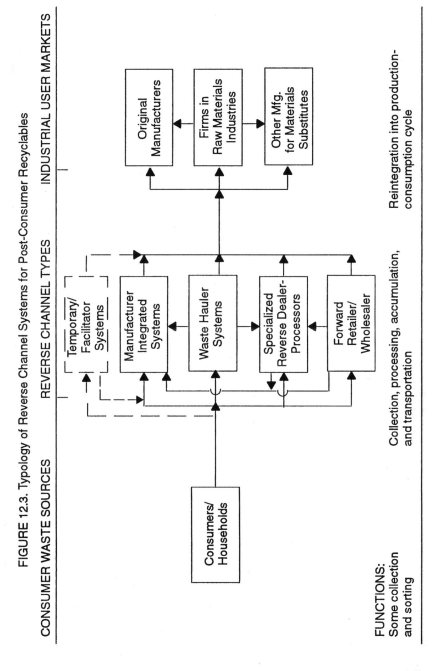

FIGURE 12.3. Typology of Reverse Channel Systems for Post-Consumer Recyclables

CONSUMER WASTE SOURCES   REVERSE CHANNEL TYPES   INDUSTRIAL USER MARKETS

Consumers/Households

Temporary/Facilitator Systems

Manufacturer Integrated Systems

Waste Hauler Systems

Specialized Reverse Dealer-Processors

Forward Retailer/Wholesaler

Original Manufacturers

Firms in Raw Materials Industries

Other Mfg. for Materials Substitutes

FUNCTIONS:
Some collection and sorting

Collection, processing, accumulation, and transportation

Reintegration into production-consumption cycle

FIGURE 12.4. Selected Characteristics of Reverse Channel Systems

Manufacturer-Integrated Systems:
- Generates steady, high volume of material to supply an internal company market
- Manufacturer controlled
- Offsets manufacturer dependence on virgin supply
- Can act as buyer from waste-hauler, dealer-processor, retailer-wholesaler, and temporary facilitator systems
- High levels of capital investment

Waste-Hauler Systems:
- Gains "first" access to materials via curbside collection programs
- Generates steady high volume of materials
- Waste-hauler has first access to materials guaranteed by local government contract
- May be required to conduct this activity at a loss in order to obtain the more lucrative basic waste collection franchise

Specialized Reverse Dealer-Processor Systems:
- Consumer materials can be a non-critical side business for large operators
- Can act as buyer from waste-hauler, smaller dealer-processor, retailer-wholesaler, and temporary/facilitator systems
- Small firms often prepared to service low volume, rural areas and re-sell to larger firms
- Presence of curbside programs may reduce volume

Forward Retailer-Wholesaler Systems:
- Based on "forced deposit" legislation
- Convenient for consumers
- Usual facilities not functionally designed to accommodate recycling activities
- Presence of curbside programs conflicts with this activity

Temporary/Facilitator Systems:
- Used by non-profit groups and charities to raise funds, etc.
- Serve as source for permanent reverse channel members
- Relatively low volume and seasonal
- Presence of curbside programs may reduce volume

(Fuller 1991). The strategy has been to maximize redemption convenience and has contributed to an industry-wide recycle rate of over 60 percent for aluminum container materials (Powell 1990).

This extraordinary recycle rate has particular significance in Florida where current legislation requires the imposition of a one cent advance disposal fee (ADF) on all consumer container materials that do not achieve a 50 percent recycle rate by mid-1993 (Florida Statutes 1988). Since all other container materials have recycle rates well below 50 percent, it appears likely that aluminum's recycling success will translate into a direct competitive cost advantage in the near future (Fuller 1991).

Partial forward integration is open to other manufacturers who have the internal volume necessary to capitalize on this approach. For example, juice bottler and glass container manufacturer Tropicana Products and paper stock maker Jefferson-Smurfitt have each integrated into the collection and processing of appropriate recyclables in moves at least partially designed to maintain stable supplies for their own operations (Fuller and Gillett 1990a).

The forward integration strategies of these manufacturers are often in direct competition against the waste-hauler systems described below, but the manufacturer-integrated system can also serve as a buyer of materials from these systems. In general, the presence of curbside collection programs tends to divert materials from manufacturer-integrated systems, so buying from waste-hauler systems is one way to make up the lost volume.

Waste-Hauler Systems

The management of the post-consumer solid waste stream has normally been treated as a local municipal responsibility. However, the escalating waste problem knows no political boundaries, and its solution clearly transcends individual local jurisdictions. In response, many states, including Florida, have passed comprehensive solid waste management legislation designed to limit landfill disposal by diverting materials through recycling systems (National Solid Wastes Management Association 1991, Florida Statutes 1988).

Such legislation typically involves the implementation of mandated curbside collection programs as a means of achieving waste diversion goals over broad areas of geography. Since these programs are legislated, they effectively remove any vestiges of "voluntary cooperation" and replace it with statutory requirements of a degree similar to those imposed on the operation of automobiles (Fuller and Gillett 1990b).

The most significant factor concerning curbside initiatives is that the initial sort of materials is made by households on a no-cost basis, thus eliminating one of the major cost barriers associated with post-consumer recyclables. As an indicator of the popularity of this solution to pollution, the number of curbside collection programs increased from approximately 1,000 in 1988 to 3,955 in 1992 (Glenn 1992b). And, there is some evidence that this approach has met with a high degree of consumer acceptance. For instance, in Winter Park, Florida, it is estimated that over 90 percent of eligible households currently participate in the community curbside recycling program and also rate it as a highly positive way to protect the environment (Kinard 1990).

Because the activities involved in curbside collection programs parallel many normal garbage collection functions, waste haulers have been in a unique position to cultivate this new business opportunity and become functionaries in these channels. For example, in the Central Florida area, Waste Management, Incorporated, a major solid waste hauler, has formed a subsidiary, Recycle America, to implement curbside collection contracts with local municipalities. The process involves the use of specialized, compartmentalized, collection vehicles and also the operation of a centralized municipal reclamation facility (MRF), which is sponsored by a consortium of local governments. The MRF is the central receiving facility at which sorting, packaging (baling, densification, etc.), and marketing activities take place (Fuller 1990). Since the geographic coverage of waste-hauler contracts is often extensive, these systems can generate significant, steady volumes of materials over time.

Waste-hauler systems provide "first access" to a steady supply of post-consumer recyclables and some firms have begun to extend their activities into the realm of sophisticated vertical marketing system arrangements. For example, Browning-Ferris Industries, a major waste hauler, has entered into a long-term contractual agreement with Wellman Industries, the nation's largest plastics recycler, to supply Wellman with all the plastics it collects via curbside programs. Similarly, Waste Management (and its subsidiary Recycle America) has entered into a 50/50 joint venture with Du Pont to supply large quantities of plastics and participate in the development of operational, large-scale plastics technologies (*Recycling Today* 1989).

In Central Florida, Waste Management also has contracts for the sale of the curbside collection aluminum component with Reynolds Aluminum Recycling Company, manufactures its own plastic collection bins from recycled materials, and has also vertically integrated into paper boxboard manufacturing as a way of internally consuming part of the volume of old newspapers (ONP) (Kinard 1990). In all of these cases, the waste hauler's immediate and contract-protected access to large volumes of recyclable materials, at costs that reflect a subsidy provided by "free" consumer sorting, may create an important differential advantage for these new market entrants over other types of reverse channels. This uniquely positions waste-hauler systems to act as suppliers to both manufacturer-integrated systems and the specialized dealer-processor systems described in the next section. However, since this system is usually tied to a openly bid waste collection franchise, the waste hauler may be forced to operate the recycling business at a loss in order to gain access to the more lucrative waste-hauling contract.

Specialized Dealer-Processor Systems

Dealer-processors, also referred to as secondary materials dealers, are independent businesses that complete the specialized marketing functions required to collect, sort, and process/upgrade materials to the industrial specifications required by end-users. Known in the past as salvage or junk yards, their scale of operations runs from "mom and pop" collectors to multimillion-dollar corporate enterprises with extensive investments in waste processing/handling equipment, specialized vehicles, and containers (Fuller and Gillett 1990a).

The traditional role of the dealer-processor has been to handle industrial solid waste, much of which requires "heavy-duty" processing to bring materials up to trade specifications. Recently, the public sector need to dispose of large quantities of post-consumer waste has caused many independent dealer-processors to expand their businesses to include post-consumer sector materials as a sideline. Large-scale dealer-processors can act as buyers in relation to waste-hauler and smaller dealer-processor systems. At the same time, the presence of curbside collection programs can also divert "direct" business away from dealer-processor systems.

At least one major manufacturer, ALCOA, has developed recycling programs that make extensive use of the existing dealer-processor intermediaries. In this regard, ALCOA has developed specialized aluminum processing equipment and promotional support programs designed to support the efforts of independent dealer-processors as they engage in competition against manufacturer-integrated systems (Fuller 1991).

A recent trend is the appearance of small-scale independent dealer-processors who specialize in a mix of post-consumer recyclables usually including old newspapers, glass, aluminum and steel containers, and plastics (Fuller and Gillett 1990a). These dealer-processors do not generally service industrial customers and their processing and transportation equipment reflects the "lightweight" handling and processing requirements associated with post-consumer recyclables. The emergence of such businesses is at least partially a result of the passage of mandated recycling legislation, which enhances public awareness and also makes available quantities of consumer recyclables on a continuing basis. These smaller operators often sell the materials collected to large dealer-processors or directly to manufacturer-integrated systems.

For instance, recent recycling legislation in Florida has created instant stocks of post-consumer recyclables in all 67 counties in the state including those in rural areas where the absolute volume of post-consumer waste is quite low (Florida Statutes 1988). In these rural areas, large scale dealer-processor, waste-hauler channels and manufacturer-integrated systems are often absent due to the limited quantities of materials available for processing, thereby opening up this business to small-scale dealer-processors by default. A recent study by Fuller and Gillett (1990a) noted an increase in the number of firms of this type operating multiple locations in rural areas of Florida.

Traditional "Forward" Retailer-Wholesaler Systems

Because the handling of recyclables requires the performance of non-traditional functions such as collecting, sorting, and large-scale storage of unsanitary materials, the adaptation of traditional "forward" middlemen to dual roles as reverse channel system members has been limited. However, reverse channels of this type have been created through "forced deposit" legislation, which requires traditional middlemen (wholesalers, retailers) to provide these functions. Several studies conducted in states that sanction container deposits (e.g., Crosby, Gill, and Taylor 1981; Crosby and Taylor 1982; Ginter and Starling 1978) have found that making recycling convenient is important in achieving acceptance of the return system and in facilitating the performance of required channel tasks. In addition, the consumer plays a more active role in such systems as they are required to bring the "product" to a channel member for the redemption of their deposits. However, the simultaneous implementation of curbside programs conflicts directly with the volume goals of "forced deposit" legislation.

Since wholesalers and retailers are functionally designed to accomplish "forward" distribution tasks, attempts to handle recyclables have resulted in relatively high-cost, inefficient operations. However, in an attempt to forestall restrictive legislation in this area, some "forward" retailers have offered voluntary recycling programs such as the installation of reverse vending machines on store premises, which provide consumers such immediate rewards as cash, receipts, tokens, stamps, or coupons for in-store discounts.

Other retailers report locating recycling stations in the rear of the store which reduces congestion in the front and generates traffic through the store (Westerman 1983). Other than profit, factors such as fostering goodwill in the community and demonstrating a commitment to a cleaner environment are cited as benefits for traditional retailers who support these types of recycling programs (*Chain Store Executive* 1982).

One example is Publix Supermarkets of Lakeland, Florida, where bins for the collection of plastic and paper bags are placed in the store to make recycling convenient for customers. In addition, the chain has developed its own private label "Green" brand of paper products, including toilet tissue, paper towels, and napkins. These products are made from 100 percent unbleached, recycled fiber, and contain no chlorine-bleaching residue, inks, dyes, or fragrance. Due to their composition, they are totally compatible with the various resource recovery alternatives available for disposable products of this type (Clark 1992).

Temporary/Facilitator Systems

Temporary or occasional intermediaries take the form of churches, civic groups, schools, and other community organizations that infrequently or occasionally collect recyclables, often for fund-raising purposes. Their primary task is to facilitate the initial accumulation sorting functions and the materials collected are immediately delivered to the various permanent channel members cited above. Much of this activity is low volume and seasonal in nature, and in many cases is actually guided and directed by permanent channel members as a means of stimulating additional volumes (Fuller 1991).

Once the immediate task is accomplished (e.g., the civic group's fund-raising drive is completed), this activity is discontinued. But despite their intermittent nature, these groups do serve as temporary middlemen between consumer sources and buyers on these occasional transactions, and are therefore counted as a facilitating reverse channel form that supports other permanent channel members. However, the presence of curbside programs will likely dampen this type of activity.

DISCUSSION

While the above typology recognizes that a variety of reverse channel types have evolved to link potential sources of post-consumer recyclables with markets, each is a response to unique conditions. Is there enough demand for recycled materials to justify the continued existence of these systems? And if so, which types are likely to prevail in the future?

Current Lack of Demand

Holding other factors constant, market demand for recyclables, as either direct or indirect substitutes for virgin materials, is a function of market price. Economic theory has long held that the efficient use of resources occurs only when total costs, which include social or ecological costs, are internalized in market prices (Cairncross 1992, Henion 1976). However, in the United States, the full payment of ecological costs does not occur and subsidies, such as the charging of below cost tipping (dumping) fees by municipalities, simultaneously encourages dumping and virgin materials production. As one specialist has noted: "To achieve market development over the long term, industry must internalize the costs of disposal. . . . Today's market system operates on the fictitious assumption that resources are unlimited and the dumps are free" (Breen 1990, p. 44).

Historically, the development of reverse channel systems for post-consumer recyclables has been impeded by high costs, poor profit prospects, and a general lack of incentives for business to include the social costs of disposal in product pricing structures (Henion 1976). As processing costs continue to exceed market prices for current recyclables, little has changed in the framework of market economics to encourage channel development (*Recycling Times* 1992, National Solid Wastes Management Association 1992). Moreover, when landfilling is an option, it costs less on average to dump materials ($28) than to process them for recycling ($50) (National Solid Wastes Management Association 1990, 1992). The one notable exception in the post-consumer waste mix is aluminum containers (UBC), which, because of inherent energy efficiency and other favorable "recycle" characteristics, remain profitable.

At present, weak demand and low prices for most recyclables are further exacerbated by monumental oversupply. This is primarily due to the so-called "success" of waste-hauler systems that are based on mandated curbside collection programs, which numbered almost 4,000 in 1992 and have created an overnight source of basic post-consumer recyclables (Glenn 1992a). Of course, the success of these programs in accomplishing the accumulation function is attributable to the public policy mandate that forces the "free" initial sort of materials by consumers, a cost barrier that had formerly plagued post-consumer recycling efforts. In the final analysis, however, the mandate to collect materials without simultaneous initiatives to develop markets is the root cause of the present dilemma.

Building Markets for Recyclables

The problem, then, is one of market development. As noted by Allen (1992) in *The Wall Street Journal*:

> The supply side of America's recycling revolution has been growing at an explosive rate, but the demand side is still barely under way. Manufacturers simply aren't geared up to absorb the huge volumes suddenly available. (p. 1)

The prospect for a turnaround in the demand for recyclables depends on several key factors, or "drivers" that are important in developing markets for the future. These drivers include: (1) a consumer commitment to green, (2) the increasing environmental costs of doing business, (3) a supportive political-legal-regulatory climate, (4) advances in technology and product design, and (5) locating manufacturing facilities near recycled materials sources.

Consumer Commitment to Green

Consumer interest in environmentalism, a phenomenon that Ottman (1992) labels "green consumerism," appears to be growing in the marketplace. Some of this interest can be traced to increased levels of awareness about environmental issues generated by the widespread media coverage of such environmental disasters as the Exxon Valdez spill, Bhopal killings, and Three Mile Island incident. In addition, several generations of children who were exposed to environmental concepts as a standard part of their primary and secondary education are now of working and voting age. Increases in awareness can also be attributed to the intense coverage of the 1992 presidential campaign in the United States, which highlighted debate on proactive environmental programs.

There is also substantial evidence that "green interest" is crystallizing into actionable consumer markets that translate into industrial markets for recyclables. Both J. Walter Thompson USA (1990) and The Roper Organization (1990) have conducted large-scale surveys in the United States that have identified relatively large and emerging consumer segments with a definite lifestyle and propensity to "buy green." Roper's two most environmentally committed segments, the True Blue Greens and the Greenback Greens, represented a combined 22 percent share in 1990, while a third somewhat green segment, called the Sprouts, commanded a 26 percent share. What is encouraging is that nearly half of those consumers surveyed exhibited at least some interest in environmental values in a marketplace setting.

Increasing Environmental Costs

In an attempt to reduce costs and increase productivity, corporate America is beginning to investigate the potential for reducing the costs of compliance with environmental regulations. In 1990, the costs for pollution abatement and control (PACO) were estimated to exceed $129 billion, and are expected to increase to over $195 billion by the year 2000 (Bezdek and Wendling 1992). These costs are associated primarily with the cleaning up of waste at the "end-of-the-pipe." Dramatic cost increases are causing firms to investigate broader aspects of the waste management problem through analysis of the production-consumption cycle shown in Figure 12.1.

Known as life-cycle assessment (LCA), the approach requires the firm to make a cradle-to-grave appraisal of how their products affect the environment. The process includes consideration of the impacts associated with raw materials extraction, product manufacturing and marketing, and ultimate disposal (final fate) at the end of a product's useful life (see Society for Environmental Toxicology and Chemistry 1991). Since post-consumer recycling reflects needs in the product disposal stage, many firms are now viewing the enhancement of recycling processes as one way to reduce costs (Freeman et al. 1992). For example, making recycling easier to accomplish through product design can simultaneously create low-cost sources of recycled materials to use in packaging and other applications. This creates end-markets for recyclables and also supports ecological goals, which represents a "win-win" situation for individual firms and the environment.

Supportive Political-Legal-Regulatory Climate

With the election of the new administration in late 1992, a continuing emphasis on ecological public policy is expected. So far, the Administration's announced strategy includes creating an Office of Environmental Policy in the White House and elevating the Environmental Protection Agency to Cabinet status (*Orlando Sentinel* 1993). Other expected political overtures include a major restructuring of taxes on energy as a means of reducing the release of pollutants into the atmosphere and an emphasis on developing new industrial processes and product design technologies that minimize the generation of waste (Gore 1992).

This aggressive approach to environmental matters dovetails nicely with a major shift in EPA regulatory direction that began in 1990. Specifically, the new focus will be on developing pollution prevention approaches instead of continuing the "command and control" philosophy embodied in regulating by forced compliance with specific end-of-pipe minimum emissions guidelines (Reilly 1992). A growing body of evidence indicates that pollution prevention costs less than pollution cleanup, and opens up the possibility of creating a sustainable competitive advantage based on innovative, hard-to-copy, or proprietary technologies that produce environmentally benign products at lower costs than their polluting predecessors (Freeman et al. 1992).

To prevent pollution, businesses must consider the recycling ramifications of products before, rather than after, product development. This should strengthen demand for post-consumer recyclables as regulatory compliance focuses on the broader picture offered by life-cycle wastes analysis and the obvious role that the effective recycling of discarded consumer products can play in solving the total waste problem. Consequently, businesses will see recycling as one necessary part of the solution, and not a problem in and of itself.

Already in place at the state level are a wide variety of laws fostering post-consumer recycling (Fuller 1993). These include supply-side statutes mandating curbside collection and requiring local governments to engage in recycling programs, as well as market development statutes on the utilization of recycled materials through a variety of financial and tax incentive programs. Further, several states have passed product contents laws, which require consumer products to be made of certain percentages of recycled materials by specific future target dates (called "rates and dates"), and state procurement regulations, which give preference to products made with recycled materials (National Solid Wastes Management Association 1990). These measures are an obvious positive force in the development of needed markets for post-consumer recyclables.

Advances in Technology, Product Design, and Development

Technology has not ignored the challenges of handling and processing recyclable materials. One example of a class of recently developed breakthrough technologies are processes that economically depolymerize polyethylene terephthalate (PET) into its original two components. This allows the use of these "recycled source" materials in direct food contact applications, a practice that was formerly avoided, and opens up previously restricted markets for these materials. As evidence of market impact, the recycle rate for PET containers has increased from virtually 0 percent in 1987 to 21 percent in 1991 (Miller 1992, p. 73).

In addition, the art and science of product design is being "greened" through design for environment (DFE) applications. The essence of DFE is to create products that take into account disposition, as well as those aspects of the product's materials, construction, use, and manufacturing processes that affect the environment (Office of Technology Assessment 1992). In short, products designed to be recyclable, easy to disassemble, and nonpolluting during use are produced through low-waste manufacturing processes, contain fewer and simpler mixes of materials, use recycled materials in their construction, and contain no toxic elements (Abler 1990, Burnette 1990). In general, DFE is a positive influence on markets for recyclables because it makes it easier to economically handle and process consumption wastes.

Locating Manufacturing Facilities Near Sources

Another major factor influencing the marketability of recyclables is distance to market. Obviously, the low unit cost and bulky nature of recyclables leads to higher prices as the distance to market increases. Conversely, many markets (i.e., mills, foundries, production facilities, etc.) were deliberately sited decades ago to be close to virgin sources.

Facilities development is a long-term investment, but numerous firms are beginning to develop facilities near sources of recyclables as it becomes clear that a steady, high-volume flow will be sustainable in the future. For example, one such expansion is presently occurring in the Southeast, while a tumultuous restructuring of the paper industry is currently underway in response to the large and readily available supplies of newsprint in major urban areas of the United States (*In Business* 1993, Glenn 1992a). An additional contributing factor is the development of state-sponsored market development organizations that serve to facilitate expansion of the recycling industry. Some of the functions performed by these organizations include implementing tax and other incentive programs, and coordinating the permitting process that accompanies industrial development (Kacandes 1991).

Weathering the Transition

Market development is a long-term proposition, not an instantaneous process. During the market development transition period, which channel types in the typology will survive the inevitable shakeout, and which will not?

Major survivors will likely include the waste-hauler systems, as well as the manufacturer-integrated and specialized dealer-processor systems that feed off waste-hauler systems. In particular, the waste-hauler channel is mandated and actually supplants routine garbage collection and disposal. As curbside sorting becomes routine consumer behavior for householders, this process will siphon off recyclables that may have been separately collected and delivered to buyback centers via other systems. Also, as a necessary public service, garbage collection, and the accumulation of recyclable materials that parallels this function, will continue despite market conditions. As operating losses occur, they will simply be viewed as public sector costs of waste disposal and be passed on to consumers in the form of increased fees or taxes. Eventually, as markets develop, local consumers may obtain some relief in the form of reduced fees or fewer increases in other local taxes.

Traditional retailer-wholesaler forward systems will also remain in place where mandated by law. Depending upon the redemption responsibilities under various statutes, the bulk of the costs of the forced repatriation of container materials will impact various "upstream" channel members, including manufacturers, who may then simply decide to pass on these costs in the form of higher prices for consumer goods.

Attrition will most likely be highest among the small independent dealer-processors and temporary/facilitator functionaries who emerged as niche marketers to take advantage of the availability of post-consumer materials. The smaller dealer-processors may simply not have the financial ability to weather the current market glut. One hope for this class of reverse channels is in servicing municipalities in rural areas where collection and recycling are mandated under state law, but limited volume precludes servicing by the larger waste-hauler and dealer-processor systems. The temporary/facilitator group, on the other hand, will likely find that routinization of the curbside programs has foreclosed their sources of materials and that available prices are not worth the collection effort.

REFERENCES

Abler, Robert A. 1990. "Design with the Waste Stream in Mind," *Innovation*, Vol. 9, No. 2 (Summer), 20-22.

Alderson, Wroe. 1958. "The Analytical Framework for Marketing," in *Proceedings-Conference of Marketing Teachers from the Far Western States*, Berkeley: University of California Press, 15-28.

Alderson, Wroe. 1965. *Dynamic Marketing Behavior*, Homewood, Illinois: Richard D. Irwin, Incorporated.

Allen, Frank E. 1992. "As Recycling Urges, Market for Materials is Slow To Develop," *The Wall Street Journal*, Vol. CCXIX, No. 12 (January 17), 1.

American Heritage Dictionary, 1985. Boston, MA: Houghton Mifflin Publishing Company.

Bezdek, Roger H. and Robert W. Wendling. 1992. "Environmental Market Opportunities," in *The Greening of American Business*, Thomas F. P. Sullivan, ed., Rockville, MD: Government Institutes, Inc.

Boone, Louis E. and David L. Kurtz. 1992. *Contemporary Marketing–7th Edition*, New York: The Dryden Press, 406.

Breen, Bill. 1990. "Selling It: The Making of Markets for Recyclables," *Garbage*, November/December, 44-49.

Burnette, Charles. 1990. "Principles of Ecological Design," *Innovation*, Vol. 9, No. 2 (Summer), 2.

Business Week. 1977. "Turning Junk and Trash into a Resource," (October), 68-75.

Cairncross, Frances. 1992. *Costing the Earth*. Boston, MA: The Harvard Business School Press.

Chain Store Executive. 1982. "Recycling Looms on Deposit Debate," Vol. 57, No 2 (December), 33-34.

Chandler, W. U. 1984. "Converting Garbage to Gold," *The Futurist*, February, 69-77.

Clark, R. 1992. Personal interview conducted with store manager of Publix Supermarket, May 5, 1992, Orlando, FL.

Crosby, L. A. and J. R. Taylor. 1982. "Consumer's Satisfaction with Michigan's Container Deposit Law," *Journal of Marketing*, Vol. 46, No. 1, (Winter), 47-59.

Crosby, L. A., J. D. Gill, and J. R. Taylor. 1981. "Consumer-Voter Behavior in the Passage of the Michigan Container Law," *Journal of Marketing*, Vol. 45, No. 2 (Spring), 19-32.

Fisk, George. 1974. *Marketing and the Ecological Crisis*. New York: Harper & Row, 15-16.

Florida Statutes. 1988. 403-9197, Advance Disposal Fee.

Freeman, Harry, Teresa Harton, Johnny Springer, Paul Randall, Mary Ann Curran, and Keith Stone. 1992. "Industrial Pollution Prevention: A Critical Review," *Journal of the Air and Waste Management Association*, Vol. 42, No. 5 (May), 616-656.

Fuller, Donald A. 1977. "Aluminum Beverage Container Recycling in Florida: A Commentary," *Atlanta Economic Review*, Vol. 27, No. 1 (January), 41-43.

Fuller, Donald A. 1978. "Recycling Consumer Solid Waste: A Commentary on Selected Channel Alternatives," *Journal of Business Research*, Vol. 6, No. 1 (January), 17-31.

Fuller, Donald A. 1979. "Materials Recycling from Consumer Sources: Concept and Case Studies," in Neil Beckwith et al., eds., *1979 Educators Conference Proceeding,* American Marketing Association, 567-571.

Fuller, Donald A. 1990. "Recycling Post-Consumer Plastic Containers: A Marketing Perspective," in Louis Capella et al., eds., *Progress in Marketing Thought*, Proceedings of the Southern Marketing Association, 177-181.

Fuller, Donald A. 1991. "Recycling Post-Consumer Aluminum Containers: A Marketing Overview," in Robert L. King, ed., *Developments in Marketing Science–Volume XIV 1991*, Proceedings of the Academy of Marketing Science, 101-105.

Fuller, Donald A. 1993. "The Role of Ecological-Legal Sanctions in Fostering Post-Consumer Recycling," *Proceedings of the 1993 Marketing and Public Policy Conference*, American Marketing Association and Association for Consumer Research, June (forthcoming).

Fuller, Donald A. and Peter L. Gillett. 1990a. *A Profile and Directory of the Recycling Industry in Florida–1989, Final Report*, Florida Department of Environmental Regulation, DER Contract No. SW-31 (December), 150 pp.

Fuller, Donald A. and Peter L. Gillett. 1990b. "Florida's Mandated Recycling Law (1988): A Marketing Commentary," in B. J. Dunlap, ed., *Developments in Marketing Science–Volume XIII 1990*, Proceedings of the Academy of Marketing Science, 249-253.

Ginter, P. M. and J. M. Starling. 1978. "Reverse Distribution Channels for Recycling," *California Management Review*, Vol. XX, No. 3 (Spring), 72-81.

Glenn, Jim. 1992a. "The State of Garbage in America–Part I," *BioCycle*, Vol. 33, No. 4 (April), 46-55.

Glenn, Jim. 1992b. "Recycling Revolution in the Paper Industry," *In Business*, Vol. 14, No. 6 (December), 40-43.

Gore, Al. 1992. *Earth in the Balance*. Boston, MA: Houghton Mifflin Company.

Guiltinan, Joseph P. and Nonyelu Nwokoye. 1974. "Reverse Channels for Recycling: An Analysis of Alternatives and Public Policy Implications," *American Marketing Association Proceedings*, No. 36 (Spring & Fall), 341-346.

Henion, Karl E. II. 1976. *Ecological Marketing*, Columbus, OH: Grid Publishing Company, 248 pp.

In Business. 1993. "If the Market Isn't There, Build Your Own," Vol. 15, No. 1 (January), 42-43.

J. Walter Thompson USA. 1990. *JWT Greenwatch*, Peter Kim, ed., Vol. 1, No. 2 (Autumn).

Kacandes, Tom. 1991. "Market Development in New York: A Report from the Field," *Resource Recycling*, Vol. 10, No. 9 (September), 53-60.

Kinard, Alan. 1990. Personal communication, September 1990. Mr. Kinard is the General Manager of Central Services, which operates the curbside recycling program in Winter Park, Florida.

Korzum, Edward, Melahat T. Duyar, and Jose Villaneuva. 1990. *The Recycling of Energy Values in Municipal Solid Waste: Current Practices and Future Trends*, A research monograph prepared for The Florida Center for Solid and Hazardous Waste, State University System of Florida, Type 1 Center, Gainesville, Florida.

Miller, Chaz. 1992. "Polyethylene Terephthalate," *Waste Age*, Vol. 23, No. 8 (August), 73-74.

National Solid Wastes Management Association. 1990. *Landfill Tipping Fees. 1990 Review*. Washington, DC.

National Solid Wastes Management Association. 1991. *Special Report: Recycling in the States–1990 Review*. Washington, DC.

National Solid Wastes Management Association. 1992. *The Cost to Recycle at a Materials Recovery Facility*. Washington, DC.

Neace, M. B. 1990. "Consumer Products and Packaging Disposal: A Normative Model," *Progress in Marketing Thought*, Proceedings of the Southern Marketing Association, 206-211.

Office of Technology Assessment. 1992. *Green Products by Design: Choices for a Cleaner Environment*, Congress of the United States, U.S. Government Printing Office, Washington, DC.

Orlando Sentinel. 1993. "Clinton Creates Environmental Office," February 9, A-7.

Ottman, Jacquelyn A. 1992. *Green Marketing: Challenges and Opportunities for the New Marketing Age.* Lincolnwood, IL: NTC Business Books.

Powell, Jerry. 1990. "How Are We Doing? The 1989 Report," *Resource Recycling*, Vol. 9, No. 5 (May), 34-37.

Recycling Times. 1992. "The Market Place," December 15.

Recycling Today, 1989. "Plastic Recycling Ventures Fighting Misconceptions," Vol. 27, No. 6 (June), 36-38+.

Reilly, William. 1992. "Environment, Inc.," *Business Horizons*, Vol. 35, No. 2 (March/April), 9-11.

The Roper Organization. 1990. *The Environment: Public Attitudes and Individual Behavior*, Commissioned by S. C Johnson & Son, Inc., Racine, Wisconsin (July).

Society for Environmental Toxicology and Chemistry. 1991. *A Technical Framework for Life-Cycle Assessment.* Washington, DC: January.

Weiner, Joshua L. and Ajay Sukhdial. 1990. "Recycling of Solid Waste: Directions for Future Research," *in W. Parasuraman et al., eds., 1990 AMA Educators Conference Proceedings: Enhancing Knowledge Development in Marketing*, Vol. I, Chicago: American Marketing Association, 389-392.

Westerman, M. 1983. "A New Way to Make Friends and Money," *Progressive Grocer*, December, 71-84.

Zikmund, William G. and W. J. Stanton. 1971. "Recycling Solid Wastes: A Channels-of-Distribution Problem," *Journal of Marketing*, Vol. 35, No. 3 (July), 34-39.

SECTION VII.
THE GREEN MOVEMENT
AND ITS IMPLICATIONS
FOR EFFECTIVE
MARKETING STRATEGY

Chapter 13

Behaviors of Environmentally Concerned Firms: An Agenda for Effective Strategic Development

C. Anthony di Benedetto
Rajan Chandran

SUMMARY. Increasing environmental awareness among consumers has encouraged many firms to implement environmentally conscious initiatives. Many of these initiatives have resulted in public skepticism directed toward these firms, and attempts by policymakers to pass legislation on product and related issues. This paper investigates product, packaging, and communication strategies implemented in selected industries in response to environmental concerns, assesses the success of these initiatives, and encourages firms to develop an agenda for implementing environmentally responsible strategies.

INTRODUCTION

Many firms have seen the trend toward increased consumer interest in environmental issues as a marketing opportunity. Many firms that have frequently been targets of environmental groups (makers of disposable diapers, detergents and bleaches, fast-food restaurants) have implemented environmentally concerned strategies for the long term. Other firms have seen this trend as an opportunity to increase sales quickly by appearing concerned about the environment. Brands marketed as having environmental benefits are increasing in market share and expected to continue to do so (Gerstman & Meyers Inc.

1989, Conway 1990, Holusha 1991b). So, as with any opportunity, there exists the potential for misuse of environmental claims by firms.

Recently, ten state attorneys general stated that "attempts to take advantage of consumer interest in the environment have led to a growing number of environmental claims that are trivial, confusing, or even misleading" (Holusha 1991b). Product packages often are marked "environmentally friendly," "recyclable," or "degradable," terms that may be too vague to convey the real benefit to the environment, and do not provide the consumer with adequate information to select correctly among brands. At the same time, there are several large consumer product firms seeking to establish national guidelines for the use of such environmental claims (Holusha 1991b). These guidelines would limit the use of environmental terms as short-term marketing gimmicks.

As consumers have become more environmentally aware, they have also become increasingly skeptical of claims. In a recent poll, nearly half of the respondents viewed environmental claims as "gimmickry" (Lublin 1990). This trend is likely to continue as time goes on and environmental claims increase (just as terms like "fresh," "lite," or "natural," often devoid of meaning, are arguably overused today) (Kiley 1990). Consumers may begin to mistrust firms that stress an environmental theme in their products and communication, or even to question their motives. Possibly, consumers might ignore all environmental messages (valid ones as well as gimmicks) if the proliferation of messages raises the level of consumer skepticism too high.

A P&G spokesperson recently stated that "at the level of concern most people have about the environment, they're not willing to make that many sacrifices in convenience, value, and performance" (Schiller 1990). Yet the quest for convenience at the expense of environmental responsibility may well be changing. In a 1990 study by the market research firm Gerstman & Meyers Inc., almost half of the respondents claimed they would pay a purchase price of 15% more for a product in an environmentally sound package. This is notable in that it is almost double the percentage obtained by the same research firm one year earlier (Gerstman & Meyers Inc. 1989, Holusha 1991b). Indeed, a substantial number of firms have responded to consumer sentiment by looking into alternative packaging materials (Kiley 1990). There is always some possibility that this kind of consumer study does not provide valid or reliable results (Were the researchers asking the right questions? unbiased questions? asking them correctly?). Still, the results lend some support to the premise that increasing environmental concern on the part of American consumers and firms is not just a fad (Coddington 1990).

Short-term quick fixes are not an appropriate response to environmental concerns, because of consumer skepticism that is likely to continue to increase (the likely perception that such moves represent "marketing ploys" by manufacturers), and (perhaps more importantly) because they are strictly tactical or responsive in nature, and do not arise from a long-term, environmentally conscious strategic posture on the part of the firm. How, then, should a firm select and develop a sound and responsible strategy for the long term? It is useful to employ the typology of environmental management strategies as proposed by Zeithaml and Zeithaml (1984) (see Figure 13.1). They suggested three categories of environmental management strategies. *Independent* strategies (in which the firm uses its own resources and abilities) can include competitive aggression as well as other approaches such as legal or political action or public relations. In choosing a *cooperative* strategy, the firm acts with other involved parties, implicitly or explicitly. Contracting, co-opting, or coalition-forming are examples of cooperative strategies. In *strategic maneuvering* such as choosing a new industry, market, or type of business, strategic implementation changes the competitive environment. The strategies are not mutually exclusive, as firms may employ a combination of these strategies simultaneously; some examples later in this report will illustrate such combination strategies.

A complementary model was presented by Hunt and Auster (1990). This is an empirically based environmental continuum model distinguishing five stages of environmental program development (see Figure 13.2). Stages 1 and 2 ("beginners" and "fire fighters") only devote minimal attention to environmental issues, while Stages 3, 4, and 5 ("concerned citizens," "pragmatists," and "proactivists") apply more aggressive policies regarding the environment. The number of Stage 5 proactivist firms was very low;

FIGURE 13.1. Zeithaml and Zeithaml's Environmental Management Strategy Typology

Strategy Types	Examples
1. Independent Strategies	
Competitive Aggression	Degradable Bunnies diapers Photodegradable trash bags P&G degradeable diaper ad campaign Coke and Pepsi both trying to be first to use recycled plastic soda bottles
Competitive Pacification	Industrywide ad campaigns
Public Relations	McDonald's ads showing chain's environmental responsibility
Voluntary Action	Tuna companies abiding by "Dolphin Safe" practices
Other possibilities include:	

Developing Dependencies (e.g.,suppliers)
   Legal or Political Action
   Demand Smoothing
   Demarketing	

2. Cooperative Strategies	
Coalition	McDonald's with EDF and other companies
Co-optation	Acquiescing with key environmental concerns–being recognized by environmental groups as a firm that has "greatly improved"
Contracting	McDonald's and Rubbermaid–turning polystyrene waste to plastic products
3. Strategic Maneuvering	
Domain Selection (entering new industries or markets)	Niche marketers in diaper industry
Diversification (investing in new businesses or products)	Phosphate-free detergents, safer paints, and spray propellants

Source: Adapted from Zeithaml and Zeithaml (1984) with examples taken from the case histories discussed in this chapter.

FIGURE 13.2. Hunt and Auster's Stages of Environmental Management Programs

Criteria	Stage 1: Beginner	Stage 2: Fire Fighter	Stage 3: Concerned Citizen	Stage 4: Pragmatist	Stage 5: Proactivist
Mindset of Corporate Managers	Envir. management unnecessary	Address issues only as necessary	Envir. management worthwhile	Envir. management important	Envir. management priority item
Support of Top Management	No involvement	Piecemeal involvement	Commitment in theory	Aware and moderately involved	Actively involved
Integration of Program with Co.	Not integrated	Piecemeal basis only	Minimal interaction with other departments	Moderate integration with other departments	Actively involved with other departments
Reporting Structures	None	Exceptions only	Internal only	Internal; some external reporting	Formalized internal and external reporting
Envir. Program's Involvement with:					
Legal	None	Moderate	Moderate	Daily	Daily
P.R.	None	None	Moderate	High	Daily
Mfg./Prodn.	None	None	None	Moderate	Daily
Prod. Design	None	None	None	Minimal	Daily

Source: Adapted from Hunt and Auster (1990).

and all firms at lower stages could be doing more to be environmentally responsible. Taken together, these two models can indicate at what stage (or stages) a firm is in terms of environmental responsibility, and what types of management strategies it can use in order to improve its position.

It is possible that a given firm may display varying degrees of environmental concern simultaneously; it is not implied that firms can always be easily categorized into one of the above stages. A fast-food chain, for example, may feel more compulsion to address the concerns of a powerful stakeholder such as an influential consumer watchdog group and change to environmentally friendly packaging, while making few other changes to its product or system of delivery.

The main objective of this work is to develop an agenda for firms seeking to respond to current or future environmental challenges from both consumer groups and government. A useful agenda would specify the roles to be played by all concerned departments within the firm: manufacturing, research and development, advertising, transportation, finance, and so on. It would be focused on long-term goals, not immediate-term market share gains. In order to develop this agenda, environmentally concerned product, packaging, and communication strategies and initiatives currently used by firms in several industries are investigated and assessed in terms of affecting public perceptions of the firm's environmental consciousness. The report concludes with a proposed environmental agenda for action specifying the tasks and roles of various concerned departments within a firm truly committed to the environment.

ENVIRONMENTALLY ORIENTED STRATEGIES EMPLOYED BY FIRMS

In compiling the following profiles, several sources were used: *The New York Times, The Wall Street Journal, Fortune, Business Week, Packaging, Earth, Marketing News, USA Today, Across the Board* and *Adweek's Marketing Week*. Both a computerized literature search and a manual library search were conducted. The Information Center of the American Marketing Association also provided pertinent documentation. This report focuses on six specific industries. These were selected because they provide excellent examples of environmentally driven actions undertaken by the competing firms, from which much can be inferred about their underlying strategies. These industries were also selected because they have all received substantial coverage in the popular press and much attention from consumer and environmental groups, therefore detailed documentation of patterns of strategy was possible. The industries selected were: detergents and related products, disposable diapers, polystyrene, trash bags, paint, and tuna.

Detergents

Detergent manufacturers have received criticism from environmental groups for two main issues: the large amount of plastic trash generated, and pollution from phosphates. Relatively simple strategies can be implemented to address the first issue, while the second involves substantial product reformulation and, therefore, a longer-term goal of developing phosphate-free detergent. Thus, many of the initiatives taken by firms in this industry have centered around product and packaging strategies designed to reduce the amount of nonrecyclable trash generated. With respect to the Zeithaml framework, leading firms appear to have employed mostly independent strategies such as voluntary action and public relations. Some strategic maneuvering (development of phosphate-free detergents) is also practiced by industry leaders.

Procter & Gamble has taken several prominent initiatives. Refills for Downy fabric softener are being sold in concentrate form. The customer buys a plastic bottle once, then adds concentrate (sold in a small cardboard box) and dilutes it with water. This procedure cuts down greatly on plastic packaging headed for landfills (Schiller 1990). "Enviro-paks" are also being tested for Downy: with this system, the customer refills the plastic bottle with a collapsible plastic pouch, or "bag-in-box." Seventy percent less plastic is used with the Enviro-pak system (Stuller 1990). P&G has also experimented with recycled plastic containers for Liquid Tide and Spic and Span, and paperboard "milk cartons" for Downy (Nelson-Horchler 1989), and has developed a detergent (Ariel Ultra concentrate), sold in Europe, that cuts down on phosphate pollutants, since less detergent needs to be used with each wash (Rolfes 1990). All of these activities are strongly supported with print and television ads, couponing, and other promotional activities. Results so far have been mixed: early Downy concentrate sales were slow due to consumer resistance to the idea of diluting concentrate (Swazy 1990), and P&G was criticized in Europe by environmental groups since animal testing was used in the development of Ariel detergent (Rolfes 1990). Colgate-Palmolive and Lever (makers of Wisk detergent and Snuggle fabric softener) have also experimented with bag-in-box systems and concentrates (Kiley 1990), and Church and Dwight is developing a nonphosphate detergent.

Disposable Diapers

The main environmental concern here is disposal. Disposable diapers alone make up over 1% of solid waste. The major manufacturers (P&G and Kimberly-Clark) seemingly ignored the problem until state lawmakers threatened bans or other measures (Kiley 1990). Thus, using the Zeithaml framework, independent strategies such as voluntary action and public relations have been reinforced by legal and political action, and some of the smaller manufacturers have used environmental claims as part of a competitive aggression strategy.

P&G and Kimberly-Clark have taken two major product initiatives to address these environmental concerns. First, "superabsorbent" diapers were developed; these cut the volume of waste for disposal in half. Second, a pilot program in Seattle designed to collect diapers and reclaim the plastic was established by P&G, and both firms have instituted composting programs (Kiley 1990, Holusha 1991c). Packaging bulk has also been reduced in recent years.

Smaller firms have used consumer environmental concern as an opportunity to gain a foothold in this very competitive market. RMED International, among others, has launched a brand of diaper that, according to its ads, is free of chemicals and almost completely biodegradable (Swazy 1990). One such small firm, American Enviro Products, claimed in ads that its Bunnies diapers biodegrade in three to five years, and the Bunnies package was very clearly marked "biodegradable." These claims were questioned, and as a result, the company had to back down from its claim and state that only the plastic back sheet and packaging was biodegradable, not the wood pulp. At the moment, the company is under investigation by the FTC for possible violation of truth-in-advertising laws (Smith 1990b, Stuller 1990).

Polystyrene

The principal environmental concern over polystyrene is its use in non-recycled packaging and foam cups, particularly by the fast-food industry. Polystyrene is indeed recyclable, but very few facilities or programs yet exist for recycling it and most used polystyrene goes to landfills.

As in previous examples, the largest firm in the industry seemingly has taken the greatest environmental initiatives. McDonald's has implemented several strategies for dealing with polystyrene waste. Most notably, it is moving away from foam "clamshell" containers for hamburgers, replacing them with paper-plastic wrap. (This move has not been without its critics; see discussion later in this report.) It has also considered selling coffee in paper cups rather than foam, but anticipates consumer resistance to this move (Swazy 1990). McDonald's had previously been recycling these containers, which were made by the Rubbermaid Company into trays. Paper products such as napkins and Happy Meal™ boxes contain recycled fiber. McDonald's has reduced the amount of packaging needed in the delivery of soft drinks and orange juice by changing its delivery method: liquids are now pumped into each outlet directly from the tanker truck (Gutfield 1990). All of these initiatives have been strongly supported with advertising programs and in-store promotions (including environmental messages on the paper tray liners). Burger King and other fast-food restaurants have also been replacing polystyrene containers with paper (Swazy 1990).

McDonald's has also formed an alliance with the Environmental Defense Fund, which is jointly studying options for reducing trash volumes and for recycling (Jacobs 1990). In cooperation with Dow, Arco Chemical, Chevron, and Mobil, McDonald's is investing in a multimillion-dollar test program for recycling polystyrene and other packaging materials (Stuller 1990). McDonald's has effectively combined independent with cooperative strategies in dealing with the criticism it has faced from environmental groups.

Firms outside the fast-food industry have taken responsible steps as well. AT&T, for one, has replaced much of the foam it uses in packaging with biodegradable cardboard (Smith 1990b). Con Agra (Swanson's and Healthy Choice microwaveable foods) has stated a company mission of selecting packaging materials that are recyclable (for example, as beverage bottles) (Kiley 1990), and both Coca-Cola and Pepsico Inc. have announced their intentions to use soft drink bottles made with recycled plastic within the next year (*Business Week* 1990).

Trash Bags

Several environmental strategies have been employed by trash bag manufacturers, mostly falling into the competitive-aggression category in the Zeithaml framework. Trash bags made by Mobil (Hefty) and First Brands (Glad) are photodegradable, that is, they break down when exposed to light. Photodegradable claims prominently figured on the packages. However, for the most part, these bags end up in landfills, where there is no light to start the breakdown process. At the time, a Mobil company spokesperson said, "Competitive pressures force (us) to market degradable trash bags, even though . . . they won't help reduce solid waste. . . . Consumers 'feel good' about having a degradable product" (Smith 1990b). This attracted the attention of environmental groups who claimed that the photodegradability claim was misleading. Eventually, these firms were required by the FTC to remove the photodegradable message from their packages, under the truth-in-advertising laws (Smith 1990b).

Other, smaller brands are biodegradable due to cornstarch content; some of these have indicated biodegradability on the package. Environmental groups have criticized these efforts as well, since the "plastic dust" resulting from breakdown of these bags may be more dangerous to health than intact plastic bags (Smith 1990b).

Paint

Solvents and oils used in paints can be hazardous to the environment. The paint manufacturers (McCloskey, Olympia, Red Devil, and Benjamin Moore) have been very responsible in developing alternate products such as acrylic-based and water-based paints. This activity might be classified as diversification (a form of strategic maneuvering) in the Zeithaml framework. Environmental initiatives in this industry are well under way, thanks to the paint manufacturers' ability to foresee stringent government regulations and their attention to new product development. As an example of the kind of legislation facing paint manufacturers, consider that in California, paint products must reduce solvent content from 80% to 20% (Kiley 1990).

Tuna

One environmental issue that has captured substantial media attention is the entrapment of dolphins in tuna drift nets. All three major American tuna packers, Starkist, Van Camp (Chicken of the Sea) and Bumble Bee, have pledged to use only "Dolphin Safe" tuna. Fishing methods that will not result in killing any dolphins are employed by American fishing fleets. Print advertising and messages on labels of canned tuna support the "Dolphin Safe" initiative (Manning 1990). Thus, implicitly cooperative strategies have been implemented in this industry, as have competitive pacification strategies (a term used in the Zeithaml framework to describe independent actions that improve relationships among competitors).

The environmental problem is not so simply resolved, however. U.S. fleets may be driven out of business because of the "Dolphin Safe" requirement, yet the fishing in the Eastern Tropical Pacific, the only place where dolphins and tuna are found together, will continue unabated by foreign fleets. Worse yet, foreign fleets are less regulated than American fleets, and kill more dolphins than their American counterparts did, so the dolphin population may be even more threatened in the long run than if American fleets continued to fish for tuna. Bumble Bee has invested in alternative fishing methods and is committed to the establishment of better international controls; these long-term programs are probably the only sure ways to protect dolphins from the nets of tuna fishing boats (Manning 1990).

Figure 13.3 summarizes the results of the initiatives and strategies described above. Wherever available, it is noted whether the strategy has been well received by the public, and also whether any criticism by consumer groups or governmental agencies was elicited.

ENVIRONMENTAL POLICIES IMPLEMENTED BY GOVERNMENTS AND RETAILERS

Many government programs have been initiated to monitor environmental issues and encourage environmental responsibility. Fed-

FIGURE 13.3. Summary of Results of Environmental Strategies

	Strategy	Result
Detergents		
P&G	Downy in concentrate; paperboard carton	Consumer resistance; low sales
	Ariel: less phosphates	Criticized: animal testing
	"Enviro-Paks"	Still in test
	Tide in recycled plastic	Still in test
Colgate-Palmolive	Palmolive liquid concentrate, plastic pouches	Still in test
Lever	Wisk, Snuggle, bag-in-boxes	Still in test
Disposable Diapers		
P&G	Superabsorbent Pampers	Favorable consumer response
	Composting program	
	Collecting/recycling program	
	Packaging reduced	
Kimberly Clark	Composting	Favorable consumer response
	Packaging reduced	
American	Biodegradable, recyclable	FTC investigation: Enviro truth-in-advertising
Polystyrene		
McDonald's	Recycling cartons	Favorable consumer response
	Uses recycled paper in pkg.	
	Reducing pkg. of beverages	
	Communications programs	
	Cooperates with companies and EDF	
Burger King	Testing paper in place of polystyrene	Still in test; generally favorable (resistance to paper coffee cups)
Trash Bags		
Mobil, First Brands	Photodegradable bags	Generally favorable consumer response Questioned by envir. groups Removed biodegradable claims after FTC investigation
Others	Biodegradable (cornstarch additive)	Generally favorable consumer response

FIGURE 13.3 (continued)

Strategy		Results
Paint		
All manu-facturers	Replacing oil and chemical solvents with water and acrylic based products	Favorable consumer response
Tuna		
All manu-facturers	"Dolphin-Safe" product Communication programs	Favorable consumer response

eral programs implemented in recent years include the Clean Air Act, the Clean Water Act, the Toxic Substances Control Act, the Resource Conservation and Recovery Act (governing the handling and disposal of hazardous waste), and the Comprehensive Environmental Response Compensation and Liability Act (managing the cleanup of contaminated sites). More recently, the FTC issued some new federal environmental guidelines in 1992. Senator Lautenberg (N.J.) has recently introduced legislation in Congress that would require the Environmental Protection Agency to establish definitions and standards on the use of environmental claims such as "biodegradable." This action is supported by groups such as the Environmental Defense Fund, the Natural Resources Defense Council, Environmental Action, the National Recycling Coalition, and the Consumers Union. All of these actions indicate that the United States government is taking a more concerted effort in controlling environmental marketing activities.

Many state and local laws and ordinances exist. Newark, for example, requires that all plastic bags be degradable (Nelson-Horchler 1989). St. Paul and Minneapolis banned the use of plastic food packaging and non-recycled grocery bags. Several states and municipalities have restricted the use of polystyrene. Maine has banned the use of aseptic packaging, due to its inability to be easily recycled (Kiley 1990, Holusha 1991c). In some Northeast states, a plastic package labeled "recycled" must contain at least 25% recycled material, including at least 15% from post-consumer waste (Smith 1990a). The Federal Trade Commission cooperates with several states in order to get companies to back up "green" and "environmentally safe" advertising claims (*CCH Trade Regulation Report* 1990).

Some foreign governments have a labeling program for environmentally sound products. One of these is Germany's "Blue Angel" label. A product that is judged to be environmentally friendly in one area (for example, reduces noise pollution; lessens damage to the ozone layer; eliminates mercury pollution) receives a Blue Angel mark on its package. Canada has an "Environmental Choice" label for recycled motor oil, water-based paints, products made from recycled plastics, and recycled office and copy papers (Smith 1990a). The Japan Environment Association labels certain products with the "Eco-Mark," but this program lacks scientific standards (*Marketing News* 1990). Recently, it has been proposed that the European Community adopt a standardized, official "green label" that would be used in all twelve nations (Simons 1990). It should be noted that creation of standards such as these is difficult. Acceptable technical definitions of what constitutes "recyclable" or "green" are hard to set, and many changes and amendments may be required as time goes on. Consider the recent parallel situation in which the FDA effectively tightened the definition of the word "fresh" when it required Procter & Gamble to remove this word from labels of Citrus Hill orange juice.

Retailers have also taken initiatives encouraging environmental responsibility. Wal-Mart's program is perhaps the best known of these. Advertising and store signage is used to recommend over 100 environmentally sound products. Ralph's and other Western supermarkets, and Canada's Loblaw's supermarkets, have labeling programs, and Kmart has instituted programs to promote environmentally friendly products (Smith 1990a, Stuller 1990). Many supermarket chains offer rebates for returning paper bags, sell eggs in recycled paper containers, or use recyclable containers for store brands. As with many of the manufacturers' initiatives, several of these programs are relatively easy to implement. They also tend to be well received. Loblaw's sold $5 million in environmentally sound products in one three-month span in 1989 (Stuller 1990).

RECOMMENDATIONS AND CONCLUSIONS

As evidenced by the growth in activity by firms, the environment is an issue of growing concern. Environmental issues are, inevitably, also marketing issues. In light of increasing consumer interest and sophistication, a new challenge is presented to firms: how to choose the correct environmental claims to make, and not elicit consumer skepticism or an unintentional backlash from environmental groups. McDonald's switch from polystyrene to paper-plastic wrap for its hamburgers has been criticized in some circles, for example. Some studies suggest that polystyrene is no worse for the environment than waxed paper if one considers total environmental impact. Thus, McDonald's did what was politically adroit and not necessarily environmentally correct when it switched to paper-plastic; the company has admitted that the change was prompted by public pressure and not inconclusive scientific evidence (Holusha 1991c). As another example, CFCs have not been in spray cans for many years (CFC aerosol propellants have been outlawed since 1978), but only recently have companies making and selling them begun placing statements to that effect on their labels. Critics have argued that these statements might be misleading to consumers. Of course, environmental claims multiply as a function of market research results like those mentioned earlier that show consumers are beginning to prefer brands that are environmentally sound. But, as consumers become more sophisticated, the mere presence of a term like "biodegradable" on a label will no longer sell a brand: consumers will require more detailed information about the actual environmental benefits delivered.

Among the case histories presented, it was found that industry leaders tended to use a combination of environmental strategies, and not to restrict themselves to only independent strategies. McDonald's has been praised for its work with environmental groups as well as its reduction of the use of polystyrene. Procter & Gamble and other leading detergent manufacturers have sought to reduce phosphate content in new detergent formulations. Indeed, many of the firms (large and small) that ran into controversy regarding their commitment to the environment seemed to be using strictly independent, competitive-aggression strategies, apparently selected according to short-term sales or market share growth objectives. The case histories suggested that the role of the industry leader might be different than that of "follower" firms. Environmental modifications can be thought of as essentially product innovations, and the industry leader takes the responsibility of launching the innovation into the market.

Although the sample of industries examined was of small size, there are some preliminary observations that can be drawn. It is suggested that firms should look beyond the simple, competitive-aggression strategies which, although not necessarily inferior *per se*, may occasionally be short-sighted. Rather, several independent strategies (including voluntary action or competitive pacification) can be used in complementary fashion, together with other types of strategies such as coalition forming, co-opting, or diversification. Cooperative strategies were very beneficial in some instances, possibly because they strengthen the working relationship between producers and suppliers. (Looked at this way, a cooperative strategy might even be consistent with a competitive-aggression strategy in some cases.) The more successful companies among those studied also seem to be particularly good at communicating their participation in environmentally oriented activities through public relations and advertising, and one might expect these to be critical support elements for most other environmental strategies.

Experts on environmental concerns have suggested several guidelines for sound environmental management policy. As many of these guidelines overlap, it is worthwhile to distill a comprehensive list of recommendations that, together, make up a useful starting point for building an agenda for environmental responsibility.

1. The firm must begin with a solid statement of their *own* responsibility to the environment (How committed are we to the environment? Do we need to be more committed?) and with an understanding of environmental attitudes and expectations on the part of the public and government (Glazer 1990).

2. A proactive stance is recommended. That is, the firm should take the initiative and not wait too long to get involved in environmentally responsible actions, so that it does not become a target of environmental groups (Glazer 1990). As

shown by the examples given above, McDonald's and Procter & Gamble are excellent examples of firms proactively seeking ways to be environmentally responsible.

3. Environmental policies should not be implemented in random, "fire-fighter" fashion when crises emerge. Corporate policies regarding environmental issues should be the key component of an integrated environmental management program (Hunt and Auster 1990).

4. The firm should strive at all times to have an impeccable environmental reputation. "Environmental accidents" such as toxic emissions, pollution, and oil spills must be foreseen and prevented before they occur (Conway 1990).

5. Realistic goals with respect to environmental responsibilities should be set, and commitment to achieving these goals must be obtained throughout the firm. This commitment includes active interest, support, and encouragement from top management (Glazer 1990; Hunt and Auster 1990) and also effective linkages between corporate management and business unit staff (Hunt and Auster 1990). In the case of detergents, minor, simple-to-implement packaging improvements have been tried; at the same time, research continues into more expensive and time-intensive product reformulation that would cut down on the amount of phosphate released into streams.

6. The firm should provide products and packages that truly are environmentally responsible. This does not mean adding "buzzwords" to the product's label. Rather, it implies an understanding of the environmental consequences of using a given package or ingredient, or of selling a given product. In order to understand this impact fully, the firm must establish the environmental impact of the product or packaging over the full life cycle; that is, from raw material through manufacture to disposal and, perhaps, recycling and re-use (Conway 1990, Holusha 1991a). This can imply the increased use of recyclable packaging, increased motivation to recycle, and the use of less packaging wherever possible. Life-cycle costing should be used to assess the long-run costs and benefits of taking an environmentally proactive stance.

7. Importantly, maintain open, honest communication with all concerned publics (Conway 1990). All forms of communication, including sales calls, labels, brochures, and broadcast and print media, can be used to spread good information about the firm's products, packaging, and environmental activities to all stakeholders (consumers, employees, shareholders, government agencies, and environmentalists).

Communications, of necessity, must be factual. Nothing will incite more bad press or attention from environmental groups than environmentally oriented communications designed to mislead. And, of course, the firm's actions must be consistent with, and actively support, the communication, lest it come to be viewed as lip service to a currently hot issue. Sometimes communication involves correcting miscommunication, such as in the controversy over whether McDonald's should use polystyrene or paper-plastic wrap. Otherwise, a statement without basis in fact made by an interest group may be reported as fact by the media and taken as truth by consumers. This last point has interesting policy implications for management. Any firm seeking to implement environmentally sound procedures actually faces several types of environmental proponents. "Preservationists" are more likely to be critical of any step taken by big business, while "environmentalists" may be more willing to make tradeoffs.

Given public perceptions and concerns, as expressed in the various surveys and studies discussed earlier and many others, any resulting government policy must be proactive in taking initiatives toward more environmental responsibility. Firms should be aware of, and responsive to, such governmental policies. In recognition of this, an Environmental Agenda is set forth in Figure 13.4 as a guideline for firms adopting a proactive stance toward environmental responsibility. It could be used by management to fix responsibilities and to coordinate actions across the firm's departments. The agenda is developed with the ultimate firm objective of manufacturing an environmentally safe product considering all life cycle stages, including use and disposition. Each department's contribution to this objective is spelled out in the agenda. The agenda states that it is the role of R&D to devote time and effort to the develop-

FIGURE 13.4. A Proposed Environmental Agenda

Manufacturing
Reduce noxious emissions from plants
Consider environmental consequences of building new plants
Examine alternate manufacturing technologies with less harsh environmental consequences
Examine use of more environmentally sound raw materials

R&D/Quality Control
R&D efforts aimed at products that are environmentally sound
Better testing methods for determining environmental consequences of new products

Advertising and Public Affairs
Communicate environmentally sound activities by firm to consumers and other interested publics
Prepare news releases and public relations activities
Cultivate relationships with media
Advise consumers of product safety; instructions for use

Transportation/ Shipping
Advise middlemen and retailers of proper use and disposition of product
Encourage middlemen and retailers to follow environmentally sound practices for storage, use and disposition of product
Enlist assistance of retailers in getting environmental messages across to consumer

Legal Affairs
Follow up on all environmental claims
Keep in touch with all current laws and regulations on the product, including initiatives by the Environmental Protection Agency
Advise management on the appropriate stance to take

Finance/Accounting
Estimate net effects on costs of environmental programs
Do studies on cost/price tradeoffs to determine likely consumer response to price increases on environmentally sound products
Estimate long-term financial impact of environmental policies

ment of products that are non-carcinogenic, biodegradable, or will not break down into hazardous components in landfills. Manufacturing must consider the pollution caused by emissions from new and existing plants and develop ways to reduce noxious emissions. Sales and distribution should be responsible for teaching middlemen and/or end users about proper use and disposition of products, and make certain that these recommendations are being practiced. Advertising and public affairs departments must plan news releases and other activities that communicate environmentally sound activities undertaken by the firm. The legal department must follow up on all environmental claims and keep up to date on all changes in applicable laws. Finance and accounting should estimate the net effects of environmental programs of overall corporate costs and profits. Other roles and responsibilities are also outlined in the agenda in Figure 13.4. Of course, the agenda requires that top management is sufficiently committed to saving the environment that they allot adequate funds to support these activities, some of which can be very expensive.

Many of the activities and policies characteristic of proactivist firms (Hunt and Auster 1990) are consistent with this Environmental Agenda: denoting environmental management as a top priority item; active involvement of top management; integration of environmental personnel with other departments; active involvement with legal, public relations, manufacturing, and product design departments, and so on. Adopting the Environmental Agenda can assist a company in achieving the proactivist stance put forth by Hunt and Auster as the ideal.

To the firm that is considering implementing an environmentally responsible strategy, several common-sense questions should be asked:

1. Does my firm's category provide a significant environmental response opportunity? Will the environmentally aware consumer respond favorably to the new strategy simply because it is good for the environment? Do we run the risk of being seen as yet another firm to drape ourselves in the "environmentally friendly" flag?

2. If we gain an advantage due to a new environmental strategy, is it sustainable? Can we keep our advantage proprietary? Can we patent it? Do we want to patent it?
3. How price sensitive is the demand for the product class or category? Will we substantially add to the cost of the product by implementing our strategy? While the research results presented earlier show that consumers are willing to pay more for environmentally sound products or packages, and the surplus they are willing to pay seems to be growing, one can assume there will always be limits.
4. Is the demand for our product class or our brand sufficiently stable for us to implement the strategy effectively?
5. Are there ways that our firm can use input from consumers effectively in designing environmentally responsible programs?

The answers to these and similar questions can help a firm assess whether an environmentally oriented strategy will pay off for them in the long run.

Though not in the scope of this study, several issues relating to environmental strategy implementation could be addressed in future research. For example, while product, packaging, and communication strategies can all be important parts of an overall environmental strategy, which should be emphasized? In developing communication claims, which product features, benefits, or attributes should be highlighted? If the market is willing to pay a price premium for more environmentally responsible packaging, how big a premium will it tolerate? Should the firm couple a minor packaging improvement with a small price increase, or offer a revolutionary new packaging concept at greater expense to the customer? What kinds of market research can support future planning and strategic control (what specific performance measures should be tracked during strategic implementation)? Additionally, the cases indicated that market leaders might respond differently to environmental challenges, being more likely to use creative combinations of environmental strategies and to cooperate with other firms and interest groups. The relationship between industry position (leader versus follower) and appropriate strategy selection could be stated as a hypothesis for further research.

REFERENCES

Business Week (1990), "Coke and Pepsi Rush to Go Green," (December 17), 38.

CCH Trade Regulation Report (1990), "Enforcement of National Advertising Regulations," No. 97 (March 20), 1.

Coddington, Walter (1990), "It's No Fad: Environmentalism Is Now a Fact of Corporate Life," *Marketing News* (October 15), 7.

Conway, Stephen J. (1990), "Short-Term Pain, Long-Term Gain Environmental Communications," speech delivered at the 1990 Marketing Conference, The Conference Board, New York.

Gerstman & Meyers Inc. (1989), *Consumer Solid Waste Management: Awareness, Attitude and Behavior Study*, New York: Gerstman & Meyers Inc. (October).

Glazer, Walt (1990), "Environmentalism Will Change Course of Research," *Marketing News* (March 19), 19.

Gutfield, Rose (1990), "Big Mac Joins with Big Critic to Cut Trash," *The Wall Street Journal* (August 2), 131-134.

Holusha, John (1991a), "'Recyclable' Claims Are Debated," *The New York Times* (January 8), D1, D5.

Holusha, John (1991b), "So What Is 'Environmentally Friendly?'" *The New York Times* (January 26), D1.

Holusha, John (1991c), "Coming Clean on Goods: Ecological Claims Faulted," *The New York Times* (March 12), D1, D10.

Hunt, Christopher B. and Ellen R. Auster (1990), "Proactive Environmental Management: Avoiding the Toxic Trap," *Sloan Management Review*, (Winter), 7-18.

Jacobs, Deborah L. (1990), "Business Takes on a Green Hue," *The New York Times* (September 2), 25.

Kiley, David (1990), "A Long, Silent Spring Awaits Wasteful Brands," *Adweek's Marketing Week* (April 16), 2-3.

Lublin, Joann S. (1990), "Creating a 'Green' Ad Campaign Risks Making Consumers See Red," *The Wall Street Journal* (December 5), B8.

Manning, Anita (1990), "More Foreign Fishing Boats Pose a Risk," *USA Today* (August 6), 1D-2D.

Marketing News (1990), "Japanese Market Products with Environmental Tie-In" (August 20), 17.

Nelson-Horchler, Joani (1989), "Old Packages Never Die . . ." *Industry Week* (September 4), 88-90.

Rolfes, Rebecca (1990), "How Green Is Your Market Basket?" *Across the Board* (January/February), 49-51.

Schiller, Zach (1990), "P&G Tries Hauling Itself Out of America's Trash Heap," *Business Week* (April 23), 101.

Simons, Marlise (1990), "A 'Green Label' for Europe's Consumer Goods," *The New York Times* (December 14), A6.

Smith, Randolph B. (1990a), "Rush to Endorse 'Environmental' Goods Sparks Worry About Shopper Confusion," *The Wall Street Journal* (March 13), B1-B3.

Smith, Randolph B. (1990b), "Environmentalists, State Officers See Red As Firms Rush to Market 'Green' Products," *The Wall Street Journal* (March 13), B1-B2.

Stuller, Jay (1990), "The Politics of Packaging," *Across the Board* (January/February), 41-48.

Swazy, Alecia (1990), "For Consumers, Ecology Comes Second," *The Wall Street Journal* (March 13), B1.

Zeithaml, Carl P. and Valarie A. Zeithaml (1984), "Environmental Management: Revising the Marketing Perspective," *Journal of Marketing*, 48 (Spring), 46-53.

Chapter 14

In Search of Market Segments for Green Products

Alma T. Mintu-Wimsatt
Don Michael Bradford

SUMMARY. The proliferation of "green" products in today's businesses suggests that there is a market that is constantly patronizing these products. Marketers agree that environmentally conscious and/or friendly products sell. However, the extent of our understanding of this market has been limited to the consumer market. While the general consuming public is a significant segment, there are other potential segments for green goods and services. This paper explores three other market segments for green goods and services. We also identify some potential problems marketers can expect in offering their products to these segments.

INTRODUCTION

One of the early lessons of the 1990s is that corporate environmentalism isn't just good public relations. Throughout America, in businesses as diverse as industrial equipment manufacturing, power generation, professional services, even restaurants and dry cleaning, management is learning that it can reap major financial benefits by going beyond compliance with environmental regulations . . .

Forbes (1991)

The "green" issue, more than any other, will affect most companies' prospects in the 1990s and beyond. Responding to the grow-

293

ing interest in the environment, companies such as Ryder Truck Rental Inc. and Lufthansa have utilized the sentiment of environmental consciousness as a means to promote and market their products and services. Consequently, claims of environmentally friendly products have become important selling points. More and more, consumers are looking for goods and services that supposedly reduce solid waste and protect the green environment . However, while some of these claims are legitimate, some companies simply take advantage of the uninformed consumer.

Currently, companies involved in "green" marketing have targeted much of their attention towards the general consuming public. This is primarily because the general consumer, as a market segment for green goods and services, is a particularly large and profitable market. In Great Britain, for example, current research indicates that approximately 12 to 15 million potential green consumers can be expected. While Americans have been slow in responding to the green movement, a survey of Fortune 500 packaging executives found that 58% agreed that consumers are willing to accept price increases for environmentally friendly packaging.

Undoubtedly, the consuming public is an important and large target segment for green goods and services. However, we contend that this segment *is not* the only avenue for green products. Businesses are fiercely competing for this one segment to gain an environmental lead (e.g., in Europe, Procter & Gamble introduced Spic and Span bottles that use recycled plastic). Meanwhile, other companies have successfully carved a niche in less traditional market segments (e.g., a waste management company in Florida is one of the state's fastest growing companies). Therefore, for companies to have a competitive advantage regarding the environment, they need to know who their target markets are and/or who their target markets ought to be.

The purpose of this chapter is to help managers identify the other potential segments available for companies offering green goods and services. There are two overriding reasons why identifying these markets is important. First, the proper identification of these markets is important if managers are to adapt competitive strategies. These strategies facilitate the initiation of new marketing programs that address environmental issues. Second, a wholistic perspective may be necessary to address the environmental issue. That is, since a symbiotic relationship exists between these markets, a collective effort (among the segments) may be necessary in order to effectively solve the "environmental" dilemma.

The remainder of this chapter is devoted to exploring the viability of four potential segments for green goods and services. A section is also provided that identifies the problems associated with each market segment. The four market segments include the following: general public (i.e., consumers); government; other for-profit organizations (i.e., private industry); and non-profit organizations (Figure 14.1).

FOUR POTENTIAL MARKET SEGMENTS

In marketing management, one of the primary steps in planning and implementing a marketing strategy is to decide on a target market. Once a target market has been developed, this becomes the basis for the marketing mix–the 4 Ps. Unfortunately, choosing a target market is not an easy task. It requires an in-depth understanding of the total market and its trends; company's distinctive competencies; and critical external factors such as the competitive and regulatory environments, among others.

This section of the chapter helps to simplify the task of a marketer whose company intends to offer green goods and services. We discuss the various markets that can aid the marketer in choosing

FIGURE 14.1. Total Market for Green Goods and Services

Segment 1	Segment 2	Segment 3	Segment 4
GENERAL CONSUMER	GOVERNMENT AGENCIES	PRIVATE INDUSTRIES	NONPROFIT COMPANIES

the "proper" market. The four segments discussed (i.e., consumer, government, private industry, and non-profit markets) are considered "direct" market segments. These markets are often directly targeted by other companies because of their sales, market share, or profit potential.

Segment 1: General Public or Consumer Market

> It's a familiar story by now. Over a year ago, marketers started capitalizing on the green euphoria of the pre-Earth Day 1990 by touting their products as "safe for the environment," "degradable," "environmentally-friendly," and so on.
>
> *Green Market Alert* (1991)

Green products are gaining visibility in West Germany, Switzerland, the Netherlands, and United Kingdom's consumer markets. This demonstrates that the green issue has become an important consumer concern. It has also provided marketers with opportunities for product improvement and differentiation. Because of these market opportunities, many companies aim to convince the public that their products are environmentally friendly and not as harmful as they may seem. At present, the window of opportunity for these companies is promising. Hence, companies like Ameritech Publishing Inc. consider proper leverage of environmental issues a "sustainable competitive advantage."

To cite additional examples, Procter & Gamble's idea of using pouches for the Lenor Fabric (known as Downy in the U.S.) liquid concentrated fabric softener (rather than bulky non-degradable plastic bottles) was well accepted in West Germany. Meanwhile, Esprit has been promoting "responsible consumption" of buying less and buying only environmentally sound goods.

A recent Gallup survey of trends and opinions concluded that consumers are willing to "pay for the privilege of buying green." This conclusion is quite appealing and encouraging for marketers. While reasons for the apparent change in the sentiments of consumers are unclear, some marketing consultants offer the following explanation:

Apart from lots of media attention, such as about the CFCs punching holes in the ozone layer, new attitudes may show a more basic disenchantment with "materialism. . . ." Most of the baby-boom generation now have families; they are said to have developed a new sense of social responsibility.

The Economist (1989, p. 75)

Segment 2: Government and Its Agencies Market

The green issue has become part of many political campaigns. Indeed, in some cases, it has become a political platform. In recent European elections, the Green Party gained 15% of the British vote. Even Margaret Thatcher, in 1988, included in her campaign her strong support for environmental issues.

In the United States, the renewed concern for the environment partly emanates from the Clinton administration's environmental mandate. By 1995, estimated annual spending on the environment will be approximately $174 billion. This spending is primarily devoted to solid-waste management, hazardous waste management, prevention of air pollution, and waste water management. Moreover, some government agencies and states have required that a proportion of their purchases be made from recycled products.

In addition, it is estimated that the Environmental Protection Agency (EPA) will spend approximately $450 billion within the next ten years for the purposes of upgrading and constructing water and sewage-treatment plants. These budget figures reflect the growing awareness among federal and state organizations of the importance of this pursuit.

The United States military can also be expected to expend valuable dollars for environmental control. Where the public's eye (if not criticism) has been focused on the environmental responsibility of most (military) installations, its viability as a potential market for green goods and services is quite likely.

Segment 3: For-Profit or Private Organizations

Business Week (1989) predicts that one of the major business trends of the 1990s will be investments into America's landscape, i.e., improving and preserving the environment. According to Scott Jay Wollins, environmental analyst for Tucker, Anthony, Inc., "Regulations and fear of liability, not conventional economic forces, drive spending on the environment." Robert Keefer, president of EnvironQuest, an environmental information company, estimates that for every dollar spent by the government, companies will spend $5 to $10 for environmental clean-up.

For Ameritech Publishing Inc., a new recycling program with Fort Howard Paper Company is being instituted. The program includes the recycling of phone books, which currently occupy approximately 1% of landfills. Both companies anticipate that this recycling project may easily become a service they can offer to other (publishing) companies given the possibility of a legislative mandate.

To further demonstrate the profitability of these markets, managers of environment-oriented companies claim that they are recession-proof. According to these managers, as long as corporate America exists, a potential and/or ready market can be found. With all the new government regulations, private industry can be expected to spend considerable resources for environmental control.

Segment 4: Not-for-Profit Organizations

Non-profit organizations such as hospitals, universities, and other charitable institutions (e.g., Red Cross) are also viable alternatives for companies that offer green products. However, many (non-profit) organizations operate under very limited budgets and are closely monitored by other regulatory agencies.

For example, several hospitals are currently re-evaluating their waste disposal systems to insure that these waste products are not illegally disposed. The cases on illegal waste dumping of hospital garbage have made the (garbage) business a lucrative service for the independent contractor.

Meanwhile, in light of the budgetary crunch in many universities, these organizations are attempting to reduce waste as much as possible. Recycling has become part of many educational institutions' budget programs. Many universities have also hired independent consultants and/or contractors to re-evaluate their operations and recommend waste reduction policies.

PROBLEMS ASSOCIATED WITH EACH MARKET SEGMENT

The previous section discussed the importance of each of the four segments. Here, the problems and/or barriers in dealing with these markets are explored.

Consumer Segment

Undoubtedly, the sentiments of consumers are hard to gauge. Despite the survey indicating consumers' willingness to purchase green products at a premium, (Schlossberg 1990) still contends that consumers are still generally concerned with economy rather than ecology. The point out that the Gallup survey is misleading. In fact, they conclude that:

> Consumers may express more concern about the ecology, but they continue to buy large luxury cars, relatively few recycle voluntarily, and most importantly, economic issues continue to dominate political campaigns.

Currently, there is a race to see which company (or companies) can churn out the most number of green goods and services. If we were to trace the product life cycle of green goods and services, these products are now entering their growth stage. If this is so, we can anticipate the flooding in the marketplace with "supposedly" green products. In the long term, this market will become very competitive and the race to see "who can reach the consumer first" as a window of opportunity will become smaller.

While competition is inevitable in any business endeavor, the presence of stricter regulations and public policies can aggravate the situation. This emanates primarily from misleading statements and claims of products being environmentally friendly. In particular, there are a number of criticisms regarding the "marketing ploy" of degradable trash bags and diapers. Manufacturers claim that it is not their fault if consumers are uninformed. Hence, consumers must interpret the degradability of these products. Debates of this nature have led to stricter policies and governing bodies.

Government Segment

The United States government has lagged behind many of its European counterparts in addressing environmental issues. Because of this, many of our legislators are playing "catch-up." That is, blanket regulations and policies are being initiated to demonstrate that the U.S. government is actually concerned with the environmental issue. Therefore, stricter legislation and/or codes of conduct can be expected. In particular, the authors quote the marketing recommendations of the Attorney General Task Force on green marketing:

> The Task Force recommends that the federal government adopt a national regulatory scheme establishing definitions for the environmental marketing claims to be used in the labeling, packaging and promotion of products on the basis of environmental attributes. This regulatory scheme should be developed with input from and after consultation with the states and should be enforceable by both state and federal officials.
>
> *The Green Report* (1990)

To any firm seeking to provide goods and services to the U.S. government and its agencies, the task will be quite difficult. The budgetary constraints mandated by the new administration are a major consideration. Additionally, regulations will have to be closely followed and monitored to ensure compliance. Several *other* agencies will have to be dealt with in order to ensure that all the necessary requirements and standards have been sufficiently met. This type of bureaucracy translates itself to the possibility of ineffective and inefficient business operations.

Private Industry Segment

Within private industry, many companies are currently undertaking environmental control and recycling programs. For example, there is BMW's car recycle center in Germany; McDonald's "McRecycle USA"; GE's millions spent on improving the environment; and Hitachi's GREEN (Global Resources, Environment, and Energy Systems) center.

The aforementioned programs and policies imply capital expenditures for their installation and maintenance. For services involved in waste management/recycling design as well as goods that offer environmentally sound substitutes, considerable market opportunities are available.

While these are compelling reasons to immediately start investing in "green" projects in order to tap into this profitable segment, several changes need to be initiated. Herein lies the problem—change can be very expensive. Expenditures will be incurred when some of the existing processes in manufacturing green goods and services have to be changed. For instance, to reduce industrial waste, 3M redefined its operation to: (1) Reformulation of the product; (2) Equipment redesign; (3) Industrial process modification; and (4) Resource recovery and/or salvaging. Obviously, 3M's four-step reorganization was an expensive endeavor.

Change also occurs in the re-establishment of standards and/or requirements. The federal government and its agencies have been quite observant. The Environmental Protection Agency is actively pursuing criminal charges, in addition to fines, for any environmental violations (Marshall and Mayer 1992). Therefore, firms dealing with the needs of private industry have to be extremely cautious.

In situations where compliance is not enough, companies have to demonstrate reasonable degrees of corporate commitment to the environmental dilemma. For example, a wholesaler for office supplies may refuse to carry a particular brand of paper unless it is made, in part, from recycled materials.

Non-Profit Segment

While not a particularly lucrative group, this segment may be especially appealing for companies that provide recycling and waste disposal services. Since part of the green dilemma is rooted in the reduction of waste, businesses connected with waste disposal will find this segment a viable customer. However, because this segment often operates as non-profit institutions, budgetary constraints will limit the extent to which they will be able to expend dollars for waste reduction purposes. Nonetheless, if the trend of environment-related regulatory policies continue, hospitals and universities (among others) will have no choice but to allocate part of their budgets for waste reduction purposes.

CHOOSING THE "RIGHT" MARKET AND STRATEGY FORMULATION

Companies offering green goods and services have various market alternatives. More importantly, this chapter points out that these opportunities are not limited to the traditional segment (i.e., consumer segment). Several non-traditional market segments (i.e., government, private industry and non-profit organizations) that are potentially large and economically feasible.

Choosing the "right" market is the foundation for sound strategy. Based on a company's target market, recommendations can be made on product, price, promotion, and distribution policies. Effectively tapping into a specific market offers marketers a leading edge. Likewise, if the segment is satisfied with the company's offerings, it may become a niche for the company's products.

Here, we have identified four probable target segments for green goods and services. Regardless of choice, each segment provides challenging pursuits for any company. With high barriers to entry, large capital expenditures, changing technology, and strong competition, the choice of the "right" target market is crucial (Figure 14.2).

While identifying the proper market is one step towards finding a niche, we also need to properly position and differentiate our products. Should we emphasize the company's use of recycled materials? Or, should the label on our packaging highlight that it is made from recycled material? Or, should our advertising focus on being environmentally friendly?

Based on current trends, environmentally friendly features of goods and services are perceived to offer unique benefits to users or buyers. This is critical in product positioning. These positive perceptions can serve as competitive advantages in gaining an environmental lead. Therefore, as a (strong) competitive advantage it be-

FIGURE 14.2. The Importance of Identifying the Proper Market

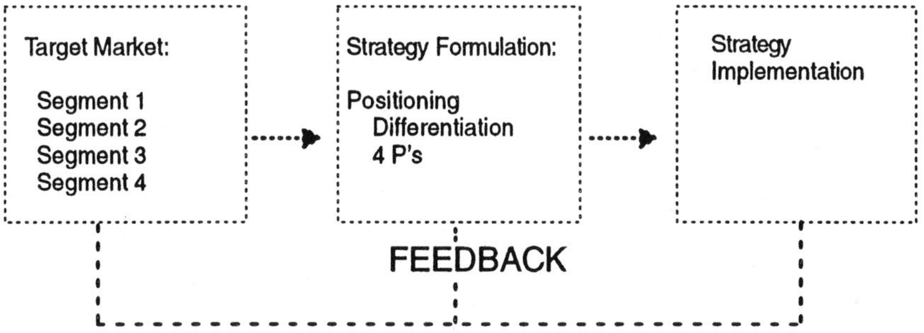

comes an important selling point in product differentiation and positioning.

CONCLUSIONS

For companies either engaged in or considering the marketing of green goods and services, this chapter serves as an eye-opener on some of the trends in this industry. The window of opportunity is wide open for prospective companies. However, based on today's environmental trends, it has become apparent that this window of opportunity is also rapidly becoming smaller.

We contend that although the biggest (and most profitable) segment seems to be the consuming public, there are several other potential segments. That is, other less traditional segments exist that can be just as profitable. Therefore, the task of the marketer is to evaluate each of these markets so that the "right" niche or market can be targeted. Once the "right" niche has been identified, strategies can be formulated that provide some environmental lead. These strategies are then implemented to effectively differentiate the company's green products from those of the competition.

Finally, it is noteworthy to mention that companies offering green goods and services are currently faced with a precarious situation. On the one hand, the rapid proliferation and growth of green products indicates that this is indeed a profitable venue. On the other hand, the sensitivity of the greening issue has put corporate America and its agenda on edge.

REFERENCES

Business Week, "Investing for the 1990s," October, 1989.

The Economist (1989) "The Perils of Greening Business," October 14, 83.

Forbes (1991), "The Profit in Preserving America," November 11, 19-22.

The *Green Market Alert* (1991) March, 4.

The Green Report: Findings and Preliminary Recommendations for Responsible Environmental Advertising, Attorneys General Task Force, November, 1990.

Marshall, M. E. and David Mayer (1992), "Enviromental Training: It's Good Business," *Business Horizons,* March/April, 54-57.

Schlossberg, Howard (1990), "Greening of America Awaits Green Light from Leaders, Consumers," *Marketing News,* March 19, 1990.

Wood Leonard and Ronald Koss (1990), "U.S. Consumers More Concerned With Economy than Ecology," *Marketing News,* March 19, 1990.

SECTION VIII.
GREEN STRATEGY
AND PUBLIC POLICY

Chapter 15

Voluntary Reaction to Green Policies Among Market-Mavens: An Application of the Parallel-Political Marketplace Conceptualization

Tom Suraphol Apaiwongse

SUMMARY. The author investigates factors that affect an individual market-maven's voluntary reaction to governmental-reformed green policy. The distinctive reform elected here is an EPA voluntary policy as a regulatory alternative. This offers a marketing approach to replace traditional mandatory regulation. Guided by Ecological-Marketing theory, this chapter adopts the parallel-political and marketplace conceptualization as a framework for delineating industrial market-mavens' reactions to green earth governmental policies. A field investigation of 88 industrial reactions suggests that benefits and uncertainties about the policy, as well as adaptability of the market-maven centers, have significant impact on a favorable reaction to the green policy. New measures of different types of policy benefit and uncertainty as well as structural and climatic adaptation in group settings are developed, validated, and offered for use in future research.

INTRODUCTION

A rapid-fire series of major world events, including wars and recessions, eclipsed environmental issues, forcing them to become a lower-

---

The research was financially supported in part by a grant from Marcia Segal and the Academic Affairs office.

order priority for business and their political overlords. The 1990s, however, have become the "Decade of the Environment," and both business and government are coming to the same conclusion: environmental protection is not an optional extra, "it is an essential part of the complex process of doing business" (Cateora 1993). Recently, at the U.N.-organized Earth Summit conference (1992) in Rio de Janeiro, world leaders and top environmental officials expressed continuing global concern over ecological issues (Taylor 1992). On paper, at least, the summit participants committed themselves to protecting the environment (D'Aquino 1992). The problem is that too many of the summiteers believe fervently that the best method of achieving the protection is the creation of new rules for everyone else's daily life. This approach is a nonstarter in the United States, and President Bush's non-committal attitude reflected that reality. Accordingly, U.S. environmental policy has been dominated by the "market failure" paradigm–the belief that environmental problems are caused by the failure of the market to provide the right signals (Smith 1992).

Decades ago, the Environmental Protection Agency (EPA) proposed several rules to regulate the environmental protection practices of such industries as steel and chemicals. Global concern about protecting the environment fostered regulatory reforms and a growing variety of specific legislation favoring environmentally friendly marketing. More recently, the Clinton Administration has favored the replacement of government regulatory programs with an innovative marketing-based policy known as the voluntary program. The voluntary policy of regulatory alternatives for industry is compatible with the concept of ecological marketing (see Henion 1978 for an elaboration of the logic of this abstraction and its extension), a term used to identify marketing that takes into consideration the environmental consequences of its actions.

Indeed, the EPA has successfully championed the innovative, economic-incentive and market-based approach that makes the Clean Air Act a model of regulatory reform. With it, the EPA can allow a business to improve cost-effectiveness without sacrificing environmental quality. The voluntary program holds more promise than the mandatory ones (Henion 1980; Schultze 1977) proposed earlier by Congress. Basically, the voluntary approach allows substantial savings to industry without relaxing government requirements.

One specific policy known as the EPA's "Bubble" links regulatory market strategies and voluntary alternatives to give industries and government a cost-effective means to accelerate pollution reduction (see Butler 1984). The voluntary policy of regulatory alternatives, however, is not without its problems, one of which emanates from the policy itself. Some industries, for instance, complain that the programs are still too restrictive to do the company much good. Another problem involves the government bureaucracy: industries complain that government officials are slow to react to firms' inquiries. The favorable or unfavorable reaction to this voluntary policy could be constrained by a firm's perceived uncertainty about the policy and the reaction of government regulators to its plans. The existence of options gives marketing practitioners the opportunity to participate creatively in the green revolution; this research considers factors affecting their willingness to become involved in the voluntary program.

Despite the increasing importance of voluntary reaction to green policies, scholarly inquiry on the topic has been hampered in two ways. First, the literature suggests that only a relatively small proportion of industrial firms react to the green voluntary policies (Apaiwongse 1993a). Second, very little academic research has attempted to document empirically the factors that affect voluntary reaction in an ecological setting. To investigate this situation, a survey was conducted to identify these factors.

This chapter develops a theory of green voluntary reaction. After describing the parallel-political marketplace conceptualization as a framework for examining the potential impact of the revolutionalized green policy on voluntary reaction, the chapter presents this as a theory and formal hypotheses. The results of an empirical study designed to test the hypotheses are then reported. Finally, the implications of the study are discussed and future research suggestions focus on further quantification and qualification of favorable reaction to green policies.

THE PARALLEL-POLITICAL MARKETPLACE CONCEPTUALIZATION

Conceptual Background

Extending prior conceptual frameworks formulated by Thorelli (1984) to examine the "political ecology of marketing," and by

Arndt (1983) as a "political economy network," the concept of a parallel-political marketplace proposed by Hutt, Mokwa, and Shapiro (1986) offers an exploratory framework with which to understand the exchange relationships that span both economic and political domains. Inevitably, marketers assume significant roles in both economic and political marketplaces: "The more marketers try to influence government decisions and the more cooperative activities have manifest political consequences, the more likely the marketer is to be recognized as a political actor" (Arndt 1979). In other words, the concept incorporates a consideration of the economic and sociopolitical forces affecting not only the marketing channel members dyad but also the regulatory body dyad found to exist in the political marketplace.

In the context of the political marketplace, exchange involves any activity between two or more organizations that has actual or expected consequences for the realization of their respective goals. While economic implications are applied to exchange relationships in the parallel-political marketplace, the dominant focus is on the political and legal features of exchange. The focal values of political exchanges are related to the benefits and costs derived from interacting with authority. Thus, political market transactions center on exchanges involving information, authority, and social legitimacy, rather than the exchange of products and monetary resources. The outcome of this exchange process depends on the bargaining, negotiation, and sources of conflict between parties (Stern and Reve 1980; Hutt, Mokwa and Shapiro 1986).

While the concept only applies to conventional consumer groups (such as trade associations), the approach shows a potential use of political action in combination with economic incentive by government to intervene in the marketing decision process and, in turn, affect voluntary response among businesses. Recently, a variety of theories and frameworks have been advanced that explore the interface between marketing and political action. Some center on the role of government as a regulator (e.g., Harris 1984; Harris and Carman 1983; Krapfel 1982; Pearce 1979), while others explore the government as a marketer (cf. Apaiwongse 1991a; Capon 1981, Mokwa and Permut 1981). In turn, there are discussions of marketing practitioners as political actors (e.g., Pearce 1983). However, relatively little attention has been given to the inherent polity and economy as an exchange within and around markets in the context of an environmental setting.

Conceptually, the parallel-political marketplace framework aggregates exchange activities from a societal perspective, and the exchange identifies the dyadic interaction between buyer and seller (see also Apaiwongse 1991b; Dwyer, Schurr, and Oh 1987). There has been, however, little attention to defining "exchange" in the voluntary interaction (Frazier, Spekman, and O'Neal 1988). More recently, an effort has begun to explore the voluntary exchange between industrial firms and regulatory agencies from the ecological marketing standpoint (Apaiwongse 1991b; 1992; 1993a).

Conceptual Application

The concept is integral to the framework devised for the present study. As formulated by Bagozzi (1977), the emerging new concept views voluntary exchange as the foundation underlying marketing.

Green Voluntary Policy

One specific existing policy known as the "Bubble" combines market strategies with voluntary policy of regulatory alternatives as an economic incentive to motivate industries to accelerate pollution reduction. This innovative "Bubble" policy of the EPA brings a flexible marketing concept to the control of air pollution. In fact, the Bubble policy capitalizes upon the exchange relationship between industry and government to achieve a specific ecologically related marketing goal.

Under the Clean Air Act, the EPA is responsible for assuring that each state enforces air pollution level standards. The approach adopted in state implementation plans has been to specify exact limits on the amount of pollutants that might be discharged by each emission source in industrial plants. The Bubble concept sets overall limits on pollutants for an entire plant instead, allowing business to determine the most appropriate mix of controls on the emission sources within the plant. A company could then be innovative in altering the pollution rates of the emission sites in the plant as long as the air pollution through the Bubble stack meets EPA requirements. In principle, the Bubble approach allows substantial savings to industry without relaxing mandated reductions in air pollution. On the contrary, the Bubble policy manifests its own problems. For instance, complaints among industrial firms focus on certain crippling restrictions of the Bubble policy and the EPA's immobilizing bureaucracy. In addition, the Bubble policy statement does not establish conclusively how the EPA resolves issues in individual cases. Certainly, the perception among industrial firms of this regulatory uncertainty will influence their policy responses.

Political Marketers' Roles

Clearly, the advancement of the political marketplace concept is enhanced by the green voluntary policy. Viewing the policy as an economic incentive in a marketplace, the author looks at the green policy as a commodity being exchanged between political marketers (as applied to business and government), who can be characterized as buyers and sellers, or vice versa. Exchanges occur when there are regulatory transactions, on the selling of regulatory ideas and information for policy reaction (buying). Additionally, the means of the exchange can be seen as ideas from submitted proposals by firms, and approval of proposals by government agencies, the EPAs. The buying function represents the submission of a proposal by a firm, and the selling function represents the approval of the proposal by the EPA. The commodities being sold and bought consist of the final submission of a green policy proposal by business to government. Thus, business plays dual marketing roles as a buyer for policy information or ideas and as a seller of a green proposal. Government attempts to sell information or policy to business, and therefore plays the role of a seller. It later attempts to approve the business policy proposal, thus playing the role of a buyer.

Market-Maven and Its Center

Marketing center is "an informal decision unit which was a more nebulous construct, reaching across functional boundaries, whose composition, hierarchical levels, lines of communication, etc. were not strictly prescribed by an organizational chart or official document" (Spekman 1978). Numerous studies (see also Deshpande and Webster 1989; McCabe 1987) have characterized marketing centers as buyers and those buying decisions often are made by committees or buying centers whose members typically represent different departments and have different interests and motivations.

Grounded by the concept of the parallel-political marketplace, this chapter offers a contemporary view of a marketing center as a dual-dyadic center whose members' roles are those of both buyer and seller. In the context of the political marketing interface between business and government, the author calls the dual buying/selling role-players "market-mavens." Extending the concept of market-maven introduced by Feick and Price (1987), market-mavens here are characterized as influencers and opinion leaders who have more detailed information and expertise or knowledge about the green policy as well as its alternatives. They also voluntarily discuss and require from regulatory agencies policy information related to the submission of a green proposal.

Thus, in this study, the "market-maven centers" are defined metaphorically (i.e., they do not exist as formal units so named) as groups of officials in a company who explore the alternatives available to them in their effort to keep air emissions within the limits set by government regulators. This center is a formal or informal cross-departmental decision unit in which the objective is the decision to submit a voluntary policy proposal to the EPA. These centers respond to the green policy and submit a green proposal to their respective EPA offices. For the present study, a market-maven center refers to a decision unit whose members participate in buying/selling-related decisions. Operationally, membership in a market-maven center is determined by the key company environmental official responsible for the decision to submit the policy proposal to the EPA.

RESEARCH CONCEPTUALIZATION

To explain voluntary reaction, this chapter investigates three sets of factors: policy benefit, policy uncertainty, and adaptability of market-maven centers. The literature from several fields suggests that these factors are likely to be the dominant explanatory variables (see Rogers and Shoemaker 1971). A detailed discussion of the independent and dependent variables and their relationships follows.

Dependent Variable

The dependent variable of interest is the voluntary reaction among market-mavens toward acceptance of the green policy. A voluntary reaction refers to voluntary commitment, and the type of voluntary response being considered here is regarded as a decision to submit a green proposal to government regulators. In light of current appeals for global concern about protecting the environment, emphasis is placed on voluntary commitment to the green policy. This commitment can be attributed to a voluntary response above and beyond that warranted by economic factors.

Broadening the Diffusion theory as pioneered by Rogers and Shoemaker (1971), favorable reaction to the innovative green policy could be divided into two explicit concepts of attitude and behavior. It is important to differentiate between these two factors because attitude does not always predict behavior; it is possible for an individual market-maven to reject a group decision attitudinally while nonetheless conforming to the buying behavior of the group, for example. Rogers and Shoemaker (1971) assert that "overt behavior can be manipulated by the organization, at least in the short run, but the members' attitudes affect continued accepting versus rejecting." Because of the potential for this dichotomy of attitude and action (Festinger 1964), voluntary reaction is a more valid dependent variable than is overt buying behavior or even actual use of an innovation. Moreover, people generally react to an innovation by assessing its usefulness, and form favorable or unfavorable beliefs accordingly (Fishbein 1963). Furthermore, confidence in a choice evaluation is also a function of belief, which produces a reaction among buyers (Farley, Howard, and Ring 1974).

Thus, the operationalization of the voluntary reaction is accomplished by having individual members in a market-maven center complete a five-point Likert scale indicating agreement/disagreement with two statements that assess the degree of belief and confidence the respondents feel about their decision to submit a green proposal to the EPA regulators.

Independent Variables

Three factors explored in this study affect voluntary reaction to the green-policy proposal: (1) the perceived benefit, (2) the perceived uncertainty (or barrier) about the green policy, and (3) adaptation of the structure and climate by market-maven centers.

1. *Policy Benefit:* This variable concerns the attributes of the green policy that affect its favorable reaction. Attributes capable of predicting responses to group innovations are extensively examined by Fliegel and Kivlin (1966), as well as Lin and Zaltman (1973). Rogers and Shoemaker (1971) conclude that "almost every research work reports a positive relationship between relative advantage and rate of adoption." The subdimensions of relative advantage are the degree of economic profitability, the low initial cost, the rate of cost recovery, the financial return, the continuing cost, the time savings and the pay-off. However, Hughes (1980) believes that the body of theory and empirical knowledge presently available does not comprehensively explain the relationship between relative advantage and the rate of favorable reaction in the areas of government-business interface and regulatory reform. This discussion suggests:

> H_1: The greater the benefit of the green policy as perceived by market-mavens, the more favorable the reaction to the policy.

> H_2: Voluntary reaction among market-mavens becomes more favorable when the green policy is (a) a more advantageous way to meet air quality standards, (b) more financially feasible to implement, (c) less expensive to operate, and (d) more energy-efficient.

2. *Policy Uncertainty:* Policy uncertainty seems to be a component of the broader concept of environmental uncertainty, as proposed by Lawrence and Lorsch (1967) and Duncan (1972). Research and theory development have shown this concept to be multidimensional (Aldrich 1979, Downey, Hillriegel and Slocum 1975) and difficult to measure (Tosi, Aldag, and Storey 1973). The

focus of the present study is more restricted. The author pursues policy uncertainty, or unpredictability of policy, as a specific component of environmental uncertainty with which market-mavens must cope.

Though there is some evidence that environmental factors tend to cause uncertainty in decision making among business (Jaworski 1988), one study indicates that "little research has been published on the effects of regulatory uncertainty on industrial innovation" (National Science Foundation 1979). The uncertainty about future policy may substantially increase the risk of commitment to adoption options. For instance, a study concludes that "the impact of regulation has delayed and even prevented innovation in a number of areas" (Rothwell 1981). Rothwell (1981) reports two main impacts of government policy on industries: first, the need to respond to the policy diverts technical and management resources away from the business innovation that enhances profit, and secondly, the firms do not have sufficient information to identify the optimum solution. Adoption decisions are clouded by unclear and rapidly changing policy, inconsistencies between local and federal policy, and the creation of an uncertainty climate (see Manners and Nason 1979). However, the concept of policy uncertainty as perceived by industrial market-mavens has not been investigated empirically. For this study, perceptual measures of uncertainty are modified from the works of Lawrence and Lorsch (1967); Duncan (1972); and the NSF (1979).

Difficulty in predicting the green policy is expected to have a negative effect on voluntary reaction. Uncertainty of the policy heightens perceived potential vulnerability with government agencies and makes a firm less susceptible to react favorably. (For an elaboration of the logic of this expectation, see Apaiwongse 1991a). The following hypotheses, therefore, flow from these considerations:

H_3: The greater the uncertainty of the green policy as perceived by market-mavens, the less favorable is the voluntary reaction to the green policy.

H$_4$: Voluntary reaction among market-mavens becomes more favorable when the green policy is (a) more predictable (b) more informative, and (c) less ambiguous.

3. *Adaptability of a Market-Maven Center:* In this chapter, the market-maven center is defined metaphorically as the group of company officials who participate in investigating acceptable methods of meeting air-emission standards. This center is a formal or informal cross-departmental decision unit in which the objective is the decision to submit a voluntary policy proposal to the EPA. Operationally, membership in a market-maven center is determined by the key company environmental official responsible for the decision to submit the policy proposal to the EPA.

Information and uncertainty theory are integral to the concept of a market-maven center. Kohli (1989) mentions that the decision unit is conceptualized as an open system in continual interaction with its environment. A crucial function the unit may carry out in adapting to environmental uncertainty is the gathering and processing of information. The decision unit's structure is viewed as the critical variable in determining the unit's information processing potential and, therefore, its adaptive response and innovative adoption. Regrettably, there are only a few empirical studies concerning marketing centers (Wind 1978; Gronhaugh and Bonoma 1980; McCabe 1987).

Although multifaceted methods of measuring group adaption are discussed in sociology literature, this chapter focuses on two dimensions introduced by Hemphill and Westie (1950): (1) flexible structure, and (2) personal climate. These dimensions have been studied extensively in the context of organizational adoption of innovations, and measures have been developed for these dimensions that have been carefully validated and replicated across a wide variety of different organizations.

The flexible structure dimension consists of autonomy, flexibility, and stratification (see Appendix). Payne and Pugh (1976) indicate that "autonomy was similar to the organizational concept of decentralization, and that flexibility was the inverse of structured work activities. Stratification resembled the organizational indicator, height of hierarchy or vertical span." The flexibility and stratification dimensions can be compared to the formalization dimension introduced by Hage and Aiken (1970).

The personal climate dimension consists of intimacy, participation, polarization, viscidity and coordination (see Appendix). Climate dimension is designated as "effective synergy" (Cattell 1948). Effective synergy is defined as the unified reaction that emerges as the dynamic intention of the group per se. The energy is expressed through the accomplishment of the outside goals for which the group works together. "Intimacy" reflects the degree of "togetherness" among members within the market-maven center. "Participation" refers to the energy invested in market-maven center activities by each member. "Polarization" identifies effective behavior among market-mavens. Finally, "high viscidity" represents a condition in which a minimum amount of internal friction exists within the market-maven center.

Several studies indicate that organizations that are low in emergent structure are likely to have more favorable attitudes toward innovation adoption than those that are more structured (Hage & Aiken 1970). Thus, effective synergy, along with its components, represents adaptability in a group structure.

The application of contingency theory to the favorable reaction (or buying) function requires the modification of the concept of environmental uncertainty and center structure. The adaptability of a marketing center structure is characterized by a high reliance on personal interaction in decision making among the individual members of a market-maven center, less emphasis on hierarchy or stratification, and a high degree of autonomy and formalization. The personal interaction among the members of a marketing center is characterized in terms of its intimacy, participation, viscidity, polarization, effective synergy, and coordination.

In this chapter, the adaptability of a market-maven center is measured against all group dimensions. The adaptability of the structure is characterized by a high reliance on some dimensions (intimacy, participation, polarization, viscidity, effective synergy, and coordination), less emphasis on hierarchy or stratification, and a high degree of flexibility and autonomy. The adaptability of the market-maven center's structure and climate is expected to be positively associated with its members' favorable reaction to the green policy.

Hence, the preceding discussion provides a conceptual foundation for the examination of the following hypotheses:

H_5: The greater the adaptability of the market-maven centers, the more favorable is the voluntary reaction to the green policy.

H_6: Voluntary reaction among market-mavens becomes more favorable when the market-maven centers' structure and climate are more (a) effectively synergistic (b) coordinated, (c) polarized (d) rule flexible, (e) autonomous, and (f) stratified.

RESEARCH METHODOLOGY

Measures

Several measures were developed for the study with a view to addressing the limitations of previously used measures. An initial pool of items was generated from available measures, extensive literature search, construct domains, and the context in which the measures were to be used. These items were revised on the basis of the comments of a panel of business executives and EPA agents. As recommended by Peter and Churchill (1986), items were not grouped by construct category wherever feasible, and the direction-ality of several items was reversed to improve the psychometric properties of the measures.

The survey questionnaire comprising the revised items was pre-tested carefully in three waves of 15 personal interviews with busi-ness executives involved in a green policy project. Each informant was asked to point out any difficulty or ambiguity in the instruc-tions or the questions asked. On the basis of the feedback received, the questionnaire was revised in successive waves until it was clear and easy to answer. The measures used in this study are listed in Tables 15.1, 15.2 and 15.3.

Data Collection

The population for this cross-sectional field study, as identified from information obtained from state and regional offices of the

EPA, was originally reported to be 63 firms. Names and addresses of participating firms, as well as the names of key executives, were obtained from the EPA. Responses from industrial firms indicated that 15 of the 63 reported by the EPA to have inquired about the green policy never decided to submit a proposal; as a result, the voluntary reaction among those market-mavens was never formed. Moreover, five firms declined to complete the questionnaire because no market-maven center of any type ever existed. Additionally, one firm withdrew its application for approval of its green policy proposal. The remaining 42 industrial firms constitute the entire population surveyed for this study and represent the steel, chemical, auto, and oil industries. Of the 42 firms actually submitting green proposals and forming market-maven centers for the policy decision, 33 (approximately 79%) responded with complete questionnaires.

A five-phase field study was used to collect data. These phases included contact with EPA officials, as well as company environmental executives, personal interviews, a pre-test, and a mail survey. Of the 88 questionnaires returned, all but five responses were complete enough to be included in the analysis. An average of three responses was obtained from each of the 33 firms having market-maven centers. In each of these firms there were four to six potential respondents. An assessment of the response rate could not be based on the number of questionnaires mailed in this study since they were not necessarily the numbers that were distributed within each market-maven center. No accurate information exists on the actual number of questionnaires distributed by key environmental officials. Thus, actual responses might be compared only approximately to the potential number of respondents as specified by key officials. Using this gross estimate, a response rate of 52% was obtained.

DATA ANALYSIS

The reliability of each of the study measures was estimated by computing its Cronbach alpha. Scale items with low interim correlations were eliminated. Next, items composing the various scales were factor analyzed (common factor method with varimax rotation) to access their convergent and discriminant validity. Each item represents an independent attempt to measure a particular construct. Accordingly, all items of a scale should load strongly on one factor if they are to satisfy the requirements of convergent validity and should load weakly on all other factors to satisfy the requirements of discriminant validity.

The factor analysis was validated using a split-half method, and

TABLE 15.1. Factor Analysis (Varimax Rotation) of Benefit from Green Policy

	Factor Description		
QUESTION CONTENT	**I**	**II**	**Communality**
1. Green Policy minimizes operation costs incurred to maintain an approved air quality control method.	**.94162**	.09503	.88665
2. Green Policy offers the most financially feasible way of implementing an approval air quality control method.	**.92394**	.16853	.85366
3. Green Policy affords the most beneficial way, among available alternatives, to meet air quality standards.	**.89862**	.27203	.80751
4. Green policy requires less energy consumption than other approved ways of meeting air quality standards.	**.76559**	.63957	.58613
Percentage of Variance	78.3		
Eigenvalue	3.13		
Cronbach's ∝	0.91		
Cumulative variance explained by one factor:	78.30%		

TABLE 15.2. Factor Analysis (Varimax Rotation) of Uncertainty from Green Policy

FACTOR DESCRIPTION

QUESTION CONTENT	I LACKNOW	II AMBIPOL	III LACKINFO	Communality
[I] LACK OF KNOWLEDGE AND EXPECTATION				
1. Can determine if a proposal will be approved. Expected Consequence	**.89940**	−0.11421	.13607	.83142
2. Can predict how the restriction of the regulations will affect the proposal approval.	**.88835**	−0.05485	.13534	.74120
3. Know what action to take to meet expectations of regulation.	**.84001**	−0.08610	.13824	.57359
[II] AMBIGUITY OF GREEN POLICY				
1. Unavailability of modified policies, in view of altered circumstances, affect the decision to submit the proposal.	.04240	**0.75145**	.01288	.38378
2. Policy is ambiguous to the point that affects the decision to submit the proposal.	.24207	**0.73798**	−.29902	.66071
3. Delays by regulators in clarifying policies will affect the decision.	−.29246	**0.68752**	−.21416	.52937

FACTOR DESCRIPTION

QUESTION CONTENT	I LACKNOW	II AMBIPOL	III LACKINFO	Communality
4. The air pollution control policies are flexible enough to encourage the proposal submission.	.24661	-0.67225	.14665	.41638
5. Revision of policies affect the decision to submit the proposal.	.15806	0.61274	.09918	.18996
[III] LACK OF ENOUGH INFORMATION				
1. The adequacy of information about conflicts and inconsistencies of policies is adequate for decision.	.14675	-0.05025	.95262	.83789
2. Can get information necessary for making the decision to submit a proposal.	.18903	-0.16661	.93310	.93922
Percentage of Variance	57.7	22.8	19.4	
Eigenvalue	3.5	1.4	1.2	
Cronbach's ∝	0.9	0.8	0.9	
Cumulative variance explained by three factors:	70.6%			

TABLE 15.3. Factor Analysis (Varimax Rotation) of Market-Maven Adaptability

QUESTION CONTENT	Factor Description						Communality
	I	II	III	IV	V	VI	
	EFFSYN	COOR	STRAT	RULFLX	POLAR	AUTO	
[I] EFFECTIVE SYNERGY							
1. Good distribution of project responsibilities.	**.86503**	.21907	.10154	-.12354	.02439	.04829	.82478
2. Share the same views.	**.85846**	.17242	.10641	-.10818	.11387	-.04989	.80516
3. Work done by capable members.	**.85612**	.29875	.07794	-.07764	.07869	.09458	.84944
4. Incompatibility among members.	**-.76565**	-.41255	.01222	.02452	-.14477	-.09363	.78690
5. Members know each other well.	**.75832**	.16739	.05499	-.07207	.33329	.14477	.74333
6. Members do small favors for one another.	**.73622**	.11388	.19199	-.06345	.15525	.09834	.62964
7. Work together as a team.	**.69098**	.28065	-.11982	-.20524	.09046	.09081	.62913
[II] COORDINATION							
1. Members do their jobs properly without getting in each other's way.	.23969	**.89502**	-.01539	-.05765	.03066	-.01937	.86339
2. All efforts geared in the direction of the proposed submission.	.22930	**.87889**	.11406	-.09904	.12060	.06658	.86679
3. Different activities fit together.	.23597	**.87371**	.12851	-.11812	.06839	.02488	.85481
4. Members make an effort to avoid creating problems.	.26507	**.85925**	.02828	-.12283	.08915	.03132	.83338
5. Related activities well timed.	.24335	**.82835**	.13568	-.16146	-.11431	-.01275	.80309

QUESTION CONTENT	Factor Description						Communality
	I EFFSYN	II COOR	III STRAT	IV RULFLX	V POLAR	VI AUTO	
[III] STRATIFICATION							
1. All members' opinions are considered equally important.	.10656	.01493	**.90714**	-.20088	.09179	-.01492	.88348
2. Mutual decision regarding the task at hand.	.08175	.09645	**.87729**	-.14646	.04800	-.12129	.82408
3. Members' standing by their contributions.	-.06732	-.20599	**.85861**	.20207	-.06292	.08724	.83658
[IV] RULE FLEXIBILITY							
1. Hold meetings at regularly scheduled times.	-.10878	-18890	-.21675	**.85260**	-.01503	.05553	.82473
2. Follow basic guidelines for making decisions.	-.13496	-.18907	-.09948	**.80205**	.05269	.12550	.72606
3. Vote on all decision matters.	-.17505	-.05528	-.27971	**.76975**	-.17600	.04632	.73757
[V] POLARIZATION							
1. Goal direction toward the proposed submission goal.	.30703	.17474	-.12269	-.01228	**.79854**	.06368	.78173
2. Division of project responsibilities.	-.04829	-.02310	.19194	-.04237	**.73567**	-.00412	.58273
3. A clear idea of a project goal.	.39844	.12870	.02650	.00346	**.71503**	.13407	.70528
4. Work under close supervision.	.18282	.34899	.12653	-.08764	**.40976**	-.03360	.34795

TABLE 15.3 (continued)

QUESTION CONTENT	Factor Description						
	I	II	III	IV	V	VI	Communality
	EFFSYN	COOR	STRAT	RULFLX	POLAR	AUTO	
[VI] AUTONOMY							
1. Members consult with various departments.	.32547	–.02071	–.04849	.14337	.02631	.88275	.90920
2. Members represent different departments.	.27076	–.06488	–.03122	.08424	.04682	.87437	.85230
3. Work independently of various departments.	.15665	–.11546	.11961	–.01143	–.04973	–.66308	.49382
Percentage of Variance	34.9	13.9	9.5	6.5	6.1	5.0	
Eigenvalue	8.7	3.4	2.4	1.6	1.5	1.2	
Cronbach's ∝	0.9	0.9	0.9	0.8	0.7	0.7	
Cumulative variance explained by six factors:	76.0%						

all factors were identified and labeled as a result of a factor vari-max.

Reliability tests showed strong Cronbach alphas ranging from 0.7 through 0.9 (see Tables 15.1, 15.2, and 15.3). It may be seen that the analysis produces a clean factor structure with items loading on the appropriate factors. With only a few items being deleted because of low or incorrect loading, the measures of all constructs show excellent validity. Factors having eigenvalues greater than 1 emerged from the factor analysis, each corresponding to a different type of construct, suggesting that the measures successfully tap the constructs they were designed to measure.

All items demonstrate very high convergent and discriminant validity by loading strongly on the factors they were designed to measure and weakly on other factors, with the exception of an item designed to measure formal polarization (item 4 of the polarization scale in Table 15.3). The item does not load strongly on any factor and it is not clear whether this loading represents a lack of discrimination validity. To avoid any possible confounding, however, the item was eliminated from further analysis. The intimacy, participation and, viscidity items load on the same factors, lending support to the argument advancing the same underlying dimension–effective synergy. The intimacy, participation, and viscidity items therefore were combined to form a measure of effective synergy.

The retained items were factor analyzed again and their reliability estimates recomputed. The results indicate that the convergent and discriminant validity and the reliability of the scales used in the subsequent analyses are very high.

The relative importance of the various individual variables was investigated by estimating the following conceptual regression model:

$$VOLREACT = \alpha + \beta_1 BENEFIT + \beta_2 UNCERTAINTY + \beta_3 ADAPTABILITY$$

[1] **BENEFIT** $= f$ { RELADV, FINFEAS, COSTMIN, ENREDUC }

Where:

VOLREACT is voluntary reaction to the green policy among market-mavens.
RELADV is relative advantage among available alternatives to meet air quality standards.

FINFEAS is financially feasible way of implementing an approval air quality control method.

COSTMIN is operating cost minimization incurred to maintain an approved air quality control method.

ENREDUC is energy reduction compared to other approved ways of meeting air quality standards.

[2] **UNCERTAINTY** = f { LACKNOW, LACKINF, AMBIPOL }

Where:

LACKNOW is lack of knowledge of outcomes, prediction, and expectation.
LACKINF is lack of information regarding the green policy.
AMBIPOL is ambiguity of the green policy and delayed feedback.

[3] **ADAPTABILITY** = f { EFFSYN, COOR, STRAT, RULFLX, POLAR, AUTO }

Where:

EFFSYN is effective synergy among market-mavens.
COOR is coordination among market-mavens.
STRAT is stratification among market-mavens.
RULFLX is rule flexibility of the market-maven centers.
POLAR is polarization of the market-maven centers.
AUTO is autonomy among market-mavens.

Thus, the purified regression model is:

$$\text{VOLREACT} = \alpha + \text{ß}_1\text{RELADV} + \text{ß}_2\text{FINFEAS} + \text{ß}_3\text{COSTMIN} + \text{ß}_4\text{ENREDUC} + \text{ß}_5\text{LACKNOW} + \text{ß}_6\text{LACKINF} + \text{ß}_7\text{AMBIPOL} + \text{ß}_8\text{EFFSYN} + \text{ß}_9\text{COOR} + \text{ß}_{10}\text{STRAT} + \text{ß}_{11}\text{RULFLX} + \text{ß}_{12}\text{POLAR} + \text{ß}_{13}\text{AUTO}$$

The next step, following the treatment suggested by developers of the measures, was to form cumulative, equally weighted indices for each of the ten measures so as to develop scores for each case. Scale items were summed to form measures of the corresponding variables. When data for any of the scale items for any construct included in the regression equation was missing, the case was eliminated. As a further validation check, the sample was split randomly and Cronbach alphas were recalculated for the indices on each subsample. Alphas continued to be excellent with a range of 0.7 to 0.9.

In order to measure Voluntary Reaction, a simple additive index was formed of the responses to the two questions on voluntary reaction. This additive index of voluntary reaction was then utilized as the dependent variable in an ordinary least squares regression. The three dimensions of uncertainty, six dimensions of adaptability, and the measure of benefit were the predictor variables. Results of the regression analysis are displayed in Table 15.4. As the table shows, the overall regression equation explains 87.1% of the total variance, a result that is statistically significant at the 0.0001 level. In order to test for internal validity of this result, the sample was

TABLE 15.4. Multiple Regression Analysis of Voluntary Reaction

Dependent Variable: Voluntary Reaction (VOLREACT)

Independent Variables:	Standardized Beta Coefficient	F	Significance
Policy Benefit:	0.85	78.30	0.0010
Relative Advantage (READV)	0.70	63.08	0.0010
Financial Feasibility (FINFEA)	0.71	67.29	0.0010
Cost Minimization (COMIN)	0.70	64.05	0.0010
Energy Reduction (ENRED)	0.53	55.03	0.0010
Policy Uncertainty:	0.50	22.01	0.0010
Lack of Knowledge (LACKNOW)	−0.62	53.79	0.0001
Lack of Information (LACKINF)	−0.30	12.89	0.0010
Ambiguity of Policy (AMBIPOL)	0.03	0.01	0.9720
Market-Maven's Adaptability:	0.60	20.70	0.0001
Effective Synergy (EFFSYN)	0.53	55.73	0.0001
Coordination (COOR)	0.53	54.82	0.0001
Polarization (POLAR)	0.21	8.24	0.0050
Flexibility of Rule (RULFLX)	−0.13	3.46	0.0670
Autonomy (AUTO)	−0.09	1.98	0.1640
Stratification (STRAT)	0.06	0.07	0.9330

Overall F = 47.11 Significance = .0001 Adjusted R^2 = 0.871

split randomly into halves and the regression recomputed. Both standardized betas and the estimate of explained variance remained stable, suggesting the results reported here are not due to chance.

Going beyond the summary R^2 statistic, the contributions of individual independent variables produce interesting findings. First, it appears that benefit, uncertainty, and adaptability are major determinants of the voluntary reaction among market-mavens. The standardized beta weights are statistically significant. In general, all independent variables are significant predictors of voluntary reaction: benefit ($ß = .85$, $p < .001$), uncertainty ($ß = .50$, $p < .001$), and adaptability ($ß = .60$, $p < .0001$). These findings substantively support H_1, H_3 and H_5.

All of the benefit attributes regarding the green policy are also significant predictors of voluntary reaction: relative advantage ($ß = 0.70$, $p < .001$), financial feasibility ($ß = 0.71$, $p < .001$), cost minimization ($ß = 0.70$, $p < .001$), and energy reduction ($ß = .53$, $p < .001$). These results support H_2.

For the uncertainty attributes, lack of knowledge about prediction or expectation ($ß = -.62$, $p < .0001$) and lack of information about the policy ($ß = -.30$, $p < .001$) are related to voluntary reaction. The ambiguity of policy, in contrast, has an insignificant effect on voluntary reaction ($ß = 0.03$, $p = .970$). Therefore, H_4 is partially supported.

Among the adaptability variables, effective synergy ($ß = .53$, $p < .0001$), coordination ($ß = .53$, $p < .0001$), polarization ($ß = .21$, $p < .005$), and rule flexibility ($ß = -.13$, $p < .067$) have significant impacts on the voluntary reaction. However, autonomy ($ß = -0.09$, $p = .16$) and stratification ($ß = 0.06$, $p = .933$) are unrelated to voluntary reaction. These results partially supported H_6.

IMPLICATIONS AND CONCLUSIONS

The survey findings seem to hold several important managerial and public policy implications for marketing practitioners, both industrial marketers and regulators. An astute business is always looking for the best deal; when market-mavens perceive greater benefit from the green policy than the conventional ones, they are more likely to react favorably to it. The study identified three positive attributes that predict favorable reaction to (or adoption) of the green voluntary policy. Its relative advantage among public policy options and financial benefit are better predictors (in a possibly differential ranking) than a third attribute, energy-consumption savings, which is a good predictor, although it exerts less impact on the decision to adopt the policy.

Conversely, uncertainty attributes imposed by the green policy itself discourage adoption. Lack of knowledge (concerning outcomes, predictions, and expectations) and the lack of enough information for decision making were both barriers. When the administrative climate of the green policy is unclear and ambiguous, companies react unfavorably. Additionally, a dearth of policy information makes market-mavens uneasy. The fact that they feel unable to predict the result of a green policy proposal submission and the general confusion about how to meet the expectation of the green policy and its regulators prompts market-mavens to react unfavorably.

Implications for Marketing Managers

In this study, the market-maven centers are groups of officials in a company who explore the alternatives available to them in their effort to keep air emissions within the limits set by government regulators. These centers make the decision to submit a green proposal to their respective EPA offices. Informed by standard organization theory, the study indicates that market-maven centers that are less formally structured and whose climate favors personal relationships are more inclined to choose the green voluntary policy as the most viable alternative. Market-maven centers that are more flexible in terms of rules and procedures for performing tasks and whose members demonstrate a cooperative spirit are significantly more likely to adopt a green voluntary policy.

The individuals in these progressive centers are team players who function in a climate marked by viscidity, intimacy, and polarization. Their relationships are close and productive, and they can, without dissension and personal conflict, work toward a single goal that is clear and specific.

The fact that regulatory choices have become more complex and that regulatory alternatives have left a communication void between government regulators and business firms (Hughes 1980) created a general climate of uncertainty within market-maven centers. Clearly, though, centers that are open, flexible, cooperative, and goal-oriented are best prepared to make choices in today's regulatory milieu. The voluntary alternative approach makes better business sense, but it requires progressive interpersonal skills and team-orientation among the market-mavens.

Implications for Policy Makers and Regulators

The concept of ecological marketing and banking of pollution rights was an outgrowth of the establishment of performance standards by the Federal EPA. A regulatory innovation such as the Bubble concept created an alternative to the command-and-control model. Market-like incentives energize the response of business to environmental mandates. A study by Hughes (1980) demonstrated that environmental goals could be reached at lesser cost when economic incentives were introduced. Within this framework, Armco devised a low-cost, dust-control program inside a steel plant, projecting a savings of $42 million in pollution abatement costs if the technique were introduced at its major steel plants (Yao 1981). The market-like incentives better serve the needs of both industry and the EPA.

Progress in environmental protection is a two-way street, however. Just as market-mavens must lay aside turfism to bring about the kind of cooperative communication that produces astute, market-worthy approaches to air emission control, regulatory agencies must likewise be willing to abandon traditional bureaucratic obstructionism and obfuscation to achieve the environmental goals for which they were purportedly created. A free flow of information between the regulatory agency and industry enhances a business firm's ability to make the most cost-effective choices. Market transaction in emission control can be made more efficient when both business firms (or buyers) and government agencies (or sellers) understand the full costs and benefits associated with the transactions they undertake (Hughes 1980). Regulatory agencies in particular need to understand that they can reap benefits by becoming more efficient and less adversarial. Frustration, unpredictable results from proposal submission, excessive government paperwork, and needless delay deal market-mavens a stressful uncertainty that tends to paralyze environmental progress, compromising the voluntary green policy in particular.

Moreover, an aggressive marketing approach on the part of regulators could stimulate market-mavens' awareness of the regulatory alternatives and their advantages. According to diffusion theory, industrial organizations require continual guidance during the voluntary reaction process if a new program is to meet with favor. The EPA can foster positive attitudes toward the green policy by accurately informing its clients in a timely manner. Information-gathering is critical to this process, and is affected by both the market-mavens' information processing activities and the amount and quality of policy information available. As the present study indicates, market-mavens generally recognize the conflicts, confusions, and inconsistencies between state and federal laws concerning environmental measures and standards, to say nothing of their sometimes inherent impracticality. These uncertainties prompt unfavorable reaction to new regulatory alternatives.

To reduce the uncertainty and make informed, cost-effective choices, the market-mavens must have clear information from the government agencies about comparative costs and benefits, risks, and social effects, and other data regarding the command-and-control and voluntary alternative options. When the government agency provides such material and it informs a company's decision, the market-mavens would become convinced that the voluntary alternative is the most attractive option. A valuable by-product of this interchange would be the development of mutual credibility and trust between regulator and regulatee.

In sum, the information exchange process just described is a powerful tool that can illuminate rational environmental choices made by market-mavens responsible for air emission control. An encounter format that trades unilateral government intervention for mutually beneficial interaction would be welcomed by business in government agencies at the federal, state, and local level. Just as environmental consciousness itself redefines our relationship to Earth, supplanting conscious or unconscious adversariality with partnership, the new green policy alternatives must redefine the interaction of business and government. An atmosphere of trust and understanding will clear the air and make faster, more efficient response to air quality mandates possible. Environmental harmony is enhanced when human beings are willing to beat their swords into plowshares and, together, get the job done.

Future Research Directions

Interpersonal relationships among market-mavens surfaced as a key to favorable response to green policies. The nature and frequency of this internal communication ought to be explored more intensively than was possible with mail surveys. On-site data collection could provide a more technical analysis of these networks. The generally flawed communication between company executives and government regulators also bears examination, particularly as it operates in negotiations about marketing. An overall study encompassing interactions between the two previously mentioned dyads would provide more global insight into the process.

Further study of the voluntary reaction could clarify the complex process that commits a company to a particular regulatory track. Longitudinal surveys of different regulatory options would provide data for causal analysis of the reaction process, especially the initiation and implementation phases.

Replication studies could verify the results of this research and strengthen its generalizations; multi-trait/multi-method investigation is suggested. Such an analysis can offer new constructs and operationalizations that may further understanding of voluntary reaction and attitude toward the green policies. Specifically, a researcher might compare the results of objective and protocol measures with their subjective, or perceptual, counterparts.

Further research could bring other relevant variables into the hypotheses. Market-maven demographic variables–size, type of industry, and so on–may have some bearing on policy reaction. A study of the consensus process and the multiple responses upon which it is built might improve the predictability of the hypotheses, although the complexity of consensus measures defy easy assessment by any one experimental design.

Although considerable further study of both business and government factors is needed, policy choices are sometimes impacted by third parties: public citizen groups, environmental organizations, and local citizens in affected communities. These groups can be very vocal and often shape public opinion in high-interest industry vs. environment cases. What role do–or should–third parties and the public play in the regulation adoption process?

Technical research could clarify the different types of regulatory alternatives, increasing our understanding of the specific factors that prompt adoption of particular regulation options. Finally, research that compares the amount and type of generalization that exists among government regulations would be useful.

APPENDIX

The structure category consists of the following dimensions:

1.1 *Autonomy*–the degree to which a market-maven center functions independently from other groups. Autonomy is reflected by the degree to which a market-maven center determines its own activities, by its absence of allegiance, dependence relative to other groups.

1.2 *Flexibility*–the degree to which a market-maven center's activities are marked by informal procedure rather than by adherence to established procedures. Flexibility is reflected in the extent to which duties of members are free from specification by company regulations.

1.3 *Stratification*–the degree to which a market-maven center orders its members into status hierarchies. Stratification is reflected by differential distribution of power, contributions, and duties.

The climate category consists of the following dimensions:

2.1 *Intimacy*–the degree to which members of the market-maven center are mutually acquainted with one another. Intimacy is reflected by modes of greeting with preferences of the other members.

2.2 *Participation*–the degree to which members of the market-maven center apply time and effort to the policy reaction.

2.3 *Polarization*–the degree to which the market-maven center is oriented and works toward the policy goal that is clear and specific to all members.

2.4 V*iscidity*–the degree to which members of the market-maven center function as a unit. Viscidity is reflected by absence of dissension and personal conflict among members, by sharing the same views on any project issues, and by working together as a team.

2.5 *Coordination*–the degree to which each member of a market-maven center operates according to the requirements of the other members and center.

REFERENCES

Aldrich, Howard E. (1979), *Organization and Environments* (Englewood Cliffs, NJ: Prentice Hall, Inc).

Apaiwongse, Tom Suraphol (1991a), "Factors Affecting Attitudes Among Buying-Center Members Toward Adoption of an Ecologically-Related Regulatory Alternative: A New Application of Organizational Theory to a Public Policy Issue," *Journal of Public Policy and Marketing*, 10, 2 (Fall), 145-160.

Apaiwongse, Tom Suraphol (1991b), "An Adaptation Among Buying Centers to a Policy Uncertainty: A Contingency Approach," *Atlantic Marketing Association Proceedings*, 370-373.

Apaiwongse, Tom Suraphol (1992), "Ecological Marketing: A Paradigm Lost," *Atlantic Marketing Association Proceedings*, 190-195.

Apaiwongse, Tom Suraphol (1993), "Market Responses to the EPA Policies," *Industrial Marketing Management*, 22, 319-330.

Arndt, Johan (1976), "Role of Product-Related Conversations in the Diffusion of New Products," *Journal of Marketing Research*, 4 (August), 291-295.

Arndt, Johan (1983), "The Political Economy Paradigm: Foundation for Theory Building in Marketing," *Journal of Marketing*, 47 (Fall), 44-54.

Bagozzi, Richard P. (1977), "Marketing at the Societal Level: Theoretical Issues and Problems," in Charles C. Slater (ed.), *Macro-Marketing: Distributive Process from a Societal Perspective* (Boulder, CO: Business Research Division, Graduate School of Business Administration, University of Colorado), 6-51.

Butler, Chad (1984), "New Source Netting and Non-Attainment Area Under the Clean Air Act," *Ecological Law Quarterly*, 3, 343-372.

Capon, Noel (1981), "Marketing Strategy Differences Between State and Privately Owned Businesses: An Exploratory Analysis," *Journal of Marketing*, 45 (Spring), 11-18.

Cateora, Philip R. (1993), *International Marketing* (Richard D. Irwin).

Cattell, R.B. (1948), "Concepts and Methods in the Measurement of Group Syntality," *Psychological Review*, 55, (January), 48-63.

D'Aquino, Niccolo (1992), "The New Green Europe," *Europe*, June, 9-10.

Deshpande, Rohit and Frederick E. Webster, Jr. (1989), "Organizational Culture and Marketing: Defining the Research Agenda," *Journal of Marketing*, 53, (January), 3-15.

Downey, H. Kirk, Don Hillriegel, and John W. Slocum, Jr. (1975), "Environmental Uncertainty: The Construct and Its Application," *Administrative Science Quarterly*, 20 (December), 613-629.

Duncan, Robert B. (1972), "Characteristics of Organizational Environments and Perceived Environmental Uncertainty," *Administrative Science Quarterly*, 7 (March), 313-327.

Dwyer, F. Robert, Paul H. Schurr, and Sejo Oh (1987), "Developing Buyer-Seller Relationships," *Journal of Marketing*, 51, (April), 11-27.

Farley, John U., John A. Howard, and L. Winston Ring (1974), *Consumer Behavior Theory and Application* (Boston: Allyn & Bacon), 11.

Feick, Lawrence F. and Linda L. Price (1987), "The Market-Maven: A Diffuser of Marketplace Information," *Journal of Marketing*, 51, 83-97.

Festinger, Leon (1964), "Behavioral Support for Opinion Change," *Public Opinion Quarterly*, 28, 404-417.

Fishbein, Martin (1963), "An Investigation of the Relationships Between Beliefs About an Object and the Attitude Toward that Object," *Human Relations*, 16, 223-240.

Fliegel, F.C. and J.E. Kivlin (1966), "Program Change and Organizational Properties," *American Journal of Sociology*, 72, (March), 313-327.

Frazier, Gary L., Robert E. Spekman, and Charles E. O'Neal (1988), "Just-In-Time Exchange Relationships in Industrial Markets," *Journal of Marketing*, 52 (October), 52-67.

Gronhaugh, Kjell and Thomas V. Bonoma (1980), "Industrial-Organizational Buying: A Derived Demand Perspective," in C. Lamb and P. Dunne (eds.), *Theoretical Development in Marketing* (Chicago: American Marketing Association), 224-228.

Hage, Jerald and Michael Aiken (1970), *Social Change in Complex Organizations*, (New York: Random House).

Harris, Robert G. and James M. Carman (1983), "Public Regulation of Marketing Activity: Part I: Institutional Typologies of Market Failure," *Journal of Macromarketing*, 3 (Spring), 49-58.

Harris, Robert G. (1984), "Public Regulation of Marketing Activity: Part II: Regulatory Responses to Market Failures," *Journal of Macromarketing*, 4 (Spring), 41-52.

Hemphill, John and Charles Westie (1950), "The Measurement of Group Dimensions," *Journal of Psychology*, 28, (April), 325-342.

Henion, Karl E. (1978), "Ecological Marketing: Will the Normative Model Become Descriptive?" in George Fisk, Johan Arndt, and Kjell Gronhaugh (eds.), *Future Direction for Marketing* (Marketing Science Institute), 301-311.

Henion, Karl E. (1980), "Values, Value Changes and Ecological Marketing," in George Fisk, Robert W. Nason, and Phillip D. White (eds.) *Macro-Marketing: Evolution of Thought* (Boulder, CO: Business Research Division, College of Business Administration, University of Colorado), 147-159.

Hughes, David G. (1980), "Marketers' Potential Contribution to Regulatory Reform," (Unpublished Working Paper, University of North Carolina, Chapel Hill), (August 15), 1-27.

Hutt, Michael D., Michael P. Mokwa, and Stanley J. Shapiro (1986), "The Politics of Marketing: Analyzing the Parallel Political Marketplace," *Journal of Marketing*, 50 (January), 40-51.

Jaworski, Bernard J. (1988), "Toward a Theory of Marketing Control: Environmental Context, Control Types, and Consequences," *Journal of Marketing*, 52, (July), 23-39.

Kohli, Ajay (1989), "Determinants of Influence in Organizational Buying: A Contingency Approach," *Journal of Marketing*, 53, (July), 50-65.

Krapfel, Robert E., Jr. (1982), "Marketing by Mandate," *Journal of Marketing*, 46 (Summer), 79-85.

Lawrence, P. and J. Lorsch (1967), *Organization and Environment, Managing Differentiating and Integration* (Boston, MA: Harvard University, Division of Research, Graduate School of Business Administration).

Lin, Nan and Gerald Zaltman (1973), "Dimensions of Innovations," in Gerald Zaltman (ed.), *Processes and Phenomena of Social Change* (New York: Wiley Interscience).

Manners, G.E. and H.K. Nason (1979), *Regulation and Innovation–Symbiote or Antithets?*, Six Countries Program National Science Foundation Workshop, The Hague, 11-13.

McCabe, Donald L. (1987), "Buying Group Structure: Constriction at the Top," *Journal of Marketing*, 51, (October), 89-98.

Mokwa, Michael P. and Steven E. Permut (1981), *Government Marketing Theory and Practice*, New York: Praeger.

National Science Foundation (NSF) (1979), "The Impact on Industrial Innovation of Environment, Health, and Safety (EHS) Regulations," paper submitted by NSF (Division of Policy Research and Analysis) to Honorable Jordan T. Baruch, Assistant Secretary for Science and Technology, U.S. Department of Commerce, March.

Payne, Roy and Derek Pugh (1976), "Organizational Structure and Climate," in Marvin D. Dunnette (ed.), *Handbook of Industrial and Organizational Psychology* (Chicago, IL: Rand McNally, College Publishing Company), 1125-1173.

Pearce, Michael (1979), "The Public Arena of Marketing," in Cynthia J. Frey, Thomas C. Kinnear, and Bonnie B. Reece, (eds.), *Public Policy Issues in Marketing*, Vol. 1 (Ann Arbor, MI: Division of Research, Graduate School of Business Administration, University of Michigan).

Pearce, Michael (1983), "The Marketing Practitioner as Political Actor," *Journal of Public Policy & Marketing*, 2, 82-99.

Peter, J. Paul and Gilbert A. Churchill, Jr. (1986), "Relationships Among Research Design Choices and Psychometric Properties of Rating Scales: A Meta Analysis," *Journal of Marketing Research*, 23 (February), 1-10.

Rogers, Everette M. and F. Floyd Shoemaker (1971), *Communication of Innovations: A Cross Cultural Approach* (New York: The Free Press).

Rothwell, Roy (1981), "The Impact of Regulation on Innovation: Some U.S. Data," *Technological Forecasting and Social Change*, 17, 7-34.

Schultze, Charles L. (1977), "The Public Use of Private Interest," *Regulation*, (September-October), 10-13.

Smith, Fred (1992), "Planning for a Better Environment," *The Wall Street Journal*, June 3, B-1.

Spekman, Robert E. (1978), "A Macro-Sociological Examination of the Industrial Buying-Center: Promise or Problem?" in Subhash C. Jain (ed.), *Research Frontiers in Marketing: Dialogues and Directions* (Chicago, IL: American Marketing Association), 111-115.

Stern, Louis W. and Troger Reve (1980), "Distribution Channels as Political Economies: A Framework for Comparative Analysis," *Journal of Marketing*, 44 (Summer), 52-64.

Taylor, Ronald A. (1992), "The Road to Rio," *Europe*, June, 12-13.

Thorelli, Hans B., "Markets as Networks: Political Science Revisited," in Paul F. Anderson and Michael J. Ryan (eds.) *1984 AMA Winter's Educators' Conference: Scientific Method in Marketing*, (Chicago: American Marketing Association, 101-105).

Tosi, Henri, Ramon Aldag, and Ronald Storey (1973), "On the Measurement of the Environment: An Assessment of the Lawrence and Lorsch Environmental Uncertainty Scales," *Administrative Science Quarterly*, 18 (March), 27-36.

Wind, Yoram (1978), "Organizational Buying Behavior," in Gerald Zaltman and Thomas V. Bonoma (eds.), *Review of Marketing* (Chicago, IL: American Marketing Association), 67-76.

Yao, Margaret (1981), "Clean Air Fight, Plain Dust Is the Key to Pollution 'Bubble' at Armco Steel Workers," *The Wall Street Journal*, (October 1), 1.

SECTION IX.
GREENING WITHIN
THE CONTEXT
OF MACRO-MARKETING

Chapter 16

Green Marketing and Selling Brotherhood

Joshua L. Wiener
Tabitha A. Doescher

SUMMARY. Many green marketing problems have a common core: the marketer is trying to "sell brotherhood." Selling brotherhood involves using a mass communication strategy to induce individuals to take actions when the actions are not in their own narrow self-interest. The authors draw on the social dilemma literature to develop a framework for selling brotherhood. In a social dilemma, a person who contributes to the community's good receives fewer personal benefits than one who does not, and all group members receive more personal benefits if all contribute than if all do not. The paper presents this framework and illustrates how the framework can be applied to a wide variety of green marketing issues.

INTRODUCTION

Many green marketing problems, such as encouraging recycling and discouraging littering, have a common core: the marketer is trying to "sell brotherhood." As discussed by Rothschild (1979), selling brotherhood involves using a mass communication strategy to induce individuals to take actions when the actions are not in their own narrow self-interest.[1]

Recently, Wiener and Doescher (1991) drew on the social dilemma literature to develop a framework for selling brotherhood. Specifically, they argue that the problem of selling brotherhood can be viewed as a problem of gaining cooperation in a social dilemma. A social dilemma is a social science construct that encompasses better-known constructs such as free riders, public goods, collective social traps, social fences, n-person prisoner dilemmas, and the tragedy of the commons. In a social dilemma, a person who contributes to the community's good receives fewer personal benefits than one who does not, and all group members receive more personal benefits if all contribute than if all do not.

This chapter presents an abridged version of Wiener and Doescher's framework and illustrates how the framework can be applied to a wide variety of green marketing issues. The first section describes the properties of social dilemmas. The second section describes general strategies for solving social dilemmas, the third section identifies the barriers to cooperation, and the fourth section discusses the ways in which these barriers can be overcome. The final section discusses implications for green marketing scholars and practitioners.

SOCIAL DILEMMAS: AN OVERVIEW

Because social dilemmas have been investigated by numerous scholars from diverse fields, there are many definitions of the construct. In this section, the most widely accepted and influential definition is reviewed.[2] Dawes (1980, p. 170) defines a social dilemma as a situation characterized by two properties:

> (a) the social payoff to each individual for defecting behavior is higher than the payoff for cooperative behavior, regardless of what other society members do; yet, (b) all individuals in society receive a lower payoff if all defect rather than cooperate.

In Dawes's definition, the terms "individual" and "social payoff" have special meanings. The term "individual" refers to any decision making unit, be it person or nation, that shares a resource with others. An individual's "social payoff" from an action is the utility s/he derives from the impact the action has on reality. The utility s/he gains from simply acting in a pro-social manner is the "nonsocial payoff." For example, a person who recycles a newspaper can gain a social payoff from the knowledge that his (her) action has both reduced landfill needs and saved trees. Although the individual can also gain utility from the act of recycling, this is part of his (her) nonsocial, not social, payoff.

The distinction between social and nonsocial payoffs can be conceptualized using a simple version of the multiattribute model of attitude:

$$A = I_sB_s + I_nB_n, \tag{1}$$

where A is the attitude towards cooperation, I is the importance of the attribute, B is the belief concerning the goodness of the attribute, s is the social payoff, and n is the nonsocial payoff. In terms of a littering example, B_s captures the individual's evaluation of the personal cost s/he will incur for not littering relative to the change in the environment brought about by her (his) action, and B_n captures the individual's beliefs concerning the goodness of not littering independent of how her (his) action alters the environment.

Green marketing communications may emphasize either social or nonsocial payoffs. When a communication emphasizes how an action, e.g., polluting a lake, harms the lake, it is focusing on the social payoff. When a communication emphasizes how the same action violates the ecological norm that man must respect and must not harm the natural environment, it is focusing on the nonsocial payoff.

The relative effectiveness of such communications will vary with both the circumstances and the target market. For example, focusing on the environmental consequences will be most effective when a person thinks that her (his) action will have a significant impact upon the environment. Focusing on norms will be most effective when the target market holds the norm. In other words, it is far easier to activate a latent norm than to create a new norm.

SOLVING SOCIAL DILEMMAS

A social dilemma can be solved by using, in Messick and Brewer's (1983) terms, either a behavioral or structural solution. A behavioral solution works by inducing individuals to cooperate for the sake of cooperation. A voluntary recycling program is an example of a behavioral solution. A structural solution, on the other hand, attempts to change the properties of the situation so that it no longer is a social dilemma. The situation is changed by altering the payoffs received by individuals who cooperate (or who defect). The most common methods of changing the payoff structure involve, (1) imposing restrictions on the ability of group members to freely access the common resource, (2) providing side payments to individuals who cooperate, (3) greatly decreasing the cost of cooperation, or (4) imposing extra costs on individuals who use the common resource.

Hardin (1968, p. 1247) has described structural solutions as "mutual coercion mutually agreed upon." His description is apt because structural solutions restrict individual freedom, and in a democratic society the imposition of a structural solution requires the consent of the group. This is true whether the structural solution involves directly limiting individual behavior (e.g., banning a product), imposing costs on defectors (e.g., placing a surcharge on nonrecycled garbage), or using tax dollars to alter the benefit-cost ratio (e.g., providing curbside pickup).

The bitter political debates that are associated with efforts to pass laws such as "Big Green" in California illustrate the importance of Hardin's view. A seeming paradox of these political battles is that many voters express both a high degree of concern about the environment and a strong degree of opposition to the proposed laws. A source of the paradox lies in the way in which environmental concern is commonly measured. Many surveys used to identify ecologically concerned consumers combine questions about willingness to make an individual sacrifice (e.g., willingness to recycle) with questions about support for laws (e.g., a bottle bill). However, recent work (e.g., Ellen, Wiener, and Cobb-Walgren 1991) suggests that there may be two different "green" segments. One segment favors (and engages in) voluntary action, while the other favors (and engages in) political action. The reason individuals who are willing to make individual voluntary sacrifices for the environment may be unwilling to support pro-environmental laws is that they see these laws as threats to their individual freedom.

In summary, the structural versus behavioral distinction defines cooperation. When the proposed solution is behavioral, cooperation means making a sacrifice for the community good. When the proposed solution is structural, cooperation entails supporting a political act that will restrict one's freedom. Key barriers to both forms of cooperation are discussed in the next section.

THE BARRIERS TO COOPERATION

Rothschild (1979) argues that scholars who seek to design strategies for selling brotherhood should first identify why people will not act in a pro-social way and then design strategies that will overcome these barriers. This section draws on both the social dilemma literature and Rothshchild's discussion of low involvement to identify the barriers to cooperation. The next section discusses how to overcome these barriers.

The Barriers Identified by Social Dilemma Research

A review of the social dilemma literature identifies four potentially important barriers to cooperation: (1) the desire to maintain one's freedom; (2) the desire to avoid being a sucker; (3) self-interest; and (4) mistrust of others (see Wiener and Doescher 1991). Whether these potential barriers will be actual barriers depends on the nature of the proposed solution, i.e., whether it is structural or behavioral. The remainder of this section discusses these barriers and explains how the nature of the solution determines whether an individual's willingness to cooperate is hindered by a particular barrier.

One reason an individual may not cooperate is that s/he wants to maintain her (his) freedom. According to Clee and Wicklund (1980, p. 401), any action that is seen as "reducing the subjective probability of attaining a choice alternative" will raise the reactance barrier. For example, the reactance barrier is raised when a person is forced to carpool in order to use a particular highway during rush hour. All social dilemma scholars acknowledge that reactance is frequently a key barrier to cooperation. Edney (1980, p. 148) goes so far as to argue that the key research question for scholars interested in solving social dilemmas is to "explore the conditions under which groups and communities will compromise individual freedoms."

A second reason an individual may not cooperate is that the individual does not want to be a sucker. An individual is a sucker if s/he makes a voluntary sacrifice (or is a member of a group that makes a collective sacrifice) to save a common resource, and that resource is destroyed. For example, a person may use the bus instead of her (his) automobile because her (his) city is in danger of violating EPA ozone standards. If the standards are violated, then the individual is a sucker.

A third reason an individual might not cooperate is that cooperating may not be in her (his) self-interest. Cooperation is not in the individual's self-interest if the social payoff s/he receives is negative. This barrier is, in many ways, the key barrier to solving a social dilemma.

A fourth reason an individual might be unwilling to cooperate is that s/he may not trust others to cooperate. In other words, researchers have found that individuals caught in a social dilemma try to meet cooperation with cooperation and defection with defection (Brewer and Kramer 1986; Dawes 1980; Kramer and Brewer 1984; Messick and Brewer 1983). For example, people are far more likely to litter an area that is already littered than one that is clean.

Whether these four barriers will actually inhibit an individual's willingness to cooperate depends on whether the solution being proposed is structural or behavioral. Recall from the previous section that a structural solution is a political act that restricts individual freedom, while a behavioral solution is one that asks individuals to make voluntary sacrifices.

Reactance will always be a barrier if the solution is structural; it will often be a barrier if the solution is behavioral. It is a barrier when the solution is structural because, by definition, a structural solution restricts individual freedom. Requiring users of a particular highway to carpool, for example, limits an individual's freedom of choice. Whether reactance is a salient barrier when the solution is behavioral depends on both the specific behavior being advocated and the type of promotion employed (Clee and Wicklund, 1980). For example, if the behavioral solution is to not purchase products that are "over"-packaged, the reactance barrier will be raised because the advocated behavior directly reduces the number of acceptable products.

The remaining three barriers (fear of being a sucker, self-interest, and mistrust) will be barriers when the proposed solution is behavioral. They may be barriers when the proposed solution is structural. A behavioral solution raises these three barriers for the following reason: if a single individual makes a sacrifice, it is possible that because others do not sacrifice, the community good will not be achieved. If one person does not pollute and others do, the community goal of having an unpolluted environment will not be attained. Since others may pollute, mistrust will be a barrier; and, because this makes the goal of having an unpolluted environment illusive, both fear of being a sucker and self-interest will also be barriers.

When a structural solution is under consideration, these three barriers will be present only if the individual is a member of a group that shares a common resource with nongroup members. In many of these situations, if nongroup members do not sacrifice, the community goal will not be achieved. For example, if one community bans the sale of a particular type of animal pelt and other communities do not, the goal of preserving the species will not be reached. Since nongroup members may sell the pelts, mistrust will be a barrier; and since the animal may become extinct, both the fear of being a sucker and self-interest will also be barriers. If, on the other hand, the group encompasses all individuals having access to the common resource, these three barriers will not be present. A worldwide ban on the sale of ivory, if enforced, might achieve the goal of preserving the elephant. In this case, there are no nongroup members to mistrust; if the ban is enforced, neither the fear of being a sucker nor self-interest will come into play, and the elephant will be preserved.

In summary, the social dilemma literature identifies four potential barriers to cooperation–the desire to maintain one's freedom, the desire to avoid being a sucker, self-interest, and one's mistrust of others. Theoretically, the salience of these barriers depends on whether the proposed solution to the social dilemma is structural or behavioral. However, for most green marketing situations, all four barriers are relevant. Most environmental problems are global in scope, and all four barriers to cooperation will usually be present unless action is taken at a global level.

The Barriers Identified by Rothschild

Rothschild (1979, p. 14-15) observes that:

> in the nonbusiness case, issues are (often of) low individual involvement . . . (because) . . . often there is a cost to the individual and benefit to the larger group. . . . Furthermore, there are nonbusiness problems where all members of society must comply for the best interests of society (and themselves).

In other words, Rothschild is arguing that when the benefit-cost ratio is low, the individual's level of involvement will be low. The problem of getting people to take pro-social actions under these conditions is the problem of "selling brotherhood," which, in turn, is isomorphic to the problem of gaining cooperation in a social dilemma.

Conceptualizing "brotherhood" in involvement terms highlights two issues that are not explicitly addressed in the social dilemma literature. The first is the importance of reinforcement. The lesson that Rothschild draws from the marketing of low-involvement consumer products is that communication tools can induce trial, but only positive product benefits (positive reinforcement) can lead to repeat purchase (continued behavior). Support for Rothschild's emphasis on the importance of positive reinforcement is found in the conservation literature (Ritchie and McDougall 1985). A second implication is that the direct link between attitudes towards the community good and trial behavior will be weak, since under conditions of low involvement, attitudes are not good predictors of behavior. Support for Rothschild's view comes from marketing studies that have found that ecological concerns have little direct influence on behavior (See Gill, Crosby, and Taylor 1986).

OVERCOMING THE BARRIERS TO COOPERATION

Rothschild (1979) argues that one effective approach to selling brotherhood would be for marketers to employ communication strategies that directly attack the barriers inhibiting cooperation. In order to use mass communication techniques to overcome these barriers, marketing practitioners must know both what information to communicate and what strategies to use to communicate this information (Fine 1990; Rothschild 1979). This section draws on the social dilemma literature to develop a series of propositions describing the information marketers should try to communicate to overcome a specific barrier. An example of the type of strategy that can be used by green marketers to convey this information follows each proposition. Table 16.1 summarizes the major conclusions of this section.

Overcoming the Reactance Barrier

Recent research has found that the willingness of an individual to accept a structural solution, when that individual is a member of a group encompassing all individuals with access to a resource, is an increasing function of the perceived likelihood that the resource will be destroyed if no action is taken. This suggests that people are more willing to sacrifice their freedom when the costs of not making the sacrifice are high.

When the individuals are either members of a group that shares the resource with others, or are being asked to voluntarily restrict their freedom, communicating that the resource is likely to be destroyed may not encourage cooperation. There are two reasons for this. First, there is no guarantee that if the individuals give up their freedom the community's goal will be achieved. Secondly, if the goal is not achieved, the sacrifice of freedom will not increase the individual's social payoff. Consequently, the first proposition applies only to the one group case, i.e., the case where all individuals who have access to the resource are members of a single group.

P_1: To reduce the reactance barrier in the one group case, emphasize the benefits of reaching the group's goal.

This information can be communicated by the "starving baby" appeal (Fine 1990). These appeals typically emphasize the negative consequences of not reaching the group's goal. Many environmental communications use this approach. For example, this is the approach used by efforts that emphasize that drilling activities will destroy a particular natural area, such as the California coastline.

Overcoming the Sucker Barrier

A common finding in the social dilemma literature is that individuals who believe the community goal will not be achieved, even if they cooperate, are less likely to cooperate than those who think the goal will be achieved (Dawes 1980; Messick and Brewer 1983). Proposition P_2 is based on this finding.

P_2: To reduce the sucker barrier, emphasize that the goal will be achieved.

TABLE 16.1. Overcoming the Barriers to Cooperation

The Barriers to Cooperation	Information that Should be Emphasized to Overcome the Barrier	Strategies for Overcoming the Barriers*
Reactance:		
One group case	Importance of reaching the goal	Starving baby appeal
Multi-group or individual case	(None suggested)	(None suggested)
Sucker	Goal will be reached	"Well baby" appeal
Self-Interest	Size of dilemma is small	Scope reduction approach, civic pride approach
	Your contribution will make the difference	Leadership appeal, phased segmentation approach
	Social payoff is larger, but not more important	Emphasize ease of cooperation
	Nonsocial payoff is larger and more important	Ethical appeal
Mistrust	Others are cooperating or will cooperate	Survey results approach, positive feedback appeal
	Group identification	Civic pride approach, common fate appeal
No Reinforcement	(Use mistrust and sucker information)	(Use mistrust and sucker strategies)
Attitude-Behavior Link	(Use sucker information)	(Use sucker strategies)

*Behavioral influence strategies are not listed because they do not rely upon changing cognitive beliefs. They should be effective in terms of overcoming the reactance and self-interest barriers (see Burns and De Vere 1982; Scott 1977).

Fine (1990) suggests a strategy that may help overcome a consumer's fear that s/he (or her (his) group) will be a sucker. Fine labels this approach the "well baby" appeal because it emphasizes that the group's goal is being reached. For example, if a marketer is trying to get people to not pollute a river, a "well baby" campaign can focus on how the river is getting cleaner and should return to its natural state in the near future.

Overcoming the Self-Interest Barrier

Because self-interest is the central barrier in social dilemmas, many experiments have investigated how this barrier can be overcome. A set of four propositions and their strategies are discussed below.

Numerous studies have investigated and found support for Olson's (1965) hypothesis that small groups are more likely to cooperate than large groups (See Dawes 1980; Messick and Brewer 1983). Proposition P_3 is based on this research.

P_3: To reduce the self-interest barrier, communicate information that reduces the perceived size of the social dilemma.

The scope reduction strategy can be used to reduce the perceived size of the social dilemma. In this type of strategy, the communication focuses upon a small but distinct part of the group's goal. For example, an individual can be asked to "save a tree" rather than to contribute to "saving a forest." As described by Fine (1990), the civic pride approach to fund-raising illustrates how scope reduction can be implemented through the use of a geographic segmentation approach. Fine uses a regionalized approach in his example of an organization dedicated to preserving threatened environments. Individuals were asked to join together with other individuals living in their region to help preserve a local area. An outstanding feature of the civic pride approach is that it reduces the actual size of the social dilemma and so relies on more than simply the power of communication.

A second approach to overcoming the self-interest barrier is to inform subjects that their contribution will influence whether the group's goal is reached. In a similar vein, research investigating perceived consumer effectiveness finds that individuals are more willing to take a pro-social action if they think their action will influence the social issue (Wiener and Doescher 1991). Proposition P_4 restates these research findings.

P_4:   To reduce the self-interest barrier, emphasize that the individual's contribution will determine whether the goal will be reached.

A person can be given a feeling that his (her) contribution can make a difference by using appeals that give a decision making unit a sense of leadership. A difference between the use of leadership appeals by social marketers and commercial marketers is that social marketers can explicitly point to the larger aggregate that the individual or community is being asked to lead. This opportunity can be exploited by the use of a phased segmentation strategy.

The phased segmentation strategy can be used to promote environmental activities when a program, such as recycling, begins with a neighborhood pilot program or with the involvement of a local civic organization. The initial group will be motivated because its members think they can lead their community. The community can be motivated by thinking in terms of leading the state. A number of statewide environmental efforts have begun and developed in this fashion.

A third approach is based on (1) social dilemma experiments that find that cooperation is an increasing function of the amount of the social payoff (see Dawes 1980; Messick and Brewer 1983) and on (2) evaluations of actual social marketing campaigns (Edney 1980; Stern and Gardner 1981). Based on their evaluations, Edney and Stern and Gardner conclude that modest incentives for cooperation can have no impact on, or can even decrease, cooperation. These scholars argue that providing incentives can reduce cooperation because this action increases both the social payoff and the importance of the social payoff. Unless the incentive is very large, the social payoff will be negative, even after the consumer receives his (her) incentive. If the social payoff is negative, then increasing its importance will, as predicted by the multiattribute model, reduce the consumer's overall attitude towards cooperation. Although communications do not directly influence the social payoff associated with cooperation, they can influence the relative importance of the social payoff. The fifth proposition is consistent with both the results of the social dilemma experiments and the evaluations of past social marketing campaigns.

P_5: To reduce the self-interest barrier, marketing communications should try to inform consumers that they will receive a higher social payoff without increasing the importance of the social payoff.

Many green marketing strategies seek to encourage cooperation by providing either incentives or disincentives, or by simply making it easier for a person to cooperate. Since both incentives and disincentives are more likely to focus attention on the social payoff, Proposition P_5 suggests that marketing communications that focus on these aspects may be counterproductive. It may be possible to reduce the self-interest barrier by using communications that focus on how easy it is for a person to cooperate (Kotler and Andreasen 1987). For example, instead of promoting the fact that individuals who agree to recycle gain a small reduction in their garbage collection costs, an effective promotion might emphasize how easy it is to recycle.

A final approach to overcoming the self-interest barrier is based on a conceptual, not empirical, foundation. Both Dawes (1980) and Olson (1965) argue that if the value and importance of the nonsocial payoff can be augmented, an individual will be more likely to cooperate. The application of the multiattribute model of attitude formation arrives at the same conclusion. Proposition P_6 is based on these conceptual arguments.

P_6: To reduce the self-interest barrier, emphasize the nonsocial payoff gained from cooperating.

Whether communications can influence the perceived nonsocial payoff is highly controversial (Wiener and Doescher 1991). Within the social dilemma literature there is little, if any, evidence that appeals emphasizing nonsocial payoffs are effective. On the other hand, the studies frequently cited as evidence that such appeals are ineffective have confounded the issue of appealing to nonsocial payoffs with the issue of ethical appeals. An ethical appeal can focus on either the nonsocial or social payoff. Most of the ethical appeals that have proven to be ineffective both in actual campaigns and experiments focus on the social payoff. In other words, appeals such as "Don't Be Fuelish–Conserve" focus attention on how the individual will benefit if the community's goal is reached. These appeals are not focusing on the intrinsic rightness of cooperating (the nonsocial payoff) as much as they are focusing on the benefits of gaining the social goal (the social payoff).

Although the existing literature does not provide strong empirical support for the sixth proposition, it is included because we think people can be motivated by communications that focus on the nonsocial payoff. These appeals can focus on emerging environmental norms or upon more basic norms such as reciprocity. The norm of reciprocity would imply that if others are helping you live in a better world, then you have a moral obligation to reciprocate by providing help.

Overcoming the Mistrust Barrier

Many studies have found that people who report they expect others to cooperate are more likely themselves to cooperate (Messick and Brewer 1983). Proposition P7 is based on these findings.

P7:   To reduce the mistrust barrier, emphasize that others are cooperating or are planning to cooperate.

This information can be communicated through the use of a survey results strategy. A survey results strategy takes advantage of the well-known phenomenon that many people who indicate they will engage in a socially desirable behavior do not do so. A social marketer can make use of this tendency by conducting a survey of intentions and then communicating that most community members plan to cooperate.

In light of the overwhelming verbal support given to the environment by the public, this survey results strategy should be highly relevant to a number of environmental issues. In other words, a common observation is that many people will express a positive attitude towards a pro-environmental action, such as recycling, but not engage in the action. In the past, this finding has been viewed with frustration. The survey results strategy views this phenomenon as an opportunity. It exploits the tendency of people to verbally support pro-environmental actions by publicizing the fact that most people surveyed indicated a willingness to sacrifice. When a person learns that most others plan to sacrifice, s/he will be motivated by various factors (including the fear of social sanctions) to sacrifice as well.

A second approach to overcoming the mistrust barrier is based on research by Kramer and Brewer (1984) and Brewer and Kramer (1986). They found that cooperation can be increased by increasing the extent to which an individual identifies with fellow group members. This has been done in social dilemma experiments by emphasizing the degree of socio-demographic similarity that exists between individual and fellow group members (Kramer and Brewer 1984) and by emphasizing that all individuals caught in the social dilemma share a common fate (Brewer and Kramer 1986). Proposition P_8 is based on this research.

> P_8: To reduce the mistrust barrier, enhance the degree to which an individual identifies with his (her) group.

There are many ways to suggest to consumers that the others caught in the social dilemma are similar to themselves. For example, promotional messages can emphasize accepted social boundaries (such as the use of region in the civic pride approach) or common fate (such as–we all share one world and if we destroy it, we all lose).

Reinforcement

The problem of little or no reinforcement has been addressed in the social dilemma literature by focusing on the effects of communicating (1) how the collective sacrifices of community members are helping the community achieve its goal, and (2) how most members of the community are cooperating. These approaches have been discussed above in the sections dealing with the "sucker" and "mistrust" barriers. The core of these approaches is that, instead of providing the individual with feedback about the consequences of his (her) action, feedback about the consequences of everyone's action is provided. Note also that social dilemma research suggests that effective feedback can focus upon process (e.g., how many others are cooperating) as well as outcome.

Weak Attitude-Behavior Link

The weak attitude-behavior link can arise when an individual places a high value on reaching a community goal, such as saving the environment, but does not think that the goal will be reached. This suggests that the root of the weak attitude-behavior link barrier is in the fear people have of being suckers.

IMPLICATIONS

The key implication of this chapter is that effective green marketing strategies can be developed by conceptualizing the task as one of gaining cooperation in a social dilemma. This approach identifies barriers that inhibit this form of pro-social behavior and provides direction to marketing practitioners who seek to develop strategies that will overcome these barriers. A direct implication of this view is that green marketers can and should borrow ideas from other efforts to "sell brotherhood." For example, within the marketing literature there are well-developed streams of research investigating conservation behavior, ecological behavior, and donation behavior. The proposed selling brotherhood perspective implies that a common theoretical framework can be applied to all of these behaviors. This in turn suggests that strategies that have been used to achieve one specific goal, such as increasing the willingness of a consumer to pay a premium for an energy-efficient appliance, should be applicable to other specific goals, such as encouraging a consumer to select a product that, although less convenient to use, is packaged in a more environmentally sound manner.

At a more tactical level, the analysis emphasizes that the green marketer must be very sensitive to whether her (his) promotions are having the unintended effect of enhancing the individual's fear of being a sucker and/or of being impotent. Promotions that emphasize impending disaster, the rapid destruction of a natural resource, the global nature of the problem, and so forth, may have this effect.

These types of "sick baby" appeals will only be effective when the decision making unit knows the problem will be solved if it acts, i.e., solving the problem does not require the cooperation of others. The analysis also suggests that educational and promotional efforts intended to create and enhance "green" norms are very important. If people hold these norms, then green marketers can motivate their behavior by nonsocial payoffs. The potential importance of norms also suggests that segmentation research and cross-cultural research should focus upon identifying ecological norms.

NOTES

1. This could occur for one or more of the following reasons: (1) the primary beneficiary of the individual's pro-social action is his or her community; (2) in general, most members of the community must cooperate for the community to benefit; and (3) the cost of the pro-social action is direct and personal (Bloom and Novelli 1981; Kotler 1982; Kotler and Andreasen 1987; Ritchie and McDougall 1985; Rothschild 1979; Scott 1977).

2. This is the view used in social psychology. See Wiener and Doescher (1991) for a discussion of the conceptualization used in economics.

REFERENCES

Bloom, P. and W. Novelli. (1981). "Problems and Challenges in Social Marketing," *Journal of Marketing*, 45: 79-88.

Brewer, M.B. and R.M. Kramer. (1986). "Choice Behavior and Social Dilemmas: Effects of Social Identity, Group Size, and Decision Framing," *Journal of Personality and Social Psychology*, 3: 543-549.

Burns, A. and S. De Vere. (1982). "An Investigation of Compliance-Gaining Techniques Applied to a Gasoline Conservation Device," *Journal of Marketing and Public Policy*, 1: 43-56.

Clee, M. and R. Wicklund. (1980). "Consumer Behavior and Psychological Reactance," *Journal of Consumer Behavior*, 6: 389-405.

Dawes, R. (1980). "Social Dilemmas," *Annual Review of Psychology*, 31: 69-93.

Edney, J. (1980). "The Commons Problem: Alternative Perspectives," *American Psychologist*, 35: 131-150.

Ellen, P., J. Wiener, and C. Cobb-Walgren. (1991). "The Role of Perceived Consumer Effectiveness in Motivating Environmentally-Conscious Behaviors," *Journal of Public Policy and Marketing*, 10: 102-117.

Fine, S. (1990). *Social Marketing*. Boston, MA: Allyn and Bacon.

Gill, J., L. Crosby, and J. Taylor. (1986). "Ecological Concern, Attitudes, and Social Norms in Voting Behavior," *Public Opinion Quarterly*, 50: 537-554.

Hardin, G. R. (1968). "The Tragedy of the Commons," *Science*, 162: 1243-1248.

Kotler, P. (1982). *Marketing for Nonprofit Organizations*. Englewood Cliffs, NJ: Prentice Hall.

Kotler, P. and A. Andreasen. (1987). *Strategic Marketing for Nonprofit Organizations*. Englewood Cliffs, N.J.: Prentice Hall.

Kramer, R.M. and M.B. Brewer. (1984). "Effects of Group Identity on Resource Use in a Simulated Commons Dilemma," *Journal of Personality and Social Psychology*, 46: 1044-1057.

Messick, M. and K. Brewer. (1983). "Solving Social Dilemmas: A Review," in L. Wheeler and P. Shaver (eds.), *Review of Personality and Social Psychology*, 4: 11-44, Beverly Hills, CA: Sage.

Olson, M. (1965). *The Logic of Collective Action*, Cambridge, MA: Harvard University Press.

Ritchie, J. and G. McDougall. (1985). "Designing and Marketing Energy Conservation Policies and Programs: Implications from a Decade of Research," *Journal of Public Policy and Marketing*, 4: 14-32.

Rothschild, M. (1979). "Marketing Communications in Nonbusiness Situations or Why It's So Hard to Sell Brotherhood like Soap," *Journal of Marketing*, 43: 11-20.

Scott, C. (1977). "Modifying Socially-Conscious Behavior: The Foot-in-the-Door Approach," *Journal of Consumer Research*, 4: 156-164.

Stern, P. and G. Gardner. (1981). "Psychological Research and Energy Policy," *American Psychologist*, 36: 329-342.

Wiener, J. and T. Doescher. (1991). "A Framework for Promoting Brotherhood," *Journal of Marketing*, 55: 38-47.

SECTION X.
AN INTERNATIONAL
CASE STUDY

Chapter 17

Environmental Issues in the Freight Transport Industry: A Qualitative Analysis of Key Stakeholders' Perceptions

Bodo B. Schegelmilch
Adamantios Diamantopoulos
Greg M. Bohlen

SUMMARY. There is a dearth of research on environmental issues in the UK service industry. This chapter attempts to partly redress this situation by focusing on the environmental image of the freight transport industry. Following a review of the literature on the greening of the transport industry, this chapter reports on a qualitative study, which was based on 65 in-depth interviews with key decision makers and different groups of influential opinion formers in the freight business. The study analyzes the perceived relative environmental impact of road and rail freight transport. Among others, views have been obtained on the importance and severity of nuisance factors arising from road and rail freight transport, the role of environmental considerations in transport decisions and the likely future environmental demands placed on this industrial service.

INTRODUCTION

The Green Challenge

In recent years, environmentalism and interest in green issues have gained a strong momentum throughout the UK. In July 1990,

NOP Market Research disclosed that 37% of adults aged 16+ spontaneously mentioned some aspect of the environment as being the *single* most important issue facing society today (Research 2000, 1990). The increased concern among the UK public has started to be expressed through purchasing behavior; in July 1989, a Mori poll revealed that the proportion of consumers choosing products on the basis of "environmental performance" had increased from 19% to 42% in less than one year (Prothero, 1990); and, by late 1992, 80% of UK consumers were expressing their concerns through the products they purchase (*Marketing*, 1992).

The "green" movement in the UK comprises about 1400 organizations (Barker, 1986). All these groups claim to be non-party political with the objective of influencing politicians and voters of all persuasions (Porritt, 1987). Indeed, the pursuit of "green" causes is no longer confined to the fringe at the left of the political spectrum, but has gained widespread support and credibility. Green organizations are showing growth in support of 20% to 30% per year, with Greenpeace recruiting between 3000 and 4000 members per week (Nelson, 1989). The 13 largest environmental bodies in the UK now have nearly five million supporters and a combined income of over £160m per annum, which is almost four times as much as that of the Trade Union Congress (Nelson, 1989). Greenpeace alone grew from just 30,000 members in 1985 to 195,000 in 1989 and reached 414,000 during 1992 (telephone enquiry to Greenpeace, October 1992).

The growing interest in environmental issues has not been confined just to consumer behavior or green pressure groups; numerous industries are now attempting to present themselves in a more environmentally friendly light: "Green is seen by major companies to bring long-term commercial advantages, even though it may be costly to implement initially" (*Marketing Research Society Newsletter*, 1990: p. 41). In March 1991, a DRT International/Touche Ross survey of 250 large industrial and commercial companies in 15 sectors across Europe revealed that 70% of companies had stated that they had specific plans to improve their environmental performance (Abbott, 1991).

Despite the growing concern/interest in environmentalism in the UK, there has been little academic research in this particular field

(Prothero, 1990). Of the research that has been conducted in Europe and the USA, the emphasis has tended to be on environmental issues relating to physical products rather than services. Furthermore, the majority of studies have focused on consumers rather than companies, using samples of the general public as opposed to other key stakeholders,[1] such as firms, government officials, and major opinion formers.

This chapter aims to partly fill the above research gap through focusing on (a) an industrial service (freight transport), (b) research conducted within a UK context, and (c) the use of multiple informants, representing non-general public interest groups. Specifically, following a review of the literature on the greening of the transport industry, the chapter reports on a qualitative study that identifies the perceived environmental problems arising from freight transportation and investigates whether environmental friendliness is a major factor in determining the modal choice. In addition, the chapter addresses some of the environment-related transport policy issues and briefly examines the expected influences on "greening" freight transport.

THE GREENING OF THE TRANSPORT INDUSTRY

Many companies operating within the transport industry view themselves as being just as concerned about green issues as any other major industry (e.g., see TNT Ltd., Annual Report, 1990), although it must be noted that the industry is very much in the center of environmental criticism: "Road transport contributes some 85% of the UK total carbon monoxide . . . pumps out 45% of the UK total of nitrogen oxides . . . produces 16% of the UK's total carbon dioxide, the major greenhouse gas" (Smith and Sambrook, 1990: p. 28).

Besides emissions and concerns arising from high levels of congestion and road traffic casualties, heavy lorries in particular are frequently attacked for the damage they cause. *The Times* (September 30th, 1987) estimated that heavy lorries cause at least £600m in damage to roads and bridges each year, while the Automobile Association (AA) has stated that roads are not worn out by cars but almost exclusively by heavy trucks (Somerset County Council,

1990). And as far as road congestion is concerned: "Traffic densities have increased by around 50% over the last decade, and by some 75% on motorways and inter-urban trunk roads" (Secretary of State, 1991: p. 3). Furthermore, the Confederation of British Industry estimates that congestion costs industry as much as £15 billion per year (Dearden, 1990).

All this has resulted in an increase in the number of voices demanding for a review of governmental transport policies. Phil Goodwin, Director of the Transport Studies Unit at Oxford University, was quoted as saying: "Up until now, transport policy has consisted of providing roads to meet the demands of drivers. Now, for the first time, there is universal recognition of the fact that there is no possibility of road planning keeping pace with demand" (Smith and Sambrook, 1990: p. 31). However, the British Government's solution to the transport problem is to encourage new developments rather than use regulatory forces: "There must now be a flourishing and substantial programme of investment by the private sector . . . we are interested in the scope for introducing private finances into the provision of overland routes" (Secretary of State, 1991: p. 13). While the UK has so far been reluctant to use regulatory forces to address transport problems, measures taken elsewhere suggest that governments are more willing to regulate transport. For example, in Germany, lorries are not permitted to drive on weekends and in Tokyo cars above a certain size are not permitted to park on the streets (Smith and Sambrook, 1990). In the USA, a total of nine states have promised to adopt tough new smog reduction rules and it seems certain that a large number of new American cars and trucks will have to run on natural gas or methanol starting in 1997 (Woodruff and Peterson, 1991). A change in political leadership may, indeed, be accompanied by a greater willingness to introduce similar regulations in the UK.

With these factors in mind, commercial users of cars and lorries have been eager to acquire a more positive environmental image. The UK's largest road transport company, BRS, revamped its environmental image in September, 1990. With the assistance of the corporate identity consultants Lloyd Northover, the company is eager to use its new fleet of "environmentally friendly vehicles" to combat public perceptions of road haulage as a dirty business (Mar-

keting, 1990). The TNT Transportation Group also addresses environmental challenges: "TNT has dedicated personnel seeking to reduce usage of fossil fuels by improving efficiency in maintenance and operation of motor vehicles and to reduce the number of motor vehicles we use" (TNT Ltd., 1990: p. 8).

Rail, of course, has not been unaffected by the increase in environmental consciousness. For example, in planning the new link between London and the Channel Tunnel, British Rail experienced considerable opposition from local residents and green pressure groups. Consequently, some 30% of the estimated costs will now be spent on environmental protection (British Railways Board, 1988/89). The opposition is particularly remarkable, as rail is widely regarded as being far more environmentally friendly than its road counterpart (e.g., see Ellwanger, 1990; TEST, 1991). In a recent document outlining proposals on a European Community railway policy, this view was reiterated by the Directorate-General for Transport. Specifically, it was pointed out that rail is less demanding in terms of space than road transport, can make a substantial contribution to the reduction of traffic congestion, reduces air pollution, and increases energy saving (Commission of the European Communities, 1990). However, having just praised the environmental virtues of rail, the Directorate-General also stresses that, according to a Directive adopted by the council in 1985, railway networks nevertheless must be evaluated for their impact on the environment. Safeguarding the environment and quality of life of neighboring populations, in its view, implies that: "the use of techniques designed to reduce nuisances, such as 'cut and cover,' should become the norm" (Commission of the European Communities, 1990: p. 149).

The tension between recognizing rail as the more environmentally-friendly mode of transport and being concerned that rail undoubtedly has *some* negative effects on the environment is also found in the UK. In a brochure entitled *Transport and the Environment*, the Department of Transport initially praises the environmental benefits of rail: "It is generally recognised that rail transport has advantages over other transport modes, in terms of its impact on the environment" (Department of Transport, 1988: p. 6). Having just stated this, the Department of Transport proceeds to comment on the same page(!): "The local environment impact of a new high-speed rail link is bound to be adverse." Thus, there is clearly a conflict between generally recognizing the environmental advantages of rail versus other modes of transport and the willingness to personally accept specific nuisances through rail transportation.

The UK government has recently announced that British Rail will soon be turned over to the private sector. As the details of the privatization have not yet been decided upon, it is difficult to foresee, at the present time, whether changes in ownership will result in changing commitments towards environmental issues in the transportation of freight on the UK railways.

METHODOLOGY

A two-stage approach was adopted for data collection purposes:

1. Discussions with "expert informants" (i.e., individuals/groups with expertise on environmental issues) to obtain initial insight into (a) key questions associated with the environmental debate, (b) research already conducted in the area of current interest, (c) past methodology used to study perceptions of environmental concern in general and transport environmental problems in particular, and (d) the types of difficulties encountered when researching environmental issues. A wide range of private organizations (e.g., Steer Davies & Gleave, Transport Consultants, who have conducted a number of studies on rail and road transport) and public organizations (e.g., The Commission of the European Communities in Brussels, particularly the Directorates-General for Transport [DG7] and for the Environment [DG11], which have conducted/commissioned a number of environmental impact studies) were contacted both in the UK and abroad. This enabled access to a number of reports, working papers, and fact sheets to be used as invaluable input to the next stage of the research.

2. First-hand, detailed information on the research issues was obtained from key interest groups. Nine such groups were identified through discussions with British Rail and the "expert informants"; covering both decision making bodies and major opinion formers (Figure 17.1). A total of sixty-five in-depth interviews were conducted with respondents in eight of these groups. Respondents were

selected according to their level of factual knowledge on freight transport issues. A large number of interviews with the final key interest group, the general public, will follow at a later date.

In organizing and scheduling the interviews, a number of hurdles had to be overcome:

1. The identification of appropriate respondents in certain interest groups proved to be anything but straightforward. For example, it took six phone calls to different government officials simply to obtain the telephone number of the political adviser to the Secretary of State for the Environment!
2. Obtaining cooperation, particularly from government officials and the media, was even more problematic, due to great initial resistance to participate in the study.
3. Efficient scheduling of the interviews, so that a number of interviews could be conducted in one day, also proved difficult. A number of respondents only granted interviews with the explicit understanding that it could take place only at a specific date/time.

In spite of the additional workload caused by the obstacles described above, the researchers eventually managed to interview all initially selected respondents, resulting in a very rich and diverse sample composition. In addition, the flexibility of the interview format allowed different emphasis on different issues according to each respondent's special knowledge and/or interests.

During the interview phase, a number of procedures were followed to safeguard data quality. First, interviews involving respondents in very senior positions were only conducted by the senior researchers; moreover, in most such cases, both researchers were involved in the interview to cross-examine the respondent and ensure comprehensive coverage of the issues. Second, all interviews were tape-recorded and subsequently transcribed to provide a verbatim record. Third, all transcripts were double-checked against the original tapes. Finally, random spot-checks by the senior researchers on the transcripts provided a final quality control mechanism.

Once the final transcripts had all been compiled and checked, the relevant information pertaining to each research objective was abstracted and summarized. Subsequently, a process of data integration and interpretation was undertaken.

FINDINGS

THE ENVIRONMENT AND FREIGHT TRANSPORT

Environmental Nuisance Factors

At the start of each interview, the respondents were asked which environmental nuisance factors spring to mind when thinking about

FIGURE 17.1

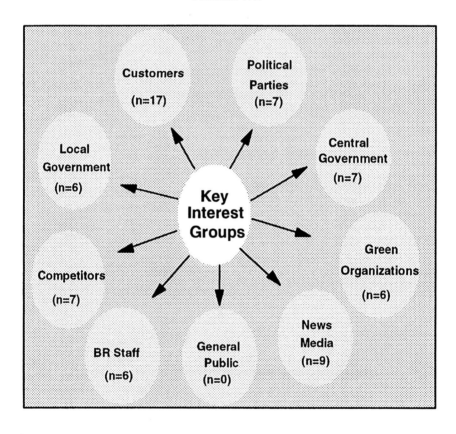

freight transport. Both the number and type of nuisance factors mentioned varied substantially across respondents, reflecting primarily different degrees of factual knowledge and/or particular concerns/interests of individual interviewees. It also became apparent that the perception of environmental issues tends to be highly politicized, particularly in terms of importance attached to each factor. Table 17.1 illustrates the issues mentioned by the interviewees.

A number of interviewees also stated how they perceived the disturbance through the nuisance factor(s) had changed during the last five years. Only a small proportion of respondents felt that the situation had improved or remained unchanged (five and two mentions respectively). The remainder of the sample believed that the situation had significantly deteriorated over the past five years (42 mentions).

It must be noted that *all* who expressed an opinion perceived a worsening of disturbances through noise and congestion during the last five years. Indeed, improvements were only perceived in terms of emission (one Railfreight customer, competitor, and journalist,

TABLE 17.1. Perception of Environmental Nuisances Arising from Freight Transport

Nuisance Factors	Importance Ranking	Number of Mentions
Noise	1	56
Emission, Air Pollution	2	53
Congestion	3	39
Dust, Dirt, Spillage	4	23
Damage to Infrastructure	5	20
Visual Intrusion	6	19
"Disturbance" to Residential Areas	7	14
Potential for Accidents	7	14
Dangerous Goods	8	13
Vibration	8	13
Effects of New Developments	8	13
Land Take	9	12
Other (e.g., pesticides in linesides)	9	12

respectively), operating safety (one Railfreight customer), and land take (one journalist).

However, some interviewees also pointed towards a number of encouraging developments, particularly where road freight is concerned: *"I think road is having a less detrimental effect. . . . Considerable efforts are being made gradually to reduce the impact. More aerodynamic bodies, more fuel efficient engines, bigger lorries,"* David Owen, Planning Manager for Transport, National Freight Corporation.

Comparisons Between Road and RailFreight Transport

Next, interviewees were prompted to compare the freight transport modes in terms of their environmental impact. Table 17.2 illustrates that the large majority of respondents who expressed an opinion view the nuisances associated with RailFreight transport to be much less severe than those associated with road freight.

The perception that RailFreight is comparatively "greener" is further highlighted by the following statements taken from the interview transcripts: *"If you just look at the individual transport [mode], I would say that rail is much more environmentally benign than road,"* C. J. Whately, Manager, Environment & External Affairs, British Coal; *"Rail is a safer mode of transport than road. . . . It is less hazardous and B. R. pay a lot more attention to safety than they used to,"* J. M. B. Gotch, Managing Director, CAIB UK Ltd.

However, despite the overall support lent to RailFreight transport, rail is not getting a totally clean bill of (environmental) health: *"You're not comparing like with like. I mean when you consider that in the UK something like less than 10% of freight goes by rail and something well over 90% by road, if you actually went 50:50 there'd be a lot less difference,"* I. C. Canadine, Company Distribution Adviser, Imperial Chemical Industries PLC; *"Clearly, if you're living in a residential area adjoining a railway system, the increased traffic going onto the rail system will be detrimental to the sort of life and the amenities you enjoy,"* J. Millard, Planning Officer, Lliw Valley Borough Council.

TABLE 17.2. Perceived Environmental Impact by Mode of Transport

Nuisance Factors	Environmental Impact:	
	Rail Freight Better	Road Freight Better
Noise	17	1
Emission, Air Pollution	28	0
Congestion	15	0
Dust, Dirt, Spillage	3	0
Damage to Infrastructure	3	0
Visual Intrusion	6	0
"Disturbance" to Residents	4	0
Potential for Accidents	4	1
Dangerous Goods	3	0
Vibration	3	1
Effects of New Developments	0	1
Land Take	3	0
TOTAL	89	4

DETERMINANTS OF MODAL CHOICE IN FREIGHT TRANSPORT

Factors Influencing Modal Choice

All choice criteria were obtained *without providing any prompts* to the interviewees. As expected, cost and reliability are the most important choice criteria (40 and 27 mentions respectively), followed by availability/convenience (19 mentions). Environmental consideration ranked lowest in determining modal choice; it was only mentioned four times, once by a politician, twice by Railfreight competitors, and once by a RailFreight customer.

When explicitly *prompted* to comment on the role of environmental factors in transport decisions, twenty-one respondents who expressed an opinion thought it was *not* considered; fifteen perceive it as being only of marginal importance. Only four interviewees, three RailFreight customers and one British Rail manager, perceived environmental considerations to be important in making transport decisions.

The feeling prevails that environmental considerations are either not at all considered, or are only deliberated when other factors determining modal choice are approximately equal: *"There are a few people within most companies who are concerned about the environment, but when it comes down to competition, you're not going to pay more to deliver your goods in an environmentally friendly fashion compared to your competitors,"* T. Brown, National Society for Clean Air.

Suggested Measures for Improving the Rail Mode

Interviewees suggested a number of measures RailFreight should undertake to transfer business from road to rail. Table 17.3 summarizes the key suggestions.

It can be seen that most suggestions would require investments;

TABLE 17.3. Perceived Scope for Improving RailFreight Transport

Suggested Measures	Number of Mentions
More Investment in Infrastructure	29
Make More Accessible / Flexible	15
Provide a Quicker Service and Delivery	12
Improve Service Quality	11
Be More Commercial / Competitive	11
Make More Reliable	9
Modernize Trains	8
Provide Better Facilities for Swap Bodies	6

inevitably there is also a certain degree of overlap between various suggestions listed in the table. A flavor for the diverse comments received on this issue is conveyed through the following: *"The trouble is that rail doesn't get its act together sufficiently or it would be truly cost efficient. . . . You're never sure that it [freight] will be unloaded in the right place, you're never sure that it will be available when you want to pick it up,"* D. Owen, Planning Manager for Transport, National Freight Corporation; *"The way that B. R. has sold off a lot of its goods yards sites for property developments–it's a particularly acute problem in London . . . They would have been really good points to bring freight and distribute it by small lorries,"* T. Bray, Friends of the Earth; *"What we're short of in this country is an enormous amount of investment in our railways. When you compare the amount of investment that goes into the French and German railway, it's enormous compared to what we're doing,"* Lord Tordoff, Liberal Democrats.

However, some respondents pointed to several recent improvements on the part of British Rail: *"Their performance in terms of economy and reliability has improved significantly,"* S. Cowie, Planning and Logistics Manager, Kuwait Petroleum (GB) Ltd. In addition, interviewees often commented on the lack of sufficient government support which, in their view, unduly constrains British Rail's efforts to improve the available services: *"I think that B. R. is trying to do the best they can within the constraints they've got . . . but the point is this: They're accepting the straight-jacket the Government has given them. . . . They should actually be standing up and saying 'Look, this isn't good enough,' "* N. Baker, Political Adviser to Mr. Simon Hughes MP, Liberal Democrats.

TRANSPORT POLICY ISSUES

The Environmental Cost of Transport

One of the issues dividing respondents most strongly was the question of the "true" cost of transport. Doubts were raised as to whether freight modes were competing on equal terms, as government policy was widely perceived to favor road freight. Specifically, it was widely argued that current lorry taxation would not adequately cover the damage lorries cause to infrastructure and the environment. Approximately two-thirds of respondents who expressed an opinion shared this view. Indeed, all interviewed representatives of Green organizations, British Rail managers, and all but one journalist perceived road transport as having an unfair competitive advantage. The overall results are outlined in Table 17.4.

The following statement emphasizes the view that levies on road freight do *not* cover the "true" cost of transport: *"The road transport is allowed to use our roads free of charge–basically the same as a car. I mean, they're just getting vast public expenditure of concealed subsidy, aren't they?"* J. Hunt, Environment Correspondent, *Financial Times*.

Not surprisingly, support for the present system was found among interviewees from the Conservative Party and the Department of Transport: *"Taxes more than cover the costs lorries impose on the infrastructure in terms of maintenance and so on and with quite a large margin on top,"* Mr. Broome, Impact Assessment–Roads, Department of Transport.

Interviewees who held the view that current taxation on road freight transport does not adequately cover the direct and/or environmental costs of this transport mode made a number of suggestions for changes. A hydrocarbon tax was most frequently mentioned, followed by the proposal to transfer expenditure onto rail and the concept that the polluter should pay for environmental damage. Table 17.5 provides an overview of these suggestions.

TABLE 17. 4. Perceived Fairness in Handling Road and Rail Competition

Levies on Lorries Reflect the "True" Cost of Road Freight Transport	Number of Mentions	% of Expressed Opinions
Yes	10	1
No	27	1
Don't Know	4	0

Government Policy and the Environment

During discussions on "true costs of road freight transport" and suggestions of "costing transport-induced environmental damage," interviewees frequently expressed their views on the role that the environment takes in shaping government transport policy. The expressed views can be categorized into three groups: those who hold the view that (a) the government takes environmental considerations *seriously*, (b) the government is only *marginally* interested in environmental issues and uses them only as "window-dressing," (c) the government does not take environmental considerations into account when formulating transport policy. The findings are summarized in Table 17.6.

A perceived neglect of the railway system was frequently found to be the reason for doubting the seriousness of environmental

TABLE 17.5. Perceived Scope for Improving Road Freight Transport

How Should "True" Cost Be Covered?	Number of Mentions
1. Hydrocarbon Taxation Policy	13
2. Cut Spending on Road/More Incentive to Use Rail	12
3. Make "Polluter Pay"	10
4. Toll Roads/Restricted Access	10
5. General Taxation to Compensate for Damage to Environment	9
6. Heavier General Taxation on Lorries	7
7. Pay According to the Weight of Lorries in Certain Areas	1

TABLE 17.6. The Environment and Government Transport Policy

Environment Taken Into Consideration In Government Transport Policy	Number of Mentions	% of Expressed Opinions
Yes - Seriously	4	12
Only Somewhat/ Window-Dressing	13	39
Not Really Considered	16	48

concern in government transport policy. Thus, it was argued that if the government was serious about the environment, it would increase support to rail. Interviewees from the government side rejected these criticisms, arguing that rail does not suffer from severe financial constraints as it is not expected to earn substantial profits. However, on balance, there was significantly more criticism than support for the green endeavors of the government: *"I am sure I am right in saying that a Labour Government would see itself much keener on rail because we are keener on infrastructure investment, we give more priority to those environmental factors, so I think that would be good news for the railways,"* N. Stanley, Political Adviser to Mr. Brian Gould MP, Labour.

EXPECTED INFLUENCES ON "GREENING" FREIGHT TRANSPORT

Expected Influence of Green Pressure Groups

The likely future influence of green pressure groups on (a) the modal choices made by companies, and (b) the formulation of government transport policy was also discussed. A substantial proportion of respondents felt able to assess these issues and Table 17.7 displays the three response categories formed.

Table 17.7 does not illustrate the widespread skepticism of both the present record of green organizations with regard to transport issues and their likely effectiveness of addressing such issues in the future. Many respondents believe that to date, the influence of green pressure groups on freight transport decisions and policies has been minimal. In addition, some respondents believe that the green organizations have had their heyday and will now lose influence: *"I think we've just passed a sort of peak. . . . I'd have thought that in the immediate future the influence of those groups is going to decline not increase,"* F. Cairncross, Environment Correspondent, *The Economist.*

It must be noted that some respondents from green organizations also share the view that, so far, they do not place sufficient emphasis on transport issues. However, all interviewees from green orga-

TABLE 17.7. The Expected Future Impact of Green Organizations on Modal
Choice and Government Transport Policy

Influence of Green Pressure Groups is Expected to	Modal Choice by Companies		Government Transport Policy	
	Number of Mentions	% Expressed Opinions	Number of Mentions	% Expressed Opinions
Gain Strength	9	33	14	52
Stay Unchanged	14	52	11	41
Weaken	4	15	2	7

nizations predicted that they will intensify their efforts to influence
freight transport decisions and policies: *"It [the shift from road to
rail] is a major issue and I think it is very hard to get away from
now. . . . If anything the pressure to do something about transportation will intensify,"* T. Brown, National Society for Clean Air.

Expected Influence of the European Community

Although many regulations of the European Commission have
been introduced into the UK, not all measures seem to be perceived
as environmentally beneficial (e.g., heavier lorries). Consequently,
interviewees were asked about their expectations regarding the impact of new EC laws/regulations on environmental policies in Britain. Twenty-nine respondents, representing 91% who expressed an
opinion, expect that EC influences will lead to stricter environmental legislation in the future. Only one respondent felt that there
would be no change in environmental laws and regulations, while
two respondents argued that environmental laws will become laxer.

Interviewees were then asked what effect such legislation might
have on the proportion of freight transport carried by road and rail
respectively. Respondents were notably unsure on this issue and,
somewhat surprisingly, more expected road to benefit than rail. The
findings are listed in Table 17.8.

The conflicting viewpoints on this issue can be identified in the
following statements: *"In the long-term if rail is confident that it is*

TABLE 17. 8. The Expected Future Influence of EC Transport Policy on Rail and Road Freight Transport

Influence of EC Transport Policy Expected to be.....	Road Freight		Rail Freight	
	Number of Mentions	% Expressed Opinions	Number of Mentions	% Expressed Opinions
Positive	13	39	7	21
Negative	6	18	9	27
Unknown Impact	14	42	17	52

a more environmentally friendly mode, then they are bound to gain from the Single Market," S. Cowie, Planning and Logistics Manager, Kuwait Petroleum (GB) Ltd.; *"Overall, it [1992] is going to be bad news for the environment,"* T. Bray, Friends of the Earth.

Perceived Impact of the Channel Tunnel on Modal Choice

Interviewees were questioned as to the perceived impact of the Channel Tunnel on freight transport decisions. Table 17.9 reveals that most respondents expect rail to gain business, but there is still a considerable degree of uncertainty.

From the government side, Ms. E. Buchanan, Special Adviser to Mr. Cecil Parkinson, pointed out that the Tunnel represents an excellent opportunity for rail to regain the custom that was taken by road. In her view, rail had previously failed due to a lack of flexibility and convenience, but the Tunnel would solve some of these problems as journeys will be longer. The following statements represent a cross-section from the interviews: *"For long distance transportation . . . there would be great advantage to use the Tunnel . . . especially if the trains will come through all the way to the inland, not just the arrival of the port,"* R. Quadranti, Sales Director (Italy), Danzas (UK) Ltd.; *"Some things will depend on how ef-*

TABLE 17. 9. Expected Impact of the Channel Tunnel on Modal Choice

Expectations	Road Freight		Rail Freight	
	Number of Mentions	% Expressed Opinions	Number of Mentions	% Expressed Opinions
Will Gain Business	6	33	17	50
Will Lose Business	2	11	2	6
Negligible Impact	2	11	2	6
Unknown Impact	8	44	13	38

fectively the system for getting freight from, say, the North of England across London and onto the Channel Tunnel works and that will be absolutely crucial to how far British Rail is open to benefit from the Tunnel in freight terms," F. Cairncross, Environment Correspondent, *The Economist.*

DISCUSSION AND CONCLUSIONS

This study has outlined a number of possible barriers to achieving competitive advantage through an emphasis on green credentials. First, the study indicates that the concept of "environmental nuisance" is of a multifaceted and complex nature and is influenced both by the factual knowledge of respondents as well as by their political/ideological disposition. This implies that any effort aimed at improving and communicating the environmental friendliness of a freight transport service is unlikely to fully satisfy *all* interested parties.

Secondly, there is evidence to suggest that customers are becoming more skeptical about "environmentally friendly" claims made by firms (*Management Consultancy*, 1989). Indeed, it could be potentially dangerous for an organization within this sector to play the "green card" and stress that its service is more environmentally sympathetic than that offered by its major competitors. For example, British Rail management is highly aware of the possible consequences of stressing RailFreight's environmental advantages over its road freight competitors: *"I think, apart from anything else, there are enough negatives to get an adverse reaction if one claims undue environmental friendliness,"* B. Scott, General Manager, British Rail Western Region; *"One must make sure that we haven't got any skeletons in the cupboard because most advertising campaigns can be shot down overnight by someone opening the door and saying 'ho, ho, ho, what have we got here.' And then you've lost all the money you've put into the advertising campaign,"* J. Harding, British Rail Research.

Finally, as far as service choice is concerned, there is little doubt that the role of environmental factors is seen as being of a *supporting* rather than *determining* nature. Currently, economic considerations are the prime influence on modal choice and, although the environment is likely to feature more strongly in the decision process, firms are generally reluctant to take unilateral steps towards greener service decisions if the latter are more costly. This implies that in order to make any service more attractive, environmental improvements should be approached in conjunction with improvements in the rest of the service package. For example, other performance areas, such as cost, reliability, availability, and convenience also need to be given equal (if not more) emphasis. The overall message appears to be this: *Being green alone does not win business.*

Nevertheless, it is believed that the environment is set to become *the* business issue of the decade (Kirkpatrick, 1990). Therefore, the importance of environmental factors in determining modal choice will undoubtedly increase in years to come, particularly since pressure is likely to mount on organizations to encapsulate Life Cycle Analysis into their operations: "As the green consumer matures and becomes better informed, the spotlight will move from the company's products to its processes" (Jolly and Charter, 1992: p. 203). Consequently, it is advisable that each firm operating within the distribution sector should consider the appointment of a Director for the Environment to oversee the formulation and implementation of environmental policy within the organization. At the very least, this would demonstrate top level commitment to environmental issues.

Future influences on the freight transport industry itself are seen to come primarily from two directions, notably (a) green pressure groups, and (b) the European Community. With regard to the former, the general expectation is that the pressure for more environmentally-responsible behavior on the part of firms and more environmentally-sensitive policies by government is unlikely to abate. Indeed, freight transport has been singled out by green organizations as an area that will come under increased scrutiny in the future. Regarding the European Community, the general feeling is that stricter environmental laws and regulations are likely to be introduced and freight transport is going to be one of the main industrial services to be affected. In this context, it must be noted that some 250 directives on green issues are currently making their way through the EC (MacKenzie, 1992). It seems prudent, therefore, for firms operating freight services to establish a line of communication with major green pressure groups and a system for monitoring developments in EC transport and environmental policy. Such a line of communication would aid the formulation of *proactive* rather than reactive marketing strategies in order to sustain/accomplish competitive advantage.

This study has illustrated that, at the very least, there is a need for more technical research to make *cost effective* environmental improvements to such industrial services as freight transport. Further research is also required to determine *how* best to incorporate a fresh environmental drive into an organization's strategic marketing plan, bearing in mind the potential pitfalls mentioned above.

There is also a need to supplement the qualitative insights obtained in this study with a quantitative analysis of environmental perceptions of both individuals and organizations. This would provide a statistical basis from which to derive broader inferences and generalizations on the topics of interest; it would also serve as a check on the stability of the present results. A survey approach targeting suitably stratified samples would be the appropriate methodology to follow to measure the extent of environmental awareness/concern within the broader consumer base. In this context, particular attention should be given to developing valid and reliable indicators of "greenness," capturing perceptions of environmental nuisances as well as levels/types of activities undertaken to combat environmental degradation.

Finally, given the growing strength of interest in environmentalism and green issues, tracking studies are required to monitor the changes in green attitudes and behavior to enable environmentally friendly firms to make the most of this key opportunity throughout the 1990s.

NOTE

1. While it is recognized that "stakeholders" are defined as individuals or organizations that have a vested interest in the activities of a particular industry, only *key* stakeholders are examined for the purpose of this chapter.

REFERENCES

Abbott, P (1991): "Action Speaks Louder than Mere Words," *Management Consultancy*, October, pp. 49-52.
Barker, M (1986) "The Directory for the Environment," Routledge & Kegan Paul.
British Railways Board (1988/89): *Annual Report & Accounts*, London.
Commission of the European Communities (1990): *Communication on a Community Railway Policy*, COM(89) 565 final, Brussels, January 25th.
Dearden, S (1990): "Road Freight Transport; Social Cost and Market Efficiency," *The Royal Bank of Scotland Review*, No. 168, December, pp. 28-42.
Department of Transport (1988): *Transport and the Environment*, London.
Ellwanger, G (1990): "The Railways in Environmentalism Conservation," *Rail International*, July, pp. 7-12.
Jolly, I. and M. Charter (1992): "'Greener' Logistics," in *Greener Marketing: A Responsible Approach to Business*, M.Charter (ed.), Sheffield, UK: Greenleaf Publishing.
Kirkpatrick, D (1990): "Environmentalism," *Fortune*, February 12, pp. 44-51.
MacKenzie, D (1992): "Greener than Thou," *Marketing Business*, April, pp. 10-13.
Management Consultancy (1989): "Keep your Head in the Green Revolution," September, pp. 56-57.
Marketing (1992): "How Green Is the UK Consumer when Shopping?" November 26, p. 16.
Marketing Research Society Newsletter (1990): "Turning Green," October.
Nelson, E (1989): "Shades of Green," *Survey*, Winter, pp. 9-11.
Porritt, J (1987): "Friends of the Earth Handbook," MacDonald & Co., London.
Prothero, A (1990): "Marketing Strategies for the 1990's," *Journal of Marketing Management*, Vol. 6, No. 2, pp. 87-103.
Research 2000 (1990): "Consumers and the Environment: The Impact of Environmental Change on Attitudes and Purchasing Behaviour," *Environmental Attitudes Survey No 1*, September, pp. 2-13.
Secretary of State (1991): "Transport in Europe–Creating the Infrastructure for the Future," *Financial Times* Conference, May 28th.

Smith, C and C Sambrook, (1990): "Dead End Street," *Marketing*, May 10th, pp. 28-31.

Somerset County Council (1990): *Environmental Committee Proposals for Lorries and the Environment.*

TEST (1991): "Wrong Side of the Tracks? Impacts of Road and Rail Freight Transport on the Environment: A Basis for Discussion." London.

TNT (1990): *TNT Limited Annual Report* 1990.

Woodruff, D and T Peterson, (1991): "Here Come the Greenmobiles," *Business Week*, November 11th, pp. 46-48.

SECTION XI.
SOME CONCLUSIONS

Chapter 18

The Future of Environmental Marketing: Food for Thought

Michael Jay Polonsky
Alma T. Mintu-Wimsatt

Every day, we reach deeper into the storehouse of the earth's resources, put more of these resources to use, and generate more waste of every kind in the process. Change begets change, then feeds on its momentum until finally the entire globe seems to be accelerating toward some kind of profound transformation.

–Al Gore, *Earth in the Balance* (1992)

This book has attempted to address some of the critical issues in green marketing. This topic is quite broad in its scope and increasingly becoming of interest to many. As such, this topic could never be comprehensively addressed in one book, especially one that is limited to a few hundred pages. Nonetheless, it was our intention to provide our readers with some insights on how the physical environment can influence the many facets of marketing practice.

So, we are now left with the crucial question: "Where will environmental marketing go from here?" Given the number of stakeholders involved and their different interests, the future of green marketing is at times uncertain. Its future direction is partially dependent on the point of view advocated by each stakeholder: consumers, government and its constituents, industry, and special interest groups.

Undoubtedly, consumers want to have their needs satisfied by various goods and services. This is what marketing strives to achieve. In addition, many consumers now feel that they must also take an active part in protecting, preserving, and conserving the environment. Is this a fad that will simply pass as it did in the 1970s? Are green issues to be incorporated into the product characteristics that consumers believe are salient when making purchase choices?

While concrete answers to these questions are presently unavailable, it is hoped that consumers will begin to realize that the consumption patterns characteristic of the 1980–waste and excess–need to be re-evaluated. In particular, consumers must take into consideration the bigger environmental picture–in other words, a holistic perspective. As consumers become more cognizant of the limitations of Mother Nature, they may change and/or modify their behaviors. These behaviors are not only in relation to what they consume, but how they consume as well.

The rise of green marketing has stimulated the most research in the area of consumer behavior. How consumers integrate green issues into the decision-making process appears to be of most interest for practitioners. The underlying rationale is that once organizations understand the green needs of their consumers, they (i.e., the organizations) can subsequently better satisfy consumer needs. Additionally, the change and/or modification of consumer behavior to integrate environmental issues in consumption patterns has also been of interest to many practitioners.

Trends in government legislation also indicate increasing environmental consciousness. As the watchdogs of society, many government institutions have played important roles in integrating green marketing issues as part of their mandate. For example, attempts to integrate mandatory recycling and bottle deposit legislation are only some of the ways that governmental activities can affect consumers and organizations. However, any government concerned with the environment is in a precarious situation. Can they "protect" the environment and simultaneously stimulate the economy? This is a major dilemma and one that will continue to be a gray area for any government and its constituents.

The topical areas of public policy and macro-marketing have also received some practitioner and academic attention. Governmental regulations relating to the environment appear to be continuously changing. These changes emanate from society's changing values as well as mankind's development of a body of environmental knowledge. Research in the green macro-marketing area is most likely to be expansive primarily due to the number of constituents involved. One key question that policy makers need to reassess is: How can government activities and legislation better direct consumer and industrial behaviors in a way that "protects" society's interest?

Currently, the least-researched area relating to green marketing appears to be industrial marketing. Despite being the least-examined topic, it is probably one of the most important. The production process, purchasing power, and control of industrial organizations deserve more interest. Unfortunately, industrial research is often more difficult, and therefore, not examined as often as consumer behavior or public policy. Indeed, marketers have to follow, and even "borrow," some of the tenets of management in order to address some of our concerns. For example, organizations' motivation is an issue that has been extensively researched in the management area. Using the concepts of organization behavior, marketers ask the following question: Are organizations motivated by profit, social responsibility, or simply compliance with legislation or other objects? Understanding motivations and how these can be modified to integrate green issues may be one of the areas that needs to be researched.

The interface between consumers and organizations is also very critical. While broader studies of this nature are more difficult and complicated to undertake, these studies are necessary if green industrial marketing is to be examined in depth.

So, one may ask: Where does this leave the future of green marketing? What should marketers embark on next?

The contributing authors of this book have provided readers with some insights on green marketing. Undoubtedly, given the numerous issues relating to green marketing, extensive research is still needed. While the studies presented here examine the state of play in green marketing in the early 1990s, the dynamic nature of the area mandates its continued investigation. In many ways, green marketing research is in its infancy. Therefore, the *challenge* lies with us, marketing practitioners and theorists, to search for answers.

Index

Page numbers in italics indicate figures; page numbers followed by t indicate tables.